Fodor's 8th Edition

Thailand

The Guide
for All Budgets

Completely
Updated

Where to Stay, Eat,
and Explore

On and Off
the Beaten Path

When to Go,
What to Pack

Maps, Travel Tips,
and Web Sites

Fodor's Travel Publications • New York, Toronto, London, Sydney, Auckland
www.fodors.com

Fodor's Thailand

EDITORS: Carissa Bluestone, Mark Sullivan

Editorial Contributors: David Dudenhoefer, Mick Elmore, Robert Tilley
Editorial Production: Tom Holton
Maps: David Lindroth, *cartographer*; Rebecca Baer, Robert Blake, *map editors*
Design: Fabrizio La Rocca, *creative director*; Guido Caroti, *art director*; Jolie Novak, *senior picture editor*; Melanie Marin, *photo editor*
Cover Design: Pentagram
Production/Manufacturing: Angela L. McLean
Cover Photo (Wat Pho Temple, Bangkok): Paul Chesley/Photographers/Aspen

Copyright

8th Edition

ISBN 1–4000–1143–4

ISSN 1064–0993

Important Tip

Although all prices, opening times, and other details in this book are based on information supplied to us at press time, changes occur all the time in the travel world, and Fodor's cannot accept responsibility for facts that become outdated or for inadvertent errors or omissions. So **always confirm information when it matters,** especially if you're making a detour to visit a specific place.

Special Sales

Fodor's Travel Publications are available at special discounts for bulk purchases for sales promotions or premiums. Special editions, including personalized covers, excerpts of existing guides, and corporate imprints, can be created in large quantities for special needs. For more information, contact your local bookseller or write to Special Markets, Fodor's Travel Publications, 1745 Broadway, New York, NY 10019. Inquiries from Canada should be directed to your local Canadian bookseller or sent to Random House of Canada, Ltd., Marketing Department, 2775 Matheson Boulevard East, Mississauga, Ontario L4W 4P7. Inquiries from the United Kingdom should be sent to Fodor's Travel Publications, 20 Vauxhall Bridge Road, London SW1V 2SA, England.

PRINTED IN THE UNITED STATES OF AMERICA

10 9 8 7 6 5 4 3 2 1

CONTENTS

Maps

ON THE ROAD WITH FODOR'S

A trip takes you out of yourself. Concerns of life at home completely disappear, driven away by more immediate thoughts—about, say, what marvels will beguile the next day, or where you'll have dinner. That's where Fodor's comes in. We make sure that you know all your options, so that you don't miss something that's around the next bend just because you didn't know it was there. Mindful that the best memories of your trip might have nothing to do with what you came to Thailand to see, we guide you to sights large and small all over the region. You might set out to bake in the sun on the island of Phuket, but back at home you find yourself unable to forget diving off the coast of Ko Samui or sampling seriously spicy cuisine in Isan. With Fodor's at your side, serendipitous discoveries are never far away.

About Our Writers

Our success in showing you every corner of Thailand is a credit to our extraordinary writers. Although there's no substitute for travel advice from a good friend who knows your style, our contributors are the next best thing—the kind of people you would poll for travel advice if you knew them.

The first time **David Dudenhoefer** visited Southeast Asia, he hitchhiked most of the way from Bangkok to Singapore. This time around he relied more on the local airlines to update the Side Trip to Laos chapter. He has contributed to six Fodor's guides during his decade and a half as a freelance journalist, during which time he has worked in 20 countries, writing and taking photos for dozens of newspapers and magazines.

Mick Elmore arrived in Bangkok in 1991, ending a four-month trek from Melbourne, Australia. He has been based in the region ever since and now calls the capital city his home. A journalist since 1984, he writes for magazines and wire services. Mick first worked for Fodor's in 1998, adding his expertise to the Java and Sumatra chapters of *Fodor's Indonesia*. He has since journeyed to Colombia to write for *Fodor's South America*. In this book he took a fresh look at the Bangkok chapter and contributed to several others.

Robert Tilley lives in a small village in Northern Thailand, his base for extensive travels throughout Southeast Asia and side trips to East Africa, where he is publicity director of a hotel management and safari company. Apart from his work for Fodor's, he writes for publications in Great Britain, Canada, Germany, Hong Kong, and Singapore. He is the author of two books on Thailand: *Beyond the Blue Mountain: a Thailand Diary* and *Noi Goes to England*.

You can rest assured that you're in good hands—and that no property mentioned in the book has paid to be included. Each has been selected strictly on its merits, as the best of its type in its price range.

How to Use This Book

Up front is **Smart Travel Tips A to Z**, arranged alphabetically by topic and loaded with tips, Web sites, and contact information. Destination: Thailand helps get you in the mood for your trip. Subsequent chapters are arranged geographically. All city chapters begin with exploring information, with a section for each neighborhood (each recommending a good tour and listing sights alphabetically). All regional chapters are divided geographically; within each area, towns are covered in logical order, and attractive stretches of road between them are indicated by the designation En Route. To help you decide what you'll have time to visit, all chapters begin with our writers' favorite itineraries. (Mix itineraries from several chapters, and you can put together a really exceptional trip.) The A to Z section that ends every chapter lists additional resources.

Icons and Symbols

★ Our special recommendations
✕ Restaurant
🏠 Lodging establishment
✕🏠 Lodging establishment whose restaurant warrants a special trip
⚠ Campgrounds
☺ Good for kids (rubber duck)
☞ Sends you to another section of the guide for more information
✉ Address
☎ Telephone number
☺ Opening and closing times

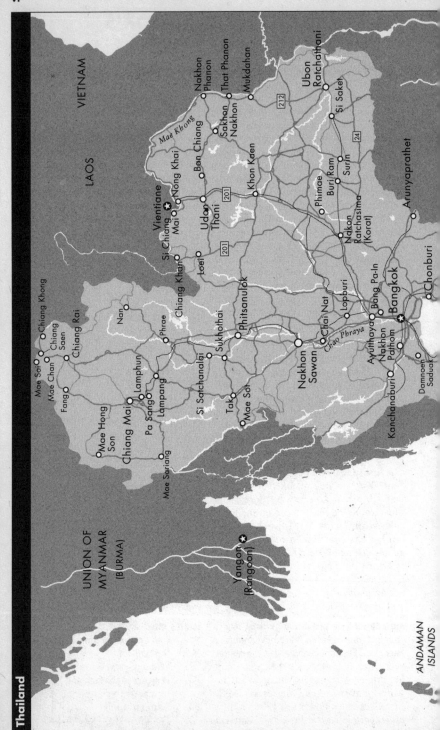

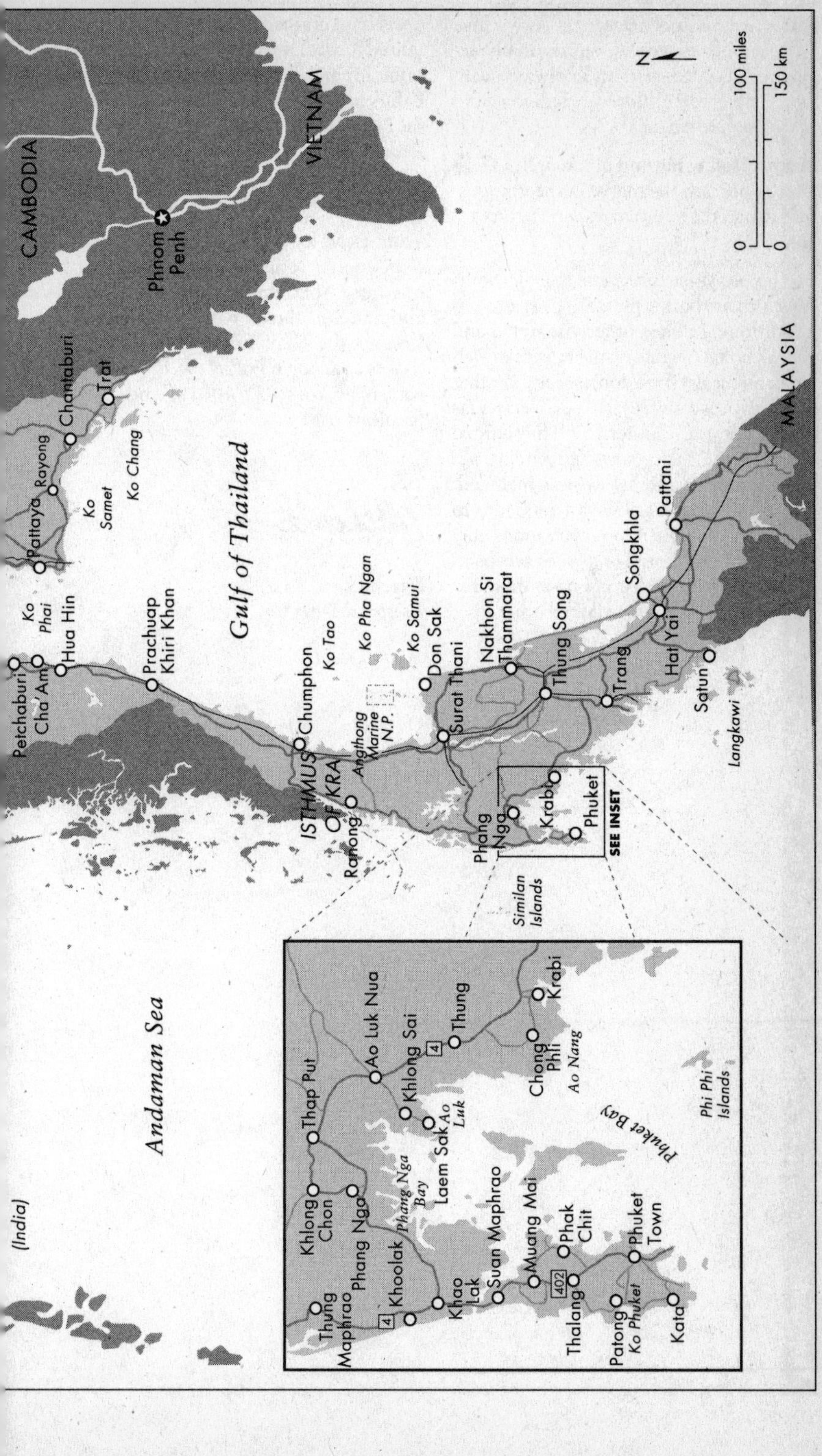
CAMBODIA
VIETNAM
Phnom Penh
Petchaburi
Cha'Am
Hua Hin
Ko Phai
Pattaya
Rayong
Chantaburi
Trat
Ko Samet
Ko Chang
Gulf of Thailand
Prachuap Khiri Khan
Chumphon
Ko Tao
Ko Pha Ngan
Ko Samui
Don Sak
Anghong Marine N.P.
ISTHMUS OF KRA
Ramong
Surat Thani
Nakhon Si Thammarat
Thung Song
Songkhla
Pattani
Hat Yai
Trang
Satun
Langkawi
MALAYSIA
Phang Nga
Krabi
Phuket
SEE INSET
Similan Islands
Andaman Sea
(India)
100 miles
150 km
0
N
Thung Maphrao
Khlong Chon
Thap Put
Ao Luk Nua
Khlong Sai
Thung
Krabi
Phang Nga
Khoolak
Khao Lak
Phang Nga Bay
Laem Sak
Ao Luk
Chong Phli
Ao Nang
Phuket Bay
Phi Phi Islands
Suan Maphrao
Muang Mai
Phak Chit
Thalang
Phuket Town
Patong
Ko Phuket
Kata
4
402

📷 Admission prices (those we give apply to adults; substantially reduced fees are almost always available for children, students, and senior citizens)

Numbers in white and black circles ③ ❸ that appear on the maps, in the margins, and within the tours correspond to one another.

For hotels, you can assume that all rooms have private baths, phones, TVs, and air-conditioning unless otherwise noted and that all hotels operate on the European Plan (with no meals) if we don't specify another meal plan. We always list a property's facilities but not whether you'll be charged extra to use them, so when pricing accommodations, do ask what's included. For restaurants, it's always a good idea to book ahead; we mention reservations only when they're essential or are not accepted. All restaurants we list are open daily for lunch and dinner unless stated otherwise; dress is mentioned only when men are required to wear a jacket or a jacket and tie. Look for an overview of local dining-out habits in Smart Travel Tips A to Z and in the Pleasures and Pastimes section that follows each chapter introduction.

Don't Forget to Write

Your experiences—positive and negative—matter to us. If we have missed or misstated something, we want to hear about it. We follow up on all suggestions. Contact the Thailand editor at editors@fodors.com or c/o Fodor's at 1745 Broadway, New York, NY 10019. And have a fabulous trip!

Karen Cure

Karen Cure
Editorial Director

ESSENTIAL INFORMATION

AIR TRAVEL

BOOKING

When you book **look for nonstop flights** and **remember that "direct" flights stop at least once.** Try to avoid connecting flights, which require a change of plane. Two airlines may operate a connecting flight jointly, so ask if your airline operates every segment of the trip; you may find that the carrier you prefer flies you only part of the way. To find more booking tips and to check prices and make on-line flight reservations, log on to www.fodors.com.

On popular tourist routes during peak holiday times, domestic flights in Thailand are often fully booked. Make sure you have reservations, and make them well in advance of your travel date. Be sure to **reconfirm your flight** when you arrive in Thailand.

CARRIERS

About 70 airlines serve Bangkok, and more are seeking landing rights. Northwest Airlines is the major U.S. carrier, flying daily from six U.S. cities, with the best connection times in Tokyo. East-coast travelers departing from New York or Washington, D.C., should consider using British Airways or Virgin Atlantic/Thai Airways via London for 19-hour flights to Bangkok. Singapore Airlines flies from Newark via Amsterdam to Bangkok.

➤ MAJOR AIRLINES: Asiana Airlines (☎ 800/227–4262). British Airways (☎ 800/247–9297). Cathay Pacific (☎ 800/233–2742). China Airlines (☎ 800/227–5118). EVA Air (☎ 800/695–1188). Gulf Air (☎ 800/553–2824). Japan Airlines (☎ 800/525–3663). Korean Air (☎ 800/438–5000). Northwest Airlines (☎ 800/447–4747). Singapore Airlines (☎ 800/742–3333). Thai Airways (☎ 800/426–5204). United Airlines (☎ 800/241–6522).

➤ FROM THE U.K.: British Airways (☎ 020/8897–4000 or 0345/222111 outside London). Qantas (☎ 0345/747767 or 0800/747767). Thai Airways (☎ 020/7499–9113).

CHECK-IN AND BOARDING

Always **ask your carrier about its check-in policy.** Plan to arrive at the airport about two hours before your scheduled departure time for domestic flights and 2½ to 3 hours before international flights. Assuming that not everyone with a ticket will show up, airlines routinely overbook planes. When everyone does, airlines ask for volunteers to give up their seats. In return, these volunteers usually get a certificate for a free flight and are rebooked on the next flight out. If there are not enough volunteers, the airline must choose who will be denied boarding. The first to get bumped are passengers who checked in late and those flying on discounted tickets, so **get to the gate and check in as early as possible,** especially during peak periods.

Always **bring a government-issued photo I.D. to the airport;** even when it's not required, a passport is best.

CUTTING COSTS

The least expensive airfares to Thailand are priced for round-trip travel and must usually be purchased in advance. Airlines generally allow you to change your return date for a fee; most low-fare tickets, however, are nonrefundable. It's smart to **call a number of airlines and check the Internet;** when you are quoted a good price, **book it on the spot**—the same fare may not be available the next day. Always **check different routings** and look into using alternate airports. Also, price off-peak flights, which may be significantly less expensive than others. Travel agents, especially low-fare specialists (☞ Discounts and Deals, *below*), are helpful.

Consolidators are another good source. They buy tickets for scheduled international flights at reduced rates from the airlines, then sell them at prices that beat the best fare available directly from the airlines. Sometimes you can even get your money back if you need to return the ticket. Carefully read the fine print detailing penalties for changes and cancellations, purchase the ticket with a credit card, and **confirm your consolidator reservation with the airline.**

When you **fly as a courier,** you trade your checked-luggage space for a ticket deeply subsidized by a courier service. There are restrictions on when you can book and how long you can stay. Some courier companies list with membership organizations, such as the Air Courier Association and the International Association of Air Travel Couriers; these require you to become a member before you can book a flight.

Many airlines, singly or in collaboration, offer discount air passes that allow foreigners to travel economically in a particular country or region. These visitor passes usually must be reserved and purchased before you leave home. Information about passes can be difficult to track down on airline Web sites, which tend to be geared to travelers departing from a given carrier's country rather than to those intending to visit that country. Try typing the name of the pass into a search engine, or search for "pass" within the carrier's Web site.

For independent travelers, check into "Circle Pacific" fares. The pricing and routing of these tickets depend on the arrangements that the airline has with the local carriers of the region. The tickets must be purchased at least 7 to 14 days in advance. You usually can add on extra stopovers, including Australian and South Pacific destinations, for a nominal charge. Several airlines work together to offer "Around the World" fares, but you must follow a specific routing itinerary and cannot backtrack. "Around the World" itineraries usually include a couple of Asian destinations before continuing through Africa and Europe.

➤ CONSOLIDATORS: **Cheap Tickets** (☎ 800/377–1000 or 888/922–8849, WEB www.cheaptickets.com). **Discount Airline Ticket Service** (☎ 800/576–1600). **Unitravel** (☎ 800/325–2222, WEB www.unitravel.com). **Up & Away Travel** (☎ 212/889–2345, WEB www.upandaway.com). **World Travel Network** (☎ 800/409–6753).

➤ COURIERS: **Air Courier Association** (☎ 800/282–1202, WEB www.aircourier.org). **International Association of Air Travel Couriers** (☎ 352/475–1584, WEB www.courier.org). **Now Voyager Travel** (☎ 212/431–1616).

➤ DISCOUNT PASSES: **All Asia Pass,** Cathay Pacific (☎ 800/233–2742, WEB www.cathay-usa.com).

ENJOYING THE FLIGHT

State your seat preference when purchasing your ticket, and then repeat it when you confirm and when you check in. For more legroom, you can request one of the few emergency-aisle seats at check-in, if you are capable of lifting at least 50 pounds— a Federal Aviation Administration requirement of passengers in these seats. Seats behind a bulkhead also offer more legroom, but they don't have under-seat storage. Don't sit in the row in front of the emergency aisle or in front of a bulkhead, where seats may not recline.

Ask the airline whether a snack or meal is served on the flight. If you have dietary concerns, **request special meals when booking.** These can be vegetarian, low-cholesterol, or kosher, for example. It's a good idea to pack some healthy snacks and a small (plastic) bottle of water in your carry-on bag. On long flights, try to maintain a normal routine, to help fight jet lag. At night, **get some sleep.** By day, **eat light meals, drink water** (not alcohol), and **move around the cabin** to stretch your legs. For additional jet-lag tips consult *Fodor's FYI: Travel Fit & Healthy* (available at bookstores everywhere).

FLYING TIMES

Bangkok is 17 hours from San Francisco, 18 hours from Seattle and Vancouver, 20 hours from Chicago, 22 hours from New York and

Toronto, 11 hours from London, and 10 hours from Sydney. Add more time for stopovers and connections, especially if you are using more than one carrier.

HOW TO COMPLAIN

If your baggage goes astray or your flight goes awry, complain right away. Most carriers require that you **file a claim immediately.** The Aviation Consumer Protection Division of the Department of Transportation publishes *Fly-Rights,* which discusses airlines and consumer issues and is available on-line. At PassengerRights.com, you can compose a letter of complaint and distribute it electronically.

➤ AIRLINE COMPLAINTS: **Aviation Consumer Protection Division** (✉ U.S. Department of Transportation, Room 4107, C-75, Washington, DC 20590, ☎ 202/366–2220, WEB www.dot.gov/airconsumer). **Federal Aviation Administration Consumer Hotline** (☎ 800/322–7873).

TRAVEL WITHIN THAILAND

Thai Airways connects Bangkok with all major cities and tourist areas in Thailand, except Ko Samui. Bangkok Airways has numerous daily flights between Bangkok and Ko Samui, using 40-seat planes. It also flies daily between Ko Samui and Phuket, daily from Bangkok to Angkor Wat in Cambodia, twice a week to Krabi, and three times a week to Chiang Mai via Sukhothai. Its fares are competitive with those of Thai Airways. The new and fast-growing Angel Airlines flies between Bangkok and Chiang Mai, Phuket, Udon Thani, and Singapore; between Chiang Mai and Phuket, Udon Thani, and Singapore; and between Phuket and Singapore.

Thai Airways offers a "Discover Thailand Pass." For $179 you can take four flights to any of the airline's Thailand destinations. You must purchase the pass outside Thailand. Be aware that this pass has its limitations: for example, if you fly from Chiang Mai to Surat Thani, you must change planes in Bangkok, meaning that you will use two of your four flights.

➤ AIRLINES: **Angel Airlines** (☎ 02/535–6287 at Don Muang airport office). **Bangkok Airways** (✉ 60 Queen Sirikit National Convention Centre, New Ratchadaphisek Rd., Klongotey, Bangkok, ☎ 02/229–3456 or 02/229–3434). **Thai Airways** (✉ 485 Silom Rd., Bangkok, ☎ 02/232–8000).

AIRPORTS

The major gateway to Thailand is Bangkok's Don Muang International Airport, which is about 25 km (15 mi) north of Bangkok. Bangkok is going ahead with plans for a second airport at Nang-Ngu Kao, 32 km (20 mi) east of town, to relieve congestion at Don Muang, but its projected opening date of late 2004 may be delayed by a year or two.

Bangkok Airways built an airport outside Sukhothai, which was once slightly off the beaten track. Now a daily flight arrives from Chiang Mai and Bangkok. The airline has also initiated direct flights between Bangkok and Siem Reap and between Singapore and Ko Samui. (Because Bangkok Airways is the only carrier with rights on Samui, flights there are already very expensive and are likely to become truly exorbitant.) There's also a new airport at Krabi with flights to and from Bangkok.

➤ AIRPORT INFORMATION: **Don Muang International Airport** (☎ 02/535–2081).

AIRPORT TRANSFERS

Bangkok has nonstop airport shuttles that serve the train stations as well as hotels (☞ Arriving and Departing *in* Bangkok A to Z). Shared hotel vans and taxis are also a popular mode of transport. It helps to **have a hotel brochure or an address in the local language for the driver.**

From the center of Bangkok to Don Muang, allow about 40 minutes in light traffic, 90 minutes at rush hour.

BUS TRAVEL

Long-distance buses are cheaper and faster than trains and reach every corner of the country. The level of comfort depends on the bus company, however, luxury "super buses" with extra-wide reclining seats, air-conditioning, video, scheduled box or buffet meals, and rest rooms are available. Be aware that air-conditioned buses are always so cold that you'll want to bring an extra sweater.

CUTTING COSTS

A typical fare for the nine-hour trip between Chiang Mai and Bangkok is anywhere from B300 to B570 depending on the travel agent with whom you book. Travel agents on Khao San Road in Bangkok offer some of the cheapest deals for private buses.

FARES AND SCHEDULES

Travel agents have bus schedules and can make reservations and issue tickets.

BUSINESS HOURS

BANKS AND OFFICES

Thai and foreign banks are open weekdays 8:30–3:30, except for public holidays. Most commercial concerns in Bangkok operate on a five-day week and are open 8–5. Government offices are generally open 8:30–4:30 with a noon–1 lunch break.

GAS STATIONS

Gas stations in Thailand are usually open at least 8–8 daily; many, particularly those on the highways, are open 24 hours a day.

MUSEUMS AND SIGHTS

Each museum keeps its own hours and may select a different day of the week to close; it's best to call before visiting. Wats are generally open to visitors from 7 or 8 in the morning to 5 or 6 PM.

SHOPS

Many stores are open daily 8–8.

CAMERAS AND PHOTOGRAPHY

Thailand, with its majestic landscapes and beautiful temples, is a photographer's dream. People here seem amenable to having picture-taking tourists in their midst, but you should always **ask permission before taking pictures of individuals.** The phrase *Tai roob dai mai?* means "Can I take a picture? The *Kodak Guide to Shooting Great Travel Pictures* (available at bookstores everywhere) is loaded with tips.

➤ PHOTO HELP: **Kodak Information Center** (☎ 800/242–2424, WEB www. kodak.com).

EQUIPMENT PRECAUTIONS

Don't pack film and equipment in checked luggage, where it is much more susceptible to damage. X-ray machines used to view checked luggage are becoming much more powerful and therefore are much more likely to ruin your film. Try to **ask for hand inspection of film,** which becomes clouded after repeated exposure to airport X-ray machines, and **keep videotapes and computer disks away from metal detectors.** Always **keep film, tape, and computer disks out of the sun.** Carry an extra supply of batteries, and **be prepared to turn on your camera, camcorder, or laptop** to prove to airport security personnel that the device is real.

FILM AND DEVELOPING

Expect to pay B100 to B125 for a roll of film with 36 exposures in most places. Some resorts may charge a bit more. The most common brands are Kodak and Fuji.

The cost of developing film is usually about B40, plus B5 to B6 per exposure. Again, resorts are likely to be a bit more expensive. The quality is usually commensurate with that of a one-hour developing shop back home.

CAR RENTAL

Cars are available for rent in Bangkok and in major tourist destinations, however the additional cost of hiring a driver is small and the peace of mind great. If a foreigner is involved in an automobile accident, he or she—not the Thai—is likely to be judged at fault.

Rates in Thailand begin at $40 a day for an economy car with unlimited mileage. This includes neither tax, which is 7% on car rentals, nor the collision damage waiver. It is better to make your car-rental reservations when you arrive in Thailand, as you can usually secure a discount.

In Chiang Mai, Ko Samui, Pattaya, and Phuket, **consider renting a jeep or motorcycle,** popular and convenient ways to get around. **Be aware that motorcycles skid easily on gravel**

roads. On Ko Samui, a sign posts the year's count of foreigners who never made it home from their vacation!

➤ MAJOR AGENCIES: **Alamo** (☎ 800/522–9696, WEB www.alamo.com). **Avis** (☎ 800/331–1084; 800/879–2847 in Canada; 0870/606–0100 in the U.K.; 02/9353–9000 in Australia; 09/526–2847 in New Zealand; WEB www.avis.com). **Budget** (☎ 800/527–0700; 0870/156–5656 in the U.K.; WEB www.budget.com). **Dollar** (☎ 800/800–6000; 0124/622–0111 in the U.K.; 02/9223–1444 in Australia; WEB www.dollar.com). **Hertz** (☎ 800/654–3001; 800/263–0600 in Canada; 020/8897–2072 in the U.K.; 02/9669–2444 in Australia; 09/256–8690 in New Zealand; WEB www.hertz.com). **National** (☎ 800/227–7368; 020/8680–4800 in the U.K.; WEB www.nationalcar.com).

INSURANCE

When driving a rented car you are generally responsible for any damage to or loss of the vehicle. You may also be liable for any property damage or personal injury that you may cause while driving. Before you rent, see what coverage you already have under the terms of your personal auto-insurance policy and credit cards.

REQUIREMENTS AND RESTRICTIONS

In Thailand, your own driver's license is acceptable unless your current driver's license is not written in English, in which case you must obtain an international driving license. It's a good idea for anyone to have an international driver's permit; it's available from the American or Canadian Automobile Associations, and, in the United Kingdom, from the Automobile Association or Royal Automobile Club. Having one in your wallet may save you a problem with the local authorities.

SURCHARGES

Before you pick up a car in one city and leave it in another, **ask about drop-off charges or one-way service fees,** which can be substantial. Note, too, that some rental agencies charge extra if you return the car before the time specified in your contract. To avoid a hefty refueling fee, **fill the tank just before you turn in the car,** but be aware that gas stations near the rental outlet may overcharge.

CAR TRAVEL

Driving in Thailand has its ups and downs. The major roads in Thailand tend to be congested, and street signs are often only in Thai. But the limited number of roads and the straightforward layout of cities combine to make navigation relatively easy. The exception, of course, is Bangkok. Don't even think about negotiating that tangled mass of traffic-clogged streets.

The main rule to remember is that traffic laws are routinely disregarded. Bigger vehicles have the unspoken right of way, motorcyclists seem to think they are invincible, and bicyclists often don't look around them. Drive carefully.

Always **avoid driving at night in rural areas,** especially north and west of Chiang Mai and in the south beyond Surat Thani, as highway robberies have been reported.

GASOLINE

A liter of gasoline costs approximately B13–B16. Many gas stations stay open 24 hours and have clean toilet facilities and minimarkets.

PARKING

In cities, the larger hotels, restaurants, and department stores have garages or parking lots. Rates vary, but count on B10 an hour. If you purchase anything, parking is free, but you must have your ticket validated.

RULES OF THE ROAD

As in the United Kingdom, **drive on the left side** of the road. Speed limits are 60 kph (37 mph) in cities, 90 kph (56 mph) outside, and 130 kph (81 mph) on expressways. If you are renting a motorcycle, **always wear a helmet;** they are now required by law, and this law is periodically enforced, particularly in Phuket.

CHILDREN IN THAILAND

Youngsters are welcome in Thailand. You will be amazed at how many people will want to hold and play with your kids, and at how their presence will actually open conversations and cut through cultural boundaries. Many activities, such as riding elephants and visiting the floating markets, will delight even the most finicky child. Places that are especially appealing to children are indicated by a rubber-duckie icon (🦆) in the margin.

If you are renting a car, don't forget to **arrange for a car seat** when you reserve. For general advice about traveling with children, consult *Fodor's FYI: Travel with Your Baby* (available in bookstores everywhere).

FLYING

If your children are two or older, **ask about children's airfares.** As a general rule, infants under two not occupying a seat fly at greatly reduced fares or even for free. When booking, **confirm carry-on allowances** if you're traveling with infants. In general, for babies charged 10% of the adult fare you are allowed one carry-on bag and a collapsible stroller; if the flight is full, the stroller may have to be checked or you may be limited to less.

Experts agree that it's a good idea to use safety seats aloft for children weighing less than 40 pounds. Airlines set their own policies: U.S. carriers usually require that the child be ticketed, even if he or she is young enough to ride free, since the seats must be strapped into regular seats. Do **check your airline's policy about using safety seats during takeoff and landing.** Safety seats are not allowed everywhere in the plane, so get your seat assignments as early as possible.

FOOD

Although Thai food can often be too spicy for children, most restaurants are happy to make make dishes that are milder. When all else fails, there are plenty of familiar fast-food restaurants in Bangkok and other large cities.

LODGING

Most hotels in Thailand allow children under a certain age to stay in their parents' room at no extra charge, but others charge for them as extra adults; be sure to **find out the cutoff age for children's discounts.**

SUPPLIES AND EQUIPMENT

Supplies are easy to find in the major supermarkets in Thailand; you can get both Huggies and Pampers brand diapers in small to extra-large sizes. Baby wipes are not commonly used, so it's a good idea to bring some from home.

COMPUTERS ON THE ROAD

The business centers of many hotels in Thailand provide Internet access. In modern upscale hotels, you'll often find in-room connections for your laptop. They use the same phone jacks as you'll find in the United States.

In Thailand's major cities, as throughout Southeast Asia, cybercafés are springing up all over; Bangkok, for example, has half a dozen or more along Silom Road and Khao San Road. You can expect to pay B1 to B2 per minute. Larger hotels and resorts can charge more—sometimes a lot more—so make sure to ask in advance.

CRUISE TRAVEL

Some cruise lines, including Cunard and Royal Viking, call at major Southeast Asian ports as part of their around-the-world itineraries. Seabourn Cruises spends 14 days cruising the waters of Southeast Asia, including the Gulf of Thailand. Cunard's Sea Goddess provides a luxury trip in the Gulf of Thailand and through the Straits of Malacca into the Andaman Sea.

Plan to spend at least four weeks cruising from the West Coast of the United States to Southeast Asia, as these ships usually visit ports in the Pacific and Australia along the way.

➤ CRUISE LINES: **Cunard's Sea Goddess** (✉ 555 5th Ave., New York, NY 10017, ☎ 212/880–7500 or 800/221–4770). **Royal Viking** (☎ 800/426–0821). **Seabourn Cruises** (✉ San Francisco St., San Francisco, CA 94133, ☎ 415/391–7444 or 800/929–9595).

CUSTOMS AND DUTIES

When shopping abroad, **keep receipts** for all purchases. Upon reentering the country, **be ready to show customs officials what you've bought.** If you feel a duty is incorrect, appeal the assessment. If you object to the way your clearance was handled, note the inspector's badge number. In either case, first ask to see a supervisor. If the problem isn't resolved, write to the appropriate authorities, beginning with the port director at your point of entry.

IN THAILAND

One liter of wine or liquor, 200 cigarettes or 250 grams of smoking tobacco, and all personal effects may be brought into Thailand duty-free. Visitors may bring in any amount of foreign currency; amounts taken out may not exceed those declared upon entry. Narcotics, pornographic materials, and firearms are strictly prohibited.

If you are bringing any foreign-made equipment from home, such as cameras, it is wise to carry the original receipt with you or register it with U.S. Customs before you leave (Form 4457). Otherwise, you may end up paying duty on your return.

IN AUSTRALIA

Australian residents who are 18 or older may bring home A$400 worth of souvenirs and gifts (including jewelry), 250 cigarettes or 250 grams of tobacco, and 1,125 ml of alcohol (including wine, beer, and spirits). Residents under 18 may bring back A$200 worth of goods. Prohibited items include meat products. Seeds, plants, and fruits need to be declared upon arrival.

➤ INFORMATION: **Australian Customs Service** (Regional Director, ✉ Box 8, Sydney, NSW 2001, ☎ 02/9213–2000 or 1300/363263; 1800/020504 quarantine-inquiry line; FAX 02/9213–4043, WEB www.customs.gov.au).

IN CANADA

Canadian residents who have been out of Canada for at least seven days may bring in C$750 worth of goods duty-free. If you've been away fewer than seven days but more than 48 hours, the duty-free allowance drops to C$200. If your trip lasts 24 to 48 hours, the allowance is C$50. You may not pool allowances with family members. Goods claimed under the C$750 exemption may follow you by mail; those claimed under the lesser exemptions must accompany you. Alcohol and tobacco products may be included in the seven-day and 48-hour exemptions but not in the 24-hour exemption. If you meet the age requirements of the province or territory through which you reenter Canada, you may bring in, duty-free, 1.5 liters of wine or 1.14 liters (40 imperial ounces) of liquor or 24 12-ounce cans or bottles of beer or ale. If you are 19 or older you may bring in, duty-free, 200 cigarettes and 50 cigars. Check ahead of time with the Canada Customs and Revenue Agency or the Department of Agriculture for policies regarding meat products, seeds, plants, and fruits.

You may send an unlimited number of gifts (only one gift per recipient, however) worth up to C$60 each duty-free to Canada. Label the package UNSOLICITED GIFT—VALUE UNDER $60. Alcohol and tobacco are excluded.

➤ INFORMATION: **Canada Customs and Revenue Agency** (✉ 2265 St. Laurent Blvd. S, Ottawa, Ontario K1G 4K3, ☎ 204/983–3500, 506/636–5064, or 800/461–9999, WEB www.ccra-adrc.gc.ca).

IN NEW ZEALAND

All homeward-bound residents may bring back NZ$700 worth of souvenirs and gifts; passengers may not pool their allowances, and children can claim only the concession on goods intended for their own use. For those 17 or older, the duty-free allowance also includes 4.5 liters of wine or beer; one 1,125-ml bottle of spirits; and either 200 cigarettes, 250 grams of tobacco, 50 cigars, or a combination of the three up to 250 grams. Meat products, seeds, plants, and fruits must be declared upon arrival to the Agricultural Services Department.

➤ INFORMATION: **New Zealand Customs** (Head office: ✉ The Customhouse, 17–21 Whitmore St., Box 2218, Wellington, ☎ 09/300–5399 or 0800/428786, WEB www.customs.govt.nz).

IN THE U.K.

From countries outside the European Union, including Thailand, you may bring home, duty-free, 200 cigarettes or 50 cigars; 1 liter of spirits or 2 liters of fortified or sparkling wine or liqueurs; 2 liters of still table wine; 60 ml of perfume; 250 ml of toilet water; plus £145 worth of other goods, including gifts and souvenirs. Prohibited items include meat products, seeds, plants, and fruits.

➤ INFORMATION: **HM Customs and Excise** (✉ Portcullis House, 21 Cowbridge Rd. E, Cardiff CF11 9SS, ☎ 029/2038–6423 or 0845/010–9000, WEB www.hmce.gov.uk).

IN THE U.S.

U.S. residents who have been out of the country for at least 48 hours may bring home, for personal use, $800 worth of foreign goods duty-free, as long as they haven't used the $800 allowance or any part of it in the past 30 days. This exemption may include 1 liter of alcohol (for travelers 21 and older), 200 cigarettes, and 100 non-Cuban cigars. Family members from the same household who are traveling together may pool their $800 personal exemptions. For fewer than 48 hours, the duty-free allowance drops to $200, which may include 50 cigarettes, 10 non-Cuban cigars, and 150 milliliters of alcohol (or perfume containing alcohol). The $200 allowance cannot be combined with other individuals' exemptions, and if you exceed it, the full value of all the goods will be taxed. Antiques, which the U.S. Customs Service defines as objects more than 100 years old, enter duty-free, as do original works of art done entirely by hand, including paintings, drawings, and sculptures.

You may also send packages home duty-free, with a limit of one parcel per addressee per day (except alcohol or tobacco products or perfume worth more than $5). You can mail up to $200 worth of goods for personal use; label the package PERSONAL USE and attach a list of its contents and their retail value. If the package contains your used personal belongings, mark it PERSONAL GOODS RETURNED to avoid paying duties. You may send up to $100 worth of goods as a gift; mark the package UNSOLICITED GIFT. Mailed items do not affect your duty-free allowance on your return.

➤ INFORMATION: **U.S. Customs Service** (for inquiries, ✉ 1300 Pennsylvania Ave. NW, Washington, DC 20229, WEB www.customs.gov,

☎ 202/354–1000; for complaints, ✉ Customer Satisfaction Unit, 1300 Pennsylvania Ave. NW, Room 5.5A, Washington, DC 20229; for registration of equipment, ✉ Office of Passenger Programs, 1300 Pennsylvania Ave. NW, Room 5.4D, Washington, DC 20229, ☎ 202/927–0530).

DINING

Thais know that eating out can be cheaper than eating in, and that inexpensive restaurants often serve food that's as good as, and sometimes better than, the fare at fancy places. That's why you see so many Thai families gathered around vendor carts or crowded around tables at a town's night market.

Thai food is eaten with a fork and spoon; the spoon held in the right hand and the fork used like a plow to push food into the spoon. Chopsticks are used only for Chinese food, such as noodle dishes. After you have finished eating, place your fork and spoon on the plate at the 5:25 position; otherwise the server will assume you would like another helping.

The restaurants we list are the cream of the crop in each price category. Unless otherwise noted, the restaurants listed in this guide are open daily for lunch and dinner.

CATEGORY	COST*
$$$$	over B400 (over US$10)
$$$	B300–B400 (US$7.50–$10)
$$	B200–B300 (US$5–$7.50)
$	B100–B200 (US$2.50–5)
¢	under B100 (under US$2.50)

*per person, for a main course at dinner

MEALS AND SPECIALTIES

Thai cuisine's distinctive flavor comes particularly from the use of fresh Thai basil, lemongrass, tamarind, lime, and citrus leaves. And though some Thai food is fiery hot from garlic and chilies, an equal number of dishes serve the spices on the side so that you can adjust the incendiary level. Thais use *nam pla,* a fish sauce, instead of salt.

If you're not sure what to order, start with some staples such as tom yam kung, which is prawn and lemongrass soup with mushrooms, then move on to pad Thai, which is fried noodles with tofu, vegetables, eggs, and peanuts. Wash it down with a Singha, a tasty Thai beer.

MEALTIMES

Restaurants tend to open in late morning and serve food until 9 or 10 in the evening. Street vendors can be found in most places 24 hours a day.

RESERVATIONS AND DRESS

Reservations are always a good idea: we mention them only when they're essential or not accepted. Book as far ahead as you can, and reconfirm as soon as you arrive.

Because Thailand has a hot climate, jackets and ties are rarely worn at dinner except in expensive restaurants, usually in the big hotels. We mention dress only when men are required to wear a jacket or a jacket and tie.

WINE, BEER, AND SPIRITS

Thai beers brewed in Thailand include Singha, Amarit, and Kloster; Singha is the most common of the three. You will also readily find Carlsberg, which is jointly owned by Danish and Thai business interests and heavily promoted in the country. San Miguel and Tuborg are other contenders in the market.

Rice whiskey, which tastes sweet and has a whopping 35% alcohol content, is another favorite throughout Thailand. Mekong is by far the most popular rice whiskey, but you will also see labels such as Sang Thip, Kwangthong, Hong Thong, Hong Ngoen, Hong Yok, and Hong Tho. Wine is increasingly available. However, the locally produced wines are likely to leave you with a nasty headache the next day, and the imported ones may do damage to your wallet. Imported wines are also likely to be in poor condition due to the tropical heat.

DISABILITIES
AND ACCESSIBILITY

Thailand is a challenge for people with disabilities. The pavements are totally unsuitable for wheelchairs, making getting around most places difficult. But traveling with a car and driver is relatively affordable here, and the Thais are so helpful that a person with disabilities can expect to have a great deal of friendly assistance.

RESERVATIONS

When discussing accessibility with an operator or reservations agent, **ask hard questions.** Are there any stairs, inside *or* out? Are there grab bars next to the toilet *and* in the shower/tub? How wide is the doorway to the room? To the bathroom? For the most extensive facilities meeting the latest legal specifications, **opt for newer accommodations.**

DISCOUNTS AND DEALS

Be a smart shopper and **compare all your options** before making decisions. A plane ticket bought with a promotional coupon from travel clubs, coupon books, and direct-mail offers or purchased on the Internet may not be cheaper than the least expensive fare from a discount ticket agency. And always keep in mind that what you get is just as important as what you save.

DISCOUNT RESERVATIONS

To save money, **look into discount reservations services** with Web sites and toll-free numbers, which use their buying power to get a better price on hotels, airline tickets, even car rentals. When booking a room, always **call the hotel's local toll-free number** (if one is available) rather than the central reservations number—you'll often get a better price. Always ask about special packages or corporate rates.

When shopping for the best deal on hotels and car rentals, **look for guaranteed exchange rates,** which protect you against a falling dollar. With your rate locked in, you won't pay more, even if the price goes up in the local currency.

➤ AIRLINE TICKETS: ☎ 800/FLY–4–LESS.

➤ HOTEL ROOMS: **Steigenberger Reservation Service** (☎ 800/223–5652, WEB www.srs-worldhotels.com). **Travel Interlink** (☎ 800/888–5898, WEB www.travelinterlink.com). **Turbotrip.com** (☎ 800/473–7829,

WEB www.turbotrip.com).
VacationLand (☎ 800/245–0050,
WEB www.vacation-land.com).

PACKAGE DEALS

Don't confuse packages and guided tours. When you buy a package, you travel on your own, just as though you had planned the trip yourself. Fly/drive packages, which combine airfare and car rental, are often a good deal.

ECOTOURISM

Tour agencies increasingly try to be eco-friendly, particularly on jungle treks in northern Thailand. This is especially true in Chiang Mai and Chiang Rai, where many people enjoy elephant treks into the mountains. Before booking a tour, **ask tough questions** about what the company does to preserve the environment.

Pay the extra few baht to buy water in glass bottles that can be recycled. Sometimes water comes in reusable plastic containers, which are clearly marked as such. However, as it stands now, too many plastic bottles are often simply strewn about, leaving an eyesore on street corners, and worse, on beaches.

ANIMAL RIGHTS

The elephant, revered for its strength, courage, and intelligence, has a long history in Thailand. These gentle giants were used to haul timber, including the teak pillars used in royal palaces and temples. In recent years, however, mechanization has made the domesticated elephant obsolete, and elephant trainers have come to rely on the tourist industry as their only source of income. To make sure they are not mistreated, the group Friends of the Asian Elephant monitors the treatment of elephants used in shows and treks. If you are going on an elephant-back trek and have concerns, check out how various companies treat their animals. Find out, for example, how many hours the elephants are worked each day and whether you will be riding in the afternoon heat.

➤ CONTACTS: **Friends of the Asian Elephant** (✉ 350 Moo 8, Ram-Indra Rd., Soi 61, Tharaeng, Bangkhen, Bangkok 10230, ☎ FAX 02/945–7124, www.elephant.tnet.co.th).

ELECTRICITY

To use your U.S.-purchased electric-powered equipment, **bring a converter and adapter.** The electrical current in Thailand is 220 volts, 50 cycles alternating current (AC); wall outlets take either two flat prongs, like outlets in the United States, or Continental-type plugs, with two round prongs.

If your appliances are dual-voltage, you'll need only an adapter. Don't use 110-volt outlets marked FOR SHAVERS ONLY for high-wattage appliances such as blow-dryers. Most laptops operate equally well on 110 and 220 volts and so require only an adapter.

EMBASSIES AND CONSULATES

Most nations maintain diplomatic relations with Thailand and have embassies in Bangkok; a few have consulates also in Chiang Mai. Should you need to apply for a visa to another country, the consulate hours are usually 8–noon daily.

➤ IN BANGKOK: **Australian Embassy** (✉ 37 Sathorn Tai Rd., ☎ 02/287–2680). **British Embassy** (✉ 1031 Wireless Rd., ☎ 02/253–0191). **Canadian Embassy** (✉ 15th floor, Abdulrahim Bldg., 990 Rama IV, ☎ 02/636–0540). **New Zealand Embassy** (✉ 93 Wireless Rd., ☎ 02/254–2530). **U.S. Embassy** (✉ 120–122 Wireless Rd., ☎ 02/205–4000).

➤ IN CHIANG MAI: **Australian Consulate** (✉ 165 Sirman Khalajan, ☎ 053/221083). **British Consulate** (✉ 201 Airport Business Park, 90 Mahidon, ☎ 053/203405). **U.S. Consulate** (✉ 387 Wichayanom Rd., ☎ 053/252629).

EMERGENCIES

Thais are generally quite helpful, so you should get assistance from locals if you need it. The Tourist Police will help you in case of a robbery or rip-off.

Many hotels can refer you to an English-speaking doctor. For serious health situations, it's best to be treated in your own country; otherwise consider flying to Singapore, which has the region's best medical facilities.

➤ CONTACTS: **Police** (☎ 191). **Tourist Police** (☎ 1699).

ENGLISH-LANGUAGE MEDIA

Thailand has by and large a free press, with only a modicum of self-censorship (particularly when referring to the monarchy) in evidence.

BOOKS

Major hotels have bookstores and tourist areas have secondhand shops where you should be able to trade or buy inexpensive books written in a variety of languages.

NEWSPAPERS AND MAGAZINES

There are two English-language newspapers published daily in Thailand: *The Bangkok Post* (morning edition) and *The Nation* (afternoon edition). The former has more of an international news staff, which is evident in the more Western-style reporting.

The Bangkok Metro magazine tells readers what's hip and happening in Bangkok. It also gives some listings for Pattaya, Phuket, and Chiang Mai.

Popular newspapers and magazines—from the *International Herald Tribune* to *Time* magazine—are widely available throughout Thailand.

RADIO AND TELEVISION

Bangkok has five VHF-TV networks, with English shows aired periodically during the day, although mostly in the mornings. Satellite and cable TV are widely available, where you can expect to see HBO, MTV Asia, CNN International, and BBC World Service Television.

There are literally hundreds of radio stations available in Thailand. Check out 107 FM for CNN hourly updates. Radio Bangkok, at 95.5 FM, also has English-speaking DJs.

ETIQUETTE AND BEHAVIOR

Displays of anger, raised voices, and confrontations are considered very bad form. Thais disapprove of public nudity and of public shows of affection. Do not step over a seated person or someone's legs. Don't point your feet at anyone; keep them on the floor, and take care not to show the soles of your feet. Never touch a person's head, even a child's (the head is considered sacred), and avoid touching a monk if you are a woman.

When visiting temples, **dress modestly.** Don't wear shorts or tank tops. If you show up improperly attired, some temples have wraps you can borrow. Others will not let you enter. Remove your shoes before entering the temple and don't point your toes at any image of the buddha, as it is considered sacrilegious.

GAY AND LESBIAN TRAVEL

Thailand has always shown tolerance toward homosexuality, though public affection between couples of any gender is frowned on. In Bangkok, Patpong III has many gay bars, and you'll also find them in Chiang Mai, Pattaya, and Phuket.

One of the best Web sites for gay travelers is Dreaded Ned's (www. dreadedned.com), which has frequently updated listings for all major destinations in the country. There are also handy maps for finding your way around the confusing streets and sois.

➤ GAY- AND LESBIAN-FRIENDLY TRAVEL AGENCIES: **Different Roads Travel** (✉ 8383 Wilshire Blvd., Suite 902, Beverly Hills, CA 90211, ☎ 323/651–5557 or 800/429–8747, FAX 323/651–3678, lgernert@tzell.com). **Kennedy Travel** (✉ 314 Jericho Turnpike, Floral Park, NY 11001, ☎ 516/352–4888 or 800/237–7433, FAX 516/354–8849, WEB www.kennedytravel.com). **Now, Voyager** (✉ 4406 18th St., San Francisco, CA 94114, ☎ 415/626–1169 or 800/255–6951, FAX 415/626–8626, WEB www.nowvoyager.com). **Skylink Travel and Tour** (✉ 1006 Mendocino Ave., Santa Rosa, CA 95401, ☎ 707/546–9888 or 800/225–5759, FAX 707/546–9891, WEB www.skylinktravel.com), serving lesbian travelers.

HEALTH

Although Thailand does not require or suggest vaccinations before traveling, the United States Centers for Disease Control offer the following recommendations:

Tetanus and polio vaccinations should be up-to-date, and you should be immunized against (or immune to) measles, mumps, and rubella. If you plan to visit rural areas, where there's questionable sanitation, you'll need a vaccination as protection against hepatitis A.

Be aware that a high percentage of sex workers in Thailand are HIV positive, and unprotected sex is extremely risky.

FOOD AND DRINK

In Thailand the major health risk is traveler's diarrhea, caused by eating contaminated fruit or vegetables or drinking contaminated water. So **watch what you eat.** Avoid ice, un-cooked food, and unpasteurized milk and milk products, and **drink only bottled water** or water that has been boiled for at least 20 minutes, even when brushing your teeth. Mild cases may respond to Imodium (known generically as loperamide) or Pepto-Bismol (not as strong), both of which can be purchased over the counter; paregoric, another antidiarrheal agent, does not require a doctor's prescrip-tion in Thailand. Drink plenty of purified water or tea—chamomile is a good folk remedy. In severe cases, rehydrate yourself with a salt-sugar solution (½ teaspoon salt and 4 table-spoons sugar per quart of water).

MEDICAL PLANS

No one plans to get sick while travel-ing, but it happens, so **consider sign-ing up with a medical-assistance company.** Members get doctor refer-rals, emergency evacuation or repatri-ation, hot lines for medical consultation, cash for emergencies, and other assistance.

➤ MEDICAL-ASSISTANCE COMPANIES: **International SOS Assistance** (WEB www.internationalsos.com; ✉ 8 Neshaminy Interplex, Suite 207, Trevose, PA 19053, ☎ 215/245–4707 or 800/523–6586, FAX 215/244–9617; ✉ 12 Chemin Riantbosson, 1217 Meyrin 1, Geneva, Switzerland, ☎ 22/785–6464, FAX 22/785–6424; ✉ 331 N. Bridge Rd., 17-00, Odeon Towers, Singapore 188720, ☎ 338–7800, FAX 338–7611).

SHOTS AND MEDICATIONS

According to the U.S. government's National Centers for Disease Con-trol(CDC) there is a limited risk of malaria, hepatitis B, dengue, rabies, and Japanese encephalitis in certain rural areas of Thailand. In most urban or easily accessible areas you need not worry. However, if you plan to visit remote regions or stay for more than six weeks, **check with the CDC's International Travelers Hotline.** In areas where malaria and dengue, both of which are carried by mosquitoes, are prevalent, use mosquito nets, wear clothing that covers the body, apply repellent containing DEET, and use spray for flying insects in living and sleeping areas. Also **talk to your doctor about taking antimalarial pills.** There is no vaccine to combat dengue, so if it's in the area, travelers should use aerosol insecticides indoors as well as mosquito repellents outdoors. Both Ko Samet and northern Thailand are known to have malarial mosquitoes, so take extra precautions if you visit these areas.

➤ HEALTH WARNINGS: **National Centers for Disease Control and Prevention** (CDC; National Center for Infectious Diseases, Division of Quarantine, Traveler's Health Sec-tion, ✉ 1600 Clifton Rd. NE, M/S E-03, Atlanta, GA 30333, ☎ 888/232–3228 general information; 877/394–8747 travelers' health line; 800/311–3435 public inquiries; FAX 888/232–3299, WEB www.cdc.gov).

HOLIDAYS

New Year's Day (January 1); Chinese New Year (January 22, 2004); Magha Puja (on the full moon of the third lunar month); Chakri Day (April 6); Songkran (April 13–15); Coronation Day (May 5); Visakha Puja, May (on the full moon of the sixth lunar month); Queen's Birthday (August 12); King's Birthday (December 5). Government offices, banks, commer-cial concerns, and department stores are usually closed on these days, but smaller shops stay open.

INSURANCE

The most useful travel-insurance plan is a comprehensive policy that in-cludes coverage for trip cancellation and interruption, default, trip delay, and medical expenses (with a waiver for preexisting conditions).

Without insurance you will lose all or most of your money if you cancel your trip, regardless of the reason. Default insurance covers you if your tour operator, airline, or cruise line goes out of business. Trip-delay covers expenses that arise because of bad weather or mechanical delays. Study the fine print when comparing policies.

If you're traveling internationally, a key component of travel insurance is coverage for medical bills incurred if you get sick on the road. Such expenses are not generally covered by Medicare or private policies. U.K. residents can buy a travel-insurance policy valid for most vacations taken during the year in which it's purchased (but check preexisting-condition coverage). British and Australian citizens need extra medical coverage when traveling overseas.

Always **buy travel policies directly from the insurance company**; if you buy them from a cruise line, airline, or tour operator that goes out of business you probably will not be covered for the agency or operator's default, a major risk. Before making any purchase, **review your existing health and home-owner's policies** to find what they cover away from home.

➤ TRAVEL INSURERS: In the United States: **Access America** (✉ 6600 W. Broad St., Richmond, VA 23230, ☎ 800/284–8300, FAX 804/673–1491 or 800/346–9265, WEB www. accessamerica.com). **Travel Guard International** (✉ 1145 Clark St., Stevens Point, WI 54481, ☎ 715/ 345–0505 or 800/826–1300, FAX 800/ 955–8785, WEB www.travelguard. com).

LANGUAGE

Thai is the country's national language. As it uses the Khmer script and is spoken tonally, it is confusing to most foreigners. In polite conversation, a male speaker will use the word "krap" to end a sentence or to acknowledge what someone has said. Female speakers use "ka." It is easy to speak a few words, such as "sawahdee krap" or "sawahdee ka" (good day) and "khop khun krap" or "khop khun ka" (thank you). With the exception of taxi drivers, Thais working with travelers in the resort and tourist areas of Thailand generally speak sufficient English to permit basic communication.

LODGING

Every town of reasonable size offers accommodations. In the smaller towns the hotels may be fairly simple, but they will usually be clean and certainly inexpensive. In major cities or resort areas there are hotels to fit all price categories. At the high end, the luxury hotels can compete with the best in the world. Service is generally superb—polite and efficient—and most of the staff usually speak English. At the other end of the scale, the lodging is simple and basic—a room with little more than a bed. The least expensive places may have Asian toilets (squat type with no seat) and a fan rather than air-conditioning.

All except the budget hotels have restaurants and offer room service throughout most of the day and night. Most will also be happy to make local travel arrangements for you—for which they receive commissions. All hotels advise that you use their safe-deposit boxes.

During the peak tourist season, October–March, hotels are often fully booked and charge peak rates. At special times, such as December 30– January 2 and Chinese New Year, rates climb even higher, and hotel reservations are difficult to obtain. Weekday rates at some resorts are often lower, and virtually all hotels will discount their rooms if they are not fully booked. Don't be reticent about asking for a special rate. Breakfast is rarely included in the room tariff. Hotel rates tend to be lower if you reserve through a travel agent (in Thailand). The agent receives a reduced room rate from the hotel and passes some of this discount on to you.

The lodgings we list are the cream of the crop in each price category. We always list the facilities that are available, but we don't specify whether they cost extra; when pricing accommodations, always ask what's included and what costs extra.

CATEGORY	COST*
$$$$	over B6,000
	(over US$150)
$$$	B4,000–B6,000
	(US$100–$150)
$$	B2,000–B4,000
	(US$50–$100)
$	B1,000–B2,000
	(under US$50)
¢	under B1,000
	(under US$25)

All prices are for a standard double room, excluding tax.

Assume that hotels operate on the **European Plan** (EP, with no meals) unless we specify that they use either the **Continental Plan** (CP, with a Continental breakfast), **Breakfast Plan** (BP, with a full breakfast), or the **Modified American Plan** (MAP, with breakfast and dinner) or are **all-inclusive** (including all meals and most activities).

APARTMENT AND VILLA RENTALS

If you want a home base that's roomy enough for a family and comes with cooking facilities, **consider a furnished rental.** These can save you money, especially if you're traveling with a group. Home-exchange directories sometimes list rentals as well as exchanges.

➤ INTERNATIONAL AGENTS: **Villas International** (✉ 4340 Redwood Hwy., Suite D309, San Rafael, CA 94903, ☎ 415/499–9490 or 800/221–2260, FAX 415/499–9491, WEB www.villasintl.com).

HOSTELS

No matter what your age, you can **save on lodging costs by staying at hostels.** In some 4,500 locations in more than 70 countries around the world, Hostelling International (HI), the umbrella group for a number of national youth-hostel associations, offers single-sex, dorm-style beds and, at many hostels, rooms for couples and family accommodations. Membership in any HI national hostel association, open to travelers of all ages, allows you to stay in HI-affiliated hostels at member rates; one-year membership is about $25 for adults (C$35 for a two-year minimum membership in Canada, £13 in the

United Kingdom, A$52 in Australia, and NZ$40 in New Zealand); hostels run about $10–$30 per night. Members have priority if the hostel is full; they're also eligible for discounts around the world, even on rail and bus travel in some countries.

➤ ORGANIZATIONS: **Hostelling International–American Youth Hostels** (✉ 733 15th St. NW, Suite 840, Washington, DC 20005, ☎ 202/783–6161, FAX 202/783–6171, WEB www. hiayh.org). **Hostelling International–Canada** (✉ 400–205 Catherine St., Ottawa, Ontario K2P 1C3, ☎ 613/237–7884 or 800/663–5777, FAX 613/237–7868, WEB www.hihostels.ca). **Youth Hostel Association Australia** (✉ 10 Mallett St., Camperdown, NSW 2050, ☎ 02/9565–1699, FAX 02/9565–1325, WEB www.yha.com.au). **Youth Hostel Association of England and Wales** (✉ Trevelyan House, Dimple Rd., Matlock, Derbyshire DE4 3YH, U.K., ☎ 0870/870–8808, FAX 0169/592–702, WEB www.yha.org. uk). **Youth Hostels Association of New Zealand** (✉ Level 3, 193 Cashel St., Box 436, Christchurch, ☎ 03/379–9970, FAX 03/365–4476, WEB www.yha.org.nz).

HOTELS

In Bangkok, the hotels we list have all the comforts of home. In the more far-flung parts of the country, hotels may be a bit more basic, with fans rather than air-conditioning. All hotels listed have private bath unless otherwise noted.

➤ TOLL-FREE NUMBERS: **Best Western** (☎ 800/528–1234, WEB www. bestwestern.com). **Choice** (☎ 800/424–6423, WEB www.choicehotels. com). **Four Seasons** (☎ 800/332–3442, WEB www.fourseasons.com). **Hilton** (☎ 800/445–8667, WEB www. hilton.com). **Holiday Inn** (☎ 800/465–4329, WEB www.sixcontinentshotels. com). **Hyatt Hotels & Resorts** (☎ 800/233–1234, WEB www.hyatt. com). **Inter-Continental** (☎ 800/327–0200, WEB www.intercontinental.com). **Marriott** (☎ 800/228–9290, WEB www. marriott.com). **Le Meridien** (☎ 800/543–4300, WEB www.lemeridien-hotels. com). **Radisson** (☎ 800/333–3333, WEB www.radisson.com). **Ramada** (☎ 800/228–2828; 800/854–7854 international reservations; WEB www.

ramada.com or www.ramadahotels. com). **Sheraton** (☎ 800/325–3535, WEB www.starwood.com/sheraton). **Westin Hotels & Resorts** (☎ 800/228–3000, WEB www.starwood.com/westin).

MAIL AND SHIPPING

Thailand's mail service is reliable and efficient. Major hotels provide basic postal services. Bangkok's central general post office on Charoen Krung (New Road) is open weekdays 8–6, weekends and public holidays 9–1. Up-country post offices close at 4:30 PM.

OVERNIGHT SERVICES

You can ship packages via DHL Worldwide, Federal Express, or UPS.

➤ CONTACTS: **DHL Worldwide** (✉ 22nd floor, Grand Amarin Tower, Phetburi Tat Mai, Bangkok, ☎ 02/ 207–0600). **Federal Express** (✉ 8th floor, Green Tower, Rama IV, Bangkok, ☎ 02/367–3222). **UPS** (✉ 16/1 Soi 44/1, Sukhumvit, Bangkok, ☎ 02/712–3300).

POSTAL RATES

Letter, packet, and parcel rates are low—B27 for a letter to the United States, B17 for a letter to Europe. Allow at least 10 days for your mail to arrive. For speedier delivery, major post offices offer overseas express mail service.

RECEIVING MAIL

You may have mail sent to you "poste restante" at the following address: Poste Restante, General Post Office, Bangkok, Thailand. There is a B1 charge for each piece collected. Thais write their last name first, so be sure to have your last name written in capital letters and underlined.

SHIPPING PARCELS

Parcels are easy to send from Thailand. Parcel rates vary by weight, country of destination, and shipping style (air or surface). Expect to pay between B700 and B1,100 for a kilo package and then an additional B300 to B350 per added kilo.

MONEY MATTERS

It is possible to live and travel quite inexpensively if you do as Thais do— eat in local restaurants, use buses, and stay at non-air-conditioned hotels.

Once you start enjoying a little luxury, prices jump drastically. For example, crossing Bangkok by bus is less than 15¢, but by taxi the fare may run to $10. Prices are typically higher in resort areas catering to foreign tourists, and Bangkok is more expensive than other Thai cities. Imported items are heavily taxed.

Sample prices: buffet breakfast at a hotel, $8; large bottle of beer at a hotel, $6, but in a local restaurant it will be under $3; dinner at a good restaurant, $15; 1-mile taxi ride, $1.50; museum entrance, 50¢–$2.

Prices throughout this guide are given for adults. Substantially reduced fees are almost always available for children, students, and senior citizens. For information on taxes, see Taxes, below.

ATMS

Twenty-four-hour automatic teller machines are widely available throughout Thailand. Some Thai ATMs take Cirrus, some take Plus, some take both.

CREDIT CARDS

Credit cards are accepted in restaurants, hotels, and shops. You may be levied a 3% to 5% charge despite the fact that this is technically against Thai law, but you will likely receive a favorable exchange rate from your home bank that could make up the difference.

Throughout this guide, the following abbreviations are used: **AE,** American Express; **DC,** Diner's Club; **MC,** Master Card; and **V,** Visa.

➤ REPORTING LOST CARDS: **American Express** (☎ 800/441–0519). **Diners Club** (☎ 800/234–6377). **Discover** (☎ 800/347–2683). **MasterCard** (☎ 800/622–7747). **Visa** (☎ 800/ 847–2911).

CURRENCY

The basic unit of currency is the baht. There are 100 satang to one baht. There are five different bills, each a different color: B10, brown; B20, green; B50, blue; B100, red; B500, purple; and B1,000, beige. Coins in use are 25 satang, 50 satang, B1, B5, and B10. The B10 coin has a gold-color center surrounded by silver.

The baht, formerly pegged to the U.S. dollar, is at press time undergoing considerable fluctuation. All hotels will convert traveler's checks and major currencies into baht, though exchange rates are better at banks and authorized money changers. The rate tends to be better in Bangkok than up-country and is better in Thailand than in the United States. Major international credit cards are accepted at most tourist shops and hotels.

At press time, B42 = US$1, B69 = £1, B28 = C$1, B26 = $A1, B23 = NZ$1.

CURRENCY EXCHANGE

Changing "old" U.S. $100 (the ones with the small heads) is increasingly difficult as these notes have been successfully counterfeited in the region. Bring the new "big head" U.S. $100. Clean, crisp notes are also preferred.

For the most favorable rates, **change money through banks.** Although ATM transaction fees may be higher abroad than at home, ATM rates are excellent because they are based on wholesale rates offered only by major banks. You won't do as well at exchange booths in airports or rail and bus stations, in hotels, in restaurants, or in stores. To avoid lines at airport exchange booths, **get a bit of local currency before you leave home.**

➤ EXCHANGE SERVICES: **International Currency Express** (☎ 888/278–6628 for orders, WEB www.foreignmoney. com). **Thomas Cook Currency Services** (☎ 800/287–7362 for telephone orders and retail locations, WEB www. us.thomascook.com).

TRAVELER'S CHECKS

Do you need traveler's checks? It depends on where you're headed. If you're going to rural areas and small towns, go with cash; traveler's checks are best used in cities. Lost or stolen checks can usually be replaced within 24 hours. To ensure a speedy refund, buy your own traveler's checks— don't let someone else pay for them: irregularities like this can cause delays. The person who bought the checks should make the call to request a refund.

PACKING

Light cotton or other natural-fiber clothing is appropriate for Thailand; drip-dry is an especially good idea, because the tropical sun and high humidity encourage frequent changes of clothing. Avoid delicate fabrics because you may have difficulty getting them laundered. A sweater is welcome on cool evenings or overly air-conditioned restaurants, buses, and trains.

The paths leading to temples can be rough, so **bring a sturdy pair of walking shoes.** Slip-ons are preferable to lace-up shoes, as they must be removed before you enter shrines and temples.

In your carry-on luggage, **pack an extra pair of eyeglasses or contact lenses and enough of any medication** you take to last a few days longer than the entire trip. You may also ask your doctor to write a spare prescription using the drug's generic name, since brand names may vary from country to country. In luggage to be checked, **never pack prescription drugs or valuables.** And don't forget to carry with you the addresses of offices that handle refunds of lost traveler's checks. Check *Fodor's How to Pack* (available in bookstores everywhere) for more tips.

To avoid customs and security delays, carry medications in their original packaging. Don't pack any sharp objects in your carry-on luggage, including knives of any size or material, scissors, manicure tools, and corkscrews, or anything else that might arouse suspicion.

CHECKING LUGGAGE

You are allowed one carry-on bag and one personal article, such as a purse or a laptop computer. Make sure that everything you carry aboard will fit under your seat or in the overhead bin. Get to the gate early, so you can board as soon as possible, before the overhead bins fill up.

If you are flying internationally, note that baggage allowances may be determined not by piece but by weight—generally 88 pounds (40 kilograms) in first class, 66 pounds (30 kilograms) in business class, and 44 pounds (20 kilograms) in economy.

Before departure, **itemize your bags' contents** and their worth, and label the bags with your name, address, and phone number. (If you use your home address, cover it so potential thieves can't see it readily.) Inside each bag, **pack a copy of your itinerary**. At check-in, **make sure that each bag is correctly tagged** with the destination airport's three-letter code. If your bags arrive damaged or fail to arrive at all, file a written report with the airline before leaving the airport.

PASSPORTS AND VISAS

When traveling internationally, **carry your passport** even if you don't need one (it's always the best form of I.D.) and **make two photocopies of the data page** (one for someone at home and another for you, carried separately from your passport). If you lose your passport, promptly call the nearest embassy or consulate and the local police.

ENTERING THAILAND

Australian, Canadian, U.S., and U.K. citizens—even infants—need only a valid passport and an onward ticket to enter Thailand for stays of up to 30 days. New Zealanders are permitted to stay up to 90 days with a valid passport and onward ticket.

The Immigration Division in Bangkok issues Thai visa extensions, but if you overstay by a few days, don't worry; you'll simply pay a B200 per diem fine as you go through immigration on departure.

➤ VISA EXTENSIONS: **Immigration Division** (✉ Soi Suan Phlu, Sathorn Rd., Bangkok, ☎ 02/287–3101).

REST ROOMS

Western-style facilities are usually available, although you still may find squat toilets in older buildings. Toilet paper is rarely provided, so it's a good idea to carry some. Often a bucket is placed under a tap next to the loo; you are expected to fill the bucket with water and flush out the toilet manually.

SAFETY

Thailand is a safe country, but normal precautions should be followed: be careful late at night, watch your valuables in crowded areas, and lock your hotel rooms securely. Credit-card scams—from stealing your card to swiping it several times when you use it at stores—are a frequent problem. Don't leave your wallet behind when you go trekking and make sure you keep an eye on the card when you give it to a salesperson.

While it's never wise to become involved in a brawl, it is particularly foolish to do this in Thailand: (a) many of the locals are accomplished martial artists and/or are carrying weapons; and (b) as a foreigner you will likely be deemed at fault, even if you weren't.

LOCAL SCAMS

Beware of touts, particularly taxi drivers, offering to take you to "their" guest house or "their brother's" shop; it's a sham. The driver will be given a commission on your spendings.

WOMEN IN THAILAND

Women should take care when walking alone on beaches or desolate areas, particularly late at night. Dress conservatively, and don't respond to verbal comments or harassment. If you're lost or need assistance, try to consult local women when possible.

SENIOR-CITIZEN TRAVEL

To qualify for age-related discounts, **mention your senior-citizen status up front** when booking hotel reservations (not when checking out) and before you're seated in restaurants (not when paying the bill). Be sure to have identification on hand. When renting a car, ask about promotional car-rental discounts, which can be cheaper than senior-citizen rates.

➤ EDUCATIONAL PROGRAMS: **Elderhostel** (✉ 11 Ave. de Lafayette, Boston, MA 02111-1746, ☎ 877/426–8056, FAX 877/426–2166, WEB www.elderhostel.org).

STUDENTS IN THAILAND

Thailand is a top destination for students. You'll run into many fellow travelers who'll clue you in to the best places to visit. Finding inexpensive dining or lodging options is easy.

➤ I.D.s AND SERVICES: **STA Travel** (☎ 212/627–3111 or 800/781–4040, FAX 212/627–3387, WEB www.sta.com). **Travel Cuts** (✉ 187 College St., Toronto, Ontario M5T 1P7, Canada, ☎ 416/979–2406 or 888/838–2887, FAX 416/979–8167, WEB www. travelcuts.com).

TAXES

A 10% value added tax is built into the price of all goods and services, including restaurant meals, and is essentially nonrefundable.

TELEPHONES

AREA AND COUNTRY CODES

The country code for Thailand is 66. When dialing a Thailand number from abroad, drop the initial 0 from the local area code. The country code is 1 for the United States and Canada, 61 for Australia, 64 for New Zealand, and 44 for the United Kingdom.

DIRECTORY AND OPERATOR ASSISTANCE

If you wish to receive assistance for an overseas call, dial 100/233–2771. For local telephone inquiries, dial 100/183, but you will need to speak Thai. In Bangkok, you can dial 13 for an English-speaking operator.

INTERNATIONAL CALLS

To make overseas calls, you should use either your hotel switchboard— Chiang Mai and Bangkok have direct dialing—or the overseas telephone facilities at the central post office and telecommunications building. You'll find one in all towns. In Bangkok, the overseas telephone center, next to the general post office, is open 24 hours; up-country, the facilities' hours may vary, but they usually open at 8 AM and some stay open until 10 PM. Some locations in Bangkok have AT&T USADirect phones, which connect you with an AT&T operator.

LONG-DISTANCE CALLS

Long-distance calls can only be made on phones that accept both B1 and B5 coins. For a long-distance call in Thailand, dial the area code and then the number.

LONG-DISTANCE SERVICES

AT&T, MCI, and Sprint access codes make calling long distance relatively convenient, but you may find the local access number blocked in many hotel rooms. First ask the hotel operator to connect you. If the hotel operator balks, ask for an international operator, or dial the international operator yourself. One way to improve your odds of getting connected to your long-distance carrier is to travel with more than one company's calling card (a hotel may block Sprint, for example, but not MCI). If all else fails, call from a pay phone.

➤ ACCESS CODES: **AT&T USADirect** (☎ 0019–991–1111; 800/222–0300 for other areas). **MCI WorldPhone** (☎ 001–999–1–2001 not from pay phones; 800/444–3333 for other areas). **Sprint International Access** (☎ 001–999–13–877; 800/877–4646 for other areas).

PUBLIC PHONES

Public telephones are available in most towns and villages and take B1 coins or both B1 and B5 pieces. Long-distance calls can be made only on phones that accept both B1 and B5 coins. For a long-distance call in Thailand, dial the area code and then the number.

TIME

Thailand is 7 hours ahead of Greenwich Mean Time. It is 12 hours ahead of New York, 15 hours ahead of Los Angeles, 7 hours ahead of London, and 3 hours behind Sydney.

TIPPING

In Thailand, tips are generally given for good service, except when a price has been negotiated in advance. A taxi driver is not tipped unless hired as a private driver for an excursion. With metered taxis in Bangkok, however, the custom is to round the fare up to the nearest 5 baht. Hotel porters expect at least a B20 tip, and hotel staff who have given good personal service are usually tipped. A 10% tip is appreciated at a restaurant when no service charge has been added to the bill.

TOURS AND PACKAGES

Because everything is prearranged on a prepackaged tour or independent vacation, you spend less time planning—and often get it all at a good price.

BOOKING WITH AN AGENT

Travel agents are excellent resources. But it's a good idea to collect brochures from several agencies, as some agents' suggestions may be influenced by relationships with tour and package firms that reward them for volume sales. If you have a special interest, **find an agent with expertise in that area**; the American Society of Travel Agents (ASTA; ☞ Travel Agencies, *below*) has a database of specialists worldwide.

Make sure your travel agent knows the accommodations and other services of the place being recommended. Ask about the hotel's location, room size, beds, and whether it has a pool, room service, or programs for children, if you care about these. Has your agent been there in person or sent others whom you can contact?

Do some homework on your own, too: local tourism boards can provide information about lesser-known and small-niche operators, some of which may sell only direct.

BUYER BEWARE

Each year consumers are stranded or lose their money when tour operators—even large ones with excellent reputations—go out of business. So **check out the operator.** Ask several travel agents about its reputation, and try to **book with a company that has a consumer-protection program.** (Look for information in the company's brochure.) In the United States, members of the National Tour Association and the United States Tour Operators Association are required to set aside funds to cover your payments and travel arrangements in the event that the company defaults. It's also a good idea to choose a company that participates in the American Society of Travel Agents' Tour Operator Program (TOP); ASTA will act as mediator in any disputes between you and your tour operator.

Remember that the more your package or tour includes the better you can predict the ultimate cost of your vacation. Make sure you know exactly what is covered, and **beware of hidden costs.** Are taxes, tips, and transfers included? Entertainment and excursions? These can add up.

➤ TOUR-OPERATOR RECOMMENDATIONS: **American Society of Travel Agents** (☞ Travel Agencies, *below*). **National Tour Association** (NTA; ✉ 546 E. Main St., Lexington, KY 40508, ☎ 859/226–4444 or 800/682–8886, WEB www.ntaonline.com). **United States Tour Operators Association** (USTOA; ✉ 275 Madison Ave., Suite 2014, New York, NY 10016, ☎ 212/599–6599 or 800/468–7862, FAX 212/599–6744, WEB www.ustoa.com).

TRAIN TRAVEL

The State Railway of Thailand has three lines, all of which have terminals in Bangkok. The Northern Line connects Bangkok with Chiang Mai, passing through Ayutthaya and Phitsanulok; the Northeastern Line travels up to Nong Khai, near the Laotian border, with a branch that goes east to Ubon Ratchathani; and the Southern Line goes all the way south through Surat Thani—the stop for Ko Samui—to the Malaysian border and on to Kuala Lumpur and Singapore, a journey that takes 37 hours. (There is no train to Phuket, though you can go as far as Surat Thani and change to a scheduled bus service.)

To save money, look into rail passes. But be aware that if you don't plan to cover many miles, you may come out ahead by buying individual tickets.

Many travelers assume that rail passes guarantee them seats on the trains they wish to ride. Not so. You need to book seats ahead even if you are using a rail pass; seat reservations are required on some trains, and are a good idea on trains that may be crowded—particularly in summer on popular routes. You will also need a reservation if you purchase overnight sleeping accommodations.

For information on schedules and passes, call the Bangkok Railway Station.

➤ TRAIN STATIONS: **Bangkok Railway Station** (☎ 02/223–3762 or 02/223–0341).

CLASSES

Most trains offer second- or third-class tickets, but the overnight trains to the north (Chiang Mai) and to the south offer first-class sleeping cabins. Couchettes, with sheets and curtains for privacy, are available in second class. Second-class tickets are about half the price of first-class, and since the couchettes are surprisingly comfortable, most Western travelers choose these. Do not leave valuables unguarded on these overnight trains.

DISCOUNT PASSES

The State Railway of Thailand offers two types of rail passes. Both are valid for 20 days of unlimited travel on all trains in either second or third class. The **Blue Pass** costs B1,100 (children B750) and does not include supplementary charges such as air-conditioning and berths; for B3,000 (children B1,500), the **Red Pass** does. Currently, a special discounted rate, available for nonresidents of Thailand, gives a reduction of B1,000 for the Red Pass and B400 for the Blue Pass.

FARES AND SCHEDULES

Train schedules in English are available from travel agents and from major railway stations.

An air-conditioned, second-class couchette, for example, for the 14-hour journey from Bangkok to Chiang Mai is B625; first class is B1,190.

PAYING

Tickets may be bought at railway stations. Travel agencies can also sell tickets for overnight trains.

RESERVATIONS

Reservations are strongly advised for all long-distance trains.

TRANSPORTATION AROUND THAILAND

SAMLORS

For short trips, these bicycle rickshaws are a popular, inexpensive form of transport, but they become expensive for long trips. Fares are negotiable, so **be very clear about what price is agreed upon.** Drivers have a tendency to create misunderstandings leading to a nasty scene at the end of the trip.

SONGTHAEWS

With a name that literally means "two rows," these pickup trucks have a couple of wooden benches in the back. They operate on routes outside of Bangkok. Drivers generally wait until they are at least half full before departing.

TAXIS

Most Bangkok taxis now have meters installed, and these are the ones tourists should take. In other cities, fares are still negotiated. Taxis waiting at hotels are more expensive than those flagged down on the street. **Never enter an unmetered taxi until the price has been established.** Most taxi drivers do not speak English, but all understand the finger count. One finger means B10, two is for B20 and so on. Ask at your hotel what the appropriate fare should be.

TUK-TUKS

So-called because of their spluttering sound, these three-wheel cabs are slightly less expensive than taxis and, because of their maneuverability, the most rapid form of travel through congested traffic. All tuk-tuk operators drive as if your ride will be their last, but, in fact, they are remarkably safe. Tuk-tuks are not very comfortable, though, and they subject you to the polluted air, so they're best used for short journeys.

TRAVEL AGENCIES

A good travel agent puts your needs first. Look for an agency that has been in business at least five years, emphasizes customer service, and has someone on staff who specializes in your destination. In addition, **make sure the agency belongs to a professional trade organization.** The American Society of Travel Agents (ASTA)—the largest and most influential in the field with more than 24,000 members in some 140 countries—maintains and enforces a strict code of ethics and will step in to help mediate any agent-client disputes involving ASTA members if necessary. ASTA (whose motto is "Without a travel agent, you're on your own") also maintains a Web site that includes a directory of agents. (If a travel agency is also acting as your tour operator, *see* Buyer Beware *in* Tours and Packages, *above*.)

➤ LOCAL AGENT REFERRALS: **American Society of Travel Agents** (ASTA; ✉ 1101 King St., Suite 200, Alexandria, VA 22314, ☎ 800/965–2782 24-hr hot line, FAX 703/739–3268, WEB www. astanet.com). **Association of British Travel Agents** (✉ 68–71 Newman St., London W1T 3AH, ☎ 020/7637–2444, FAX 020/7637–0713, WEB www. abtanet.com). **Association of Canadian Travel Agents** (✉ 130 Albert St., Suite 1705, Ottawa, Ontario K1P 5G4, ☎ 613/237–3657, FAX 613/237–7052, WEB www.acta.ca). **Australian Federation of Travel Agents** (✉ Level 3, 309 Pitt St., Sydney, NSW 2000, ☎ 02/9264–3299, FAX 02/9264–1085, WEB www.afta.com.au). **Travel Agents' Association of New Zealand** (✉ Level 5, Tourism and Travel House, 79 Boulcott St., Box 1888, Wellington 6001, ☎ 04/499–0104, FAX 04/499–0827, WEB www.taanz.org.nz).

VISITOR INFORMATION

➤ TOURIST INFORMATION: **Tourism Authority of Thailand** (✉ c/o World Publications, 304 Park Ave. South, 8th Floor, New York, NY 10010 U.S., ☎ 212/219–7447, FAX 212/219–4697; ✉ 611 N. Larchmont Blvd., 1st floor, Los Angeles, CA 90004 U.S., ☎ 213/461–9814, FAX 213/461–9834).

➤ IN THE U.K.: **Thailand Tourist Board** (✉ 49 Albemarle St., London W1X 3FE, ☎ 0207/499–7679).

➤ IN AUSTRALIA AND NEW ZEALAND: **Tourism Authority of Thailand** (✉ 75 Pitt St., Sydney 20000, NSW, ☎ 02/9247–75719).

➤ U.S. GOVERNMENT ADVISORIES: **U.S. Department of State** (✉ Overseas Citizens Services Office, Room 4811 N.S., 2201 C St. NW, Washington, DC 20520, ☎ 202/647–5225 for interactive hot line; 301/946–4400 for computer bulletin board; FAX 202/647–3000 for interactive hot line).

WEB SITES

Do check out the World Wide Web when planning your trip. You'll find everything from weather forecasts to virtual tours of famous cities. Be sure to visit **Fodors.com** (www.fodors.com), a complete travel-planning site. You can research prices and book plane tickets, hotel rooms, rental cars, vacation packages, and more. In addition, you can post your pressing questions in the Travel Talk section. Other planning tools include a currency converter and weather reports, and there are loads of links to travel resources.

Other sites worth checking out are: www.tat.or.th, www.amazingsiam. com, www.thailand-travelsearch.com, and www.nectec.or.th for more information on Thailand.

WHEN TO GO

Thailand has two climatic regions: tropical savannah in the northern regions and tropical rain forest in the south. Three seasons run from hot (March through May) to rainy (June through September) and cool (October through February). Humidity is high all year, especially during the hot season. The cool season is pleasantly warm in the south, but in the north, especially in the hills around Chiang Mai, it can become quite chilly. The cool season is the peak season. Prices are often twice as high then as in the low seasons, yet hotels are often fully booked.

CLIMATE

➤ FORECASTS: **Weather Channel Connection** (☎ 900/932–8437), 95¢ per minute from a Touch-Tone phone.

The following are average daily maximum and minimum temperatures for Bangkok. The north will generally be a degree or two cooler.

Jan.	89F	32C	May	93F	34C	Sept.	89F	32C
	68	20		77	25		75	24
Feb.	91F	33C	June	91F	33C	Oct.	88F	31C
	72	22		75	24		75	24
Mar.	93F	34C	July	89F	32C	Nov.	88F	31C
	75	24		75	24		72	22
Apr.	95F	35C	Aug.	89F	32C	Dec.	88F	31C
	77	25		75	24		68	20

FESTIVALS AND SEASONAL EVENTS

The festivals listed below are national and occur throughout the country unless otherwise noted. Many events follow the lunar calendar, so dates vary from year to year.

➤ JAN.: **New Year celebrations** are usually at their best around temples. In Bangkok, special ceremonies at Pramanae Ground include Thai dancing.

➤ FEB.: **Magha Puja,** held on the full moon of the third lunar month, commemorates the day when 1,250 disciples spontaneously heard Lord Buddha preach the cardinal Doctrine. The **Flower Festival,** held in Chiang Mai during the early part of the month when the province's flowers are in full bloom, features a parade with floral floats, flower displays, and beauty contests.

➤ APR.: **Songkran** marks the Thai New Year and is an occasion for setting caged birds and fish free, visiting family, dancing, and splashing everyone with water in good-natured merriment. The festival is at its best in Chiang Mai.

➤ MAY: On the full moon of the sixth lunar month, the nation celebrates the holiest of Buddhist days, **Visakha Puja,** commemorating Lord Buddha's birth, enlightenment, and death. Monks lead the laity in candlelight processions around their temples.

➤ AUG.: On the 12th, **Queen Sirikit's birthday** is celebrated with religious ceremonies at Chitlada Palace, and the city is adorned with lights.

➤ NOV.: Held on the full moon of the 12th lunar month, **Loi Krathong** is the loveliest of Thai festivals. After sunset, people make their way to a body of water and launch small lotus-shape banana-leaf floats bearing lighted candles to honor the water spirits and wash away the sins of the past year. Of all Bangkok's fairs and festivals, the **Golden Mount Festival** is the most spectacular, with sideshows, food stalls, bazaars, and large crowds of celebrants.

➤ DEC.: On the 5th, the **King's birthday,** a trooping of the colors is performed in Bangkok by Thailand's elite Royal Guards.

1   DESTINATION: THAILAND

Traversing Thailand

What's Where

Pleasures and Pastimes

Fodor's Choice

Great Itineraries

TRAVERSING THAILAND

A BLUR OF ORANGE AND GREEN is all you can make out as you tear past the temples in the heart of the Old City. There's so much to explore here in Bangkok that you've hopped in a tuk-tuk, one of the open-sided vehicles hurtling at such breakneck speeds that no more than two of their three wheels ever seem to touch the street. Soon you're dodging in and out of traffic, your heart in your throat.

As you maneuver your way around this most colorful of capitals, your choice of transportation tells a lot about you. If you like to get your bearings before you head out to explore, you'll probably hop aboard one of the ferries sailing up and down the Chao Phraya. As you float toward the Old City, you get to know the lay of the land—the porcelain-covered temple of Wat Arun appears on the western side of the river, then the glint of gold of Wat Phra Kaeo comes into view on the east. In the distance a dozen or so sparkling spires mark other temples.

Many of the city's attractions—the Grand Palace, the National Museum, and the National Gallery of Art—are found along the river. If your destination is farther afield, you'll have to find another means of transportation. Comfort-minded travelers are drawn to taxis, where you can roll up the window if the dust and dirt become overwhelming. If you're the type that doesn't waste any time getting to your destination, you'll prefer a tuk-tuk. These speedy vehicles, named for the sound made by their sputtering engines, are one of the quickest ways around the city. Even faster are the motorcycle taxis found downtown. You simply agree on a fare with the red-vested driver and hop on the back.

Remember, though, that the average speed on Bangkok's roads is less than 3 miles per hour. This is why many people, especially when they are exploring vibrant neighborhoods like Chinatown, set out on foot. Here, in the twisting alleys lined with vendors, you can take a break at a noodle shop filled with old men playing mah-jongg. Another great place for a stroll is Sanam Luang, the so-called "field

of kings." This expansive park, not far from the Grand Palace, is one of the few verdant spots in the city. If you're here on a sunny day, the sky above will be filled with kites.

Although it's west of Bangkok, the community of Damnoen Saduak has a gridlock problem of its own. Here the labyrinth of canals is jammed with wooden boats overloaded with mangoes, guavas, and other fruits and vegetables. The best way to navigate the floating market is to hire a *ruilla pai* (rowboat) and paddle among the vendors. If you are headed to the ancient ruins of Ayutthaya, to the north of the capital, there's no better way to get there than by cruising up the river on a *rua hang yao* (long-tail boat).

Outside of Bangkok and a handful of other cities, the modes of transportation change dramatically. Instead of taxis and tuk-tuks you're more likely to find *samlors* and *songthaews*. Basically a tricycle with a bench attached, the samlor resembles a tuk-tuk without an engine. You usually sit in the back, but in Sukhothai and a couple of other towns you may find yourself on a seat in front that obscures the driver's view. The songthaew, a pickup truck with two parallel benches in the back, is the most common means of transportation in rural areas. Although not at all comfortable, they are a great way to meet the Thai people.

If you're an intrepid traveler, you're most likely going to head up into the hills of Northern Thailand. Where the roads end you can always find other transportation. Imagine surveying the countryside from atop an elephant. As the tiny wooden benches propped on their backs rock you to and fro, you'll be amazed at how adept these bulky animals are at climbing the rocky slopes. When they've deposited you at your destination, the elephants are likely to head to the nearest river to cool off.

In Thailand, getting there is often an adventure in itself. Climbing into a samlor or piling into the back of a songthaew probably won't be the fastest way to get to your destination, but you'll doubtless have experiences that will stick with you long after the trip is over.

WHAT'S WHERE

Bangkok

Bangkok never seems to slow down. Stand on any corner and watch the city swirl around you. The only way to escape this pace is by taking to the river. A ferry ride on the Chao Phraya River is a great way to get your bearings, while a ride in a long-tail boat along the adjoining canals called *klongs* brings you past rickety stilt houses and fragrant floating markets. Bangkok is home to some of Thailand's most impressive temples, and a few steps from the river are Wat Pho, where you'll find the golden statue of the Reclining Buddha, and Wat Phra Keo, which holds the country's most revered icon, the Emerald Buddha. Also near the river is the National Museum, where Asian masterpieces are among the crowning jewels of a world-class art collection. The National Theater next door showcases traditional dancers. Don't worry if you miss one of the all-too-rare productions; you'll surely stumble onto an impromptu street performance. For edge-of-your-seat action, catch one of the daily Thai boxing matches, which are held at the Lumphini and Ratchadamnoen stadiums.

The Central Plains

The Central Plains are irresistible to those who want to delve deep into the region's fascinating history. A side trip from Bangkok to the former capital of Ayutthaya is a good start, but you must venture farther north to the even older cities at Sukhothai and Sri Satchanalai to discover how these disparate communities finally became a country. Compared to some of the ancient cities found in Thailand, Sukhothai is a fairly recent addition to the landscape; the amazingly intact ruins you will find here are merely 800 years old. Such temples as Wat Mahathat evoke the city's role in unifying and enlightening the land that eventually would become Thailand. Sukhothai's sister city, Si Satchanalai, has hilltop temples where you can meditate for hours without seeing another soul. All around are the scenes of an age-old way of life, such as teams of water buffalo working the rice paddies.

Northern Thailand

In the country's northernmost reaches, you'll find Thailand's most dramatic landscapes, most distinctive temples and palaces, most independent peoples, and most flavorful food. Make your first stop the walled city of Chiang Mai, where you can marvel at the spectacular ruins of Wat Chedi Luang, felled by an earthquake in 1545. Make sure to pay a visit to mountaintop Wat Phrathat Doi Suthep, one of four royal temple compounds. To the south there are the ancient cities of Lamphun, where you can sample a small, sweet fruit called the lamyai, and Lanpang, where one means of transportation, oddly enough, is horse-drawn carriage. Toward Myanmar is Mae Hong Son, which is surrounded by verdant countryside and villages populated by hill tribes. In the far north, more tribal villages surround the town of Chiang Rai, gateway to the so-called Golden Triangle. Once known for opium production and warlords, the region remains exhilarating, especially if you take an elephant trek into the bamboo-covered mountains.

Isan

The country's heartland runs from the border of Myanmar to those of Cambodia and Laos. Mist-covered fields are interspersed with ancient ruins. At Ban Chiang, tucked away in the northeast near the border of Laos, jewelry and pottery are among the artifacts of a civilization that flourished 7,000 years ago. Tour buses are rare on the roads of the sprawling northeast plateau. Consequently, the few travelers you'll see here are in search of the relatively undisturbed culture or remnants of its fascinating history.

The Southern Beaches

Thailand's southern region is paradise—a long peninsula washed by the Gulf of Thailand on one side and the Andaman Sea on the other. Phuket, the country's largest island, offers worldly pleasures. Here you can succumb to *nuat boroan* (traditional massage), watch pearl workers glean their prizes from local waters, dine poolside at luxurious resorts, or simply sunbathe on west coast sands. The nearby Phi Phi Islands, with their secret silver-sand coves, are more laid-back than Phuket. Phang Nga Bay is a true hideaway, where limestone outcroppings rise hundreds of feet above the sea and caves accessible only by boat wait to be explored. You can veer still farther off the path by heading to the tranquil fishing island of Ko Pha Ngan, where luxury means a bungalow on the beach. If you're eager for close-up views of extraordinary marine life, sail off to the Similan Islands, where the diving visibility is 60 to 120 ft, or explore the waters around the 40 islets of Angthong Marine National Park, full of astonishing multicolor coral. Although few strands and coves in even these remote places are completely untrammeled, many are idyllic nonetheless.

Laos

Landlocked Laos shares borders with Thailand, Myanmar, China, Vietnam, and Cambodia. Its western border, defined in many places by the Mekong River, abuts Thailand. Most of Laos's more accessible attractions—including its two major cities, Vientiane and Luang Prabang—are concentrated in the northern part of the country, close to Chiang Mai.

PLEASURES AND PASTIMES

Architecture

Successfully staving off occupation by European powers, Thailand has architecture that is refreshingly free of colonial touches. That isn't to say that other artistic styles aren't present. Throughout history, Thai architects borrowed ideas from Indian, Sri Lankan, and Cambodian structures, and Thai artists often used symbolic elements that began as Hindu concepts. Despite these antecedents, what emerged was uniquely Thai. The stolid stone temples built by the Khmers in the northeast, the lotus-topped spires of Sukhothai found in the Central Plains, and the gracefully curved roofs constructed by the Lannas in the north are unlike anything you'll find elsewhere.

Beaches

Thailand's two coasts, along the Gulf of Thailand and the Andaman Sea, lie slowly steaming below the Tropic of Cancer. This makes the beaches here a sun-worshipper's dream come true. They come in every flavor—lively shores lined with raucous bars and clubs, quiet coves sheltering exclusive hotels, isolated islands with thatched bungalows, and a few stretches of sand with no footprints at all.

Dining

Food is a consuming passion for the Thais. Nowhere is this more evident than on just about any street corner. Throughout the day, one food cart replaces another, each vendor stirring up a different tasty morsel. The range of Thai cuisine is vast; no restaurant worth its salt has fewer than 100 dishes on its menu. There are seasonal delights, and of course, regional differences and specialties. You'll find a delicious spicy pork sausage in the north, where meals are usually eaten with sticky rice kneaded into balls and dipped in various sauces. In the northeast you'll find barbecued chicken, minced beef, and a spicy papaya salad. Along the southern coast, seafood reigns supreme. Thousands of boats return each day filled with lobster, crabs, and shrimp. Because traders from neighboring lands often stopped here, you'll find dishes that remind you of Malaysia, Indonesia, and even India.

Lodging

In no other country will you find such a wide range of accommodations, all at reasonable prices. If you're staying at the beach, a few dollars can get you cocooned in a mosquito net inside a thatch-roof hut. Not much more money and you can be ensconced in a comfortable suite overlooking the ocean. Even in Bangkok you could pamper yourself at the Oriental, considered one of the finest hotels in the world, and spend less than you would for a nondescript hotel back home. Where you stay, then, depends more on your personality than your purse.

Massage

Every visit to Thailand should include a massage or two. They came in a variety of styles, from gentle kneading of the muscles to joint-breaking pulls. Make sure to talk with your practitioner about what to expect. Traditional nuat boroan aims to release blocked channels of energy through methods similar to reflexology. Your aches and pains will melt away, and you'll find yourself invigorated as well. If you'd like to learn the techniques yourself, there are plenty of schools that teach massage.

Shopping

The first time you set foot in one of Thailand's ubiquitous night markets you will find yourself hooked. These centers of commerce—ranging in size from a handful of stalls in smaller villages to vast buildings filled with hundreds of shops in the larger cities—are a shopper's delight. You'll find everything from hand-carved figurines and woven baskets to watches with recently affixed Rolex logos and polo shirts with the alligator slightly askew. The prices, after a little negotiating, are tantalizingly low. If you're in Bangkok or another larger city, you'll also find a slew of department stores, shopping centers, and malls. The prices are significantly lower than in shopping meccas like Singapore or Hong Kong.

Trekking

The forests surrounding the northern cities of Chiang Mai and Chiang Rai would make good trekking just for their rugged beauty. But these misty hills are also home to villages belonging to various hill tribes, descendents of people who migrated here centuries ago from China. The various tribes—Karen, Hmong, Yao, and many others—have held onto ancient customs, making their communities a fascinating window into the past. Reaching the villages, however, is not always so easy. The easiest way to maneuver up the steep grades is often on the back of an elephant.

FODOR'S CHOICE

Beaches

Ao Phra Nang, Krabi. Towering pinnacles of limestone rising from the ocean grab your attention at this stretch of sand not far from Krabi.

Nai Harn, Phuket. Yachts from around the world drop anchor in this protected bay. You can't beat the views of sunset on the Andaman Sea from Phromthep Cape.

Pansea Beach, Phuket. On the western coast of Phuket, this exclusive enclave draws those in search of rest and relaxation.

Haad Tong Nai Pan, Ko Pha Ngan. One of the country's most idyllic retreats, this beachcomber's paradise lets you shut out the rest of the world.

Dining

Le Normandie, Bangkok. Atop the legendary Oriental Hotel, this French restaurant commands a panoramic view across the Chao Phraya River. $$$$

Sala Rim Naam, Bangkok. Sala Rim Naam is a great place to experience royal Thai cuisine while watching a show of classical dancing. $$$$

Ban Klang Nam, Bangkok. Superbly prepared seafood is served up with a view of ships anchored on the river. $$

Tum Tum Cheng, Laos. You can't leave Luang Prabang without trying Mekong catfish—and this is *the* place to do so. $

Huen Phen, Chiang Mai. Browse through the many small dining rooms, each full of antiques, then settle in to enjoy good northern Thai fare. ¢

Prachak, Bangkok. This unprepossessing place serves up portions of the best roast duck in town for less than a dollar. ¢

Vientiane Kitchen, Bangkok. Live Laotian music gives this thatch-roof restaurant a festive feel. ¢

White Orchid, Phuket. Dine beneath towering palms at this outdoor café at the water's edge. You'll always get fresh fish and a warm welcome. ¢

Lodging

Chiva-Som, Hua Hin. This spa resort offers an escape from stress with top-notch treatments and a peaceful setting right on the beach. $$$$

Manee's Retreat, Si Saket. The real Thailand is revealed at this one-of-a-kind guest house. $$$$

Oriental Hotel, Bangkok. The Oriental's prestigious clientele and unbeatable location on the Chao Phraya are just two of the reasons it continues to be an institution. $$$$

Rayavadee Premier Resort, Ao Nang. Talk about secluded—the only way to reach your thatch-roof bungalow is by longtail boat. $$$$

The Regent, Bangkok. The cabana rooms, whose private patios look onto a small garden with a lotus pond, are exquisite. *$$$$*

The Regent, Chiang Mai. Luxury is taken for granted here among the Lanna Thai buildings, which encircle rice fields and landscaped gardens. *$$$$*

Santiburi, Ko Samui. Details like beautifully polished teak floors make you feel as if you're staying at a billionaire's holiday hideaway. *$$$$*

Villa Santi, Laos. The royal family had a hand in creating this resort around one of their former residences, so you know you'll be staying in style. *$$$*.

Imperial Tara Mae Hong Son, Mae Hong Son. Whether taking a dip in the pool or enjoying traditional Thai food on the porch, you'll have a full view of a tranquil, terraced valley. *$$*

Panviman Resort, Ko Pha Ngan. Bungalows are staggered up a cliff, which means you'll always have fantastic views of the bay. *$*

River View Lodge, Chiang Mai. This small hotel is a charming alternative to the highrise hotels of the north. *$*

The Atlanta, Bangkok. Classical music at teatime and old movies after dinner draw people back to this small, quirky hotel. *¢*

Number 4 Guest House, Sukhothai. Set in overgrown tropical gardens, these handhewn bungalows couldn't be more charming. *¢*

Quintessential Thailand

National Museum, Bangkok. Trace the region's rich history or view one of the world's best collections of Southeast Asian art at Thailand's finest museum.

Night Market, Chiang Mai. One of Thailand's most exciting bazaars offers a little bit of everything, from hand-carved statues to knock-off Rolexes.

Phang Nga Bay, Southern Thailand. Canoe around the pillars of limestone that rise majestically from the sea at this fascinating spot.

Suan Pakkard Palace, Bangkok. Five antique teak houses, home to the gold-paneled Lacquer Pavilion, magnificently exemplify the region's architectural style.

Temples and Shrines

Wat Benjamabophit, Bangkok. The illustrious Marble Temple, clad in glistening gray stone, is home to more than 50 different images of Buddha.

Wat Chedi Luang, Chiang Mai. An earthquake may have toppled the spire of this temple, but you can still marvel at the unfinished masterpiece.

Wat Phanan Choeng, Ayutthaya. This small temple on the banks of the Lopburi River commemorates the death of a king's beloved bride.

Wat Pho, Bangkok. It's the largest wat in Bangkok, and for good reason: inside is an immense statue of the Reclining Buddha.

Wat Phra Keo, Bangkok. Home of the revered Emerald Buddha, this sacred temple is among the most ornate in the country.

Wat Pumin, Nan. To reach this temple you climb a flight of steps flanked by two superb nagas, their heads guarding the north entrance and their tails the south.

Wat Traimit, Bangkok. The world's largest solid-gold Buddha is a striking presence within this otherwise unassuming temple.

Wat Xieng Thong, Laos. A stunning "tree of life" mosaic is just one of the things that makes this temple on the banks of the Mekong famous.

GREAT ITINERARIES

Highlights of Thailand

9 days.

Almost every trip to Thailand begins in Bangkok, the chaotic capital city. Don't be afraid to linger there a few days, because some of the country's most astounding sights can be found in and around the Old City. You'll probably be exhausted by the pace in a few days, so slow down by heading to one of the smaller cities in the north. Most people pick Chiang Mai, often called the "Rose of the North." It's the most popular base for visits to villages belonging to hill tribes. Thailand is famed for its beaches, and the grandest of grand finales to a trip here is a stop on the island of Phuket.

Around Bangkok
3 days.

Start your first day with the most famous of all Bangkok sights, the Grand Palace. Make sure not to miss the gorgeously ornate Wat Phra Keo, home of the Emerald Buddha, and Wat Pho, the temple that holds the Reclining Buddha. Take a ferry across the Chao Phraya to the western bank to visit Wat Arun, the Khmer-style Temple of the Dawn. Later, return to the eastern bank and spend the afternoon exploring the National Museum and the National Gallery of Art.

On Day Two, head to one of the city's most beautiful temples, Wat Benjamabophit. The century-old structure is made of marble. Nearby is Dusit Park, a refuge from the heat and dust. Here you'll find the Vimarnmek Mansion, the largest teak structure in the world. A short tuk-tuk ride away is Sun Pakkard Palace, a series of five teak houses built on high columns. After lunch take in Jim Thompson's House. These up-country buildings were brought to Bangkok by Thompson, an American entrepreneur who single-handedly revived the country's silk industry. The houses are filled with priceless pieces of Asian art.

On Day Three, rise early so you can take in the famed floating market at Samnoen Saduak. Continue on to see the towering temple at Nakhon Pathom, then continue to Kanchanaburi, site of the famous bridge over the River Kwai. Return late in the day to Bangkok. ☞ Chapter 2

Chiang Mai
3 days.

Fly north to Chiang Mai, an enchanting walled city. On the first day, rise early to explore the beautiful temples inside the walls, including Wat Phra Singh, Wat Chedi Luang, and Wat Chiang Man. In the afternoon check out the wonderful carvings in the crafts stores along Sankamphaeng Road. In the evening you'll want to walk through the city gates to the Night Market. On the second day go to Wat Phrathat Doi Suthep, the temple on a mountain overlooking the city. Ring the dozens of bells surrounding the main

building for good luck. On the way back to Chiang Mai, visit the seven-spired temple called Wat Chedi Yot. Grab your camera on the third day, when you'll head into the hills north of the city to take an elephant trek to a hill-tribe village. ☞ Chiang Mai and West to the Border in Chapter 4

Phuket
3 days.

After all this sightseeing, you'll probably be in the mood for some rest and relaxation. Most people fly down to Phuket, one of the country's prettiest islands. If you want to take a day trip, a popular one is to Phang Nga Bay, where you can see the gravity-defying limestone formations that rise out of the sea. Another is to the Phi Phi Islands, where you'll find some astounding snorkeling. ☞ Phuket and Phuket Bay Resorts in Chapter 6

Architectural Marvels
14 days.

The principal building materials of Thailand's religious buildings have varied over the years. Khmer architects were fond of stone. Sukhothai and Lanna builders worked with brick, while in Ayutthaya they used bricks cemented by mortar and covered with one or more coats of stucco. Ironically, this means that the structures from the ancient Khmer empire, which lasted from the 9th to the 13th centuries, are better preserved than those built by later kingdoms. But you can find examples of temples from all the peoples who ruled this land if you wander a bit off the beaten path.

Isan
3 days.

After arriving in Bangkok, take the night train to Nakhon Ratchasima, a city known as the gateway to the northeast. From here it's easy to see the region's most spectacular sites, including Prasat Hin Phimae. Built during the late 11th or early 12th century, the central prang of this Hindu temple is especially stunning in the light of early morning. On the next day take a car to Prasat Hin Khao Phanom Rung, a supreme example of Khmer architecture. Because there were no later additions to the complex, you can clearly how it appeared when it was built in the 10th century. ☞ Isan in Chapter 5

Ayutthaya
6 days.

On Day Four, head back to Bangkok and take a boat up the Chao Phraya River to the ancient capital of Ayutthaya. The style of architecture found here, which drew on elements of the much older Khmer empire, arose during the mid-14th century. Ayutthaya was destroyed after the Burmese attacked the city in 1767, so only a handful of the original structures remain. While you're in the area, make sure to visit Lopburi, one of Thailand's oldest cities.

It's easy to spend three days in and around Bangkok, where you can poke around the Grand Palace, which has some good examples of Rattanakosin architecture. This building style, which came into its own in the late 18th century, attempts to recreate the opulence of Ayutthaya architecture. The more recent structures also employ Western building techniques. ☞ North from Bangkok in Chapter 2

Chiang Mai
3 days.

At about the same time Ayutthaya was flourishing in the south, the Lanna empire controlled the north. Fly to Chiang Mai to see fine examples of this people's graceful architecture. One particularly lovely building is the *ho trai*, or library, at Wat Phra Sing. Like similar structures from this period, it is raised off the ground so that the books inside would not be damaged by insects. There are other wonderful examples of Lanna architecture in the nearby towns of Lamphun and Lampang. ☞ Chiang Mai and West to the Border in Chapter 4

Sukhothai
2 days.

Fly from Chiang Mai to Sukhothai, a dusty town in the Central Plains. Thailand's first capital, it deserves at least a day or two of exploration. The central temple of Wat Mahathat is splendid, with a frieze of walking monks surrounding a huge platform supporting several lotus-topped spires. Don't miss the outlying sights such as Wat Sri Chum, home to a huge Buddha almost totally enclosed in a towering building. Spend the night in town, making sure to explore the Night Market. The next morning take the hour's trip to Si Satchanalai, a nearby city with hilltop temples that impart a wonderful sense of calm. ☞ The Central Plains in Chapter 3

2 BANGKOK

Seen from a long-tail boat floating down the
Chao Phraya River, Bangkok appears to be
the most ancient of cities. It's only when you
get closer to the towering temples that you
realize they are set in a modern metropolis.
But it's still possible to turn a corner and find
a tidy shrine holding a golden Buddha
statue or a ramshackle shop selling the most
aromatic of spices.

FRANTIC, FRENZIED, AND FRENETIC, Bangkok defies all attempts
to get from one place to another. That's not surprising, as the capital has no real center, and the streets seem to veer off in every
direction. Follow any road for long and you're sure to be surprised where
you end up. No wonder newcomers can only scratch their heads in be-
wilderment.

Updated by
Mick Elmore

Admittedly, there is much to criticize about this city of more than 10
million. Some people complain about the heat, the humidity, and the
haze that hovers over the city. (Traffic cops often wear face masks when
directing traffic at busy intersections.) Others sneer at block after
block of concrete buildings where you'll see nary a tree. Some days it
seems that no one has a good word to say about Bangkok.

Yet there's a reason Thais refer to their capital as Krung Thep, which
means "City of Angels." When King Rama I moved the capital here
in 1782, he set out to build a city as beautiful as Ayutthaya was before it was sacked by the Burmese. In many ways, Bangkok is the most
mesmerizing spot in Thailand—here you'll find some of the country's
most beautiful temples and shrines. It's hard to imagine a lovelier sight
than Wat Arun when the sun is sitting low in the sky. And a walk through
the grounds of the Grand Palace takes your breath away.

Bangkok's stark contrasts will require an adjustment on your part, but
amid the chaos you soon come to appreciate the gentle nature of the
Thais and their genuine respect for other people. You may not fall in
love with Bangkok, but you'll never forget it.

Pleasures and Pastimes

Architecture and the Arts

Bangkok is, without doubt, the chief repository of the nation's most
amazing art and artifacts. The wonderful *wats* (temples) contain some
of the country's most beautiful buildings and images of Lord Buddha.
At Wat Pho you'll find the golden statue of the Reclining Buddha, and
at Wat Phra Keo is the much revered Emerald Buddha. The palaces,
with traditional peaked roofs of green, orange, and red, call to mind
the region's architectural history. The National Museum houses a fascinating collection of Southeast Asian masterpieces. The most venerable pieces are more than 5,000 years old.

Boating

Krung Thep used to be known as the Venice of the East. Sadly, many
of the *klongs* (canals) that once distinguished this area have been paved
over. Several klongs remain, though, and traveling along these water-
ways is one of the delights of Bangkok. They have been cleaned up in
the last decade, and the water is no longer black and smelly. In the long-
tail boats and ferries, not only do you beat the stalled traffic, but you
get to see houses on stilts, women washing clothing, and kids jumping
in with a splash. A popular trip to the Royal Barge Museum, and the
Khoo Wiang Floating Market starts at the Chang Pier on the Chao Phraya
River and travels along Klong Bangkok Noi and Klong Bangkok Yai.

Dining

In Bangkok there are endless places—from swanky hotel dining rooms
where you can sit down for a multicourse meal to sidewalk stalls
where you can grab a quick noodle lunch. In between are informal restaurants where wonders await the gastronomically curious. Don't miss
out on Royal Thai cuisine, based on the elaborate meals once served
to the kings and their families.

CATEGORY	COST*
$$$$	over B400 (over US$10)
$$$	B300–B400 (US$7.50–$10)
$$	B200–B300 (US$5–$7.50)
$	B100–B200 (US$2.50–5)
¢	under B100 (under US$2.50)

*per person, for a main course at dinner

Lodging

Few cities in the world rival Bangkok for first-class lodging. The half dozen or so deluxe hotels are superb, offering unparalleled comfort, attentive service, and at those along the Chao Phraya River, stunning views. In the past, the opulent Oriental has been rated among the best in the world, but now the city has others, such as the Regent, that offer the grand dame some competition. These high-end hotels are surprisingly affordable, with rates comparable to standard hotels in New York or London. If you are on a budget, you can spend far less. There are many moderately priced lodgings with excellent facilities.

CATEGORY	COST*
$$$$	over B6,000 (over US$150)
$$$	B4,000–B6,000 (US$100–$150)
$$	B2,000–B4,000 (US$50–$100)
$	B1,000–B2,000 (under US$50)
¢	under B1,000 (under US$25)

*All prices are for a standard double room, excluding tax.

Nightlife

Although in recent years it has tried to improve its image, Bangkok is still known for its strips of seedy bars catering to foreign tourists. With their garish neon, flashy facades, and barkers describing just how far the dancers are willing to go, the clubs of the the Patpong and Soi Nana areas have an anything-goes atmosphere. However, more and more bars are becoming places where those of both genders may go to relax, have a drink, and listen to live music.

Shopping

In the past, Hong Kong and Singapore were Asia's main shopping destinations, but now you would do well to hold off until you reach Bangkok, which is less expensive and offers much more in the way of traditional crafts. And if Bangkok's endless shops are not enough, the sidewalk vendors present bargains just about wherever you walk.

EXPLORING BANGKOK

Because its endless maze of streets is part of its fascination, finding your way around Bangkok is a challenge. The S curve of the Chao Phraya River can throw you off at first, until you realize that the great waterway is an important navigational tool. Not only are most of the popular sights close to the river, you can also use it to get quickly from one place to another. There's no faster way to get from Thonburi to Chinatown, for example, than by boat.

The Old City is the most popular destination for travelers, as it is home to opulent temples like Wat Pho and Wat Phra Keo. Across the river is Thonburi, where you'll find Wat Arun. North of the Old City is Dusit, the royal district since the days of Rama V. The highlight of a visit to this neighborhood of elegant buildings lining wide avenues is Dusit Park, one of the most appealing patches of green in the city.

East of the Old City is Chinatown, a labyrinth of streets with restaurants, shops, and warehouses. Head east along Rama IV Road and you'll reach the parallel commercial streets of Silom Road and Suriwong Road. Between them lies Patpong, the city's most notorious red-light district. Continue farther south and you reach the riverbank and some of the city's leading hotels, the Royal Orchid, the Oriental, and the Shangri-La.

To the north of Rama IV Road is Bangkok's largest green area, Lumphini Park, a patch of green in the midst of endless blocks of concrete buildings. Continue north and you'll reach Sukhumvit Road, once a residential neighborhood. In the last quarter century it has developed into a bustling district filled with restaurants, hotels, and shops.

Knowing your exact destination, its direction, and its approximate distance are important in planning your itinerary. They also assist you in negotiating *tuk-tuk* (three-wheeled taxi) fares. Note, however, that many sights have no precise written address and the spelling of road names changes from map to map and even block to block, thus Ratchadamri is often spelled *Rajdamri,* Ratchadamnoen is sometimes seen as *Rajdamnern,* Charoen Krung can be *Charoennakorn* or even *New Road.* Crossing and recrossing the city is time-consuming, and you can lose many hours stuck in traffic jams. Remember that Bangkok is enormous, and distances are great; it can take a half hour or more to walk between two seemingly adjacent sites.

Great Itineraries

If you aren't melted by the heat or sluggish from jet lag, you can cover Bangkok's attractions in three days. In another two days you have plenty of time to make short trips outside the city. It would take at least a week to get to know your way around Bangkok.

Numbers in the text correspond to numbers in the margin and on the Exploring Bangkok map.

IF YOU HAVE 2 DAYS

Start your first day with the most famous of all Bangkok sights, the **Grand Palace** ①. In the same complex is the gorgeously ornate **Wat Phra Keo** ②. Not far south of the Grand Palace is Bangkok's oldest and largest temple, **Wat Pho** ③, famous for its enormous Reclining Buddha. If you are feeling a bit tense, remember that the temple is also home to a school of traditional massage. Take a tuk-tuk to Chinatown and visit **Wat Traimit** ⑱ so you can pay respects to this perfectly harmonious and glittering image. At the Chao Phraya River, catch an express boat to the Oriental Hotel and have a cup of tea. In the evening, stroll along bustling Silom Road to check out the goods for sale. Afterward you can catch a dinner show featuring traditional dancing.

The next day visit **Jim Thompson's House** ㉒, then continue on to **Wat Benjamabophit** ⑬, which contains Bangkok's much-photographed Marble Temple. Spend the afternoon in the **National Museum** ⑥.

IF YOU HAVE 3 DAYS

Start your first day with breakfast on the terrace at the Oriental Hotel, then take an express boat up the Chao Phraya River to the **Grand Palace** ①. Visit the Emerald Buddha at **Wat Phra Keo** ②, then walk to **Wat Pho** ③ to see the Reclining Buddha. Cross the river to **Wat Arun** ④, the beautiful Temple of the Dawn, and climb the large spire for views of the entire city. Then take the boat upstream to the **Royal Barge Museum** ⑤; the barges displayed are used on ceremonial occasions. Cross the bridge and spend the rest of the afternoon browsing around the **National Museum** ⑥.

On Day Two visit **Jim Thompson's House** ㉒ and **Suan Pakkard Palace** ㉑. Then go on to the **Vimarnmek Mansion** ⑩ before visiting **Wat Ben-**

jamabophit ⑬. South of the Marble Temple is the golden dome of **Wat Saket** ⑮, and the metal temple of **Wat Rachanada** ⑭. Now head for Chinatown for a little shopping before finding harmony at **Wat Traimit** ⑱. In the evening, if you have the energy, you might explore Sukhumvit Road.

On Day Three rise at dawn and take an early bus tour to **Damnoen Saduak,** home of the famous floating market. From there go on to **Nakhon Pathom,** where the main attraction is the ancient Phra Pathom Chedi, the tallest Buddhist monument in the world. By early afternoon a train or bus can get you to **Kanchanaburi,** site of the notorious bridge over the River Kwai.

When to Tour Bangkok

November to March is the best time to see Bangkok. The city is at its coolest—a mere 85°—and driest. In April the humidity and heat build up to create a sticky stew until the rains begin in late May.

The Old City

Most of Bangkok's major attractions are in this part of the city, which was founded in 1782. The Grand Palace and other sights are within a short distance of the Chao Phraya River, making them easily accessible from most parts of the capital. When the heat gets too much for you, enjoy the cooling breezes off the water as you take a ferry to see the sights on the other side.

A Good Tour

Start at the **Grand Palace** ①, Bangkok's most enduring landmark, then head to the adjoining **Wat Phra Keo** ② to see the Emerald Buddha. Head south on Sanamchai Road (take a taxi if the heat gets to you) to **Wat Pho** ③ for a glimpse of the Reclining Buddha. From Wat Pho, head west to the river and then north (toward the Grand Palace) about 250 yards to the Tha Thien jetty and take the ferry across to Thonburi to visit **Wat Arun** ④. For a breathtaking view of the city, climb the staircase to the top.

Also in Thonburi is the **Royal Barge Museum** ⑤, easily reached by boat. These beautiful boats are used only on special occasions. Cross back to the eastern shore to visit the **National Museum** ⑥. Plan on several hours to explore this museum and the adjacent **National Gallery** ⑦. Also nearby is the **National Theatre** ⑧, which in the evening hosts traditional dance performances.

Timing

This is a full day of sightseeing. Ideally, you would begin early in the morning, take a break to escape the midday heat, and end late in the afternoon. If you have a few days, you might want to break this up into two tours. You will want to spend a few hours wandering around the Grand Palace and Wat Phra Keo. Wat Pho won't take as long unless you opt for a traditional massage. Allow at least two hours at the National Museum and an hour at the National Gallery. Both are closed on Monday, Tuesday, and public holidays.

Sights to See

❶ **Grand Palace.** In 1782, when King Rama I moved the capital across the river from Thonburi, he built this walled city. The palace and adjoining structures only got more opulent as subsequent monarchs added their own touches here and there. The compound is open to visitors, but all the buildings, which are used only for state occasions and royal ceremonies, are not. The official residence of the king—although he actually lives at Chitlada Palace in north Bangkok—is the Chakri

14

Exploring Bangkok

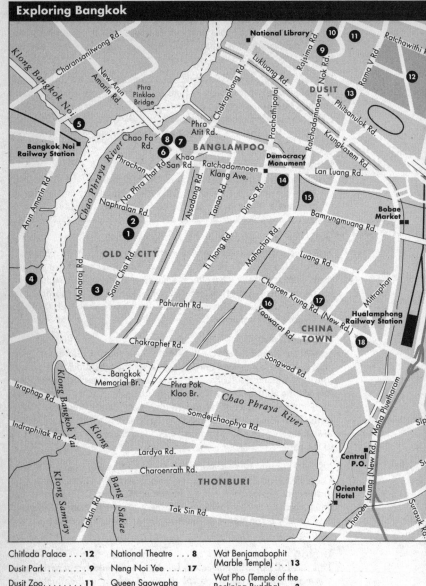

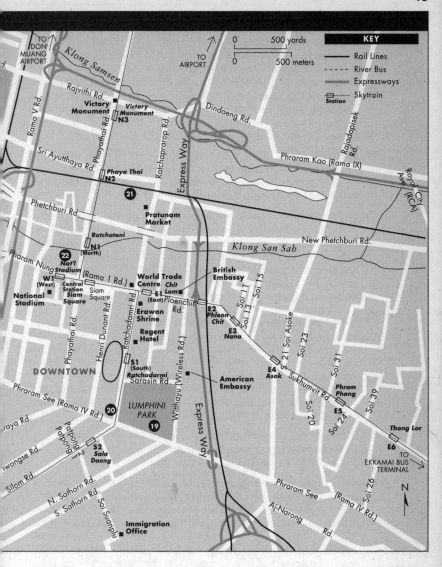

KEY

— Rail Lines
---- River Bus
— Expressways
▭ Skytrain
Station

KEY

— Rail Lines
---- River Bus
— Expressways
▭ Skytrain
Station

TO DON MUANG AIRPORT

Klong Samsen

TO AIRPORT

0   500 yards
0   500 meters

Rajvithi Rd.

Rama V Rd.

Victory Monument

Victory Monument N3

Phayathai Rd.

Dindaeng Rd.

Ratchaprarop Rd.

Sri Ayutthaya Rd.

Phraram Kao (Rama IX)

Rajadapisek Rd.

Royal City Ave. (RCA)

Phaya Thai N2

Phetchburi Rd.

21

Pratunam Market

Ratchateni N1 (North)

Pharam Nung

New Phetchburi Rd.

Klong San Sab

22 Nat'l Stadium (Rama 1 Rd.)

W1 (West)

Central Station Siam Square

Siam Square

National Stadium

Soi 15

Soi 11

World Trade Centre Chit

E1 (East) Lom

Ploenchit Rd.

British Embassy

Soi 13

Erawan Shrine

Regent Hotel

Ratchadamri Rd.

Phayathai Rd.

E2 Phleon Chit

E3 Nana

Soi 21 Soi Asoke

Soi 23

Sukhumvit Rd.

Soi 31

Soi 39

Henri Dunant Rd.

S1 (South)

Ratchadarmi Sarasin Rd.

Withayu (Wireless Rd.)

American Embassy

E4 Asok

Soi 20

E5 Soi 24

Phrom Phong

Soi 26

DOWNTOWN

Phraram See (Rama IV Rd.)

20

LUMPHINI PARK

19

Express Way

Thong Lor

E6

TO EKKAMAI BUS TERMINAL

raya Rd.

Patpong 2 Patpong

iwongse Rd.

Silom Rd.

S2 Sala Daeng

N. Sathorn Rd.

S. Sathorn Rd.

Soi Suanplu

Phraram See (Rama IV Rd.)

Aj-Narong Rd.

N

Immigration Office

Maha Prasat palace, whose rooms are sometimes open to visitors on special occasions. The Dusit Maha Prasat, on the right, is a classic example of palace architecture, and Amarin Vinichai Hall, on the left, the original audience hall, is now used for the presentation of ambassadors' credentials. Note the glittering gold throne. Just east of the Grand Palace compound is the **City Pillar Shrine**, containing the foundation stone (Lak Muang) from which all distances in Thailand are measured. The stone is believed to be inhabited by a spirit that guards the well-being of Bangkok. ⊠ *Sana Chai Rd.,* ☎ *02/224–1833,* WEB *www. palaces.thai.net.* 🖃 *Admission.* ◷ *Daily 8:30–3:30.*

❼ National Gallery. Opposite the National Theatre, the National Gallery exhibits both modern and traditional Thai art. The building itself once housed the royal mint. ⊠ *Chao Fa Rd.,* ☎ *02/281–2224,* WEB *www. thailandmuseum.com.* 🖃 *Admission.* ◷ *Wed.–Sun. 9–4.*

★ ❻ National Museum. There's no better place to acquaint yourself with Thai history than the National Museum, which holds one of the world's best collections of Southeast Asian art. Most of the masterpieces from the northern provinces have been transported here, leaving up-country museums looking a little bare. You'll have a good opportunity to trace Thailand's long history, beginning with the ceramic utensils and bronze ware of the Ban Chiang people (3000–4000 BC). The main building was built in 1783 as a palace for surrogate kings (a position abolished in 1874). Head to the artifact gallery, at the left of the ticket counter, for a historical overview. Afterward, explore the galleries that portray the Dvaravati and Khmer periods. This will prepare you for the different styles of Thai art, from the Sukhothai period (13th–14th centuries) to the Ayutthaya period (14th–18th centuries). There are free guided tours in English on Wednesday and Thursday at 9 AM. ⊠ *Na Phra That Rd.,* ☎ *02/224–1333,* WEB *www.thailandmuseum. com.* 🖃 *Admission.* ◷ *Wed.–Sun. 9–4.*

❽ National Theatre. Classical dance and drama can usually be seen here on the last Friday and Saturday of each month. ⊠ *Na Phra That Rd.,* ☎ *02/224–1342.* 🖃 *Admission.*

❺ Royal Barge Museum. These splendid ceremonial barges are berthed on the Thonburi side of the Chao Phraya River. The boats, carved in the early part of the 19th century, take the form of mythical creatures in the *Ramakien,* a traditional tale of the human incarnation of Vishnu. The most impressive is the red-and-gold royal vessel called *Suphannahongse* (Golden Swan), used by the king on special occasions. Carved from a single piece of teak, it measures about 150 ft and weighs more than 15 tons. Fifty oarsmen propel it along the river, accompanied by two coxswains, flag wavers, and a rhythm-keeper. ⊠ *Khlong Bangkok Noi,* ☎ *02/424–0004.* 🖃 *Admission.* ◷ *Daily 9–5.*

❹ Wat Arun. If the Temple of the Dawn is inspiring at sunrise, it is even more marvelous toward dusk when the setting sun throws amber tones over the entire area. The temple's design is symmetrical, with a square courtyard containing five Khmer-style *prangs* (spires). The central prang, which reaches to 282 ft, is surrounded by its four attendant prangs at each of the corners. All five are covered in mosaics made from broken pieces of Chinese porcelain. Energetic visitors climb the steep steps of the central prang for the view over the Chao Phraya; the less ambitious can linger in the small park by the river, a peaceful spot to gaze across at the city. ⊠ *Arun Amarin Rd.,* ☎ *02/466–3167.* 🖃 *Admission.* ◷ *Daily 8:30–5:30.*

★ ❸ Wat Pho. The Temple of the Reclining Buddha, the largest wat in Bangkok, houses what is perhaps the most unusual representation of the Buddha in Bangkok. The 150-ft sculpture, covered with gold, is so large it fills an entire *viharn* (temple). Especially noteworthy are the mammoth statue's 10-ft feet, with the 108 auspicious signs of the Buddha inlaid in mother-of-pearl. Many people ring the bells surrounding the image for good luck.

Don't be perturbed by the statues that good-natured poke fun at *farangs* (foreigners). These towering figures, which are supposed to scare away evil spirits, were modeled after the Europeans who plundered China during the Opium Wars. These statues, some of whom wear farcical top hats, guard the entrance to the northeastern quarter of the compound and a very pleasant three-tier temple containing 394 seated Buddhas. Usually a monk sits cross-legged at one side of the altar, making himself available to answer questions (in Thai). On the walls, bas-relief plaques salvaged from Ayutthaya depict stories from the Ramakien. Around this temple area are four tall *chedis* (spires) decorated with brightly colored porcelain. Each represents one of the first four kings of the Chakri dynasty.

Behind the viharn holding the Reclining Buddha is Bangkok's oldest open university. A century before Bangkok was established as the capital, a monastery was founded here to teach traditional medicine. Around the walls are marble plaques inscribed with formulas for herbal cures, and stone sculptures squat in various postures demonstrating techniques for relieving pain. The monks still practice ancient cures, and the massage school is now famous. A massage lasts one hour, growing more and more pleasurable as you adjust to it. Massage courses of up to 10 days are also available. ⊠ *Chetuphon Rd.* ☒ *Admission.* ☉ *Daily 8–5.*

★ ❷ **Wat Phra Keo.** No single structure within the Grand Palace elicits such awe as the adjacent Temple of the Emerald Buddha, the most sacred temple in the kingdom. No other wat in Thailand is so ornate and so embellished with glittering gold. You may prefer the simplicity of some other wats, but you'll never quite get over Wat Phra Keo's opulence. As you enter the compound, take note of the 20-ft-tall statues of fearsome creatures in traditional battle attire standing guard. They set the scene—mystical, majestic, and awesome. Turn right as you enter, because on the inner walls are lively murals depicting the whole epic tale of the Ramakien.

Several *aponsis* (mythical half-woman, half-lion creatures) stand guard outside the main chapel, which has a gilded three-tier roof that dazzles the eye. Inside sits the Emerald Buddha. This most venerated image of Lord Buddha is carved from one piece of jade 31 inches high. No one knows its origin, but history places it in Chiang Rai in 1464. From there it traveled first to Chiang Mai, then to Lamphun, and finally back to Chiang Rai, where the Laotians stole it and took it home with them. The Thais sent an army to get it back, and it reached its final resting place when King Rama I built this temple. The statue is high above the altar, so you can see it only from afar. Behind the altar and above the window frames are murals depicting the life and eventual enlightenment of the Buddha. At the back of the royal chapel you'll find a scale model of Angkor Wat. ⊠ *Sana Chai Rd.,* ☎ *02/224–1833,* WEB *www.palaces.thai.net.* ☒ *Admission.* ☉ *Daily 8:30–3:30.*

Dusit

Unlike any other neighborhood in the city, Dusit seems calm and orderly. Its tree-shaded boulevards lined with elegant buildings befit the district that holds Chitlada Palace, the official residence of the king and queen. All the planning was the work of King Rama V, the first of the country's monarchs to visit Europe. He returned with a grand plan to remake his capital after the great cities he had visited.

A Good Tour

Begin at **Dusit Park** ⑨, a square of green that sits like a postage stamp in this quiet corner of Bangkok. Here you'll find **Vimarnmek Mansion** ⑩, the largest teak structure in the world. An elegant pavilion on the water is a great place to gaze across the lake. On the other side of Ratchadamnoen Nok Road you can see eye to eye with white-handed gibbons and other rare creatures at the **Dusit Zoo** ⑪. Lovely **Chitlada Palace** ⑫, the king's private residence, is in a private compound just beyond.

On the corner of Nakhon Pathom Road and Si Syutthaya Road is **Wat Benjamabophit** ⑬, the elegant palace made of marble where the king spent his days as a monk. It's one of the most photographed sights in the city. Take a tuk-tuk south to **Wat Rachanada** ⑭. Walk east across Maha Chai Road to towering **Wat Saket** ⑮, one of the city's best-known landmarks.

TIMING

The sights in and around Dusit are fairly close together, so this tour could be done in a morning or an afternoon.

Sights to See

⑫ **Chitlada Palace.** When in Bangkok, the king resides at Chitlada Palace, which takes up an entire block across from Dusit Park. The extensive grounds are home to a herd of royal white elephants. Although the palace is closed to the public, the outside walls are a lovely sight when lit up to celebrate the king's birthday. ⊠ *Ratchawith Rd. and Rama V Rd.*

⑨ **Dusit Park.** The Vimarnmek Mansion may get all the attention, but there are several other sights within these formal gardens that will make you want to wander off the well-tended paths. The **Royal Carriage Museum**, near the park's entrance, is filled with unusual vehicles used by the country's monarchs. In the **Royal Family Museum** hang the official portraits of some of the region's most colorful rulers. ⊠ *Ratchawith Rd. and Rama V Rd.*

☝ ⑪ **Dusit Zoo.** Komodo dragons and other rarely seen creatures are on display at this charming little zoo. While adults sip coffee at the cafés, children can ride elephants (though not the white ones, which are of "royal blood"). ⊠ *Ratchawith Rd. and Rama V Rd*, ☎ 02/281–0021 ▦ *Admission.* ☉ *Daily 8:30–6.*

⑩ **Vimarnmek.** The largest teak structure in the world, Vimarnmek was moved to its present location in the early 19th century by King Rama V. The three-story mansion is now in the administrative center of Bangkok. The place fits its name, which means "Cloud Mansion," as its extraordinary lightness is enhanced by a reflecting pond. King Rama V's fascination with Western architecture shows in its Victorian style, but the building retains an unmistakably Thai delicacy. Many of the furnishings were gifts from European monarchs. Some are exquisite— porcelain, handcrafted furniture, and crystal—and some have novelty value, like the first typewriter brought to Thailand. Exhibitions of Thai dancing take place daily at 10:30 and 2. ⊠ *Ratchawith Rd.,* ☎ 02/ 628–6300. ▦ *Admission.* ☉ *Daily 9:30–4.*

★ ⑬ **Wat Benjamabophit.** Bangkok's most photographed wat, the Marble Temple was built in 1899. Thailand's present king spent his days as a monk here before his coronation. Statues of the Buddha line the courtyard, and the magnificent interior has cross beams of lacquer and gold, but Wat Benjamabophit is more than a splendid temple. The monastery is a seat of learning that appeals to Buddhist monks with intellectual yearnings. ⊠ *Nakhon Pathom Rd.* 🖾 *Admission.* ⊘ *Daily 8–5.*

⑭ Wat Rachanada. The Temple of the Metal Castle intentionally resembles the mythical castle of the gods. According to legend, a wealthy and pious man built a fabulous castle, Loha Prasat, from the design laid down in Hindu mythology for the disciples of the Buddha. Wat Rachanada, meant to duplicate that castle, is the only one of its kind remaining. There are stalls selling amulets that protect you from harm or increase your chances of finding love. They tend to be rather expensive, but that's the price of good fortune. ⊠ *Saran Rom Rd.* 🖾 *Admission.* ⊘ *Daily 8–6.*

⑮ Wat Saket. A well-known landmark, the towering gold chedi of Wat Saket was once the highest point in the city. King Rama III began construction of this temple, but it wasn't completed until the reign of Rama V. To reach the gilded chedi you must ascend an exhausting 318 steps, so don't attempt the climb on a hot day. On a clear day, the view from the top is magnificent. Every November, at the time of the Loi Kratong festival, the temple hosts a popular fair with food stalls and performances. ⊠ *Chakkaphatdi Phong Rd.* 🖾 *Admission.* ⊘ *Daily 8–5.*

Chinatown

Teahouses, dim sum restaurants, and bustling markets still abound in Chinatown, one of the oldest neighborhoods in Bangkok. It's a delight to wander through the maze of alleys, ducking into herb shops and temples along the way. Yaowarat Road, the main thoroughfare, is crowded with gold and jewelry shops. Pahuraht Road is full of textile shops, with nearly as many Indian dealers as Chinese.

A Good Tour

Start at the northwest end of Yaowarat Road, where you can browse for treasures at **Nakorn Kasem** ⑯, better known as the Thieves Market. Head east on Yaowarat Road, the main thoroughfare, to experience the sights and sounds of this vibrant neighborhood. Head north on Mankon Road to reach **Neng Noi Yee** ⑰, a beautiful Buddhist temple topped by dragons gazing heavenward. Return to Yaowarat Road and continue east until it leads into Charoen Krung Road. On the opposite corner stands **Wat Traimit** ⑱, home of the Golden Buddha. If you're in need of sustenance at this point, hop in a tuk-tuk and head to the Oriental Hotel for a barbecue on the banks of the Chao Phraya.

TIMING
Allow a few hours to visit Chinatown, especially if you enjoy browsing at the many markets.

Sights to See

⑯ Nakorn Kasem. The Thieves Market was once known for its reasonable prices for antiques. You won't find the same bargains today, but it's still fun to browse among the stalls. ⊠ *Yaowarat Rd. and Chakraphet Rd.*

⑰ Neng Noi Yee. Unlike most temples you'll see in Bangkok, Neng Noi Yee has a glazed ceramic roof topped with fearsome dragons. Although it's a Buddhist shrine, it incorporates elements of Confucianism and Taoism as well. ⊠ *Mankon Rd.*

★ **⑱ Wat Traimit.** The Temple of the Golden Buddha has little architectural merit, but off to the side is a small chapel containing the world's largest solid-gold Buddha, cast about nine centuries ago. Weighing 5½ tons and standing 10 ft high, the statue gleams with such richness and purity that even the most jaded are inspired by its strength and power. The statue, sculpted in Sukhothai style, is believed to have been brought first to Ayutthaya. When the Burmese were about to sack the city, it was covered in plaster. Two centuries later, still in plaster, it was thought to be worth very little. When it was being moved to a new temple in Bangkok in the 1950s it slipped from a crane and was left in the mud by workmen. In the morning, a temple monk, who had dreamed that the statue was divinely inspired, went to see the Buddha image. Through a crack in the plaster he saw a glint of yellow, and soon discovered that the statue was pure gold. ⊠ *Tri Mit Rd.* ☎ *Admission.* ☉ *Daily 9–5.*

Downtown

To many people, this mass of business towers is Bangkok's center. Among the shopping centers you'll find the city's largest undeveloped space, Lumphini Park. South of Rama IV Road is Silom Road, one of the main financial districts. Suriwong Road, where you'll find many upscale hotels, runs parallel to Silom. Between them lies Patpong, home to the city's most notorious nightspots.

A Good Tour

Start in **Lumphini Park** ⑲, a swath of green where Thais go the escape the heat. Across Ratchadamri Road is **Queen Saowapha Snake Farm** ⑳, where you can watch deadly snakes being milked for their venom. To the north is **Suan Pakkard Palace** ㉑, consisting of several teak houses. The serene atmosphere makes the palace one of the most relaxing places in which to absorb the local culture. If you're interested in the silk trade, there's no better place to learn about it than at **Jim Thompson's House** ㉒. The American businessman was very wealthy, as you'll see at his home filled with fine antiques spanning 14 centuries.

TIMING
The sights in this part of the city are spread out, so make sure to allow several hours to get from one to another.

Sights to See

㉒ **Jim Thompson's House.** Formerly an architect in New York City, Jim Thompson decided after World War II that he would single-handedly revitalize Thailand's moribund silk industry. His project met with tremendous success, which in itself would have made him a legend. Thompson imported parts of several up-country buildings, some as old as 150 years, to construct his compound of six Thai houses. Three are exactly the same as their originals, including details of the interior layout. With true appreciation and a connoisseur's eye, Thompson then furnished them with what are now priceless pieces of Southeast Asian art. Adding to Thompson's notoriety is his disappearance: in 1967 he went to the Malaysian Cameron Highlands for a quiet holiday and was never heard from again. The entrance to the house is easy to miss: it's at the end of an unprepossessing lane, leading north off Rama I Road, west of Phayathai Road (the house is on your left). A good landmark is the National Stadium skytrain station—it's down the street from it. ⊠ *Soi Kasemsong 2,* ☎ *02/612–3668.* ☎ *Admission.* ☉ *Daily 9–5:30.*

⑲ **Lumphini Park.** Two lakes enhance this popular park, one of the few in the center of the city. You can watch children feed bread to the turtles or teenagers taking a rowboat to more secluded shores. ⊠ *Rama IV Rd.*

☙ ⑳ **Queen Saowapha Snake Farm.** In 1923 the Thai Red Cross established this unusual snake farm. Venom from cobras, pit vipers, and other deadly snakes is collected and used to make antidotes for people who are bitten. At 11 AM milking sessions (and weekdays at 2:30 PM) you can watch the staff fearlessly handle the slithery creatures. ⊠ *1871 Rama IV Rd.,* ☎ *02/252–0161.* ▣ *Admission.* ⊙ *Weekdays 8:30–4:30, weekends 8:30–noon.*

★ ㉑ **Suan Pakkard Palace.** Five antique teak houses, built high on columns, complement the undulating lawns, shimmering lotus pools, and lush shrubbery at this compound. The center of attraction, the Lacquer Pavilion that sits serenely at the back of the garden, houses gold-covered paneling with scenes from the life of the Buddha. Other houses display porcelains, stone heads, traditional paintings, and Buddha statues. ⊠ *352 Si Ayutthaya Rd.,* ☎ *02/245–4934.* ▣ *Admission.* ⊙ *Daily 9–4.*

DINING

Thais are passionate about food. Finding an out-of-the-way shop that prepares some specialty better than anywhere else, then dragging groups of friends to share the discovery, is a national pastime. The tastes and smells of Thailand are all around you day and night, since the Thais always seem to be eating. Want a midnight snack? More than likely there's a night market nearby serving up delicious dishes late into the evening.

Former fishing boats or refurbished rice barges often serve a traditional dinner while cruising the Chao Phraya River. These two-hour evening cruises are usually strictly for tourists. **The Horizon** (⊠ Shangri-La Hotel, 89 Soi Wat Suan Phu, New Rd., ☎ 02/236–7777) departs each evening at 7:30 PM. It costs B1,400 per person. **The Manohra Moon** (⊠ Marriott Royal Garden Riverside Hotel, 257/1–3 Charoen Krung Rd., Thonburi, ☎ 02/476–0021) has both lunch and dinner cruises. They are a bargain at B1,100 per person.

Chinese

$$$$ ✗ **Dynasty.** Government ministers and corporate executives come here to feast on the outstanding Cantonese cuisine. In addition to the main dining rooms, 11 smaller nooks provide unsurpassed settings for business lunches or romantic dinners. The crimson carpeting, carved screens, lacquer furniture, and porcelain objets d'art contribute to the quietly elegant atmosphere. The Peking duck is among the draws. Only the freshest ingredients are used for seasonal specialties that include everything from hairy crabs (October–November) to Taiwanese eels (March). The service is efficient and friendly without being obtrusive. ⊠ *Sofitel Central Plaza Bangkok, 1695 Phaholyothin Rd.,* ☎ *02/ 541–1234. Reservations essential. AE, DC, MC, V.*

$$$$ ✗ **Jade Garden.** If you're looking for a place to enjoy a dim sum brunch, you couldn't do better than the fine Cantonese cuisine at Jade Garden. The superb dishes are made without the aid of MSG, a rare practice in this part of the world. The decor is similarly assured in its effects, with a remarkable wood-beam ceiling and softly lighted Chinese-print screens. Private dining rooms are available with advance notice. Two good dinner specials are fried Hong Kong noodles and pressed duck with tea leaves. Look for the monthly "special promotion" dish featuring seasonal ingredients. ⊠ *Montien Hotel, 54 Suriwong Rd.,* ☎ *02/233–7060. AE, DC, MC, V.*

$$$$ ✗ **Mayflower.** Captains of industry, heads of state, and members of the royal family are among the regular customers of the five stylishly opulent private rooms of the Mayflower. The carved wood screens and porcelain vases in the main dining room lend an air of refinement that

is perfectly in keeping with the outstanding Cantonese food. Two of the best items on the menu are the piquant abalone-and-jellyfish salad and the drunken chicken, made with steamed, skinned, and boned chicken doused with Chinese liquor and served with two sauces, one sweet and one spicy. The excellent wine list assumes that price is no object. Two- to three-day advance notice is required for private rooms. ⊠ *Dusit Thani Hotel, Rama IV Rd.,* ☎ *02/236–0450. Reservations essential. AE.*

$$–$$$$ ✕ **Sui Sian.** This longtime favorite serves delicious, if a bit inconsistent, Cantonese cuisine. Certainly the decor of both the main dining rooms and the adjoining private rooms make it a good spot for lunch or dinner meetings. The larger rooms with bamboo-tile eaves give the feeling of dining in an outdoor courtyard, an impression reinforced by the display of jade trees. The Peking duck is particularly good. If you're in an extravagant mood, try a pricey dish called "ancient master jumps the wall"—a soup incorporating black chicken, deer tendons, abalone, shark's fin, dried scallops, fish maw, turtle, sea cucumber, mushrooms, and a selection of secret Chinese herbs. ⊠ *Landmark Hotel, 138 Sukhumvit Rd.,* ☎ *02/254–0404. AE, DC, MC, V.*

$$ ✕ **Shangrila.** The menu has a wide range of entrées from Peking duck
★ to thinly sliced pork with garlic, but it is hard to pass up the marvelous selection of dim sum favorites. Waiters will help you choose individual dishes, but it's difficult to make a mistake because each is around B35. The service is pleasantly attentive. The small restaurant's split levels make it more comfortable than restaurants in the neighborhood. Bright white tablecloths and gleaming glassware make for an upbeat dining experience. ⊠ *154/4–7 Silom Rd.,* ☎ *02/234–9147 or 02/234–9149. AE, DC, MC, V.*

$ ✕ **Tien Tien.** For years, Tien Tien has catered to busy business executives. If you happen to be in the neighborhood you'll find that dinner is just as tasty. The roast pork is superb; order it any way you want, but it's so juicy and tender that the most popular accompaniment is simple steamed rice. The Peking duck is also a must; its skin is crisp and the pancakes are light and fluffy. The decor, which doesn't get much beyond white tablecloths and red walls, is the only disappointment. ⊠ *105 Patpong, Silom Rd.,* ☎ *02/234–8717. MC, V.*

¢   ✕ **Coca Noodles.** On evenings and weekends, these raucous restaurants are full of Chinese families downing a daunting variety of noodle dishes. Both wheat- and rice-based pastas are available in abundance, in combination with a cornucopia of meats, fish, shellfish, and crunchy Chinese vegetables. Try some of the green, wheat-based noodles called *mee yoke,* topped with a chicken thigh, red pork, or crab meat. You can also try an intriguing Chinese variant of sukiyaki that you prepare yourself on a hot plate built into your table. ⊠ *461 Henri Dunant Rd., near Siam Square,* ☎ *02/251–6337 or 02/251–3538;* ⊠ *6 Soi Tantawan, Suriwong Rd.,* ☎ *02/236–0107. No credit cards.*

¢   ✕ **Prachak.** Families from wealthy neighborhoods send their maids here
★ to bring home the superb *ped* (roast duck) and *moo daeng* (red pork). You may want to follow their lead, as the tile floors and bare walls hardly make you want to linger. Whatever you do, get here early, as by 6 PM there's often no duck or pork left, and by 9 PM the place has closed for the night. The problem is in *finding* this hole in the wall, located across from the Shangri-La Hotel. Once you're there, the grandson of the restaurant's founder welcomes you with a bit of English. ⊠ *1415 Charoen Krung (New Road), Silom Bansak,* ☎ *02/234–3755. Reservations not accepted. No credit cards.*

Eclectic

$$ ✕ **Pickle Factory.** Originally from Chicago, Jeff Fehr started making pickles in this art deco–style house that feels right out of south Florida. That's where the name came from, although now this unpretentious place serves ample plates of pasta and the best pizza in town. And if you like pickles, this is your place. It's an intimate setting with some tables set beside the swimming pool. ⊠ *55 Soi Ratchawithi 2,* ☎ *02/ 246–3036. No credit cards.*

$–$$ ✕ **Kuppa.** Looking a bit like a refurbished warehouse, this light and airy space has plenty of polished metal and wood. Unlike many downtown eateries, each table has plenty of space. The menu offers traditional fare as well as a wide range of international dishes. In a short time Kuppa has picked up a dedicated following because of the coffee roasted on the premises. Then again, it might just be the impressive desserts. ⊠ *39 Sukhumvit Soi 16,* ☎ *02/663–0450. AE, DC, MC, V.*

French

$$$$ ✕ **Le Banyan.** You might never guess that inside this traditional Thai home you'll find first-rate French cooking. The chef occasionally experiments with Asian influences, adding to his Continental fare a note of lemongrass, ginger, or Thai basil. A large silver-plated duck press normally takes center stage in the elegant dining room. Pressed duck à la Rouennaise, in a sauce prepared with red wine, is one of the specialties of the house. Panfried foie gras and king lobster in mustard sauce make delicious alternatives. ⊠ *59 Sukhumvit Soi 8,* ☎ *02/253–5556,* WEB *www. lebanyan.net. Reservations essential. AE, DC, MC, V. Closed Sun.*

$$$$ ✕ **Le Normandie.** Perched atop the Oriental Hotel, this legendary
★ restaurant commands a peerless view of the Chao Phraya River. The most highly esteemed chefs in France periodically take over the kitchen. These artists usually import ingredients from the old country, which means patrons can feast on phenomenal cuisine. Even when no superstar is on the scene, the food is remarkable; the menu often including classic dishes like slow-cooked shoulder of lamb. ⊠ *48 Oriental Ave.,* ☎ *02/659–9000. Reservations essential. Jacket and tie required. AE, DC, MC, V. No lunch Sun.*

German

$$ ✕ **Bei Otto.** Berlin comes to Bangkok in the form of Bei Otto, which serves food so fabulous that it wouldn't be out of place back in Germany. Otto Duffner came to Bangkok more than 20 years ago to open this longtime favorite. The walls of the main dining room are covered with photos of the owner with people of note who've dropped by to sample the cuisine. The dining room is comfortable, if a tad cramped, but the food is tasty and the portions tremendous. ⊠ *1 Sukhumvit Soi 20,* ☎ *02/262–0892. AE, DC, MC, V.*

$ ✕ **Tawandang German Brewery.** A boisterous atmosphere makes this
★ taproom a fun place for dinner. There is seating for 1,500, and live music performed by local bands often packs the place. German brew master Jochen Neuhaus produces 40,000 liters of lagers and other beers each month. The restaurant serves Thai, German, and Chinese fare. You can't miss the place—it resembles a big barrel. ⊠ *462/61 Rama III Rd.,* ☎ *02/678–1114. AE, DC, MC, V.*

Indian

$ ✕ **Himali Cha Cha.** Although Cha Cha, who was once Indian Prime Minister Jawaharlal Nehru's cook, died in 1996, his recipes live on.

Bangkok Dining and Lodging

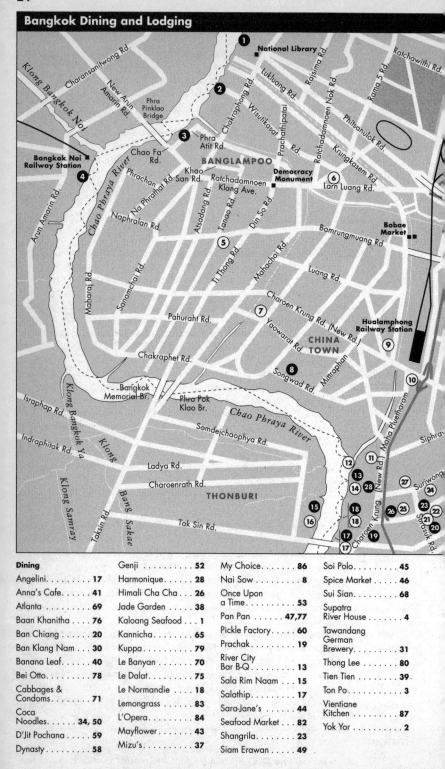

National Library

Ratchawithi Rd.

Charansanitwong Rd.

Klong Bangkok Noi

New Arun Amarin Rd.

Lukluang Rd.

Rajsima Rd.

Pama 5 Rd.

Phra Pinklao Bridge

Chakraphong Rd.

Wisutikasat

Prachathipatai Rd.

Ratchadamnoen Nok Rd.

Phitsanulok Rd.

Bangkok Noi Railway Station

Phra Atit Rd.

Chao Fa Rd.

Phrachan

Na Phrathat Rd.

Khao San Rd.

BANGLAMPOO

Ratchadamnoen Klang Ave.

Democracy Monument

Larn Luang Rd.

Krungkasem Rd.

Arun Amarin Rd.

Naphralan Rd.

Atsadang Rd.

Tanao Rd.

Din So Rd.

Bamrungmuang Rd.

Bobae Market

Maharaj Rd.

Chao Phraya River

Sanamchai Rd.

Ti Thong Rd.

Mahachai Rd.

Luang Rd.

Pahuraht Rd.

Charoen Krung Rd. (New Rd.)

Hualamphong Railway Station

Chakraphet Rd.

Yaowarat Rd.

CHINA TOWN

Maha Puetharam

Israphap Rd.

Bangkok Memorial Br.

Phra Pok Klao Br.

Songwad Rd.

Mitraphan

Siphra

Indraphithak Rd.

Somdejchaophya Rd.

Chao Phraya River

Suriwong

Klong Bangkok Ya

Klong

Ladya Rd.

THONBURI

Charoenrath Rd.

Charoen Krung (New Rd.)

Surasak

Klong Samray

Taksin Rd.

Bang Sakae

Tak Sin Rd.

Dining

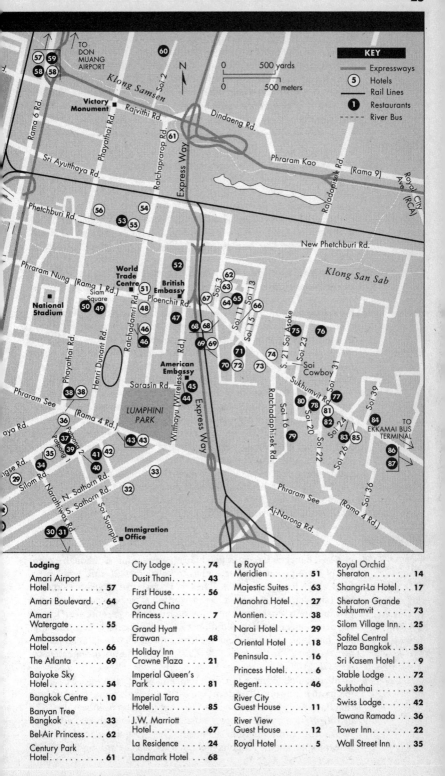

KEY

—	Expressways
⑤	Hotels
—	Rail Lines
❶	Restaurants
- - - -	River Bus

They are currently prepared with equal ability by his wife. The quality of the food remains top-notch. The tandoori chicken is locally famous, and the daily specials, precisely explained by the staff, are usually too intriguing to pass up. The breads and the mango-flavor *lassis* (yogurt drinks) are delicious. The northern Indian cuisine is served in a pleasantly informal setting with the usual Mogul decor. A second branch recently opened near the Phrom Phong skytrain station. ⊠ *1229/11 New Rd.*, ☎ *02/235–1569*; ⊠ *Sukhumvit Soi 35*, ☎ *02/258–8834. AE, DC, MC, V.*

Italian

$$$$ ✕ **Angelini.** Although the competition is stiff, many consider this the
★   best Italian restaurant in Bangkok. It's a comfortable place where you can relax at a table overlooking the river. Especially soothing is a duo that plays jazz in the evenings. The Italian dishes are all good, with the rack of lamb head and shoulders above the rest. The desserts, such as the chocolate soufflé, alone are worth the visit. ⊠ *Shangri-La Hotel, 89 Soi Wat Suan Phu, New Rd.*, ☎ *02/236–7777. Reservations essential. AE, DC, MC, V.*

$$ ✕ **L'Opera.** Specializing in a variety of homemade pastas, this family-run restaurant draws a loyal clientele. The staff takes pride in their work, and many of them have remained over the years despite overtures from the competition. Consider the large ravioli stuffed with spinach and cheese or the *spadarrata*, a combination of different types of seafood in a garlic-and-white-wine sauce. The table in the bay window is the nicest, but given its proximity to the air-conditioner you might want to wear a sweater. ⊠ *53 Sukhumvit Soi 39*, ☎ *02/258–5606. AE, DC, MC, V.*

$ ✕ **Pan Pan.** The two branches of this eatery have remained enormously popular for many years, despite the proliferation of Italian restaurants in Bangkok. The relaxed atmosphere in both places invites intimate conversions. The long menu includes such favorites as linguine with a sauce of salmon, cream, and vodka that is a taste of high-calorie heaven, and "chicken godfather," served with a cream-and-mushroom sauce that is disappointment-proof. Save room for the ice cream—traditional gelato. ⊠ *6–6/1 Sukhumvit Rd., near Soi 33*, ☎ *02/258–9304 or 02/258–5071*; ⊠ *45 Soi Lang Suan, off Ploenchit Rd.*, ☎ *02/252–7104. AE, DC, MC, V.*

Japanese

$$ ✕ **Genji.** Bangkok has many good Japanese restaurants, although a number of them give a chilly reception to newcomers. Genji, with warm service, is a happy exception. The fact that it's in a large international hotel shouldn't deter you—it has an excellent sushi bar and several small private rooms where you can enjoy such dishes as the succulent grilled eel. Set menus for lunch and dinner are well conceived, and the Japanese breakfasts are a nice change from typical Thai fare. ⊠ *Hilton International, 2 Witthayu Rd.*, ☎ *02/253–0123. Reservations essential. AE, DC, MC, V.*

$ ✕ **Mizu's.** Opened by a Japanese man almost 50 years ago, Mizu's remains an institution. The decor is a bit dated, with some travel posters that have hung around since the '70s, but the food is unbeatable. The menu offers a range of spicy curries and sizzling charcoal-broiled steaks from cattle raised in the north. This is a good place for dinner before exploring the Patpong night market. ⊠ *32 Patpong Rd.*, ☎ *02/233–6447. AE, MC, V.*

Laotian

¢ **✕ Vientiane Kitchen.** Laotian cuisine is similar to that of northeast Thai-
★ land, with a few differences here and there. This open-air restaurant
named after the capital of Laos is set under thatched roofs, giving the
place a festive feeling. Live Laotian music and dance add to the atmosphere. It's best to go with a group so you can share several dishes, as
is custom in Laos. Some odd dishes might prove a bit much for many
people, but standards like grilled chicken, papaya salad, and sticky rice
are all recommended. ⊠ *8 Sukhumvit Soi 36,* ☎ *02/258–6171. AE,
DC, MC, V.*

Thai

$$$$ **✕ Sala Rim Naam.** To reach this elegant dining room you must take
★ a boat across the Chao Phraya River from the Oriental Hotel. This is
one of the best places to sample Royal Thai cuisine, elaborate dishes
once served only to the king and his family. You may not want to van-
dalize the platters of fruits and vegetables carefully carved to resemble flowers. Try some of the spicy salads, especially the shrimp version
called *yam koong.* Make reservations for 7:30 PM and plan to stay on
for the beautifully staged Thai dancing. The delicious lunch buffet is
always less crowded and, during the hot season serves rarely found light
recipes. ⊠ *48 Oriental Ave., across from the Oriental Hotel,* ☎ *02/
437–6211. Reservations essential. AE, DC, MC, V.*

$$$ **✕ D'Jit Pochana.** Convenient for those staying near the airport, D'Jit
Pochana has numerous rooms—including several large private rooms
suitable for business dinners—on different levels. Request a table with
a view of the pond in the garden. Among the many specialties are *gai
hor bai toey* (deep-fried chicken in pandan leaves) and *tom kha gai* (spicy
soup with chicken and coconut milk). ⊠ *26/368–80 Gp 6 Phaholyothin
Rd.,* ☎ *02/531–1644. AE, DC, MC, V.*

$$ **✕ Ban Klang Nam.** This open-air restaurant is upstream from the
★ Hanging Bridge, so you'll need a taxi to get here. Choose a table next
to the railing so you can gaze at the river; you can also opt for a seat
on the dock. The difficult-to-make *mee krob* (panfried rice noodles)
shows off the skill of the kitchen. The fried sea bass in garlic and pepper and the snapper in an oyster sauce are superb, as is the smooth
tom yam kung (hot and sour shrimp soup). ⊠ *3792/106 Pharam 3,
Soi 14,* ☎ *02/292–0175 or 02/292–2037. Reservations essential. AE,
MC, V.*

$$ **✕ Kaloang Seafood.** This local favorite is a bit off the beaten track,
but it's worth the effort if you want the fantastic fish you can only get
at a riverside restaurant. An alley near the National Library leads to
the open-air restaurant, built on a ramshackle pier. The breeze off the
river keep things comfortably cool most evenings. More observant cus-
tomers will notice right away that almost all the workers are in drag.
The generous grilled seafood platter is a bargain, as is the plate of grilled
giant river prawns. Try the *yam pla duk foo.* This grilled fish salad is
rather spicy, but it goes great with a cold beer. ⊠ *2 Sri Ayutthaya Rd.,*
☎ *02/281–9228. AE, DC, MC, V.*

$$ **✕ Salathip.** On a veranda facing the Chao Phraya River, this intimate
restaurant practically guarantees that you'll have a romantic evening.
Be sure to reserve a table outside so you can enjoy the breeze. Although
the food may not have as many chilies as some would like, it hasn't
been adulterated to suit Western tastes. On Sunday night you are
treated to what is possibly the best buffet in Bangkok. The traditional
music makes everything taste even better. ⊠ *Shangri-La Hotel, 89 Soi
Wat Suan Phu, New Rd.,* ☎ *02/236–7777. Reservations essential.
AE, DC, MC, V. No lunch.*

$$ ✕ **Seafood Market.** Although it's miles from the ocean, this vast restaurant has fish so fresh that it feels like the boats must be somewhere nearby. You take a cart and choose from an array of seafood—crabs, prawns, lobsters, clams, oysters, fish. The waiter takes it away and instructs the chef to cook it any way you like. Typically your eyes are bigger than your stomach, so select with prudence, not gusto. The location on Sukhumvit Road has fluorescent lighting that adds to the supermarket feel. ✉ *388 Sukhumvit Soi 24,* ☎ *02/258–0218. Reservations not accepted. AE, DC, MC, V.*

$$ ✕ **Siam Erawan.** If you're in the Siam Square area, this popular bistro across from the Novotel is worth a try. On the wooden tables you'll find an eclectic mix of European antiques and Thai artifacts. The menu is varied, combining standard favorites such as chicken and coconut milk soup and roast duck with red curry with more unusual entries like spicy stir-fried boar meat. The best dish, however, is the spicy crab soup. ✉ *458/7–9 Soi 7, Siam Square,* ☎ *02/250–1733. Reservations not accepted. MC, V.*

$ ✕ **Anna's Café.** This restaurant exudes optimism and cheer. It has dining areas separated with potted plants, so you always feel you have some privacy. Although there is a smattering of European dishes, most of the menu is modern Thai. The green curry with chicken and eggplant is mild and served with a salted boiled egg to counter its sweetness. The *tod mun kung* (fried prawn cakes) served with stir-fried vegetables and fried rice makes a full and tasty meal. A good appetizer to share is the extremely spicy grilled fish salad. ✉ *118 Soi Saladaeng, at the top of Silom Rd.,* ☎ *02/632–0619;* ✉ *Diethelm Tower B, Witthayu Rd.,* ☎ *02/632–0620. AE, DC, MC, V.*

$ ✕ **Baan Khanitha.** Half the pleasure of eating here is the attractive setting. Wood paneling, traditional prints, and copper serving pieces create just the right mood for a relaxing evening. The food is strictly Thai, and the dishes are explained well by the English-speaking waiters. The recipes have been altered a bit to appeal more to tourists, which explains the absence of Thais in the dining room. Ask for the complimentary appetizer called *mieng khum* (spinach wraps). The fried soft-shell crabs in a hot-and-sour sauce and the *gaeng keow wan gai* (green curry with chicken and Thai eggplant) are two of the better choices. ✉ *Sukhumvit 23 Soi Prasan,* ☎ *02/258–4181;* ✉ *49 Soi Ruamrudee 2,* ☎ *02/253–4638. Reservations essential. MC, V.*

$ ✕ **Ban Chiang.** The decor here is turn-of-the-20th-century Bangkok, so the walls are adorned with antique prints, old photographs, and a clock with a slowly ticking pendulum. The extensive menu can be quite spicy, especially the shrimp-and-vegetable soup and the roasted duck curry. Other dishes, such as the fried fish cakes and grilled prawns, are much milder. The service is not one of the place's strong points, and you need to know your way around a Thai menu to order a good selection of dishes. ✉ *14 Srivieng Rd.,* ☎ *02/236–7045. MC, V.*

$ ✕ **Cabbages & Condoms.** Don't be misled by the restaurant's odd name or disconcerted by the array of contraceptive devices for sale. The popular place raises funds for the Population & Community Development Association, the country's family planning program. You'll find the food here excellently prepared, with such dishes as chicken wrapped in pandanus leaf, crisp fried fish with chili sauce, and shrimp in a mild curry sauce being the standouts. The eatery lost some of its charm when it expanded a few years ago, but still serves up good food for a good cause. ✉ *10 Sukhumvit Soi 12,* ☎ *02/229–4610. AE, DC, MC, V.*

$ ✕ **Harmonique.** Choose between tables on the terrace or in the dining rooms of this small house near the river. The decor, from bouquets of flowers tumbling out of vases to chests scattered with bric-a-brac, gives the place a casual feel. The menu is small, but the entries are carefully selected. Guests from the Oriental and Royal Orchid Sheraton are ably assisted by the staff in selecting the right entrées. Try the crisp fish sautéed in garlic, the mild crab curry, or the Chinese cabbage topped with salted fish—all are excellent. ⊠ *22 Charoen Krung Soi 34,* ☎ *02/237–8175. AE.*

$ ✕ **Kannicha.** The starched tablecloths, dramatic lighting, and waiters with scarlet suspenders over their white shirts sets the stage for sophisticated Thai fare. The menu is wide and varied. While perusing your many choices, choose a tasty appetizer such as mieng khum (spinach wraps) or *kung tod* (fried shrimp). Favorite main dishes range from pork sautéed in garlic and young peppers to sea bass in "sauce of three tastes." ⊠ *17 Sukhumvit Soi 11,* ☎ *02/651–1573. AE, MC, V.*

$ ✕ **Lemongrass.** A feeling of adventurousness has made this elegant restaurant a favorite with Thais as well as resident Westerners. Embellished with Southeast Asian antiques, the dining rooms and the garden have plenty of atmosphere. Over the years the cuisine has become geared to the milder palate of Westerners, which makes for a good introduction to Thai food. Be sure to try a glass of *nam takrai,* the cold, sweet drink brewed from lemongrass. It's pricey but good. ⊠ *5/1 Sukhumvit Soi 24,* ☎ *02/258–8637. AE, DC, MC, V.*

$ ✕ **My Choice.** Thais with a taste for their grandmothers' traditional recipes flock to this restaurant off Sukhumvit Road. The *ped aob,* a thick soup made from beef stock, is particularly popular. Foreigners may prefer the *tom kha tala,* a hot-and-sour soup with big pieces of shrimp. The interior is plain, so when the weather is cool most people prefer to sit outside. ⊠ *Sukhumvit Soi 36,* ☎ *02/258–6174. AE, DC, MC, V.*

$ ✕ **Once Upon a Time.** Period photos of the royal family, movie stars, and beauty queens grace the wooden walls of this old teak house. The dining room is filled with delightful antiques. The music, often by local performers, is traditional Thai. The menu is nothing if not authentic. *Miang kham,* a traditional snack of dried shrimp, dried coconut, peanuts, pineapple, chili pepper, and sweet tamarind sauce rolled together in a green leaf, makes an excellent appetizer. Afterward move on to the chopped pork with chili sauce or the beef fillet with pickled garlic. ⊠ *Soi 19, Phetchburi Rd., near Juladis Tower,* ☎ *02/255–4948. AE, DC, MC, V.*

$ ✕ **River City Bar B-Q.** This is a place where you can be the chef—a waiter brings to your table a hot plate and a mound of different meats and vegetables. You grill them to your own taste. Order some appetizers to nibble on while dinner is cooking—the northern Thai sausage is excellent. The tables at the edge of the roof of the River City Shopping Centre have romantic views of the Chao Phraya River. ⊠ *River City Shopping Centre,* ☎ *02/237–0077. MC, V.*

$ ✕ **Spice Market.** This popular place recreates the interior of a well-
★ stocked spice shop, with sacks of garlic, piles of dried chilies, and heavy earthenware jars of fish sauce lined up as they were when the only way to get to Bangkok was by steamer. The dishes are tempered to suit the tender mouths of Westerners, but you may ask for your curry to be prepared Thai-style. From the middle of January to the end of March you can try the *nam doc mai* (mango with sticky rice). Many people arrange trips to Bangkok at this time of year just for this dessert. If that doesn't satisfy your sweet tooth, there is also a comprehensive selection of old-fashioned Thai candies. ⊠ *Regent of Bangkok Hotel, 155 Ratchadamri Rd.,* ☎ *02/251–6127. Reservations essential. AE, DC, MC, V.*

$ ✕ Supatra River House. Its location on the Chao Phraya River makes this restaurant worth a visit, especially because it is across from the Grand Palace. The free ferry from Maharaj Pier shuttles diners back and forth. Housed in the former home of Khunying Supatra, founder of the city's express boat business, it has a small museum dedicated to the art she collected. The traditional food happens to be quite good. ⊠ *17/1 Chao Fa Rd.,* ☎ *02/411–0305. AE, MC, V.*

$ ✕ Yok Yor. Step down the gangplank to reach this restaurant aboard a boat on the Chao Phraya River. The well-prepared entrées are served with dispatch, and the cool darkness of the river lends a romantic aura. Most dishes are Thai, but you'll also find Japanese, Chinese, and even some European dishes on the menu. There's live music beginning at 6 PM. The management also runs a dinner-and-music cruise along the Chao Phraya every night from 8:30 to 10:30. Your spot on the 400-seat boat coasts B70. ⊠ *Wisutikasat Rd. at Yok Yor Pier,* ☎ *02/863–0565. AE, DC, MC, V.*

¢ ✕ Atlanta. Although it looks like a coffee shop in a budget hotel, the Atlanta serves surprisingly good Thai fare, thanks to reclusive innkeeper Charles Henn and longtime chef Khun Anong. The menu, which explains the ingredients and their origin, makes interesting, amusing reading. Don't pass up the *tom yam kung* (spicy shrimp soup)—it's especially smooth. Vegetarian dishes are being added to the menu every week. Classical jazz begins the evening, followed by a movie of some repute. ⊠ *78 Sukhumvit Soi 2,* ☎ *02/252–1650 or 02/252–6069. No credit cards.*

¢ ✕ Banana Leaf. If you need a break from shopping on Silom Road, this restaurant is worth a visit. The delicious food here is quite a bargain. Try the baked crab with glass noodles, spicy papaya salad, grilled black band fish, or grilled pork with coconut milk dip. The decor is basic, but the staff is extremely friendly. ⊠ *Silom Complex, Silom Rd.,* ☎ *02/231–3124. No credit cards.*

¢ ✕ Nai Sow. The city's best tom yam kung is found at this Chinese-Thai restaurant next to Wat Plaplachai in Chinatown. Chefs come and go, but the owner somehow manages to keep the recipe to this signature dish a secret. Other equally tasty entrées range from curried beef to sweet-and-sour mushrooms. For an unusual and delicious dessert, finish with the fried taro. Forget about ambience—plain tables and chairs are about the only furnishings. ⊠ *3/1 Maitrichit Rd.,* ☎ *02/222–1539. Reservations not accepted. MC, V.*

¢ ✕ Sara-Jane's. Formerly of Massachusetts, the owner moved here
★ when she married a Thai more than 20 years ago. She has two branches of her restaurant offering cuisine that draws on the traditions of the northeastern part of the country. Both locations are big and plainly furnished and serve lunch to a populous clientele. Many types of salads are served with *larb,* made from marinated minced pork, chicken, or tuna. A favorite here is the grilled fish salad, always on the spicy side. There's also Italian food and wine. ⊠ *Narathiwat Rd. near Sathorn Rd.,* ☎ *02/679–3338;* ⊠ *Sindhorn Tower, Witthayu Rd.,* ☎ *02/650–9992. No credit cards.*

¢ ✕ Soi Polo. Although the beat-up plastic tables and lack of air-condi-
★ tioning make this joint seem unappealing, for more than 40 years it has been a popular lunch spot for nearby office workers. The reason is its world-class fried chicken flavored with black pepper and plenty of golden-brown garlic. The chicken should be sampled with sticky rice and a plate of *som tam,* a hydrogen bomb of hot-and-sour raw papaya salad. The place is a bit hard to find; it's the last of the shops on your left as you enter Soi Polo. Don't get lost, as you need to get here a bit before noon if you expect to get a table. Otherwise the restaurant will deliver to your hotel for B30. ⊠ *Soi Polo, off Witthayu Rd.,* ☎ *02/*

251–2772 or 02/252–0856. *Reservations not accepted. No*
cards. No dinner.

¢ ✕ **Thong Lee.** This small but attractive restaurant draws a devoted cr
to its air-conditioned dining room on the second floor. The menu
not very adventurous, but every dish has a distinct personality—evi
dence of the cook's vivid imagination. Almost everyone orders the *muu*
phad kapi (pork fried with shrimp paste). The *yam hed sod* (hot-and-
sour mushroom salad) is memorable, but might be too spicy for some
people. ⊠ *Sukhumvit Soi 20,* ☎ *no phone. Reservations not accepted.*
No credit cards.

¢ ✕ **Ton Po.** A covered veranda overlooking the Chao Phraya River is
★ the setting for this often-packed eatery. To enjoy the breezes that blow
even on the hottest days, try to secure a waterfront table. Many of the
dishes are well known, but none more so than the delectable *tom kh-*
long plaa salid bai makhaam awn, a hot-and-sour soup made from local
dried fish, chili, lime juice, lemongrass, young tamarind leaves, mushrooms, and a full frontal attack of other seasonings. Less potent but
equally good are the *gai hor bai toey* (deep-fried chicken in pandan
leaves) and *haw moke plaa* (a curried fish custard thickened with coconut cream and steamed in banana leaves). ⊠ *Phra Atit Rd.,* ☎ *02/*
280–0452. Reservations not accepted. AE, DC, MC, V.

Vietnamese

$$ ✕ **Le Dalat.** This classy restaurant, a favorite with Bangkok residents,
★ consists of several intimate dining rooms in what was once a private
home. The Vietnamese cuisine is served with style. Don't pass up the
naem neuang, which requires you to place a garlicky grilled meatball
on a piece of rice paper, then pile on bits of garlic, ginger, hot chili,
star apple, and mango before you wrap the whole thing up in a let-
tuce leaf and pop it in your mouth. ⊠ *51 Sukhumvit Soi 23, opposite*
the Indian Embassy, ☎ *02/260–1849. Reservations essential. AE, DC,*
MC, V.

LODGING

Even after the economic crisis of the last decade that saw businesses
raising their prices to offset the beleaguered baht, hotels in Bangkok
are still less expensive than those in Singapore and Hong Kong. They
are certainly not pricy by European standards. Rates at the city's lux-
ury hotels are about what you'd pay for a standard room elsewhere.
Business hotels have fine service, excellent restaurants, and amenities
like health clubs. Even budget hotels have comfortable rooms and ef-
ficient staffs. Wherever you stay, remember that prices fluctuate enor-
mously and that huge discounts are the order of the day. Always ask
for a better price.

The four main hotel districts are along the parallel streets of Silom and
Suriwong; around Siam Square; near Lumphini Park; and along
Sukhumvit Road. Backpackers head to the neighborhood just north
of Ratchadamnoen Road. The main thoroughfare, Khao Sahn Road,
is full of cheap cafés, secondhand bookstalls, and hundreds of small
guest houses renting tiny rooms for as little as B150 a night.

$$$$ ▣ **Banyan Tree Bangkok.** After checking in on the ground floor, you
soar up to your room at this 60-story hotel. The light-filled suites in
the slender tower all have sweeping views of the city. The generous use
of native woods in everything from the large desks to the walk-in clos-
ets gives the rooms a warm glow. With a two-line telephone system
equipped with a data port and an in-room printer-fax-scanner, there's

need to head to the business center. For those in need of pam-
..g, a fully equipped spa offers the latest treatments, and a sun deck
.n the 53rd floor beckons with a relaxing whirlpool. For meals there's
the rooftop Vertigo, a fair-weather restaurant that the hotel claims is
the world's highest alfresco eatery. In September you can test your fitness in the annual "vertical marathon" up the hotel's stairs. ⊠ 21/100
S. Sathorn Rd., 10120, ☎ 02/679–1200, FAX 02/679–1199, WEB www.
banyantree.com. 216 suites. 4 restaurants, pool, health club, spa, bar,
business services, meeting rooms. AE, DC, MC, V.

$$$$ 🏨 **Dusit Thani.** This high-rise has a distinctive pyramid shape that
makes it immediately identifiable. A popular Chinese restaurant, an
elegant Thai restaurant, and a sprawling shopping arcade occupy the
street level. One floor up is the reception area, where a sunken lounge
overlooks a small garden. The pool is in a central courtyard filled with
trees, making it a peaceful oasis from the heat and humidity. It's proximity to the skytrain makes this hotel a convenient base for exploring
the city. Rooms here are spacious, especially the high-priced suites. Rates
include an American breakfast. ⊠ Rama IV Rd., 10500, ☎ 02/236–
0450, FAX 02/236–6400, WEB www.dusit.com. 470 rooms, 30 suites. 8
restaurants, coffee shop, in-room VCRs, pool, health club, bar, shops,
nightclub, business services, meeting rooms. AE, DC, MC, V.

$$$$ 🏨 **Grand Hyatt Erawan.** This stylish hotel hovers over the Erawan Shrine.
With an extensive modern art collection, the impressive atrium soars
up four stories to a stained-glass roof. Rooms are spacious, with bay
windows holding a desk and a couple of chairs. The wood floors are
strewn with tasteful rugs, and the walls are hung with original art. Everything is high-tech, with your messages displayed on the TV monitor.
Baths have separate showers, oversize tubs, and private dressing areas.
The Italian fare at Spasso, created by a Milanese chef, is especially creative; lunch here is a must whether or not you stay in the hotel. The
pool, set on a gorgeous terrace, is surrounded by lush ferns. ⊠ 494
Ratchadamri Rd., 10330, ☎ 02/254–1234; 800/233–1234 in the U.
S.; FAX 02/254–6308, WEB www.hyatt.com. 387 rooms. 8 restaurants, 2
tennis courts, pool, health club, squash, bar, business services, meeting rooms. AE, DC, MC, V.

$$$$ 🏨 **Holiday Inn Crowne Plaza.** With two towers of glass and steel, the
Holiday Inn Crowne Plaza is impressive. It might be too big for some,
however. The vast public areas make it seem rather like New York City's
Grand Central Terminal, especially with the clusters of airline employees
and tour groups running to and fro. Less hectic are two executive floors
with their own concierge and lounge. Rooms are generously propor-
tioned, with lots of light streaming in. For meals, try the traditional
fare at the Thai Pavilion. ⊠ 981 Silom Rd., 10500, ☎ 02/238–4300,
FAX 02/238–5289, WEB www.crowneplazabangkok.com. 715 rooms, 9
suites. 3 restaurants, 2 tennis courts, pool, health club, bar, business
services, meeting rooms. AE, DC, MC, V.

$$$$ 🏨 **Imperial Queen's Park.** With two gleaming white towers, the Imperial Queen's Park is the largest hotel in Bangkok. To keep its 1,300
rooms filled, the hotel makes special arrangements with guests staying a month or more. The hotel is just off busy Sukhumvit Road, next
to a small park that is ideal for jogging. Standard rooms are spacious
and have large desks, but the junior suites have separate work areas
and plenty of natural light. Many rooms have whirlpool tubs (although not the latest models). If you want to take a swim, choose between the two pools. ⊠ 199 Sukhumvit Soi 22, 10110, ☎ 02/261–
9000, FAX 02/261–9530, WEB www.imperialhotels.com. 1,145 rooms, 155
suites. 7 restaurants, 2 tennis courts, 2 pools, health club, bar, business services, convention center, meeting rooms. AE, DC, MC, V.

$$$$ 🏨 **J. W. Marriott Hotel.** Try as it might, this dow[n]
doesn't stand out in the crowd. Rooms have the s[t]
although the firm beds makes for a good night's sleep[.]
extra bucks to stay on the executive floors, which have a sep[a]
where you are offered complimentary breakfast, afternoon t[e]
evening cocktails. The fitness center is superb, with the latest equipment for retooling the body. When you want to relax, there are steamy
saunas nearby. Restaurants include the Man Ho serving Cantonese fare,
the White Elephant specializing in Thai favorites, and the New York
Steakhouse. ⊠ *4 Sukhumvit Soi 2, 10110,* ☎ *02/656–7700,* FAX *02/656–*
7711, WEB *www.marriot.com. 446 rooms. 4 restaurants, pool, health*
club, sauna, bar, business services, meeting rooms. AE, DC, MC, V.

$$$$ 🏨 **Landmark Hotel.** Although it prides itself on being thoroughly modern, the Landmark's generous use of polished wood in its reception area
suggests a grand European hotel. Rooms, elegant enough to satisfy the
pickiest guest, are geared to corporate travelers, with good-size desks
equipped with video monitors that can be linked to the business center. There's a staff of 950, so it's no surprise that the service is attentive. Rates include a buffet breakfast. ⊠ *138 Sukhumvit Rd., 10110,*
☎ *02/254–0404,* FAX *02/253–4259,* WEB *www.landmarkbangkok.com.*
395 rooms, 55 suites. 4 restaurants, coffee shop, snack bar, pool,
health club, suana, squash, shops, business services, meeting rooms.
AE, DC, MC, V.

$$$$ 🏨 **Oriental Hotel.** For many years the opulent Oriental Hotel has set
★   the standard that few of the city's newer hotels approach. Part of its
fame stems from the celebrities that stayed here in the past, but the recent guest book reveals no less impressive names. The hotel's location
on the Chao Phraya is unrivaled. The original building, now called the
Author's Residence, has been carefully refurbished. Rooms here and
the luxury suites of the River Wing are the most comfortable. Among
its well-known restaurants are Sala Rim Naam, renowned for its Thai
food, and Le Normandie, the best French restaurant in Bangkok. In
addition, the hotel hosts a riverside barbecue every night. There are
cooking classes that teach you the secrets of Thai cuisine, and a smart
spa on the other side of the river that lets you indulge in all sorts of
luxurious treatments. ⊠ *48 Oriental Ave., 10500,* ☎ *02/659–9000;*
00800/2828–3838 in the U.K.; 800/526–6566 in the U.S.; FAX *02/659–*
0000, WEB *www.mandarinoriental.com. 393 rooms. 8 restaurants, 2 ten-*
nis courts, 2 pools, health club, jogging, squash, bar, business services,
helipad. AE, DC, MC, V.

$$$$ 🏨 **Peninsula.** All the latest technology, like bedside controls that dim
the lights, turn on the sound system, and close curtains, is found in the
Peninsula. Baths not only have a separate shower stall but a hands-
free telephone and a television with a mist-free screen at the end of the
tub. The spacious rooms look out onto the river and the skyscrapers
that make up the skyline of Bangkok. Because the Peninsula is in
Thonburi, you'll have to take the free shuttle across the river every time
you come and go. The restaurants are adequate, though not exceptional,
serving Cantonese and Pacific Rim cuisine. Barbecue buffets are often
held in the evening. The hotel has a long, attractive swimming pool
with private gazebos where you can lounge about in sun or shade. ⊠
333 Charoennakorn Rd., Klonsan, 10600, ☎ *02/861–2888,* FAX *02/861–*
2355, WEB *www.peninsula.com. 370 rooms. 3 restaurants, health club,*
bar, business center, meeting rooms, helipad. AE, DC, MC, V.

$$$$ 🏨 **Regent.** Long one of Bangkok's leading hotels, the Regent reigns
★   over the embassy district. Stride up the palatial steps and into the formal lobby where local society meets for morning coffee and afternoon
tea, Classical art adds a note of sophistication. Off a delightful court-

yard there are plenty of shops where you can browse. The generously sized rooms are decorated with furniture upholstered with silk. The best rooms overlook the racetrack, but ask for a high floor so that the skytrain doesn't block the view. A quartet of "cabana rooms," whose private patios look onto a small garden with a lotus pond, are exquisite. Be sure to indulge yourself with the Regent's fragrant-oil massage. ✉ *155 Ratchadamri Rd., 10330,* ☎ *02/251–6127,* 🖷 *02/253–9195,* 🕸 *www.regenthotel.com and fourseasons.com. 346 rooms, 10 suites. 7 restaurants, pool, health club, massage, shops, business services. AE, DC, MC, V.*

$$$$ 🏨 **Le Royal Meridien.** Towering over the city's business district, the Royal Meridien is perfectly situated for corporate travelers. The executive floor has rooms with plenty of added amenities, including fax machines with dedicated lines. Guests here can also enjoy the pleasant lounge with great city views while sipping complimentary evening cocktails. The hotel's leading restaurant, the Summer Palace, prides itself on massive tables than can seat 10 to 24 people. The rooftop pool, however, is surprisingly intimate. ✉ *973 Ploenchit Rd., Lumphini, Pathumwan, 10330,* ☎ *02/656–0444,* 🖷 *02/656–0555,* 🕸 *lemeridienbangkok.com. 381 rooms. 2 restaurants, pool, health club, spa, business services, meeting rooms. AE, DC, MC, V.*

$$$$ 🏨 **Royal Orchid Sheraton.** Of the luxury hotels along the riverfront, this 28-story palace is more oriented toward tour groups than neighbors like the Oriental, Shangri-La, and Peninsula. All the well-appointed rooms face the river. The color scheme, low-key peaches and creams, is a little uninspired. Standard rooms tend to be long and narrow, leaving some people feeling slightly cramped. The Thai Thara Thong restaurant is memorable, with subtle classical music accompanying your meal. You can also choose Japanese, Indian, or Italian cuisine. A glassed-in bridge leads to the adjacent River City Shopping Centre. ✉ *2 Captain Bush La., 10500,* ☎ *02/266–0123 or 02/237–0022,* 🖷 *02/ 236–8320,* 🕸 *www.sheraton.com. 771 rooms. 8 restaurants, coffee shop, 2 tennis courts, 2 pools, health club, 2 bars, shops, business services, meeting rooms, helipad. AE, DC, MC, V.*

$$$$ 🏨 **Shangri-La Hotel.** Although it's one of Bangkok's best hotels, the Shangri-La has never managed to achieve the fame of the Oriental. That's a shame, because the spacious marble lobby illuminated by crystal chandeliers is palacial. The adjacent lounge, with its floor-to-ceiling windows, offers a marvelous view of the Chao Phraya River. The peace of the gardens is only interrupted by the puttering of passing boats. Many of the large rooms, decorated in soothing pastels, are beginning to show their age. In the luxurious Krungthep Wing, a separate tower across the garden, all room balconies overlook the river. Angelini's is considered by many the city's finest Italian restaurant. The Sunday brunch, served near the river, is the best in Bangkok. ✉ *89 Soi Wat Suan Phu, New Rd., 10500,* ☎ *02/236–7777,* 🖷 *02/236–8579,* 🕸 *www.shangrila.com. 801 rooms, 65 suites. 9 restaurants, 2 tennis courts, 2 pools, health club, squash, 3 bars, shops, business services, helipad. AE, DC, MC, V.*

$$$$ 🏨 **Sheraton Grande Sukhumvit.** Soaring 33 floors above noisy city streets, the Sheraton Grande Sukhumvit is hard to miss. The light-filled suites on the upper floors each have spacious baths angled off the bedrooms. A 24-hour butler service will bring you coffee or iron your clothes at the push of a button. You'll never go hungry here. On street level is Riva's, a restaurant serving up contemporary cooking, while off the marble lobby on the second floor the Orchid Café lays out an international buffet. In the afternoon you can enjoy tea in the lounge or cocktails in the rotunda. On the third floor, the health club and the serpentine swimming pool are laid out in the lovely garden. Here you'll find a Thai restaurant and, during the dry months, a barbecue. ✉ *250 Sukhumvit Rd., 10110,* ☎ *02/653–0333,* FAX *02/653–0400,* WEB *www.sheratongrandesukhumvit.com. 418 rooms, 27 suites. 4 restaurants, pool, health club, bar, business services. AE, DC, MC, V.*

$$$$ ⊞ **Sofitel Central Plaza Bangkok.** Catering to corporate travelers, this huge hotel is in the heart of the business district. To the west is a view of the Railway Golf Course; the other side looks out onto the city's astounding vertical growth. The refreshingly cool lobby, with a cascading waterfall, is a welcome retreat from the city streets. Rooms are gracefully appointed. Antique prints, bronze statues of mythological figures, and temple-dog lamp stands remind you that you are in Thailand. Among the hotel's numerous restaurants and bars is Dynasty, a popular spot for Chinese cuisine. ✉ *1695 Phaholyothin Rd., 10210,* ☎ *02/541–1234,* FAX *02/541–1968,* WEB *www.centralhotelsresorts.com. 577 rooms, 7 suites. 6 restaurants, pool, health club, bar, business services, meeting rooms. AE, DC, MC, V.*

$$$$ ⊞ **Sukhothai.** On six landscaped acres near Sathorn Road, the Sukhothai has numerous courtyards that make the hustle and bustle of Bangkok seem worlds away. The hotel's well-regarded restaurant is set in a pavilion on an artificial lake. The dining room serving Continental fare is comfortable, but the prices are high. Standard rooms are spacious, but not exceptionally well furnished. The one-bedroom suites have splendidly oversized baths paneled in teak with his and hers washbasins and mirrors. ✉ *13/3 S. Sathorn Rd., 10120,* ☎ *02/287–0222,* FAX *02/287–4980,* WEB *www.sukhothai.com. 136 rooms, 76 suites. 2 restaurants, tennis court, pool, health club, massage, sauna, squash, bar. AE, DC, MC, V.*

$$$ ⊞ **Amari Airport Hotel.** If you want to stay within walking distance of the airport, this is your only option. A covered passageway leads from the international terminal to the utilitarian lobby. Rooms are functional. The daytime (8 AM–6 PM) rate for travelers waiting for connections is B1,000 for stays up to three hours, and video screens in public areas display schedules of flight arrivals and departures. ✉ *333 Chert Wudhakas Rd., Don Muang 10210,* ☎ *02/566–1020,* FAX *02/566–1941,* WEB *www.amari.com. 420 rooms. 2 restaurants, coffee shop, pool, nightclub, meeting rooms. AE, DC, MC, V.*

$$$ ⊞ **Amari Boulevard.** This pyramid-shape tower certainly has a dashing profile. Rooms in the newer glass tower are modern and airy, with plenty of amenities. The use of dark wood in the older rooms lend them a traditional ambience. Particularly attractive are those overlooking the pool. The ground-floor lobby is vast, with plenty of places to have a quiet conversation. The casual Peppermill restaurant serves a range of Thai and Japanese dishes. The hotel is on a one-way soi near Sukhumvit Road, so it's convenient to shops and restaurants. ✉ *2 Sukhumvit Soi 5, 10400,* ☎ *02/255–2930,* FAX *02/255–2950,* WEB *www.amari.com. 315 rooms. Restaurant, pool, health club, bar, business services, meeting rooms. AE, DC, MC, V.*

$$$ ⊞ **Amari Watergate.** This flagship hotel has spacious and comfortable rooms, all decked out in silks and other rich fabrics. Baths are also quite large, although the separate showers are rather small. The executive floor has a lounge where complimentary cocktails are served in the afternoon. The restaurants serve up delicious Italian and Vietnamese fare. A Thai eatery specializes in fare from the country's four major regions. A coffee shop serves a tasty buffet. The swimming pool is one of the largest you'll find in the city. ✉ *847 Phetchburi Rd., 10400,* ☎ *02/653–9000,* FAX *02/653–9045,* WEB *www.amari.com. 549 rooms, 29 suites. 4 restaurants, pool, health club, bar, business services, meeting rooms. AE, DC, MC, V.*

$$$ ⊞ **Montien.** Across from Patpong, this hotel has been remarkably well maintained since it was constructed in 1970. The rooms are spacious, but the decor is not inspired. They do, however, have extras like private safes. Prices are slightly higher than you would expect, but the hotel often gives discounts. This is the only hotel with in-house fortune-tellers who will read your palm for a small fee. ⊠ *54 Suriwong Rd., 10500,* ☎ *02/234–8060,* FAX *02/236–5218,* WEB *www.montien.com. 475 rooms. 2 restaurants, coffee shop, in-room safes, pool, bar, nightclub, business services, meeting rooms. AE, DC, MC, V.*

$$ ⊞ **Baiyoke Sky Hotel.** Although this 88-story hotel brags that it is the tallest in the world, you can't stay above the 50th floor. The rooms are very plainly furnished and not particularly restful. They are spacious, however and have large bathrooms with separate showers. There's a great view from the revolving observation deck on the 84th floor, but even guests must pay for the privilege. The lobby, on the 18th floor, has a coffee shop that is open 24 hours. ⊠ *222 Ratchaprarop Rd., Rajthawee, 10400,* ☎ *02/656–3000,* FAX *02/656–3555,* WEB *www. baiyokehotel.com. 224 rooms, 7 suites. 2 restaurants, pool, business services. AE, DC, MC, V.*

$$ ⊞ **Bel-Air Princess.** Down a quiet side street, this well-managed hotel is just steps from clamorous Sukhumvit Road. It gets its fair share of tour groups, but for the most part the lobby and lounge are peaceful retreats. The bowl of fruit on each floor is a thoughtful touch. Nicely decorated rooms are large enough for a table and chairs. Rooms at the back of the hotel look down on Soi 7, while those on the front have a view of the pool. ⊠ *16 Sukhumvit Soi 5, 10110,* ☎ *02/253–4300,* FAX *02/255–8850,* WEB *www.dusit.com. 160 rooms. 2 restaurants, in-room safes, pool, health club, bar. AE, DC, MC, V.*

$$ ⊞ **Century Park Hotel.** Its location in the northern part of downtown makes the Century Park Hotel convenient to the airport. The rooms, though neat and clean, are a bit dark. The coffee shop is open 24 hours, a plus for travelers with early-morning flights. ⊠ *9 Ratchaprarop Rd., 10400,* ☎ *02/246–7800,* FAX *02/246–7197,* WEB *www.centuryparkhotel. com. 383 rooms. Coffee shop, pool, bar. AE, DC, MC, V.*

$$ ⊞ **Grand China Princess.** One good reason for staying in Chinatown is the chance to experience the sights and sounds of the city's oldest neighborhood. Another reason is this hotel, which occupies the top two-thirds of a 25-story tower. Rooms have panoramic views of the city. The furnishings are plain, but there are plenty of little extras. The 10th-floor lobby has a welcoming bar, lounge, and coffee shop. Siang Ping Loh, serving Cantonese and Szechuan fare, is well worth a visit. ⊠ *215 Corner of Yaowarat and Ratchawongse Rds., Samphantawongse, 10100,* ☎ *02/224–9977,* FAX *02/224–7999,* WEB *www.dusit.com. 155 rooms. Restaurant, coffee shop, in-room safes, cable TV, health club, business services. AE, DC, MC, V.*

$$ ⊞ **Imperial Tara Hotel.** This hotel is on a side street near Sukhumvit Road, which means restaurants and clubs are practically at your doorstep. While you check in, enjoy a cup of tea in the spacious lobby lined with teak carvings. Rooms, all of which are on the small side, have nice views. Many overlook the eighth-floor terrace with a swimming pool. ⊠ *Sukhumvit Soi 26, 10110,* ☎ *02/259–0053,* FAX *02/ 258–8747,* WEB *www.imperialhotels.com. 183 rooms, 12 suites. Restaurant, coffee shop, pool, meeting rooms. AE, DC, MC, V.*

$$ ⊞ **Narai Hotel.** This hotel's name refers to the god Vishnu (Narai is the Thai name for Vishnu), and an elegant bas-relief of the Hindu deity can be seen on the wall in front of the main staircase. Conveniently near the business district on Silom Road, this modern edifice has utilitarian but comfortable rooms. It is a good value, given its cheerful rooms

and friendly service. ⊠ *222 Silom Rd., 10500,* ☎ *02/237–0100,* FAX
02/236–7161, WEB *www.narai.com. 452 rooms, 12 suites. 3 restaurants,
coffee shop, pool, health club, nightclub, business services. AE, DC,
MC, V.*

$$ 🏨 **Swiss Lodge.** This small hotel not far from Silom Road is the city's
closest equivalent to a boutique hotel. Nicely furnished rooms have a
fresh feel. Single rooms are really the size of doubles; doubles are large
enough to hold king-size beds. All have ample work space and data
ports where you can plug in your computer. A business center with com-
puter facilities and a small meeting room holding up to six people are
also available. There are a lounge and bar on the second floor and a
very small pool and sundeck on the fifth floor. On the ground floor, a
coffee shop serves Thai and Continental food. ⊠ *3 Convent Rd.,
10500,* ☎ *02/233–5345,* FAX *02/236–9425,* WEB *www.swisslodge.com.
57 rooms. Restaurant, in-room safes, pool, bar, business services; no-
smoking floors. AE, DC, MC, V.*

$$ 🏨 **Tawana Ramada.** Although it has hosted tourists for many years,
a careful eye on the details keeps this hotel looking smart. Rooms have
wood floors and tasteful furnishings that call to mind the region's history. A few have balconies overlooking the very modest pool, but they
are not worth the extra cost. The hotel's location, in the heart of the
Silom-Suriwong district, gives you easy access to Bangkok's sights. The
Grill offers an international buffet. A coffee shop stays open until 2
AM. ⊠ *80 Suriwong Rd., 10500,* ☎ *02/236–0361,* FAX *02/236–3738,*
WEB *www.tawanahotel.com. 265 rooms. 2 restaurants, in-room safes,
pool, health club, business services, meeting rooms. AE, DC, MC, V.*

$$ 🏨 **Wall Street Inn.** Most of the guests at this hotel on Suriwong Road
are from Japan, perhaps because of the many Japanese businesses in
the immediate area. But the location near Lumphini Park makes it an
appealing option for anyone. Standard rooms are small and window-
less, so make sure to ask for one of the deluxe rooms. There's not much
of a view, however. The hotel also offers traditional Thai massage. ⊠
37/20–24 Soi Suriwong Plaza, Suriwong Rd., 10500, ☎ *02/233–4164,*
FAX *02/236–3619. 75 rooms. Coffee shop, massage, business services.
AE, DC, MC, V.*

$–$$ 🏨 **Princess Hotel.** Not far from Wat Rachanada and Wat Saket, this
medium-size hotel is ideally located for exploring Dusit and the Old
City. The one drawback is that the neighborhood, dominated by merchants by day, is virtually deserted in the evening. It's a short taxi ride
to a number of fine riverside restaurants, however, or you can pick one
of the hotel restaurants serving Chinese, Italian, Japanese, and Thai
cuisine. Enter through the tranquil lobby, which has gardens on two
sides. The rooms are decorated in subdued colors that set off the dark-
wood furnishings. Well-lighted desks provide adequate work space. The
baths and tubs, however, are very small. ⊠ *269 Larn Luang Rd.,
10100,* ☎ *02/281–3088,* FAX *02/280–1314,* WEB *www.dusit.com. 160
rooms. 4 restaurants, pool, business services. AE, DC, MC, V.*

$ 🏨 **Ambassador Hotel.** One of Bangkok's biggest hotels, the Ambas-
sador has three wings of rooms, a dozen restaurants, and a shopping
center with scores of shops. It's a virtual city, which may explain the
impersonal service. Rooms are compact, decorated in standard-issue
pastels. The Tower Wing is more comfortable, especially because the
Sukhumvit Wing overlooks a busy street. Ask for a room above the
sixth floor to avoid noise from the hotel's popular outdoor beer garden. ⊠ *171 Sukhumvit Soi 11–13, 10110,* ☎ *02/254–0444,* FAX *02/254–
7516,* WEB *www.amtel.co.th. 726 rooms, 24 suites. 12 restaurants, coffee shop, snack bar, 2 tennis courts, pool, health club, massage, bar,
business services, meeting rooms. AE, DC, MC, V.*

$ ⊞ **Bangkok Centre.** There are few hotels around the Hualamphong Railway Station, on the edge of Chinatown. If you have an early train, Bangkok Centre has clean, comfortable rooms. The restaurant, which serves Brazilian fare, is known for its lunch buffet. ⊠ *328 Rama 4, 10500,* ☎ *02/238–4848,* ℻ *02/236–1862,* ⟦WEB⟧ *www.bangkokcentrehotel. com. 80 rooms. Restaurant, coffee shop, pool, meeting rooms. AE, DC, MC, V.*

$ ⊞ **City Lodge.** There are two City Lodges off Sukhumvit, but this one on Soi 19 is the better choice. The compact rooms are functional, designed to fit a lot into a small space. Business services are minimal, but you can use those at the nearby sister hotel, the Amari Boulevard. La Gritta specializes in Italian food. ⊠ *Sukhumvit Soi 19, 10110,* ☎ *02/ 254–4783,* ℻ *02/255–7340,* ⟦WEB⟧ *www.amari.com. 35 rooms. Restaurant. AE, DC, MC, V.*

$ ⊞ **First House.** Tucked behind the Pratunam Market, the First House is an excellent value for a hotel in this price range. In the small lobby you can catch up on the latest with the complimentary newspapers. The 24-hour coffee shop serves Thai dishes. The compact rooms are nicely furnished, but rather dark. ⊠ *14/20–29 Phetchburi Soi 19, Pratunam, 10400,* ☎ *02/254–0303,* ℻ *02/254–3101. 84 rooms. Coffee shop, travel services. AE, DC, MC, V.*

$ ⊞ **Majestic Suites.** There are no actual suites here, but there are a wide selection of standard rooms. They range from studios barely big enough to fit a queen-size bed to much larger deluxe rooms that have thoughtful amenities as fluffy robes hanging in your closet. The hotel is still fairly new, so the furnishings are bright and fresh. ⊠ *110 Sukhumvit Rd., between Soi 4 and Soi 6, 10110,* ☎ *02/656–8220,* ℻ *02/656– 8201,* ⟦WEB⟧ *www.majesticsuites.com. 55 rooms. Coffee shop, in-room safes, minibars, bar, business services. AE, DC, MC, V.*

$ ⊞ **Manohra Hotel.** An expansive marble lobby is your first clue that this hotel is head and shoulders above others in its price range. Rooms have pleasant furnishings and spotless baths. There is a swimming pool and rooftop garden for sunbathing. The best asset, though, may be the friendly staff. They are more than happy to arrange for a traditional massage. ⊠ *412 Suriwong Rd., 10500,* ☎ *02/234–5070,* ℻ *02/237– 7662,* ⟦WEB⟧ *www.manohra-hotel-bangkok.com. 230 rooms. 2 restaurants, coffee shop, indoor pool, nightclub, meeting rooms. AE, DC, MC, V.*

$ ⊞ **La Residence.** You'd expect to find this charming little hotel on the Left Bank of Paris, not in the business district of Bangkok. It's one of the few low-key lodgings in this area dominated by office towers. The rooms are small, but the details—pale-wood furniture, sheer draperies, flowery wallpaper —give them a fresh, airy feel. The staff, however, can be abrupt at times. The restaurant, with Thai and European food, also serves as a sitting room for guests. ⊠ *173/8–9 Suriwong Rd., 10150,* ☎ *02/233–3301,* ℻ *02/237–9322,* ⟦WEB⟧ *www.sawadee.com. 23 rooms. Restaurant, laundry service. AE, DC.*

$ ⊞ **Royal Hotel.** Nearer to the Grand Palace and the Old City than any other of the city's lodgings, this hotel is a carefully kept secret of many frequent visitors. Its clean and comfortable rooms have homey touches like small writing tables. Several banquet rooms on the ground floor are popular with wedding parties. The lobby café is a good place to take a break from sightseeing. ⊠ *2 Rajdamnoen Ave., 10200,* ☎ *02/ 222–9111,* ℻ *02/224–2083. 300 rooms. 3 restaurants, coffee shop, in-room VCRs, pool, bar, meeting rooms. AE, DC, MC, V.*

$ ⊞ **Silom Village Inn.** Extremely reasonable rates are but one of the draws
★ at this small hotel. It's also carefully run, with rooms that are as neat as a pin. The king-size beds leave just enough space for a desk and a couple of chairs. Ask for a room at the back of the hotel to avoid the ruckus on Silom Road. The staff at the reception desk is helpful and

reliable at taking messages. A small restaurant serves Italian food, but many other choices are just outside your door. ⊠ *Silom Village Trade Centre, 286 Silom Rd., 10500,* ☎ *02/635–6810,* FAX *02/635–6817. 34 rooms. Restaurant. AE, DC, MC, V.*

$ 🛏 **Stable Lodge.** On a residential street near Sukhumvit Road, this small hotel feels more like a guest house. The rooms are clean and comfortable, and a few have private balconies where you can have your breakfast. The rooms at the back are the quietest. The pool is a delightful place to relax in the afternoon. Make sure to return in the evening, when there's a barbecue in the garden. The coffee shop serves Thai and Danish food. ⊠ *39 Sukhumvit Soi 8, 10110,* ☎ *02/653–0017,* FAX *02/ 253–5125,* WEB *www.stablelodge.com. 40 rooms, most with private baths. Restaurant, pool. AE, MC, V.*

$ 🛏 **Tower Inn.** Head to the top of this slender tower on Silom Road where there's a health club with the latest equipment and a rooftop swimming pool with views of the skyline. The rooms are spacious, with plenty of light from picture windows, though the furnishings are a bit utilitarian. ⊠ *533 Silom Rd., 10500,* ☎ *02/237–8300,* FAX *02/237–8286,* WEB *www.towerinnbangkok.com. 150 rooms. Restaurant, pool, health club, travel services. AE, DC, MC, V.*

¢ 🛏 **The Atlanta.** Writers in search of inspiration should head to this ven-
★ erable hotel, which opened its doors in 1952. It retains its original art deco lobby, making it the oldest in Bangkok. The leatherette banquettes and circular sofas are often used for magazine fashion shoots. Just beyond the lobby is a swimming pool set next to a pleasant garden filled with tables and chairs. Owner Charles Henn, a part-time professor, caters to frugal travelers who return again and again for the spacious accommodations. Simply decorated rooms come with fans or air-conditioning. The restaurant off the lobby serves excellent Thai food, including a good selection of vegetarian options. Classical music is played before 5 PM, jazz thereafter, and a movie is screened after dinner. ⊠ *78 Sukhumvit Soi 2, 10110,* ☎ *02/252–1650 or 02/252–6069,* FAX *02/ 656–8123. 49 rooms. Restaurant, fans, pool, travel services; no room TVs. No credit cards.*

¢ 🛏 **River City Guest House.** Although it's a block from the water's edge, this lodging has no view of the river. But if it did, the price would probably double. As it is, B500 gives you a modest air-conditioned room with a double bed, a table, and a chair. The prime location gives you easy access to the restaurants of Chinatown and puts you within walking distance of the nightlife on Suriwong and Silom roads. The trick is finding the place. It's north of the River City Shopping Centre where the soi bends to the right. ⊠ *11/4 Soi Rong Nam Khang 1 (Soi 24), Charoen Krung Rd., 10100,* ☎ *02/235–1431. 17 rooms. Coffee shop. MC, V.*

¢ 🛏 **River View Guest House.** On the edge of Chinatown, this family-run hotel is unique for being a budget hotel that overlooks the river. The eighth-floor coffee shop has a spectacular view. The accommodations, calling to mind college dorm rooms, are clean and comfortable. The staff will go out of its way for you, even staying up to meet you if your flight arrives late in the evening. The one problem is that even tuk-tuk drivers sometimes have difficulty locating the place. The easiest way to find it is to head north from the Royal Orchid Sheraton. You'll soon see the guest house's sign pointing down a side street. ⊠ *768 Soi Panurangsri, Songvad Rd., 10100,* ☎ *02/234–5429,* FAX *02/ 236–6199. 45 rooms. Restaurant. V.*

¢ 🛏 **Sri Kasem Hotel.** Across a canal from Hualamphong Train Station, this small hotel is ideally located if you arrive on a late train or are departing early in the morning. It's more than 30 years old, so don't expect modern amenities. The sparsely furnished rooms are air-conditioned, the baths are clean, and the price is right. ⊠ *1860 Krung Kasem Rd., 10500,* ☎ *02/225–0132,* FAX *02/225–4705. 26 rooms. Coffee shop. No credit cards.*

NIGHTLIFE AND THE ARTS

The English-language newspapers the *Bangkok Post* and *The Nation* have the latest information on current festivals, exhibitions, and nightlife. The Tourist Authority of Thailand's weekly *Where* also lists events. Monthly *Metro* magazine has an extensive listings section and offers reviews of new hot spots.

Nightlife

Although the law requires that bars and nightclubs close at 2 AM, Bangkok is a city that never sleeps. Many restaurants and other establishments stay open for late-night carousing. The city is awash with bars catering to all tastes, from classy watering holes to sleazy strip clubs. Off Sukhumvit Road, Soi 55 (also called Soi Thonglor) has several good bars and nightclubs. Soi Sarasin, across from Lumphini Park, is packed with friendly pubs and cafés that are popular with yuppie Thais and expats. Narathiwat Road, which starts at Suriwong, intersects Silom, then runs all the way to Rama III, sees trendy bars and restaurants opening every month.

Many tourists, most out of curiosity more than anything else, take a stroll through the city's most infamous neighborhoods. Live sex shows, though officially banned, are still found in three areas. Patpong is the largest, and it includes three streets that run between Suriwong and Silom roads. Lining Patpong 1 and 2 are go-go bars with hostesses by the dozen. Shows are generally found one flight up. The Patpong area is well patrolled by police, so it is quite safe. It even has a Night Market patronized by Thais.

Soi Cowboy, off Sukhumvit Road at Soi 21, is a less raunchy, more easygoing version of Patpong. Some bars have go-go dancers, while others are good for a quiet beer (with or without a temporary companion). Nana Plaza, at Soi 4, is popular with expats. The plaza is packed with three floors of hostess bars. The newest bars have spilled out along Soi 4.

Most gay bars and clubs happen to be located near Patpong on a pair of dead-end alleys off Silom Road. Soi 2 is filled with thumping discos, and Soi 4 is a bit more sedate. Other gay establishments are found near Sukhumvit Road.

Bars and Pubs

PATPONG AREA

A good place to start carousing is **Brown Sugar** (⊠ 231/20 Soi Sarasin, Ratchadamri skytrain station, ☎ 02/250–0103). More stylish than most, **The Barbican** (⊠ Soi Thaniya, off Silom Rd., Sala Daeng skytrain station, ☎ 02/234–3590) is as popular for its food as it is for its drinks.

You can get a decent pint of beer at the **Bobbies Arms** (⊠ Patpong 2, Sala Daeng skytrain station, ☎ 02/233–6828), a rough approximation on an English pub. This longtime favorite remains popular even with the proliferation of pubs.

The lively **O'Reillys** (⊠ 62/1-4 Silom Rd., Sala Daeng skytrain station, ☎ 02/632–7515) sometimes has live music. It is convenient to many hotels. Off Silom Road, **Shenanigans** (⊠ 1/5–6 Convent Rd., Sala Daeng skytrain station, ☎ 02/266–7160) is standing room only from Tuesday to Friday. Beers on tap include Guinness.

SUKHUMVIT ROAD AREA

The popular **Bull's Head Pub** (✉ Sukhumvit Soi 33, Phrom Phong skytrain station, ☎ 02/259–4444) has a Quiz Night on the second Tuesday of each month. Amid the swinging nightlife of Soi 4, **Bus Stop** (✉ 14 Sukhumvit Soi 4, ☎ 02/251–9222) is a pleasantly relaxed pub with outdoor seating. Gather around the two large-screen TVs to watch whatever sport happens to be on.

OTHER PARTS OF BANGKOK

The Old Dragon (✉ 29/78–81 Royal City Ave., ☎ 02/203–0972) is filled with oddities, from wooden cinema seats to old mirrors etched with Chinese characters. The owner claims that little here besides the customers is less than 50 years old. The snacks served here are a mix of Chinese and Thai. Celebrating the famous American highway, **Route 66** (✉ 29/37 Royal City Ave., ☎ 02/203–0407) is often packed. **Saxophone** (✉ 3/8 Victory Monument, Phayathai Rd., Victory Monument skytrain station, ☎ 02/246–5472) is popular with locals and expats.

Clubs

Concept CM2 (✉ 392/44 Rama 1, Soi 6, ☎ 02/255–6888) is a posh nightclub in the Novotel Siam. Bands hit the stage at 9 PM. If you want to really cut loose, try **Deeper** (✉ 82 Silom Rd. Soi 4, ☎ 02/233–2830). It tries hard for an underground vibe.

Gay Bars

Open to the street, **Balcony** (✉ 86–88 Silom Soi 4, Sala Daeng skytrain station, ☎ 02/235–5891) is the perfect place to watch people amble past. The most venerable of Bangkok's gay bars, **Telephone** (✉ 114/11–13 Silom Soi 4, Sala Daeng skytrain station, ☎ 02/235–5891) gets going on weekends.

On crowded Soi 2, **DJ Station** (✉ Silom Soi 2, ☎ 02/266–4029) draws a young crowd. Around the corner from DJ Station, **Freeman** (✉ 60/18-21 Silom Rd., ☎ 02/632–8033) has a balcony where you can watch the dance floor.

Jazz Bars

To hear easy-on-the-ears jazz, try the Oriental Hotel's **Bamboo Bar** (✉ Oriental La., ☎ 02/236–0400). **Fabb Fashion Café** (✉ In the Mercury Tower, 540 Ploenchit Rd., ☎ 02/843–4946) is the place to go for live music early in the evening. **Witch's Tavern** (✉ Sukhumvit Soi 55, ☎ 02/391–9791) has musicians on Friday, Saturday, and Sunday. The bar also serves hearty English fare.

The Foreign Correspondents Club of Thailand (✉ Maneeya Center, Chit Lom skytrain station, ☎ 02/652–0580) has live music Friday nights, when it is open to the public.

The Arts

Dance

For Thais, classical dance is more than graceful movements. The dances actually tell tales from the Ramakien. A series of controlled gestures convey the stories. Performances are accompanied by a woodwind called the *piphat,* which sounds like an oboe, as well as a range of percussion instruments. At the **National Theatre** (✉ Na Phra That Rd., ☎ 02/224–1342), performances begin most days at 10 AM and 3 PM. Special performances start at 5:30 PM on the last Friday of each month. **Silom Village** (✉ 286 Silom Rd., ☎ 02/234–4448) may seem to appeal most to foreigners, but it draws many Thais. The block-size complex, open 10 AM–10 PM, features performances of classical dance.

Many restaurants also present classical dance performances. **Baan Thai** (⊠ Sukhumvit Soi 32, ☎ 02/258–5403) is a popular destination for those staying in the eastern part of Bangkok. At the Oriental Hotel, **Sala Rim Naam** (⊠ Oriental La., ☎ 02/236–0400) stages a beautiful show accompanied by an excellent dinner.

OUTDOOR ACTIVITIES AND SPORTS

Participant Sports

Golf

There are several good golf courses in and around Bangkok. Greens fees are around B700 weekdays and B1,500 weekends, with caddy fees about B200. Book early for the weekends, when tee times are harder to come by. **Navatanee Golf Course** (⊠ 22 Mul Sukhaphiban 2 Rd., Bangkapi, ☎ 02/376–1422), designed by the legendary Robert Trent Jones, is the area's most challenging. **Rose Garden Golf Course** (⊠ 32 km [20 mi] west of Bangkok, ☎ 034/322588 to 593) is a relatively undemanding course.

Health Clubs

The well-regarded **Clark Hatch Athletic Club** (⊠ Thaniya Plaza, Silom Rd., ☎ 02/231–2250; ⊠ Charn Issara Tower II, 2922/215 New Petchburi Rd., ☎ 02/308–2779; ⊠ Amari Watergate Hotel, 847 Petchburi Rd., ☎ 02/653–9000; ⊠ Amari Atrium Hotel, 1880 New Petchburi Rd., ☎ 02/718–2000; ⊠ Century Park Hotel, 9 Ratchaprarop Rd., ☎ 02/246–7800) charges B400 per day for nonmembers. With the best fitness facility of any hotel, the **Grand Hyatt Erawan** (⊠ 494 Ratchadamri Rd., ☎ 02/254–1234, ext 4437) charges B589 if you are not a guest.

Jogging

If you want to run a few miles before breakfast, the small running tracks found at many hotels may be the best bet. You are safe in public parks during the day, but not at night. North of the city, **Chatuchak Park** has a loop that is 4 km (2½ mi). The well-paved paths at **Lumphini Park,** measure about 2 km (1 mi). They are popular among serious joggers. On Sukhumvit Road between sois 22 and 24, **Queen Sirikit Park** is small but pleasant with a jogging trail.

Sanam Luang, the open space near the Grand Palace, is another popular park for runners.

Massage

Venues offering traditional massage are quite commonplace in Bangkok—you can even pamper yourself while sightseeing at Wat Pho. The staff at your hotel can recommend reputable therapists. If you have the time, pull out all the stops with a two-hour massage.

A gentle massage in genteel surroundings is what you'll get at **Oriental Spa** (⊠ 48 Oriental Ave., ☎ 02/236–0400). Amid the wood-paneled sophistication of the Oriental Hotel you can treat yourself to facials, wraps, and even a "jet lag solution." A most relaxing massage with deliciously warm oils is available at the **Regent Hotel** (⊠ 155 Ratchadamri Rd., ☎ 02/251–6127).

Spectator Sports

Horse Racing

Betting on the horses is a popular pastime in Bangkok, where a typical day at the track might involve a dozen races. Two tracks hold races on alternating Sundays. The **Royal Bangkok Sports Club** (⊠ Henri Dunant Rd. between Rama I and Rama IV Rds., ☎ 02/251–0181) is across from Lumphini Park. The **Royal Turf Club** (⊠ On the north side of Phitsanulok Rd. just east of Rama V Rd., ☎ 02/280–0020) is a stone's throw from Chitlada Palace.

Thai Boxing

The national sport of Thailand draws an enthusiastic crowd in Bangkok. Here it's the real thing, unlike some shows you may see in the resort areas. Understanding the rules is difficult, as the sport is fast and furious. Daily matches alternate between the two main stadiums. **Lumphini Stadium** (⊠ Rama IV Rd., ☎ 02/251–4303) has matches on Tuesday, Friday, and Saturday at 6 PM. **Ratchadamnoen Stadium** (⊠ Ratchadamnoen Nok Rd., ☎ 02/281–4205) has bouts on Monday, Wednesday, and Thursday at 6 PM and Sunday at 1 PM. Tickets (B200–B1,000) may be purchased at the gate.

SHOPPING

The city's most popular shopping areas are Silom Road and Suriwong Road in Downtown for silk, Sukhumvit Road in Downtown for leather goods, Yaowarat Road in Chinatown for gold, and along Oriental Lane and Charoen Krung Road for antiques. The shops around Siam Square and at the World Trade Centre attract both Thais and foreigners. Peninsula Plaza, across from the Regent Hotel in the embassy district, has very upscale shops. If you're knowledgeable about fabric, you can find bargains at the textile merchants who compete along Pahuraht Road in Chinatown and Pratunam Road off Phetchburi Road. You can even take it to a tailor and have something made just for you.

You can reclaim the 7.5% VAT (Value Added Tax) paid for purchases at the airport if you have a receipt. Ask the shopkeeper about the VAT refund. If you still want the convenience of duty-free shopping, try **King Power International Group** (⊠ World Trade Center, Rajadamri Rd., ☎ 02/252–3633; ⊠ Mahatun Plaza, Phoenchit Rd., ☎ 02/253–6451). Both are open daily 9:30 AM to 10:30 PM. You pay for the items at the shop, then pick them up at the airport when you leave. You need your passport and an airline ticket, and you need to make your purchase at least eight hours before leaving the country.

Markets

You can purchase virtually anything at the sprawling **Chatuchak Weekend Market** (⊠ Phaholyothin Rd.), from fountains to place in your rock garden to roosters ready to do battle. Sometimes you'll find great buys on clothing, including silk items in a *mudmee* (tie-dyed before weaving) design that would sell for five times the price in America. Strategically placed food vendors mean you don't have to stop shopping to grab a bite. Though it's open on Friday from 5 to 9 PM and weekends from 9 AM to 9 PM, the city's largest market is best on Saturday and Sunday in the late morning. It's easy to reach, as it's across the street from the northern terminus of the skytrain and near the Northern Bus Terminal.

In late 2001, the **Suan Lum Night Bazaar** (⊠ Rama IV and Witthayu Rds.), opened across from Lumphini Park. It has attracted some attention, but nowhere near that of the weekend market.

Hundreds of vendors jam the sidewalk each day at **Pratunam Market** (⊠ Corner of Phetchburi and Ratchaprarop Rds). The stacks of merchandise consist mainly of inexpensive clothing. It's a good place to meet Thais, who come in the evening to sample the inexpensive Thai and Chinese street food.

In Chinatown you'll find **Nakorn Kasem** (✉ Yaowarat Rd. and Charoen Krung Rd.), the so-called thieves market where you can buy anything from housewares to porcelains. Bargains are hard to find nowadays, but these small, cluttered streets are fascinating. **Pahuraht Market** (✉ Near Yaowarat Rd.), operated mostly by Indians, is known for its bargain textiles. A man with a microphone announces when items at a particular stall will be sold at half price, and shoppers surge over to bid. **Soi Sampeng** (✉ Parallel to Yaowarat Rd.) also has lots of fabrics—it is Bangkok's best-known and oldest textile center.

Specialty Stores

Antiques

Note that Thai antiques and old images of the Buddha need a special export license. Suriwong Road, Charoen Krung Road, and the Oriental Plaza (across from the Oriental Hotel) have many art and antiques shops, as does the River City Shopping Centre. Original and often illegal artifacts from Angkor Wat are sometimes sold there as well.

As you wander around the Old City, don't miss the small teak house that holds **123 Baan Dee** (✉ 123 Fuengnakorn Rd., ☎ 02/221–2520). Antique silks, ceramics, beads, and other fascinating artifacts fill two floors. If you need sustenance, there's a small ice-cream parlor at the back. **Peng Seng** (✉ 942 Rama IV, at Suriwong Rd., ☎ 02/234–1285) is one of the city's most respected dealers of antiquities. Prices may be high, but articles are most likely to be genuine. **Rasi Sayam** (✉ 32 Sukhumvit Soi 23, ☎ 02/258–4195), in an old teak house in a garden, has a wonderful collection of fine Thai crafts.

Clothing and Fabrics

Thai silk gained its reputation only after World War II, when technical innovations made it less expensive. Two fabrics are worth seeking out: mudmee silk, produced in the northeastern part of the country, and Thai cotton, which is soft, durable, and easier on the wallet than silk.

Design Thai (✉ 304 Silom Rd., ☎ 02/235–1553) has a large selection of silk items in all price ranges. If you ask, you can usually manage a 20% discount. For factory-made clothing, visit the **Indra Garment Export Centre** (✉ Ratchaprarop Rd., behind the Indra Regent Hotel), where hundreds of shops sell discounted items.

The **Jim Thompson Thai Silk Company** (✉ 9 Suriwong Rd., ☎ 02/234–4900) is a prime place for silk by the yard and ready-made clothes. The prices are high, but the staff is knowledgeable. A branch has opened in the Oriental Hotel.

Napajaree Suanduenchai studied fashion design in Germany; 22 years ago she opened the **Prayer Textile Gallery** (✉ Phayathai Rd., near Siam Square, ☎ 02/251–7549) in her mother's former dress shop. She makes stunning items in naturally dyed silks and cottons and in antique fabrics from the farthest reaches of Thailand, Laos, and Cambodia.

Many people who visit Bangkok brag about a custom-made suit that was completed in just a day or two, but the finished product often hangs on the shoulders just as one would expect from a rush job. If you want an excellent cut, give the tailor the time he needs. One of the best in Bangkok is **Marco Tailor** (✉ 430/33 Siam Square, Soi 7, ☎ 02/252–0689), which sews a suit equal to those on Savile Row. For women's apparel, **Stephanie Thai Silk** (✉ 55 Soi Shangri-La Hotel, New Rd., Bangrak, ☎ 02/233–0325) is among the city's finest shops. A skirt with blouse and jacket made of Thai silk starts at B5,000.

Jewelry

Thailand is known for its sparkling gems, so it's no surprise that the country exports more colored stones than anywhere in the world. There are countless jewelry stores on Silom and Suriwong roads. Be wary of deals that are too good to be true, as they probably are. Scams are common, so it's best to stick with established businesses.

A long-established firm is **Johny's Gems** (⊠ 199 Fuengnakorn Rd., ☎ 02/224–4065). If you telephone, they will send a car to take you to the shop near Wat Phra Keo (a frequent practice among the city's better stores). **Oriental Lapidary** (⊠ 116/1 Silom Rd., ☎ 02/238–2718) has a long record of good service. **Pranda Jewelry** (⊠ 333 Soi Rungsang, Bangna-Trad Rd., ☎ 02/361–3311) is a well-known store with separate branches for gems and jewelry. **Than Shine** (⊠ 84/87 Sukhumvit Soi 55, ☎ 02/381–7337), run by sisters Cho Cho and Mon Mon, offers classic as well as modern designs.

Leather

It's easy to find good buys on leather goods in Bangkok, which has some of the lowest prices in the world for custom work. Crocodile leather is popular, but be sure to obtain a certificate that the skins came from a domestically raised reptile; otherwise U.S. Customs may confiscate the goods. The River City Shopping Centre, next to the Royal Orchid Sheraton Hotel, has a number of leather shops. For shoes and jackets, try 25-year-old **Siam Leather Goods** (⊠ River City Shopping Centre, 23 Trok Rongnamkhaeng, ☎ 02/233–4521).

Precious Metals

Chinatown is the place to go for gold. There is no bargaining, but you are likely to get a good price. For bronze try **Siam Bronze Factory** (⊠ 1250 Charoen Krung Rd., ☎ 02/234–9436). It's located near the Oriental Hotel.

SIDE TRIPS FROM BANGKOK

Although you'll never run out of things to do and see in Bangkok, there may come a time when you want to escape the heat and noise. Exotic markets in Damnoen Saduak, a mammoth temple at Nakhon Pathom, and the bridge over the River Kwai at Nakhon Pathom can all be seen on day trips from the City of Angels.

Muang Boran

❶ *20 km (12 mi) southeast of Bangkok.*

Southeast of the capital is Muang Boran (Ancient City), an odd park shaped like Thailand. After entering through the southern tip you find, placed more or less as in their geographical areas, 108 smaller but proportionally correct replicas of Thailand's most important architectural sites and monuments. You really need a car—the area is too vast to cover on foot. Small, discreetly placed restaurants are scattered throughout the grounds, and crafts are sold in a "traditional Thai village." Allow a good four hours to cover most of the sites. By car, take the Samrong–Samut Prakan expressway and turn left at the Samut Prakan intersection onto Old Sukhumvit Road. At Km 33, Muang Boran is on your left. You can also take air-conditioned bus 11 and get off at Pak Nam, transferring to bus 36, which passes Muang Boran. ⊠ *Old Sukhumvit Rd., Samut Prakan,* ☎ *02/226–1936.* ▣ *Admission.* ☉ *Daily 8–5.*

Damnoen Saduak

❷ *109 km (65 mi) southwest of Bangkok.*

At Damnoen Saduak, the first thing you should do is hire a *ruilla pai* (rowboat) for about B300. Then you can witness gridlock as challenging

Side Trips from Bangkok

as any in Bangkok as dozens of boats clog the klong. Woman dressed in baggy pants, long-tail shirts, and straw hats sell produce from their own boats, paddling back and forth (or pulling their way through the more crowded sections) to reach customers. Other women, cooking tasty treats on little stoves, sit ready to deliver sustenance to the hungry. The scene couldn't be more colorful.

If you want to rest, a wharf alongside the klong is lined with tables and chairs. Buy your drinks from the nearby stand. Go early, because by 11 AM you will have seen the best of Damnoen Saduak; any later and the novelty wears thin.

Nakhon Pathom

56 km (34 mi) west of Bangkok.

Reputed to be Thailand's oldest city, Nakhon Pathom is thought to date from 150 BC. It marks the region's first center of Buddhist learning, established here about a millennium ago. Its main attraction is **Phra Pathom Chedi,** the tallest Buddhist monument in the world. At 417 ft, it stands a bit higher than the chedi at Shwe Dagon in Myanmar.

The first chedi on this site was erected in the 6th century, but the large chedi you see today, constructed in 1860, completely encloses the ruins of the original. The man responsible for reconstructing the chedi was King Rama IV, who understood the historical role Phra Pathom Chedi had played in the the establishment of Buddhism in Thailand. Believing that the chedi, then in a state of disrepair, contained the ashes of the Buddha, he ordered that the crumbling structure be incorporated into a dazzling new structure.

In the outer courtyard are four viharns facing in different directions that contain images of Lord Buddha in various postures. The terraces around the temple complex are full of fascinating statuary, including an unusual Buddha seated in a chair. The museum contains some interesting Dvaravati (6th–11th-century) sculpture. Traditional dances are sometimes performed in front of the temple, and during the Loi Krathong festival a fair is set up in the adjacent park. ⊠ *South of train station.* ⊙ *Wed.–Sun. 9–noon and 1–4.*

Sanan Chan Palace was built during King Rama IV's reign. The palace is closed to the public, but the surrounding park is a lovely place to relax in the shade before heading back to Bangkok. ⊠ *West of Phra Pathom Chedi.*

On the Bangkok Road out of Nakhon Pathom is the **Rose Garden,** a complex designed to resemble a Thai village. Amid gardens of more than 20,000 rosebushes are traditional-style houses and a stage where a "cultural show" featuring dancing, boxing, sword fighting, and even a wedding ceremony begins at 2:45 PM. The park, popular with Thai families, has restaurants and a hotel. The B350 admission is fairly steep, but you can while away a few pleasant hours here far from the heat of Bangkok. ⊠ *Petchkasem Rd.,* ☎ *02/295–3261,* WEB *www.rose-garden.com.* ☜ *Admission.* ⊙ *Daily 8–6.*

Next door to the Rose Garden you'll find the **Samphran Elephant Ground & Zoo.** Although there is a lot to see and do here, the elephants definitely steal the show. A score of these great pachyderms haul logs, play football, and dance on their hind legs. The finale reenacts the Yutha Harti, the 16th-century elephant-back battle between a Thai king and an invading Burmese prince. During the 40-minute show a sound track explains the role of elephants in Thai history, including their centuries-long role as beasts of burden. ⊠ *Petchkasem Rd.,* ☎ *02/295–2939,* WEB *www.elephantshow.com.* ☜ *B350.* ⊙ *Daily 8:30–5.*

Kanchanaburi

4 *140 km (87 mi) west of Bangkok.*

Kanchanaburi Province's jungles, rivers, and waterfalls make it one of Thailand's most beautiful regions. But it is also known for the Death Railway built during World War II, immortalized in the film *The Bridge Over the River Kwai.* About 16,000 prisoners-of-war and between 50,000 and 100,000 slave laborers from neighboring countries were forced by the Japanese to construct a rail link through the jungles of Thailand and Burma. The death toll was staggering—one person died for every railway tie that was laid. Two cemeteries are a testament to the thousands who died here.

Don't expect to see the bridge used in the 1954 movie, which was filmed in a river gorge in Sri Lanka. The original bamboo bridge that inspired the film can still be seen in Kanchanaburi where the Kwai Noi and Kwai Yai rivers meet to form the Mae Khlong River. A few hundred meters upstream is another span with arched steel supports that the Japanese built later in the war. Two square center sections were rebuilt after being bombed during the war. You can walk across this bridge, which is next to a plaza packed with restaurants and souvenir shops.

The **Kanchanaburi War Cemetery,** next to noisy Saengchuto Road just south of the train station, has row upon row of neatly laid-out graves of 6,982 Australian, British, and Dutch prisoners of war. The remains of the American POWs were returned to the United States during the Eisenhower administration. All the dead here are remembered at a service held every April 25, Australia's Anzac Day. The **Chong-Kai War Cemetery,** on the grounds of a former hospital for prisoners of war, is a serene site with simple, neatly organized grave markers of the soldiers forced to work on the railway. Rarely visited because it's a little out of the way, this graveyard is worth the trek. To get there, hire a tuk-tuk or take a ferry across the river and walk just over 500 meters down the road. The cemetery will be on your left.

The **Japanese War Memorial Shrine** is near the bridge, 1 km (½ mi) northwest of the Kanchanaburi War Cemetery. Be sure to read the plaque on the Japanese War Memorial—it has an English translation.

About 2 km (1 mi) downriver from the bridge and in town is the **JEATH War Museum** (JEATH is an acronym for Japan, England, America, Australia, Thailand, and Holland). Founded in 1977 by a monk from the adjoining temple, the museum consists of a reconstructed bamboo hut—the type used to house prisoners of war—and a collection of utensils, railway spikes, clothing, aerial photographs, newspaper clippings, and illustrations designed to show the conditions under which the POWs lived during the construction of the railway. ⊠ *Admission.* ۞ *Daily 8–5.*

About 1 km (½ mi) inland from Chong-Kai War Cemetery you'll find **Wat Thum Khao Pun,** one of the best cave temples in the area. At the small shrine outside stands a guide who directs you into the cave. Inside are calm images of the Buddha sitting between the stalagmites and stalactites.

DINING AND LODGING

Most restaurants are near the River Kwai Bridge or farther downstream where the Kwai Noi and Kwai Yai join to form the Mae Khlong. Because most foreigners visit Kanchanaburi on day trips from Bangkok, the hotels lining the riverbanks are intended primarily for Thai families. A few of the resorts offer thatched bungalows that have lovely river views. They tend to be hot and muggy at night, however.

$ ✕ **River Kwai Floating Restaurant.** The most attractive—and crowded—open-air restaurant is adjacent to the bridge. Fish dishes, either fried with pungent spices or lightly grilled, dominate the menu. The specialty is *yeesok,* a fish reeled in from the Kwai Yai and Kwai Noi rivers. Another tasty choice is the *tom yum gong,* hot and sour shrimp soup. Arrive ahead of the tour groups to snag a table alongside the river. ⊠ *River Kwai Bridge,* ☎ *034/512595. No credit cards.*

¢ ✕ **Pae Karn Floating Restaurant.** For authentic local cuisine, try this little restaurant on a dock where the Kwai Noi and Kwai Yai rivers meet. The food is better than in the tourist restaurants scattered around the bridge, but the decor adds up to little more than a few tables set around a bare-walled room. ⊠ *Song Kwai Rd.,* ☎ *no phone. No credit cards.*

$$ ✕▥ **River Kwai Village.** In the jungles of the River Kwai Valley, this resort consists of five single-story log cabins. The air-conditioned rooms are simply furnished in teak, with pretty colored stones embedded in the walls. For more adventurous types there are a few "raftels," rooms set on rafts floating in the river. The cafeteria-style restaurant offers a combination of Thai and Western dishes, but it's more fun to eat at the casual restaurant on one of the rafts. The resort provides transportation from Bangkok. Rates include a buffet breakfast. ⊠ *72/12 Moo 4, Tambon Thasao, Amphoe Sai Yok, 71150,* ☎ *034/634454; 02/251–7552 in Bangkok;* FAX *034/634456,* WEB *www.bkk2000.com/rkvh. 60 rooms, 7 raft houses. 2 restaurants, pool, meeting rooms, travel services. AE, DC, V.*

$$ ▥ **Kasem Island Resort.** Perched on an island in the middle of the river, this resort has one of the area's most enviable locations. Choose between standard rooms, bungalows, or raft-houses. Not all rooms have air-conditioning, so remember to ask. Rates include a buffet breakfast. ⊠ *44 Thaichumpon St., 71000,* ☎ *034/513359; 02/255–3604 in*

Bangkok. 29 rooms, 10 bungalows, 19 raft houses. Restaurant, fans; no a/c in some rooms. MC, V.

$ 🏨 **Felix River Kwai Resort.** This luxury hotel is on the banks of the river, within sight of the bridge. Polished wood floors and wicker headboards give a cool airiness to the rooms. Each has niceties like a private safe and cable TV. A large free-form pool set amid tropical gardens is a great place to relax. The hotel is within walking distance of most of Kanchanaburi's attractions. Rates include a buffet breakfast. ✉ *9/1 Moo 3, Tambon Thamakham, 71000,* ☎ *034/515061; 02/655–7949 in Bangkok;* 🅵🅰🆇 *034/515095,* 🆆🅴🅱 *www.felixriverkwai.co.th. 150 rooms. Restaurant, pool, health club, massage. AE, DC, MC, V*

$ 🏨 **Pavilion Rim Kwai Thani Resort.** Toward the Erawan Waterfall, this resort caters to wealthy Bangkok residents who want to retreat into the country without giving up their creature comforts. Tropical flora surrounds the complex, and the River Kwai flows serenely past. Rooms with the shining wood floors are sparsely furnished. The large dining room serves Thai and Western dishes. A buffet breakfast is included. ✉ *79/2 Moo 4, Km 9 Ladya-Erawan Rd., Tambon Wangdong, 71190,* ☎ *034/515772,* 🅵🅰🆇 *034/515774. 200 rooms. Restaurant, pool, gym. AE, MC, V.*

¢ 🏨 **River Kwai Hotel.** On the main road through town you'll find the first large-scale hotel constructed in Kanchanaburi. It's a comfortable place very popular with tour groups, but the river is quite a distance away. Rates include a buffet breakfast. ✉ *284/4–6 Saengchuto Rd., 71000,* ☎ *034/513348,* 🅵🅰🆇 *034/511269. 150 rooms. Restaurant, travel services. AE, MC, V.*

OUTDOOR ACTIVITIES AND SPORTS

Rafting trips on either the Kwai Yai or Mae Khlong river, which take at least a full day, let you venture far into the tropical jungle. The mammoth rafts, which resemble houseboats, are often divided into separate sections for eating, sleeping and sunbathing. Be careful when taking a dip—the currents can sometimes suck a swimmer down. The cost of a one-day trip starts at about B300. Longer trips are also available.

SHOPPING

Blue sapphires from the Bo Phloi mines, 45 km (28 mi) north of Kanchanaburi, are generally a good buy, but prices are marked up at the shops in the plaza before the bridge. You're better off buying the sapphires at the small shops in the center of town.

Erawan Waterfall

❺ *65 km (40 mi) northwest of Kanchanaburi.*

To see some of the spectacular scenery of Kanchanaburi Province, take the trip to the Erawan Waterfall. Set in the beautifully forested Khao Salop National Park, it is perhaps the most photographed in Thailand. It's lovely at any time of year, but is at its best in early autumn. You can take a tour from Kanchanaburi or hop on the public bus that leaves every hour for the 90-minute journey. Once you arrive it's a 1½-km (1-mi) walk or taxi ride to the foot of the falls. Allow two hours to climb up all seven levels of the falls. The name comes from the rock at the top thought to resemble an elephant; Erawan refers to the god Indra's three-headed elephant.

Sai Yok Noi Waterfall

❻ *77 km (46 mi) from Kanchanaburi.*

The trip out of Kanchanaburi to Sai Yok Noi (also called Kao Phang) is a memorable one, since you travel there on the Death Railway. The train leaves each day at 10:33 AM, passing through thick jungles and rushing waterfalls as it clings to the mountainside on a two-hour journey that is not for the faint-hearted. From Nam-Tok, the last stop, it's a 1½-km (1-mi) walk to Sai Yok Noi. Although a lot smaller than the Erawan Waterfall, it has pools where you can swim during the rainy season running from May to August. On weekends the area is packed with Thai families. There's a bus back to Kanchanaburi that takes half the time of the train.

BANGKOK A TO Z

To research prices, get advice from other travelers, and book travel arrangements, visit www.fodors.com.

AIR TRAVEL

Dozens of airlines fly into Bangkok each day. Thai Airways, the national airline, has direct flights from the West Coast of the United States and from London. It also flies from Hong Kong, Singapore, Taiwan, and Japan.

The U.S. carrier with the most frequent flights is Northwest Airlines. It has service through Tokyo from New York, Detroit, Seattle, Dallas, San Francisco, and Los Angeles. British Airways flies nonstop to Bangkok from London. Singapore Airlines flies to Bangkok through Singapore.

Air New Zealand and Qantas both fly to Bangkok, with the latter offering several flights a day. Two Taiwanese airlines, China Airlines and Eva Air, both fly frequently through Bangkok to many points in Asia, as does Hong Kong-based Cathay Pacific.

➤ CARRIERS: **Air New Zealand** (✉ Charoen Krung Rd., ☎ 02/233–5900). **British Airways** (✉ 990 Rama IV Rd., ☎ 02/636–1747). **Cathay Pacific** (✉ 11th floor, Ploenchit Tower, Ploenchit Rd., ☎ 02/263–0606). **China Airlines** (✉ Peninsula Plaza, 153 Ratchadamri Rd., ☎ 02/253–5733). **Eva Air** (✉ 2nd floor, Green Tower, Rama IV Rd., ☎ 02/367–3388). **Northwest** (✉ 153 Ratchadamri Rd., Peninsula Shopping Plaza, 4th floor, ☎ 02/254–0789). **Qantas** (✉ Charn Issara Tower, 942/51 Rama IV Rd., ☎ 02/267–5188). **Singapore Airlines** (✉ Silom Centre Bldg., 2 Silom Rd., ☎ 02/236–0440). **Thai Airways** (✉ 485 Silom Rd., ☎ 02/280–0060).

AIRPORTS AND TRANSFERS

Bangkok's new international airport is scheduled to open in 2005. For the time being, most flights to Thailand land at Don Muang International Airport, 25 km (16 mi) north of the city. The airport has more than its share of hustlers out to make a quick baht, many wearing uniforms and name tags that make them look official. Many try to get you to change your hotel to one that pays them a large commission, often claiming your hotel is overbooked. They will also hustle you into overpriced taxis or limousines. Do not get taken in by these ruses.

There are many ways to get into Bangkok from the airport. A bus service costing B100 runs approximately every 30 minutes between the airport and four sectors of downtown Bangkok. A1 travels to Ratchadamri and Silom roads. A2 covers the central area that includes Chinatown. A3 travels down Sukhumvit Road. A4 weaves its way to Hualamphong, the main train station. A detailed listing of each route is available from the Tourist Authority of Thailand office and at the bus stop outside the arrivals hall. You can also catch local air-conditioned buses costing B25 on the main road that passes the airport.

If you take a taxi, count on a B200–B250 fare plus a B50 expressway toll charge and a B50 airport surcharge. (Taxis bound for the airport do not add the surcharge.) To make sure that your driver knows where you are headed, state your destination to the person in the kiosk near the curb. The dispatcher will write it down for the driver, who will lead you to the taxi. The expressways are often congested, meaning that the trip from the airport can take anywhere from 30 minutes to more than an hour.

Bangkok Airport Express trains make the 35-minute run every 90 minutes from 8 AM to 7 PM. Check the schedule at the information booth in the arrival hall. The fare is B45. You can also take the regular trains from 5:30 AM to 9 PM. The fare is B5 for a local train and B13 for an express. The train is not convenient for many travelers, as most hotels are not near the train station.

For about B6,000 per person you can whiz into the city in a helicopter. Sri Chang Flying Services flies between the airport and several downtown hotels, including the Peninsula, Oriental, Royal Orchid Sheraton, and Shangri-La. The new expressways have greatly diminished the need for this service, however.

➤ AIRPORT INFORMATION: **Don Muang International Airport** (☎ 02/504–2701).

➤ TRANSFERS: **Bangkok Airport Express** (☎ 02/223–0341). **Sri Chang Flying Services** (☎ 02/652–2550).

BOAT AND FERRY TRAVEL

Ferries (sometimes called "river buses") ply the Chao Phraya River. The fare for these express boats is based on the distance you travel, but B5 will cover most trips. At certain piers you must add a B1 jetty fee. The pier adjacent to the Oriental Hotel is convenient to many of the city's hotels. You can get to the Grand Palace in about 10 minutes, or to the other side of Krungthon Bridge in about 15 minutes.

Long-tail boats (so called for the extra-long propeller shaft that extends behind the stern) operate as taxis that you can hire for about B400 an hour. They are the most convenient way to cross the river to get to Thonburi.

BUS TRAVEL TO AND FROM BANGKOK

Bangkok has three major terminals for buses headed to other parts of the country. The **Northern Bus Terminal,** called Morchit, serves Chiang Mai and points north. The **Southern Bus Terminal,** in Thonburi, is for buses bound for Hua Hin, Ko Samui, Phuket, and points south. The **Eastern Bus Terminal,** called Ekkamai, is for buses headed to Pattaya, Rayong, and Trat provinces.

The air-conditioned orange-color 999 buses are the most comfortable. They have larger seats that recline. A hostess serves drinks and snacks and even shows a movie. If no 999 bus is available on your route, stick with the air-conditioned blue VIP buses. They aren't as luxurious, but are still comfortable.

Buses leave from Bangkok's Southern Bus Terminal every 20 minutes starting at 6 AM for Damnoen Saduak. The fare is B30 to B90. From the station, walk along the canal for 1½ km (1 mi) to the floating market. Buses leave from the Southern Bus Terminal every 20 minutes for the 2½-hour trip to Kanchanaburi. Buses also run to Nakhon Pathom from Damnoen Saduak.

Most bus companies do not take reservations, and tickets are sold on a first-come, first-served basis. This is seldom a problem, however, because the service is so regular that the next bus is sure to depart before long. For example, VIP buses from Bangkok to Kanchanaburi depart every 15 minutes.

➤ BUS STATIONS: **Eastern Bus Terminal** (✉ Sukhumvit Soi 40, ☎ 02/391–2504). **Northern Bus Terminal** (✉ Phaholyothin Rd., behind Chatuchak Park, ☎ 02/936–2852). **Southern Bus Terminal** (✉ Pinklao-Nakomchaisri Rd., Talingchan, ☎ 02/391–9829).

BUS TRAVEL WITHIN BANGKOK

Although city buses can be very crowded, they are convenient and inexpensive. For a fare of B3.50 to B5 on the non-air-conditioned buses and B8 to B20 on the air-conditioned ones, you can travel virtually anywhere in the city. Air-conditioned microbuses, in which you are guaranteed a seat, charge B25. Most buses operate from 5 AM to around 11 PM, but a few routes operate around the clock.

The bus routes are confusing, but someone at the bus stop should know the number of the bus you need. You can pick up a route map at most bookstalls for B35. Buses can be very crowded, so be alert for pickpockets.

CAR RENTALS

Most rental agencies in the capital let you drop off the car in a different city. This means, for example, you can pick up your car in Bangkok and leave it in Chiang Mai. Of the international chains, Avis, Hertz, and National have offices at the airport and in downtown Bangkok.

➤ AGENCIES: **Avis** (✉ 2/12 Witthayu Rd., ☎ 02/255–5300). **Budget** (✉ 19/23 Bldg. A, Royal City Ave., 10320, ☎ 02/203–0180, FAX 02/203–0249. **Hertz** (✉ 1620 New Phetburi Rd., ☎ 02/251–7575). **National** (✉ 727 Srinakarin Rd., ☎ 02/722–8487).

CAR TRAVEL

Thailand's highway system is good (and getting better), so driving is a more popular option than in years past. There are plenty of sights around Bangkok that are within easy driving distance.

As for driving in Bangkok—don't bother. The maze of streets is difficult enough for taxi drivers to negotiate. Throw in bumper-to-bumper traffic and you'll wish that you were on a water taxi on the river or the skytrain soaring above the streets.

DISABILITIES AND ACCESSIBILITY

Bangkok has made precious few steps toward improving things for people with disabilities. Most sights are reached by at least one daunting set of steps. This means getting around the city will be a challenge for those in a wheelchair. Your best bet is hiring a guide who can drive you from sight to sight. The good news is that most of the larger hotels have rooms that are designed for people with handicaps.

EMBASSIES

Most of the embassies in the capital are located around Lumphini Park, especially along Witthayu Road. The U.S. embassy is open weekdays 7 to 4.

➤ CONTACTS: **Australia** (✉ 37 Sathorn Rd., ☎ 02/287–2680). **Canada** (✉ 990 Rama IV Rd., ☎ 02/636–0540). **New Zealand** (✉ 93 Witthayu Rd., ☎ 02/254–2530 up to 3). **United Kingdom** (✉ 1031 Witthayu Rd., ☎ 02/253–0191). **United States** (✉ 120 Witthayu Rd., ☎ 02/205–4000).

EMERGENCIES

In case of emergency, it's a good idea to contact the Tourist Police. The force has mobile units in major tourist areas.

Bangkok has a number of reputable dental clinics, among them Ambassador Dental Clinic and Thaniya Dental Centre. If you want a private dentist, see Khun Phira Sithiamnuai, who trained in Massachusetts. For medical attention, Bunrungrad Hospital, near Sukhumvit Road, and Bangkok Nursing Hospital, near Silom Road, are considered the best by most expatriates. Nonthavej Hospital, not far from Don Muang International Airport, has an excellent staff accustomed to foreign patients. Other good facilities include Bangkok Adventist Hospital, Bangkok Christian Hospital, and Chulalongkorn Hospital.

There are many pharmacies in Bangkok, including Foodland Supermarket Pharmacy. Compared with the United States, fewer drugs require prescriptions. If you need one, the prescription must be written in Thai. Over-the-counter drugs do not necessarily have the same ingredients as those found elsewhere, so read the label carefully. If you cannot find a pharmacy, the ubiquitous 7-Eleven, AM/PM, and other convenience stores carry nonprescription medications.

➤ DOCTORS AND DENTISTS: **Ambassador Dental Clinic** (✉ 171 Sukhumvit Soi 11, ☎ 02/255–2279). **Khun Phira Sithiamnuai** (✉ Sukhumvit 24, ☎ 02/661–1156). **Thaniya Dental Centre** (✉ 52 Silom Rd., ☎ 02/231–2100).

➤ EMERGENCY SERVICES: **Ambulance** (☎ 1669). **Fire** (☎ 199). **Police** (☎ 191). **Tourist Police** (✉ 4 Ratchadamnoen Rd., ☎ 1155).

➤ HOSPITALS: **Bangkok Adventist Hospital** (✉ 430 Phitsanulok Rd., ☎ 02/281–1422). **Bangkok Christian Hospital** (✉ 124 Silom Rd., ☎ 02/233–6981 or 02/233–6989). **Bangkok Nursing Home** (✉ 9 Convent Rd., ☎ 02/632–0550). **Bunrungrad Hospital** (✉ Sukhumvit Soi 3, ☎ 02/253–0250). **Chulalongkorn Hospital** (✉ Rama IV Rd., ☎ 02/252–8181). **Nonthavej Hospital** (✉ 30/8 Ngam-wongwan Rd., Bangkhen Nonthaburi, ☎ 02/589–0102).

➤ 24-HOUR PHARMACIES: **Foodland Supermarket Pharmacy** (✉ No. 9 Patpong 2 Rd., ☎ 02/233–2101; ✉ 1413 Sukhumvit Soi 5, ☎ 02/254–2247).

ENGLISH-LANGUAGE MEDIA

The English-language dailies the *Bangkok Post* and *The Nation* and the monthly *Metro* are available at most newsstands.

With two locations, Asia Books has a wide selection of books and magazines. Bookazine is a chain with a good selection and several locations, including one in the CP Tower. Kinokuniya Books has one of the city's largest selections of English-language books. And for older hard-to-find used books try Merman Books.

➤ ENGLISH-SPEAKING BOOKSTORES: **Asia Books** (✉ 221 Sukhumvit Soi 15, ☎ 02/651–0428; ✉ Peninsula Plaza, ☎ 02/253–9786). **Bookazine** (✉ 313 Silom Rd., ☎ 02/231–0016). **Kinokuniya Books** (✉ Emporium Shopping Complex, Sukhumvit Rd., ☎ 02/664–8554). **Merman Books** (✉ 191 Silom Rd., ☎ 02/231–3155).

HEALTH

Use common sense to stay healthy in Bangkok. There's no need to avoid most foods, even those sold by street vendors. Simply make sure what you are eating was cooked in front of you or is still hot. Never eat food that has been allowed to cool to room temperature. The rule of thumb is to look for the vendors patronized by long lines of locals. Spicy food may be too much for sensitive stomachs, so try to take it easy your first few days. Bottled water is available everywhere in Bangkok.

Sexual transmitted diseases should be taken seriously in Bangkok. AIDS is a big problem, especially among sex workers. Condoms are available everywhere, even from street vendors.

MAIL AND SHIPPING

All neighborhoods have at least one post office, and the staff at your hotel can tell you where to find the nearest one. The city's main post office is on Charoen Krung Road south of Chinatown. It is more efficient than smaller ones, which can have dreadfully slow service.

The major international courier services, Federal Express, DHL and UPS, have offices in Bangkok.

➤ COURIER SERVICES: **DHL Worldwide** (✉ Grand Amarin Tower, 22nd floor, New Phetchburi Rd., ☎ 02/207–0600). **Federal Express** (✉ Green Tower, 8th floor, Rama IV Rd., ☎ 02/367–3222). **UPS** (✉ Soi 44/1, Sukhumvit Rd., ☎ 02/712–3300).

MONEY MATTERS

Major banks all exchange foreign currency, and most have easily accessible ATMs that accept foreign bank cards. Bangkok has come great strides in the past decade, with ATMs proliferating in areas popular with tourists.

Currency exchange offices are common, but don't wait until the last minute. It's distressing to try to find one when you're out of baht.

TAXIS AND TUK-TUKS

Taxis are an economical way to get around, especially if you don't hit gridlock. A typical journey of 5 km (3 mi) runs about B60. Most taxis have meters, so avoid those that lack one or claim that it is broken. The rate for the first 2 km (1 mi) is B35, with an additional baht for every 50 meters after that. If the speed drops to below 6 kph, a surcharge of one baht per minute is added.

Unmetered tuk-tuks are usually slightly cheaper than taxis. They are a better options when traffic is light so that you don't choke on fumes when stuck in traffic. The drivers are tough negotiators, and unless you are good at bargaining you may well end up paying more than for a metered taxi. Unscrupulous tuk-tuk drivers—all too common, especially around touristy areas—offer tours at a bargain rate, then take you directly to jewelry shops and tailors who, of course, give the drivers a commission. Don't fall for it.

At many sois you will find groups of motorbikers. These "soi boys" once only took passengers down the side streets, but their operations have expanded so that they can travel anywhere in Bangkok. The risk and discomfort limit their desirability, but if you are late for a date they are the fastest way between two points. Fares are negotiable, usually about the same as or perhaps a little less than taxis. Always ask for a helmet.

TELEPHONES

Telephone information from an English-speaking operator is available by dialing 1133. Getting through, however, can often be difficult.

TOUR OPERATORS

Virtually every major hotel has a travel desk that books tours in and around Bangkok. With only slight variations, companies usually offer half-day tours of Wat Pho, Wat Benjamabophit, and Wat Traimit; half-day tours of the Grand Palace and Wat Phra Keo; and dinners featuring traditional dance.

Several established agencies are good bets. Try Diethelm, East West Siam, or World Travel Service.

➤ AGENCIES: **Diethelm** (✉ Kian Gwan Bldg. 11, 140/1 Witthayu Rd., ☎ 02/255–9150). **East West Siam** (✉ Bldg. One, 11th floor, 99 Witthayu Rd., ☏ 02/256–6153 or 02/256–6155). **World Travel Service** (✉ 1053 Charoen Krung Rd., ☏ 02/233–5900).

TRAIN TRAVEL TO AND FROM BANGKOK

Hualamphong Railway Station, the city's main station, is where you'll find most long-distance trains. Bangkok Noi Railway Station, on the Thonburi side of the Chao Phraya River, is used by local trains to Hua Hin and other nearby destinations.

Trains from both the Hualamphong and Noi stations stop in Nakhon Pathom. Trains for Kanchanaburi leave Noi Station at 8 AM and 1:55 PM. The State Railway of Thailand also runs a special excursion train (B75) on weekends and holidays that leaves Hualamphong Station at 6:15 AM and returns at 7:30 PM, stopping at Nakhon Pathom and Kanchanaburi. There is no train to Damnoen Saduak.

➤ TRAIN STATIONS: **Bangkok Noi** (✉ Arun Amarin Rd., ☏ 02/411–3102). **Hualamphong** (✉ Rama IV Rd., ☏ 02/223–0341).

TRAIN TRAVEL WITHIN BANGKOK

The skytrain transformed the city when it opened on the king's birthday in 1999. It now has 25 stations on two lines that intersect at Siam Square. Although it covers just a fraction of the capital (it bypasses the Old City and Dusit, for example), it is surprisingly convenient for visitors. The routes above Sukhumvit, Silom, and Phaholyothin roads make traveling in those areas a breeze. If you are traveling between two points along the route, the skytrain is by far the best way to go. The fare is B10 to B40, determined by the distance you travel. It runs from 5 AM to midnight.

➤ CONTACT: **Bangkok Transit System** (☏ 02/617–7300).

VISITOR INFORMATION

Bangkok's downtown branch of the Tourist Authority of Thailand, open 8:30 to 4:30, tends to have more in the way of colorful brochures than hard information, but it can supply useful material on national parks and various out-of-the-way destinations. A 24-hour hot line provides information on destinations, festivals, arts, and culture. You may also use the hot line to register complaints or request assistance from the tourist police. There is also a TAT branch at the international terminal at Don Muang International Airport.

For those traveling west of the capital, there is a TAT office in Kanchanaburi.

➤ TOURIST INFORMATION: **Bangkok** (✉ 1600 New Phetburi Rd., 10320, ☏ 02/694–1222, FAX 02/694–1361). **Kanchanaburi** (✉ 325 Saeng Chuto Rd., ☏ 034/511200).

3 THE CENTRAL PLAINS

In their rush to get south to the beaches or north to the mountains, many visitors to Thailand ignore the country's heartland. They are missing out on one of the best parts of this land, as the fertile fields are studded with the ruins of ancient capitals with such mystical names as Ayutthaya and Sukhothai. Here you'll find tantalizing clues to the region's proud past.

T HE STONE-STREWN PATH up the hillside doesn't look as if any-one has passed this way for ages. Could this really be the way? You glance over to your guide, who nods. After mopping the sweat from your forehead you continue your climb. At the top, the path opens onto a huge plaza with a sweeping view of the valley below. Just ahead is a stone wall, and beyond that is a spire that points heavenward. No tour buses here. This temple is yours alone.

Updated by
Robert Tilley

This is the Central Plains, one of the most overlooked regions of Thai-land. Some people take a side trip from Bangkok to the ancient capi-tal of Ayutthaya, but fewer venture farther north to the even older cities at Sukhothai and Sri Satchanalai. This means that you are likely to en-counter few other people as you wander among some of the most breath-taking ruins in the country.

Thailand was founded in 1238, when the cornerstones were laid for the towering temples at Sukhothai. The Sukhothai period was relatively brief—a series of eight kings—but it witnessed lasting accomplishments. The Thais gained their independence, which was maintained despite the efforts of Europe. King Ramkhamhaeng formulated the Thai al-phabet by adapting the Khmer script to suit the Thai tonal language, Theravada Buddhism was established and became the dominant na-tional religion, and, toward the end of the Sukhothai dynasty, such a distinctive Thai art flourished that the period is known as Thailand's Golden Age.

Thailand's most glorious period began when Ayutthaya became the king-dom's seat of power in 1350. Toward the end of the 16th century, Eu-ropeans described the city, with its 1,700 temples and 4,000 golden images of the Buddha, as more striking than any capital in Europe. In 1767, the Burmese conquered Ayutthaya and destroyed its temples with such vengeance that little remained standing. The city never recovered, and today it is a small provincial town with partially restored ruins. The site is particularly striking at sunset, when the silhouetted ruins glow orange-brown and are imbued with a melancholy charm.

Although off the beaten track, it isn't difficult to reach the Central Plains. If you have more than a passing interest in Thailand's history, you won't be able to resist spending a few days rooting around in its majestic ruins. Accommodations here aren't luxurious, but a night or two in a charm-ing guest house amid beautiful gardens or a bamboo hut in the mid-dle of a rice field brings you remarkably close to the people.

Pleasures and Pastimes

Architecture
The optimism that accompanied the birth of the nation at Sukhothai is reflected in the art and architecture of the period. Strongly influenced by Sri Lankan Buddhism, the monuments left behind by the architects, artisans, and craftsmen of those innovative times had a light, often play-ful touch. Statues of the Buddha show him as smiling, serene, and con-fidently walking toward a better future. There were impudent touches in the temple decoration, such as the impossibly graceful elephants por-trayed in supporting pillars.

Dining
Although the region is not known for its cuisine, it's possible to eat well in the Central Plains. Although most of the dishes you'll be served are the same as those found elsewhere in the country, you can often find fare that is fresh and flavorful. Do rely on local markets, which

are full of delicious things to eat. Choosing one dish from a vendor and another from the next, you can put together quite a feast for next to nothing.

CATEGORY	COST*
$$$$	over B400 (over US$10)
$$$	B300–B400 (US$7.50–$10)
$$	B200–B300 (US$5–$7.50)
$	B100–B200 (US$2.50–5)
¢	under B100 (under US$2.50)

*per person, for a main course at dinner

Lodging

Because relatively few tourists visit the Central Plains, most hotels and guest houses cater chiefly to a business clientele. There are some top-class hotels, but most accommodations are much more modest. As elsewhere in Thailand, standards of cleanliness are high and even the most basic room will invariably have fresh linen and towels.

A new phenomenon is the appearance of lodgings run by hospitable and knowledgeable local people anxious to help visitors get to know this seemingly remote region. They open up their homes to paying guests and show them around for a modest fee. Listed here are a few of the most reputable.

For budget-conscious travelers, rooms in the Central Plains are truly a bargain—even the most expensive hotels charge less than $60 a night. Don't expect the full range of facilities, however. Such refinements as room telephones, televisions, and even hot water can be rare outside the cities.

CATEGORY	COST*
$$$$	over B6,000 (over US$150)
$$$	B4,000–B6,000 (US$100–$150)
$$	B2,000–B4,000 (US$50–$100)
$	B1,000–B2,000 (under US$50)
¢	under B1,000 (under US$25)

*All prices are for a standard double room, excluding tax.

Shopping

Because a relatively small number of travelers venture this way, there are fewer crafts for sale here than elsewhere in the country. One notable exception is around Sukhothai and Sri Satchanalai, where you can find reproductions of the pottery that was made here when this was the capital of the country.

Exploring the Central Plains

In the best of all possible worlds you'd spend at least at least a week in this region, gazing down from its mysterious temples, strolling through the strongholds of long-gone civilizations, and wandering along the banks of the rivers. You would browse in the markets and explore the villages. But on a trip of any length, you're sure to discover classic architecture at ancient cities like Ayutthaya and Sukhothai in the Central Plains.

Great Itineraries

Numbers in the text correspond to numbers in the margin and on the Central Plains, Ayutthaya, and Sukhothai maps.

IF YOU HAVE 1 DAY

If you have little time to venture into the Central Plains, the easiest trip is to **Ayutthaya** ①–⑧, which became the country's capital after

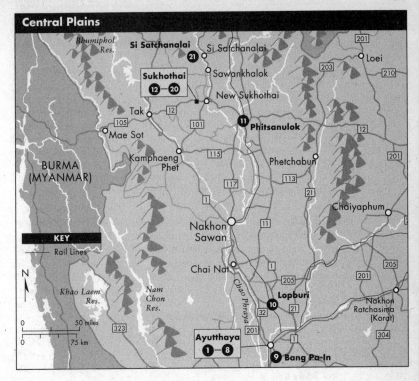

Central Plains

Sukhothai's influence waned. You can reach the ancient city several ways, but none is more atmospheric than by long-tail boat up the Chao Phraya River. If you have time, take a side trip to see the summer palace of **Bang Pa-In** ⑨.

IF YOU HAVE 3 DAYS
Leave Bangkok early on a journey up the Chao Phraya River to the old capital of **Ayutthaya** ①–⑧. While you're here, take in **Bang Pa-In** ⑨, the opulent summer palace. Return to Bangkok, where you can take the train or plane to **Phitsanulok** ⑪ to see the Phra Buddha Chinnarat and the Pim Buranaket Folklore Museum. Board a bus for the hourlong trip to 🖼 **Sukhothai** ⑫–⑳. You'll need the best part of a day to see highlights of the country's first capital. The next morning take the hour's trip to **Si Satchanalai** ㉑, an ancient satellite city. In the afternoon you can grab a plane at Sukhothai for the trip back to Bangkok or Chiang Mai.

When to Tour the Central Plains

The dry months between November and March are also the coolest and therefore the best time to visit. After March, this central area of Thailand becomes almost unbearably hot. It is only slightly cooled by the rains that fall between June and early October.

AYUTTHAYA AND ENVIRONS

Ayutthaya

72 km (45 mi) north of Bangkok.

Ayutthaya lies in a bend of the Chao Phraya River where it meets the Pa Sak River and the Lopburi River. To completely encircle their capital by water, the residents dug a curving canal along the northern perimeter, linking the Chao Phraya to the Lopburi. Although the modern town is on the eastern bank of the Pa Sak, most of the ancient temples are on the island. An exception is Wat Yai Chai Mongkol, a short tuk-tuk ride away.

Try to get an early start so you can see as much as possible before 1 PM, when the heat becomes unbearable. Take a long lunch and, if you have time, continue your tour in the late afternoon so you can catch the sunset.

A Good Tour

Two impressive temples sit outside the boundaries of the old city. East of the Pa Sak River lies **Wat Yai Chai Mongkol** ①, constructed in 1357. Notice how the chedi is leaning. Restored without replacing the foundation, it is slowly sinking. Nearby is **Wat Phanan Choeng** ②, a small temple that was built before Ayutthaya's rise to power.

Head to Rotchana Road, where you can cross the bridge to the island. Take a right on Chikun Road. At the corner of Naresuan Road you'll reach two adjacent temples, **Wat Phra Mahathat** ③ and **Wat Ratburana** ④. Many treasures were unearthed here, and most can be seen in the National Museum in Bangkok. Continue west on Naresuan Road, then turn right on Si San Phet Road, where you'll reach **Wat Phra Si Samphet** ⑤, a shining structure made of white marble. Just to the south is **Viharn Phra Mongkol Bopitr** ⑥.

To learn more about the history of Ayutthaya, head south to the **Chao Sam Phraya National Museum** ⑦. If that doesn't satisfy your curiosity about the culture, a short walk to the east is the **Ayutthaya Historical Study Centre** ⑧.

TIMING

Most people find that a morning or afternoon is sufficient to see Ayutthaya. For a three-hour tour of the sights, tuk-tuks can be hired for about B500; a four-wheel samlor (small bicycle cab) costs a bit more than B700.

Sights to See

⑧ **Ayutthaya Historical Study Centre.** Financed by the Japanese government, this educational center houses fascinating audiovisual displays about Ayutthaya. Models of the city as a rural village, as a port city, as an administrative center, and as a royal capital reveal the city's history. Students get in for B50, everyone else pays B100. ⊠ *Rotchana Rd. between Si San Phet Rd. and Chikun Rd.,* ☎ *035/245123.* ⊡ *Admission.* ⊙ *Weekdays 9–4:30, weekends 9–5.*

⑦ **Chao Sam Phraya National Museum.** Although Ayutthaya's best pieces are in Bangkok's National Museum, a guided visit can illuminate the four centuries of art created here. One of the highlights is a jewel-covered sword that was found in a tomb at Wat Ratchaburana. ⊠ *Rotchana Rd. at Si San Phet Rd.,* ☎ *035/241587.* ⊡ *Admission.* ⊙ *Wed.–Sun. 9–4.*

Elephant Kraal. Thailand's only intact royal kraal was last used during King Chulalongkorn's reign in 1903 to hold wild elephants to be trained for martial service. ⊠ *5 km (3 mi) north of Ayutthaya.*

⑥ **Viharn Phra Mongkol Bopitr.** This shining white-marble temple, south of Wat Phra Si Samphet, is one of the modern structures in the old city. Built in 1956, the viharn houses a large bronze image of the Buddha, one of the few that escaped the destruction wrought by the Burmese. ⊠ *Off Naresuan Rd.* ⊡ *Admission.* ⊙ *Daily 8–5.*

★ ② **Wat Phanan Choeng.** This small temple on the banks of the Lopburi River predates Ayutthaya's rise to power. One of the U-Thong kings,

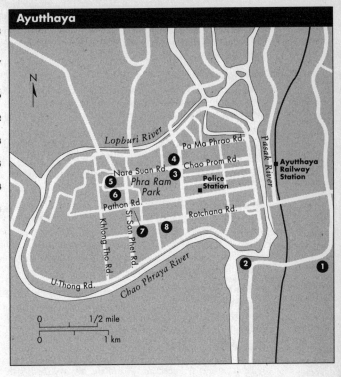

Ayutthaya

who had arranged to marry a daughter of the Chinese emperor, came to this spot on the river in 1324. Instead of entering the city with his fiancée, he arranged an escort for her. But she, thinking that she had been deserted, threw herself into the river in despair and drowned. The king tried to atone for his thoughtlessness by building the temple. The story has great appeal to the Chinese, many of whom make romantic pilgrimages here. ⊠ *East of the old city.* ▧ *Admission.* ⊙ *Daily 8–6.*

3 **Wat Phra Mahathat.** Built in 1384 by King Ramesuan, the monastery was destroyed by the Burmese. In 1956, during a restoration project, a buried chest was found containing a relic of Lord Buddha, golden Buddha images, and other objects that are now housed in Bangkok's National Museum. If you climb up what is left of the monastery's 140-ft prang, you'll be able to envision just how grand the structure must have been. ⊠ *Naresuan Rd. and Chee Kun Rd.* ▧ *Admission.* ⊙ *Daily 8:30–4:30.*

5 **Wat Phra Si Samphet.** Wat Phra Si Samphet was the largest temple in Ayutthaya, as well as the place where the royal family worshiped. The 14th-century structure lost its 50-ft Buddha in 1767, when the invading Burmese melted it down for its 374 pounds of gold. The trio of chedis survived, and are the best existing examples of Ayutthaya architecture. Enshrining the ashes of several kings, they stand as eternal memories of a golden age. If the design looks familiar, it may be because Wat Phra Si Samphet was used as a model for Wat Phra Keo at the Grand Palace in Bangkok. Beyond the monuments you'll find a grassy field where the royal palace once stood. The foundation is all that remains of the palace that was home to 33 kings. The field is a cool, shady place in which to stop for a picnic. ⊠ *Naresuan Rd.* ▧ *Admission.* ⊙ *Daily 8–5.*

4 **Wat Ratburana.** This temple across from Wat Phra Mahathat was built in 1424 by the seventh Ayutthaya king in memory of his brothers, who died during an elephant-back battle over the throne. ⊠ *Naresuan Rd. and Chee Kun Rd.* ☞ *Admission.* ☉ *Daily 8:30–4:30.*

1 **Wat Yai Chai Mongkol.** The enormous chedi at Wat Yai Chai Mongkol, the largest in Ayutthaya, was constructed by King Naresuan after he defeated the Burmese crown prince during a battle atop elephants in 1593. (A recent painting of the battle is one of the highlights of the temple.) The chedi is now leaning a bit, as later enlargements are weighing down on the foundation. The complex, dating from 1357, was totally restored in 1982. Linger a while to pay your respects to the huge Reclining Buddha. ⊠ *East of the old city.* ☞ *Admission.* ☉ *Daily 8–5.*

Dining and Lodging

If you're a romantic, you may want to stay in Ayutthaya so you can wander among the ruins at night. Since most tourists leave Ayutthaya by 4 PM, those who stay the night are treated to genuine Thai hospitality. Don't expect luxury, however; Ayutthaya has only modest hotels and simple restaurants.

$ ✕ **Pae Krung Kao.** If you can't resist dining outdoors beside the Pa Sak River, this is the better of the two floating restaurants near the Pridi Damrong Bridge. You can also drop by for a leisurely beer. ⊠ *4 U-Thong Rd.,* ☎ *035/241555. AE, MC, V.*

$ ✕ **Tevaraj.** For good, spicy food, head for this unpretentious restaurant behind Ayutthaya's railway station. The *tom kha gai* (chicken soup with coconut) is excellent, as are the always-fresh fish dishes. ⊠ *74 Wat Pa Kho Rd.,* ☎ *no phone. No credit cards.*

$$$$ ⌂ **Manohra Song.** This 60-ft rice barge has, with the help of lots of taste and even more money, been brought back to life as a luxury cruiser on the Chao Phraya. For a day and a half, you'll relax in suites decorated with rich woods like mahogany and teak and yards of flowing silks. Pampered by a private chef, you'll watch the world drift by between Bangkok and Ayutthaya. ⊠ *Marriott Royal Garden Riverside Hotel, 257/1–3 Charoen Nakorn Rd., Thonburi, Bangkok 10600,* ☎ *02/476–0021; 02/276–0022 in Bangkok;* ℻ *02/477–0811,* ⱳⴱ *www.manohracruises.com. 4 suites. Dining room. AE, MC, V.*

$ ⌂ **Krungsri River Hotel.** A welcome addition to Ayutthaya, the Krungsri River Hotel is conveniently close to the train station. The spacious marble-floor lobby is refreshingly cool, and the rooms, although not distinguished in any way, are clean, fresh, and filled with modern furnishings. For the best views, choose a room overlooking the river. Because Ayutthaya has few overnight visitors, try to negotiate a discounted rate. Rates include a buffet breakfast. ⊠ *27/2 Rojana Rd., 13000,* ☎ *035/244333,* ℻ *035/243777. 200 rooms. Restaurant. MC, V.*

Bang Pa-In

9 *20 km (12 mi) south of Ayutthaya.*

A popular attraction near Ayutthaya is found in the village Bang Pa-In—the extravagant **Royal Palace,** set in well-tended gardens. The original structure, built by King Prusat on the banks of the Pa Sak River, was used by the Ayutthaya kings until the Burmese invasion. After being neglected for 80 years, it was rebuilt during the reign of Rama IV and became the favored summer palace of King Rama V until tragedy struck. When the king was delayed in Bangkok, he sent his wife ahead on a boat that capsized. Although she could easily have been rescued, people stood by helplessly because a royal could not be touched by a commoner on pain of death. The king could never forgive himself. He built a pavilion in her memory; be sure to read the touching inscription engraved on the memorial. ▨ *Admission.* ☉ *Tues.–Thurs. and weekends 8–3.*

King Rama V was interested in the architecture of Europe, and many Western influences are evident here. The most beautiful building, however, is the **Aisawan Thippaya,** a Thai pavilion that seems to float on a small lake. A series of staggered roofs lead to a central spire. The structure is sometimes dismantled and taken to represent the country at worldwide expositions.

Phra Thinang Warophat Phiman, nicknamed the Peking Palace, faces a stately pond. The replica of a palace of the Chinese imperial court, it was built from materials custom-made in China—a gift from Chinese Thais eager to win the king's favor. It contains a collection of exquisite jade and Ming-period porcelain.

Take the cable car across the river to **Wat Nivet Thamaprawat,** built in Gothic style. Complete with a belfry and stained-glass windows, it looks as much like a Christian church masquerading as a Buddhist temple.

Shopping

The **Bang Sai Folk Arts and Craft Centre** was set up by the queen to train families to make handicrafts. Workers at the center are happy to demonstrate their techniques. The crafts on sale include woven baskets, wood carvings, dyed silks, and handmade dolls. There's also a small restaurant and a nearby park that's a pleasant place for a picnic. ⊠ *24 km (14½ mi) south of Bang Pa-In,* ☎ *035/366090 or 035/366666,* WEB *www.bangsai.net.* ▨ *Admission.* ☉ *Daily 8:30–4:30.*

Lopburi

⑩   *75 km (47 mi) north of Ayutthaya, 150 km (94 mi) north of Bangkok.*

One of Thailand's oldest cities, Lopburi has been inhabited since the 4th century. After the 6th century, its influence grew under the Dvaravati rulers, who dominated northern Thailand until the Khmers swept in from the east. From the beginning of the 10th century until the middle of the 13th, when the new Thai kingdom drove them out, the Khmers used Lopburi as their provincial capital. During the Sukhothai and early Ayutthaya periods, the city's importance declined until, in 1664, King Narai made it his second capital to escape the heat and humidity of Ayutthaya. He employed French architects to build his palace; consequently, Lopburi is a strange mixture of Khmer, Thai, and Western architecture.

Lopburi is relatively off the beaten track for tourists. Few foreigners stay overnight. The rarity of foreigners may explain why locals are so friendly and eager to show you their town—and to practice their English. Samlors are available, but most of Lopburi's attractions are within easy walking distance.

Wat Phra Si Rattana Mahathat, built by the Khmers, is near the railway station. It underwent so many restorations during the Sukhothai and Ayutthaya periods that it's difficult to discern the three original Khmer prangs—only the central one is intact. Several Sukhothai- and Ayutthaya-style chedis are within the compound. ⊠ *Na Phra Karn Rd.* ▨ *Admission.* ☉ *Daily 8:30–4:30.*

Past Wat Phra Si Mahathat is **Phra Narai Ratchaniwet.** The palace's well-preserved buildings, completed between 1665 and 1677, have been converted into museums. Surrounding the buildings are castellated walls and triumphal archways grand enough to admit an entourage mounted on elephants. The most elaborate structure is the Dusit Mahaprasat Hall, built by King Narai to receive foreign ambassadors. The roof is gone, but you'll be able to spot the mixture of architectural styles: the square doors are Thai and the domed arches are Western. North of Phra Narai Ratchaniwet is the restored Wat Sao Thong Thong. Notice the windows of the viharn, which King Narai intended to imitate those found in Europe. ⊠ *Ratchadamnern Rd.* 🔳 *Admission.* ⊙ *Daily 8:30–4:30.*

North of Wat Sao Thong Thong is **Vichayen House,** built for French King Louis XIV's personal representative, De Chaumont. The house was later occupied by King Narai's infamous Greek minister, Constantine Phaulkon, whose political schemes eventually caused the ouster of all Westerners from Thailand. When King Narai was dying in 1668, his army commander, Phra Phetracha, seized power and beheaded Phaulkon. During the attack, Vichayen House was nearly destroyed. ⊠ *Vichayen Rd.* 🔳 *Admission.* ⊙ *Wed.–Sun. 9–noon and 1–4.*

East on Vichayen Road is a Khmer shrine called **Phra Prang Sam Yot,** Lopburi's most famous landmark. The three prangs symbolize the sacred triad of Brahma, Vishnu, and Shiva. King Narai converted the shrine into a Buddhist temple, and a stucco image of the Buddha sits serenely before the central prang. ⊠ *Vichayen Rd.*

East of Phra Prang Sam Yot is **San Phra Kan.** The residents of the temple, a troop of monkeys, often perform for visitors. ⊠ *Vichayen Rd.*

Lodging

$ 🏨 **Lopburi Inn.** This hotel has achieved a certain amount of fame by hosting an annual dinner party for the town's resident monkeys each November. It's a pleasant place with modern facilities. Even so, don't expect your room to have much more than a clean bed and a private bath. The dining room serves Thai and Chinese food. A buffet breakfast is included in the rates. ⊠ *28/9 Narai Maharat Rd.,* ☏ *036/412300,* 𝔽𝔸𝕏 *036/411917. 142 rooms. Restaurant, coffee shop. AE, DC, V.*

SUKHOTHAI AND ENVIRONS

Phitsanulok

⓫ *377 km (234 mi) north of Bangkok.*

For a brief span in the 14th century, after the decline of Sukhothai and before the rise of Ayutthaya, Phitsanulok was the kingdom's capital. Farther back in history, Phitsanulok was a Khmer outpost called Song Kwae—only an ancient monastery remains. The new city, which had to relocate 5 km (3 mi) from the old site, is a modern provincial administrative seat with few architectural blessings. There are outstanding attractions, however, such as the Phra Buddha Chinnarat inside Wat Phra Si Ratana Mahathat. Make sure to take time to walk along the Nan River, lined with numerous tempting food stalls in the evening. On the far side you'll see many houseboats, which are popular among Thais. Disregarding the Naresuan Bridge, some locals still paddle across the river in small boats.

With modern conveniences, Phitsanulok is an ideal base for exploring the region. Most of the sights in Phitsanulok are within walking distance, but bicycle samlors are easily available. Bargain hard—most trips should be about B20. Taxis are available for longer trips; you'll find a few loitering around the train station.

Naresuan Road runs from the railway station to the Nan River. North of this street you'll find **Wat Phra Si Ratana Mahathat,** a temple commonly known as Wat Yai. Built in the mid-14th century, Wat Yai has developed into a large monastery with typical ornamentation. Particularly noteworthy are the viharn's wooden doors, inlaid with mother-of-pearl in 1756 at the behest of King Boromkot. Behind the viharn is a 100-ft prang with a vault containing Buddha relics. The many religious souvenir stands make it hard to gain a good view of the complex, but the bot is a fine example of the traditional three-tier roof with low sweeping eaves, designed to diminish the size of the walls, accentuate the nave, and emphasize the image of the Buddha.

Within the viharn is what many consider the world's most beautiful image of the Buddha, Phra Buddha Chinnarat. It was probably cast in the 14th century, during the late Sukhothai period. Its mesmerizing beauty and the mystical powers ascribed to it draw streams of pilgrims—among the most notable of them was the Sukhothai's King Eka Thossarot, who journeyed here in 1631. According to folklore, the king applied with his own hands the gold leaf that covers the Buddha. Many copies of the image have been made, with the best known residing in Bangkok's Marble Temple. ⊠ *Off Ekethosarot Rd.* ⊠ *Free.* ⊙ *Daily 8–6.*

★ Phitsanulok also has a little-known museum, **Pim Buranaket Folkcraft Museum,** that alone would justify a visit to the city. In the early 1980s, Sergeant-Major Khun Thawee traveled to small villages, collecting traditional tools, cooking utensils, animal traps, and handicrafts that were rapidly disappearing, and crammed them into a traditional house and barn. For a decade nothing was properly documented; visitors stumbled through tiger traps and cooking pots. Then Khun Thawee's daughter came to the rescue: the marvelous artifacts are now systematically laid out. You can now understand the use of everything on display, from the simple wood pipes hunters played to lure their prey to elaborately complex rat guillotines. The museum is a 15-minute walk south of the railway station, on the east side of the tracks. ⊠ *Wisut Kasat Rd.* ⊠ *Donation.* ⊙ *Daily 9–5.*

Dining and Lodging
Phitsanulok lacks fine dining establishments, although there are a couple of good pontoon restaurants on the north bank of the river. You can also get a bite at the Night Market, on the river near Naresuan Bridge.

$ ✕ **Phraefahthai.** Reserve a riverside table at this floating restaurant and you can watch the fishermen as they land the catch of the day. You'll soon see why the place is popular among local businessmen and their families. The fish, of course, is fresh and prepared from traditional recipes—start with the spicy shrimp soup, then try the *tabtim* (tilapia) fried in garlic. ⊠ *60 Wangjan Rd.,* ☎ *055/242743. No credit cards.*

$ 🏨 **Pailyn Hotel.** Located in downtown Phitsanulok, this gleaming white high-rise is within walking distance of most of the city's attractions. The rooms are quite large, with picture windows—choose one on a higher floor for the best view of the river. The comfortable furnishings are covered in restful pastels. The large lobby and coffee shop are full of activity in the morning as tour groups gather, as well as in the evening when the disco attracts locals and travelers alike. ⊠ *38 Baromatrailokart Rd., 65000,* ☎ *055/252411; 02/215–7110 in Bangkok;* FAX *055/258185. 125 rooms. 2 restaurants, coffee shop, minibars, cable TV, nightclub, meeting rooms, travel services. AE, DC, MC, V.*

$ 🏨 **La Paloma.** It may have a fancy name, but La Paloma is a business hotel with enough comforts to make it a good base for exploring the area. Rooms are quite plush, with queen-size beds and a couple of easy chairs. The nightclub is a popular local haunt. ⊠ *103 Srithumtripdork*

Rd., ☎ *055/217930. 249 rooms. Restaurant, coffee shop, minibars, cable TV, pool, massage, billiards, nightclub, laundry service, business services, convention center. AE, MC, V.*

¢ 🏨 **Rajapruk Hotel.** The best deal in Phitsanulok, the Rajapruk Hotel charges budget prices for the city's best accommodations. Rooms are decorated with warm colors that accentuate the hotel's intimate feel. There are plenty of amenities, including a swimming pool. A small coffee shop off the lobby is a good place for light meals; a more formal restaurant serves Thai and Chinese entrées. The hotel's main drawback is its location, away from the center of town. ✉ *99/9 Pha-Ong Dum Rd.*, ☎ *055/258477; 02/251–4612 in Bangkok;* 📠 *055/251395. 110 rooms. Restaurant, coffee shop, refrigerators, cable TV, pool, hair salon, nightclub, laundry service, travel services, car rental. AE, DC, MC, V.*

Sukhothai

56 km (35 mi) northwest of Phitsanulok, 427 km (265 mi) north of Bangkok.

Sukhothai, which means "the dawn of happiness," holds a unique place in Thailand's history. Until the 13th century, most of Thailand consisted of many small vassal states under the thumb of the Khmer Empire based in Angkor Wat. But the Khmers had overextended their reach, allowing the princes of two Thai states to combine forces. In 1238 one of the two princes, Phor Khun Bang Klang Thao, marched on Sukhothai, defeating the Khmer garrison commander in an elephant duel. Installed as the new king of the region, he took the name Sri Indraditya and founded a dynasty that ruled Sukhothai for nearly 150 years. His youngest son became the third king of Sukhothai, Ramkhamhaeng, who ruled from 1279 to 1299. Through military and diplomatic victories he expanded the kingdom to include most of present-day Thailand and the Malay peninsula.

By the mid-14th century, Sukhothai's power and influence had waned, and Ayutthaya, once its vassal state, became the capital of the Thai kingdom. Sukhothai was gradually abandoned to the jungle, and a new town grew up about 14 km (9 mi) away. New Sukhothai, where all intercity buses arrive, is a quiet market town where most inhabitants are in bed by 11 PM.

In 1978, a 10-year restoration project costing more than $10 million created the Sukhothai Historical Park. The vast historical park (70 square km/27 square mi) has 193 historic monuments, of which about 20 can be classified as noteworthy and six have particular importance.

A Good Tour

Frequent songthaews from New Sukhothai will take you to the old city for about B10. They will drop you on the main street just outside the park entrance, about 500 yards from the **Ramkhamhaeng National Museum** ⑫. This repository of some of Sukhothai's greatest treasures should be your first stop.

Because the sights are so spread out, the best way to explore the park is by bicycle; you can rent one along the main street. You can also book a tour with a guide. Either way, bring along a bottle of water with you—the sun is hotter than you think. Head first to **Wat Mahathat** ⑬, the spiritual center of the old city. More than 200 structures are a part of this massive complex. It's quite a contrast to the adjacent site of the **Royal Palace** ⑭, where almost nothing remains. To the south is one of the city's most fascinating structures, **Wat Sri Sawai** ⑮. Because of its Hindu images in the stonework, many believe the three-prang tem-

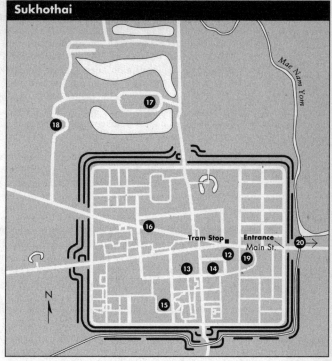

ple was here before construction began on the city itself. To the north of Wat Mahathat is **Wat Sra Sri** ⑯, which is built of a pair of islands in a tranquil lake.

Just beyond the northern city walls is **Wat Phra Phai Luang** ⑰ second in importance to Wat Mahathat. Look for the remains of what was an immense reclining Buddha. Southwest of Wat Phra Phai Luang is **Wat Sri Chum** ⑱, worth visiting for its sheer size. The Buddha statue seated within is one of the most impressive in the old city.

On the eastern side of the old city, the most notable temple is **Wat Traphang Thong Lang** ⑲. On the walls are well-preserved carvings that depict the Buddha preaching. To the east is **Wat Chang Lom** ⑳, where you can still make out the stone elephants that once supported the temple.

TIMING

Depending on your means of transportation, this tour could take a few hours or the best part of a day. Many people come late in the day to enjoy the cooler temperatures and the sight of the sunset painting the ruins vivid shades of pink and orange.

Sights to See

⑫ **Ramkhamhaeng National Museum.** Most of the significant artifacts from Sukhothai are in Bangkok's National Museum, but this open, airy museum has more than enough fine pieces to demonstrate the gentle beauty of this period. Here you'll learn about how refinements in the use of bronze let artisans create the graceful walking Buddhas found here. A relief map gives you an idea of the layout of the old city. ▧ Admission. ⊙ Wed.–Sun. 9–noon and 1–4.

⑭ **Royal Palace.** Thais imagine Sukhothai's government as a monarchy that served the people, stressing social needs and justice. Slavery was abolished, and people were free to believe in their local religions, Hinduism and Buddhism (often simultaneously), and to pursue their trade without hindrance. In the 19th century, a famous stone inscription of King Ramkhamhaeng was found among the ruins of the palace across from Wat Mahathat. Sometimes referred to as Thailand's Declaration of Independence, the inscription's best-known quote reads: "This city Sukhothai is good. In the water there are fish, in the field there is rice. The ruler does not levy tax on the people who travel along the road together, leading their oxen on the way to trade and riding their horses on the way to sell. Whoever wants to trade in elephants, so trades. Whoever wants to trade in horses, so trades."

⑳ Wat Chang Lom. The bell-shape chedi of this temple outside the city walls is raised on a square base atop now-damaged elephant buttresses (a few have been reconstructed). In front of the chedi are a viharn and solitary pillars; the remains of nine other chedis have been found within this complex.

⑬ Wat Mahathat. Sitting amid a tranquil lotus pond, Wat Mahathat is the largest and most beautiful monastery in Sukhothai. Enclosed in the compound are some 200 tightly packed chedis, each containing the funeral ashes of a nobleman. Towering above them, a large central chedi, notable for its bulbous, lotus-bud prang. Wrapping around the chedi is a frieze of 111 monks, their hands raised in adoration. Probably built by Sukhothai's first king, Wat Mahathat owes its present form to King Lö Thai, who in 1345 erected the lotus-bud chedi to house two important relics brought back from Sri Lanka by the monk Sisatta. This Sri Lankan–style chedi became the symbol of Sukhothai and classical Sukhothai style. Copies of it were made in the principal cities of its vassal states, signifying a magic circle emanating from Sukhothai, the spiritual and temporal center of the empire.

⑰ Wat Phra Phai Luang. This former Khmer structure, once a Hindu shrine, was converted to a Buddhist temple. Surrounded by a moat, the sanctuary is encircled by three laterite prangs, similar to those at Wat Sri Sawai—the only one that remains intact is decorated with stucco figures. In front of the prangs are the remains of the viharn and a crumbling chedi with a seated Buddha on its pedestal. Facing these structures is the *mondop* (a square structure with a stepped pyramid roof, built to house religious relics). It was once decorated with Buddha images in four different poses. Most of these are now too damaged to be recognizable; only the reclining Buddha still has a definite form.

⑯ Wat Sra Sri. Another one of Sukhothai's noteworthy attractions is this peaceful temple that sits on two connected islands encircled by a lotus-filled lake. The rolling mountains beyond add to the monastery's serenity. The lake, called Traphong Trakuan Pond, supplied the monks with water and served as a boundary for the sacred area. A Sri Lankan–style chedi dominates six smaller chedis, and a large, stucco, seated Buddha looks down a row of columns, past the chedis, and over the lake to the horizon.

Especially wondrous is the walking Buddha beside the Sri Lankan–style chedi. The walking Buddha is a Sukhothai innovation and the most ethereal of Thailand's artistic styles. The depiction of the Buddha is often a reflection of political authority and is modeled after the ruler. Under the Khmers, authority was hierarchical, but the kings of Sukhothai represented the ideals of serenity, happiness, and justice. The walking Buddha is the epitome of Sukhothai's art; he appears to be floating on air, neither rooted on this earth nor placed on a pedestal above the reach of the common people. Later, after Ayutthaya had become the capital, statues of Buddha took on a sternness that characterized the new dynasty.

⑱ Wat Sri Chum. Like many other sanctuaries, Wat Si Chum was originally surrounded by a moat. The main structure is dominated by a breathtaking statue of the Buddha in a seated position. The huge stucco image is one of the largest in Thailand, measuring 37 ft from knee to knee. Enter the mondop through the passage inside the left inner wall. Keep your eyes on the ceiling: more than 50 engraved slabs illustrate scenes from the *Jataka,* which are stories about the previous lives of Lord Buddha.

⑮ Wat Sri Sawai. Sukhothai's oldest structure may be this Khmer-style structure, with three prangs—similar to those found in Lopburi—surrounded by a laterite wall. (Laterite, made from red porous soil that hardens when exposed to air, is the building material used most often in Sukhothai.) The many stucco Hindu images and scenes suggest that Sri Sawai was probably first a Hindu temple, later converted to a Buddhist monastery. Historians believe that Brahmanism probably played an important role throughout the Sukhothai period.

⑲ Wat Traphang Thong Lang. The square mondop of Wat Traphang Thong Lang is the main sanctuary, the outer walls of which boast beautiful stucco figures in niches—some of Sukhothai's finest art. The north side depicts the Buddha returning to preach to his wife. On the west side, he preaches to his father and relatives. Note the figures on the south wall, where the story of the Buddha is accompanied by an angel descending from Heaven.

Dining and Lodging

There are many inexpensive cafés near the old city. Several low-priced guest houses are also nearby, but most visitors stay in the new city, where there are a number of good eateries in and around the covered marketplace.

$ ✕ **Dream Café.** While waiting for your meal, you can feast your eyes
★ on the extraordinary collection of antiques that fill this charming restaurant. This is Sukhothai's finest restaurant, and possibly the best in the entire Central Plains. The rustic tile floor, the glowing teak tables and chairs, and the nooks and crannies packed with fascinating odds and ends—everything from old lamps to fine ceramics—combine in a perfect harmony. The traditional food is excellent, too. If you can't bear to leave this paradise, behind the restaurant are five romantic rooms, aptly named Cocoon House, set in a fairy-tale garden. ✉ *86/1 Singhawat Rd., 64000,* ☎ *055/612081,* 🇫🇦🇽 *055/622157. MC, V.*

$ ⊡ **Pailyn Sukhothai Hotel.** The staff is proud to point out that King
★ Bhumibol Adulyadej has spent the night at the Pailyn Sukhothai Hotel, the only luxury hotel near Sukhothai. It's an imaginatively styled building, incorporating a typical stepped roof. Large, comfortable rooms surround an airy central atrium. The pool is a welcome sight after a day exploring the dusty ruins. For dinner, the Supankanlaya restaurant serves Thai and Chinese cuisine. Halfway between New Sukhothai and the old city, it makes up for its isolated location with a free chauffeur service. ✉ *Jarodvithithong Rd., 64210,* ☎ *055/613310; 02/215-5640 in Bangkok;* 🇫🇦🇽 *055/613317. 238 rooms. 3 restaurants, minibars, cable TV, pool, health club, massage, sauna, travel services. MC, V.*

$ ⊡ **Rajthanee Hotel.** The traditional Thai entrance of this well-run hotel leads into a modern building filled with comfortable rooms. There's a terrace where you can also enjoy a Thai whisky and the stylish restaurant that serves good Asian cuisine. ✉ *229 Jarodvithitong Rd., 64000,* ☎ *055/611531. 83 rooms. Restaurant, café, minibars, cable TV, lounge, meeting rooms. AE, MC, V.*

$ ⊞ **Thai Village House.** This cluster of thatched bungalows is usually jammed with tour groups. The hotel's advantage is its location—a five-minute bicycle ride from the old city. Rooms, most of which are air-conditioned, have two queen-size beds, but little else. The open-air dining room is pleasantly relaxing. ⊠ *214 Jarodvithithong Rd., Muang Kao, 64000,* ☎ *055/611049 or 055/612075,* ⅏ *055/612583. 123 rooms. Restaurant, shops. MC, V.*

¢ ⊞ **Lotus Village.** The lotus-flower ponds that dot the lush gardens of this attractive Thai-style lodging give the place its name. It's run by a charming French-Thai couple who are happy to help organize tours of Sukhothai and the surrounding area. The teak bungalows—some with fans, others with air-conditioning—are comfortably furnished and have private verandas. The inn is tucked away near the Yom River. It's best reached via Rajuthit Road, which runs along the river from the center of town. There's a breakfast room but no restaurant. ⊠ *170 Ratchathani Rd., 64000,* ☎ *055/621484,* ⅏ *055/621463,* ⅏ *www. lotus-village.com. 10 rooms. Breakfast room, travel services. No credit cards.*

¢ ⊞ **Number 4 Guest House.** It's a bit difficult to find this lodging on the
★ outskirts of town (even taxi drivers sometimes scratch their heads), but once you're here you will wonder how you could have stayed elsewhere. These bamboo bungalows are set in an overgrown garden where golden bananas and scarlet birds of paradise hang just outside your door. Just beyond are seemingly endless rice fields. On your veranda is a comfortable day bed, while inside is delightfully worn antique furniture. There's no dining room, but the hosts are happy to cook you dinner and serve it in the garden. The guest house is west of the Yom River, off Charodvithitong Road. ⊠ *140/4 Soi Khlong Mae Lumpung Rd., 64000,* ☎ *055/610165. 13 rooms. Travel services. No credit cards.*

Si Satchanalai

➋➊ *80 km (50 mi) north of Sukhothai.*

With its expanse of neatly mown lawns, Sukhothai is sometimes criticized for being too well groomed. But Si Satchanalai, spread out on 228 acres on the banks of the Mae Yom River, remains a quiet place with a more ancient, undisturbed atmosphere. This is a place where it isn't difficult to find the ruins of a temple where you won't be disturbed for hours.

Most visitors to Si Satchanalai reach it as part of a tour from Sukhothai (most hotels can set you up with a guide). If you want to go on your own, hop on a bus bound for the town of Sawankhalok. Take a taxi to the historical park, asking the driver to wait while you visit the various temples. You can also tour the site by bicycle or on top of an elephant, if that's your choice of transportation. Accommodations near the park are only relatively expensive bungalows. Most visitors stay in Sukhothai.

Si Satchanalai, a sister city to Sukhothai, was governed by a son of Sukhothai's reigning monarch. Despite its secondary position, the city grew to impressive proportions, and no less than 200 of its temples and monuments survive, most of them in a ruined state but many well worth seeing. Near the entrance, **Wat Chang Lom** shows strong Sri Lankan influences. The 39 elephant buttresses are in much better condition than at the similarly named temple in Sukhothai. The main chedi was completed by 1291; as you climb the stairs that run up the side, you'll find seated images of the Buddha. The second important monument, **Wat Chedi Jet Thaew,** is to the south of Wat Chang Lom. The complex has seven rows of ruined chedis, some with lotus-bud tops that are reminiscent of the larger ones at Sukhothai. The chedis contain the ashes of members of Si Satchanalai's ruling family. **Wat Nang Phya,** to the southeast of Wat Chedi Jet Thaew, has well-preserved floral reliefs on its balustrade and stucco reliefs on the viharn wall. As you leave the park, stop at **Wat Suam Utayan** to see a Si Satchanalai image of Lord Buddha, one of the few still remaining.

Sukhothai grew wealthy on the fine ceramics it produced from the rich earth around the neighboring town of Sawankhalok. The ceramics were so prized that they were offered as gifts from Sukhothai rulers to the imperial courts of China, and they found their way as far as Japan. Fine examples of 1,000-year-old Sawankhalok wares are on display at the **Sawankhalok Museum,** about 1 km (½ mi) from the town. ✉ *Phitsanulok Rd., Sawankhalok.* ☒ *Admission.* ⊙ *Weekdays 10–6, Sat. and Sun. 10–8.*

THE CENTRAL PLAINS A TO Z

To research prices, get advice from other travelers, and book travel arrangements, visit www.fodors.com.

AIR TRAVEL
All air traffic to the Central Plains radiates from Bangkok, with the exception of daily flights from Chiang Mai to Sukhothai and thrice-weekly flights between Chiang Mai and Phitsanulok, all on Thai Airways. There are several Thai Airways flights each day from Bangkok to Sukhothai and Phitsanulok. Sukhothai is roughly equidistant between its own airport (a beautiful open-air terminal built by Bangkok Airways but also used by Thai Airways) and the one in Phitsanulok, which is less than an hour away by taxi or bus.
➤ CARRIER: **Bangkok Airways** (✉ 10 Moo 1, Jarodvithithong Rd., Sukhothai, ☎ 055/633266).

AIRPORTS
There are two airports in the Central Plains that make exploring this out-of-the-way area far easier. In Sukhothai, the terminal is about 10 km (6 mi) from town. The terminal at Phitsanulok is 25 (15 mi) from the city center.

BUS TRAVEL TO AND FROM THE CENTRAL PLAINS
Most of the towns in the Central Plains are served by direct buses from Bangkok. Buses bound for Ayutthaya and Lopburi depart from Bangkok's Northern Bus Terminal every 30 minutes between 6 AM and 7 PM. Minibuses frequently leave Ayutthaya's Chao Prom Market for Bang Pa-In beginning at 6:30 AM. The 50-minute trip costs B10.

Buses to Sukhothai depart from Bangkok's Northern Bus Terminal and Chiang Mai's Arcade Bus Station. Fares are remarkably low—never more than B200 for the longest journey.
➤ BUS STATIONS: **Ayutthaya** (✉ Naresuan Rd., ☎ no phone). **Phitsanulok** (✉ Singhawat Rd. and Ekethosarot Rd., ☎ 055/242061). **Sukhothai** (✉ Prasertpong Rd., ☎ no phone).

BUS TRAVEL WITHIN THE CENTRAL PLAINS
From Phitsanulok, there is a bus to Sukhothai that departs every half hour. From Sukhothai, buses to the old city depart from Charodvithitong Road.

CAR RENTALS
Two major rental agencies, Avis and Budget, are located at the airport in Phitsanulok.

➤ AGENCIES: **Avis** (✉ Phitsanulok Airport, ☎ 055/242060). **Budget** (✉ Phitsanulok Airport, ☎ 055/258556).

CAR TRAVEL

A car is a good way to explore the archaeological sites around Phitsanulok. The roads leading to Sukhothai, Sri Satchanalai, and other sites are paved and reasonably well maintained. You may, however, prefer to hire a car and driver, as some of the roads are not marked.

EMERGENCIES

There are reliable hospitals in both Ayutthaya, Phitsanulok, and Sukhothai. In Ayutthaya, there's the Ratcha Thani Hospital. In Phitsanulok, try Phitsanuwej Hospital on Khun Piren Road.

AYUTTHAYA

➤ EMERGENCY NUMBERS: **Ratcha Thani Hospital** (✉ 111 Moo 3, Rotchana Rd., ☎ 035/335555). **Tourist Police** (☎ 035/242352).

PHITSANULOK

➤ EMERGENCY NUMBER: **Police** (☎ 055/240199).
➤ HOSPITAL: **Phitsanuwej Hospital** (✉ Khun Piren Rd., ☎ 055/252762).

SUKHOTHAI

➤ EMERGENCY NUMBER: **Police** (☎ 055/611199).
➤ HOSPITAL: **Sukhothai Hospital** (✉ Charodvithitong Rd., ☎ 055/611782).

HEALTH

The same precautions apply in the Central Plains as in the rest of Thailand. Drink bottled water and avoid fruits and vegetables that may have been washed in tainted water. Foods from street vendors and night markets should be fine if you make sure they are still hot. In most cases the foods are cooked to order, so you can observe whether the seller is cutting corners.

Locals will proudly state that no cases of malaria have been reported for years. There are still plenty of mosquitoes, so bring along plenty of repellent. If there are no screens in the window of your hotel, a mosquito net will probably be hung over the bed. If not, ask for one.

MAIL AND SHIPPING

The employees at most post offices are invariably friendly and helpful, often delighting in covering your mail with the colorful pictorial stamps that are a speciality in Thailand. Allow for at least a week for post to reach addresses in the United States. All hotels catering to international travelers will mail your letters, which is an easier option than seeking out the local post office.

➤ POST OFFICES: **Ayutthaya** (✉ U-Thong Rd). **Phitsanulok** (✉ 1145 Buddhabucha Rd.). **Sukhothai** (✉ Nikhon Kasem Rd.).

MONEY MATTERS

You'll have no difficulty at all finding ATM machines in Phitsanulok and Sukhothai. They're easily identifiable by blue-on-white signs. In smaller towns you might have to seek out the foreign exchange counter of a local bank. They will exchange foreign currency, particularly U. S. dollars, and cash traveler's checks. There's usually a nominal fee.

TOUR OPERATORS

The Chao Phraya Express Boat Company runs a Sunday excursion to Bang Pa-In Summer Palace. It departs at 8 AM and arrives in time for lunch. On the return trip, the boat stops at the Bang Sai Folk Arts and Craft Centre before arriving in Bangkok at 5:30 PM. The trip costs B350.

In Sukhothai, Dhanasith Kampempool's one-man agency is *the* place to go for a tour of the area. Dhanasith (or Tom, as he prefers to be called) studied and worked for more than 20 years in the United States. His English is, of course, perfect. His office is next to the Vitoon Guesthouse in Old Sukhothai: just tell Tom what you want to see and where you want to go and he'll arrange it.

➤ TOUR COMPANIES: **Chao Phraya Express Boat Company** (✉ Maharat Pier, 2/58 Aroon-Amarin Rd., Bangkok, ☎ 02/222–5330). **Dhanasith Kampempool** (✉ 49 Moo 3, Jarodvithithong Rd., Old Sukhothai, ☎ 055/697045 or 055/633397, ℻ 055/633397).

TRAIN TRAVEL

The Northeastern Line, which heads into Isan, has frequent service from Bangkok to Ayutthaya and Lopburi. Beginning at 4:30 AM, trains depart frequently from Bangkok's Hualamphong Station, arriving in Ayutthaya 80 minutes later. Since Don Muang International Airport lies between the two cities, many travelers returning from Ayutthaya get off at the airport to fly to their next destination.

Trains from Bangkok's Hualamphong Station regularly make the hour-long trip to Bang Pa-In Station, where you can catch a minibus to the palace. Three morning and two afternoon trains depart for the three-hour trip to Lopburi. Trains back to Bangkok run in the early and late afternoon.

To reach Phitsanulok, the closest station to Sukhothai and Sri Satchanalai, trains depart from Bangkok and Chiang Mai. Either way, the journey takes approximately six hours from either city. Some trains between Bangkok and Phitsanulok stop at Lopburi and Ayutthaya, enabling you to visit these two historic cities en route.

A special express train between Bangkok and Phitsanulok takes just over five hours. Tickets for this service, which cost considerably more, are purchased at a separate booth inside the stations at Bangkok or Phitsanulok. Reservations are essential.

VISITOR INFORMATION

The Tourist Authority of Thailand has offices in Ayutthaya and Phitsanulok. Here you can find helpful maps and brochures.

➤ TOURIST INFORMATION: **Ayutthaya** (✉ Si Sanphet Rd., ☎ 035/246076). **Phitsanulok** (✉ Sithamtraipidok Rd., ☎ 055/252742).

4 NORTHERN THAILAND

The mist-shrouded mountains of Northern Thailand are a gateway to the ancient world. The walled city of Chiang Mai, once capital of the Lanna empire, still shines with 12th-century temples pointing toward the heavens. To the north is Chiang Rai, which leads to the legendary Golden Triangle. Here you can seek out hill tribes that live as they have for centuries. But past and present coexist in much of the region. In Mae Hong Son you will see mahouts and their elephants working alongside bulldozers carving out new highways.

Updated by
Robert Tilley

THE FABLED **"GOLDEN TRIANGLE"** is an irresistible draw for many visitors to Thailand. This mountainous region, bordered by Myanmar to the west and Laos to the east, was once ruled by the opium warlord Khun Sa. The opium trade still flourishes in the more remote parts of the region, despite determined efforts by government officials to stamp it out.

Northern Thailand, once the home of the Lanna people, could not be mistaken for another region. Set foot in Chiang Mai, the so-called "rose of the north," and you feel as if you're in another country. The old walled city with newer neighborhoods spreading in every direction is not a smaller version of Bangkok, but a bustling metropolis in its own right. Chiang Mai lays claim to a longer history, richer culture, tastier cuisine, and friendlier people than the country's capital—opinions that only longtime visitors can confirm or dismiss. Looking to escape urban life altogether? To the north is Chiang Rai, a regal capital 30 years before Chiang Mai was built. This quieter, less-developed town is slowly becoming a base for exploring the country's northernmost reaches.

From Chiang Mai, the highways and byways extend into mountains that appear on the map but are often hidden in the haze that descends on the city for much of the year. Chiang Mai is an ideal base for exploring the hill tribe villages where people live as they have for centuries. The communities closest to the city have been overrun by tourists, but if you strike out on your own with a good map you may still find some that haven't become theme parks. Most of the villages are bustling craft centers where the colorful fabrics you see displayed in Bangkok shop windows take shape before your eyes. The elaborately costumed villagers descend into Chiang Mai and Chiang Rai every evening to sell their wares in the night markets that transform thoroughfares into tented bazaars.

There's also plenty of excitement, from riding elephants into the mountains to rafting down the rivers that cut deep into the jungle-swathed hills. Here you'll find Thailand's highest mountain, Doi Inthanon, regarded as an eastern buttress of the Himalayas. You can trek to the foot of the mountain and still be back at your hotel in time for a sumptuous dinner followed by a night on the town.

Pleasures and Pastimes

Dining

The cuisine in the northern part of the country differs significantly from the rest of Thailand, although most restaurants serve both types. Locals prefer the glutinous *kao nio* (sticky rice), using handfuls of it to scoop up delectable sauces and curries, but you'll have no problem ordering plain *kao suay* (steamed rice). Popular *hang led* (red curry) is tasty, as are *sai ua* (crispy pork sausage) and *mu yo* (spicy sausage). Noodles of nearly every variety can be bought for a few baht from food stalls everywhere, and some fried-noodle dishes have found their way onto many menus. Western food is served at all larger hotels, although the local version of an "American" or "English" breakfast can sometimes be a bit of a shock.

CATEGORY	COST*
$$$$	over B400 (over US$10)
$$$	B300–B400 (US$7.50–$10)
$$	B200–B300 (US$5–$7.50)
$	B100–B200 (US$2.50–5)
¢	under B100 (under US$2.50)

per person, for a main course at dinner

Lodging

Chiang Mai's luxury hotels are the equal of any in Bangkok, both in terms of comfort and amenities. One of them, an architectural wonder called the Regent Chiang Mai, is among the finest in Southeast Asia. Resorts outside Chiang Mai offer a range of outdoor activities that surpasses those in Bangkok. Golfers, in particular, are sure to be pleased. Resorts in nearby towns such as Chiang Rai, Chiang Saen, and Mae Sai are less expensive, and those in distant villages like Phrae and Nan are downright cheap.

Smaller hotels and guest houses range from simple accommodations with fan-cooled rooms and shared baths to stylish establishments with lovely gardens and homey rooms. The cheapest can be quite simple indeed—perhaps a bit shabby, but never dirty—while spending a bit more will get you home-away-from-home comfort.

CATEGORY	COST*
$$$$	over B6,000 (over US$150)
$$$	B4,000–B6,000 (US$100–$150)
$$	B2,000–B4,000 (US$50–$100)
$	B1,000–B2,000 (under US$50)
¢	under B1,000 (under US$25)

All prices are for a standard double room, excluding tax.

Shopping

The region is world famous for its silks, of course, but a stroll through the night markets of Chiang Mai and Chiang Rai will uncover an astonishing range of handicrafts, many of them originating in the nearby hill tribe villages. Hand-painted ceramics, delicately woven fabrics, carefully tooled leather—the list is almost endless. Chiang Mai has a silversmith district where exquisite pieces are found for incredibly low prices. The city is also famous for its lacquered umbrellas, and a visit to one of the local workshops should be on every itinerary. Some of the smaller border towns have unusual imported goods—in Chiang Khong, for instance, you can find fine lace from Laos. Mai Sai, on the Myanmar border, is the place to find Burmese rubies and other precious and semi-precious stones.

Trekking

Trekking is more than a popular pastime in Northern Thailand—it's big business. Scores of private travel agencies offer trips of one to seven days into the mountains, many offering stays in hill tribe villages so you can experience their simple way of life. Some of the more accessible villages, particularly those inhabited by the long-necked women of the Karen people, have consequently come to resemble theme parks. Be clear about what you expect when booking a trek. Insist on the real thing, perhaps offering a bit more to achieve it. Better still, ask your hotel to recommend a good local guide. Gather as much information as you can from those who have just returned from a trek. Their advice will save you time, money, and frustration.

Exploring Northern Thailand

Chiang Mai, Thailand's second-largest city, is the region's most popular destination for travelers. To the south you'll find the dazzling wats and ancient architecture of Lamphun and Lampang, while to the southwest is Doi Inthanon National Park, dominated by the country's highest mountain. Northwest of Chiang Mai is the little market town of Mae Hong Son, a good base for visits to the villages of the Karen people. Northeast of Chiang Mai is the so-called "Golden Triangle," where the frontiers of Thailand, Myanmar, and Laos meet. Chiang Rai, a town older even than Chiang Mai, is the place to go for treks into the region's wild countryside.

Great Itineraries

To get a feeling for Northern Thailand, it would be ideal to spend at least a week or two. This would allow time to make a trek to one or two hill tribe villages.

IF YOU HAVE 2–3 DAYS

Numbers in the text correspond to numbers in the margin and on the Northern Thailand, Chiang Mai, Mae Hong Son, and Chiang Rai maps.

Spend your first day exploring the well-ordered streets of ⊞ **Chiang Mai** ①–⑫. In the morning you can poke around Wat Phra Singh and the other sights in the Old City. Check out the crafts stores that line several kilometers of Sankamphaeng Road in the afternoon. After a hard day of shopping, treat yourself to the luxury of a Thai massage. On the second day rise early and drive up to **Wat Phra That Doi Suthep** ⑦, the breathtaking temple overlooking Chiang Mai. On the way back, visit the Elephant Training Centre at Mae Sa. In the afternoon, stop by **Wat Chedi Yot** ⑨ and the **National Museum** ⑩. For the evening's entertainment, wander among the stalls at the justifiably famous Night Bazaar. If you have a day to spare, head south to see the wats of **Lamphun** ⑭ and the markets of **Pa Sang** ⑮, then continue on to see the Burmese and Chinese architecture at ⊞ **Lampang** ⑯.

IF YOU HAVE 5 DAYS

On your first two days, cover the major sights in and around ⊞ **Chiang Mai** ①–⑫. On the third day, fly to ⊞ **Mae Hong Son** ⑳–㉓ and take a tour of a nearby Karen village. Fly to ⊞ **Chiang Rai** ㉔–㉖ the next day, making sure to take a ride on the Mae Kok River in a long-tail boat. On the fifth day make a circular tour to **Chiang Saen** ㉗ to see its lovely wats, then to **Ban Sop Ruak** ㉙ to learn about the opium lords, and finally to **Mae Sai** ㉚ for a look at Burmese crafts.

IF YOU HAVE 7 DAYS

If you are lucky enough to have a week or more in Northern Thailand, you have plenty of time to stay for a few nights with a hill tribe family. Treks to these mountain villages, most often on the back of an elephant, can be arranged from Chiang Mai, Chiang Rai, Mae Hong Son, and other communities.

When to Tour Northern Thailand

Northern Thailand has three seasons. The region is hottest and driest from March to May. The rainy season runs from June to October, with the wettest weather in September. Unpaved roads are often impassable at this time of year. The best season to visit is in the winter months from November to March. At higher altitudes it can then be quite cold in the evening, so take a sweater if you are heading to the mountains.

CHIANG MAI AND ENVIRONS

Because of the distance, most visitors to Northern Thailand decide to fly from Bangkok to Chiang Mai. The 70-minute flight to Chiang Mai is relatively inexpensive, and the city's splendid airport is conveniently located. The overnight train from Bangkok is comfortable, especially if you insist on a first-class sleeper. Luxury buses, with television and fully reclining seats, offer the cheapest mode of transportation.

Regional buses connect Chiang Mai to nearby towns such as Lamphun and Lampang, which make them easy excursions. The Golden Trian-

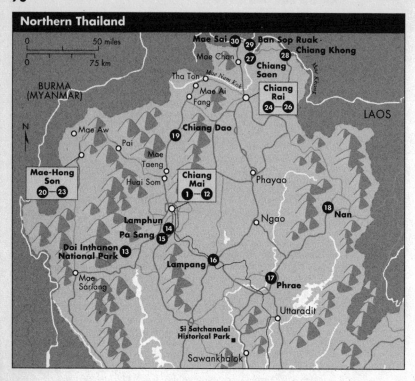

Northern Thailand

gle and the mountains near the Myanmar border, home of many hill tribes, are farther afield, but are readily accessible by air or by bus.

Chiang Mai

696 km (430 mi) north of Bangkok.

Chiang Mai's rich history stretches back 700 years to the time when several small tribes, under King Mengrai, banded together to form a new nation called Anachak Lanna Thai. Their first capital was Chiang Rai, but after three decades they moved it to the fertile plains near the Mae Ping River to a place they called Napphaburi Sri Nakornping Chiang Mai.

The Lanna Thai eventually lost its independence to Ayutthaya and, later, to Burma. Not until 1774—when the Burmese were finally driven out—did the region revert to the Thai kingdom. After that, the region developed independently of southern Thailand. Even the language is different, marked by a more relaxed tempo. In the last 50 years the city has grown beyond its original borders; the provincial town has exploded beyond its moat, expanding into the nearby countryside.

The Old City

Chiang Mai's Old City can be explored easily on foot or by bicycle, with the occasional use of tuk-tuks or taxis for trips outside the ancient walls. If you hire a taxi for a day (B1,000–B1,400, depending on mileage), negotiate the price in advance or, better yet, arrange it the evening before and have the driver collect you from your hotel in the morning. Do not pay the driver until you have completed the trip.

Motorcycles are a cheap and popular option. Rental agencies are numerous, and most small hotels have their own agency. A car and driver is the most convenient way to visit the temples outside the city. If you're planning on driving yourself you'll need an international license—and strong nerves. Chiang Mai's traffic is scarcely less dense than Bangkok's, and a well-planned but initially confusing one-way system confounds newcomers.

A GOOD TOUR

Start your tour at the Tha Pae Gate, which leads through the ancient city walls into the oldest part of Chiang Mai. Head west on Ratchadamnoen Road, turning north on Ratchaphakhina Road. After a few blocks you'll reach **Wat Chiang Man** ①, the oldest temple in Chiang Mai. Check out the pair of Buddha statues in the viharn. Backtrack down Ratchaphakhina Road and head west on Ratchadamnoen Road. On Phra Pokklao Road, between Rajmankha and Ratchadamnoen roads, stands **Wat Chedi Luang** ②. Most striking is the ruined chedi, destroyed by lightning before it was completed. A bit farther west is **Wat Phra Singh** ③, whose colorfully decorated viharn typified Lanna Thai architecture.

Several other worthwhile temples are outside the city walls. to the east is the serene **Wat Chaimongkol** ④. It's an easy walk from the Tha Pae Gate if the sun isn't too strong. You'll want to take a tuk-tuk to **Wat Suan Dok** ⑤, one of the largest temples in the region. A bit farther away are the verdant grounds of **Wat Umong** ⑥.

TIMING

If you don't venture beyond the city walls, you can see the three main temples in a few hours. If you want to visit the nearby wats, plan on at least half a day.

SIGHTS TO SEE

★ ❹ **Wat Chaimongkol.** Although rarely visited, this small temple is well worth the journey. Located outside the Old City near the Mae Ping River, it has only 18 monks in residence. Its little chedi contains holy relics, but its real beauty lies in the serenity of the grounds. ⊠ *Charoen Prathet Rd.*

★ ❷ **Wat Chedi Luang.** In 1411, King Saen Muang Ma ordered his workers to build a chedi "as high as a dove could fly." He died before the structure was finished, as did the next king. During the reign of the following king, an earthquake knocked down about a third of the 282-ft spire. Wat Chedi Luang is now a superb ruin. Don't miss the naga balustrades at the steps to the viharn, considered the finest of their kind. ⊠ *Phra Pokklao Rd., between Rajmankha and Ratchadamnoen.*

NEED A BREAK?

Chiang Mai has no shortage of massage parlors (the respectable kind) where the aches of a day's strenuous sightseeing can be kneaded away with a traditional massage. The full body massage takes two hours and costs around B200. Your hotel can usually organize either an in-house massage or recommend one of the city's numerous centers. One of the best massage parlors is **O.T. Traditional Thai Massage Center** (⊠ 459/100 Charoenmuang Bazaar, Charoenmuang Rd., ☎ 053/302665). **Petngarm Hat Wast** (⊠ 33/10 Charoen Prathet Rd., ☎ 053/270080), in the Diamond Hotel, offers a range of traditional and herbal massages. Good massages with or without herbs are given at **Suan Samoon Prai** (⊠ 105 Wansingkham Rd., ☎ 053/252716).

❶ **Wat Chiang Man.** Chiang Mai's oldest monastery, dating from 1296, is typical of northern Thai architecture. It has massive teak pillars inside the bot, and two important images of the Buddha sit in the small building to the right of the main viharn. They are supposedly on view only on Sunday, but sometimes the door is unlocked. ⊠ *Ratchaphakhina Rd.*

★ ❸ **Wat Phra Singh.** In the western section of the Old City stands Chiang Mai's principal monastery, Wat Phra Singh. The beautifully decorated wat contains the Phra Singh Buddha, with a serene and benevolent expression that is enhanced by the light filtering in through the tall windows. Note the temple's facades of splendidly carved wood, the elegant teak beams and posts, and the masonry. Don't be surprised if a student monk approaches you—he doubtless wants to practice his English. ⊠ *Phra Singh Rd. and Singharat Rd.*

❺ **Wat Suan Dok.** To the west of the Old City is one of the largest of Chiang Mai's temples, Wat Suan Dok. It is said to have been built on the site where bones of Lord Buddha were found. Some of these relics are believed to be inside the chedi; others were transported to Wat Phra That Doi Suthep. At the back of the viharn is the bot housing Phra Chao Kao, a superb bronze Buddha figure cast in 1504. Chiang Mai aristocrats are buried in stupas in the graveyard. ⊠ *Suthep Rd.*

❻ **Wat Umong.** The most unusual temple in Chiang Mai is Wat Umong, dating from 1296. According to local lore, a monk named Jam liked to go wandering in the forest. This irritated King Ku Na, who often wanted to consult with the sage. So he could seek advice at any time, the king built this wat for the monk in 1380. Along with the temple, tunnels were constructed and decorated with paintings, fragments of which may still be seen. Beyond the chedi is a pond filled with hungry carp. Throughout the grounds the trees are hung with snippets of wisdom such as "Time unused is the longest time." ⊠ *Off Suthep Rd., past Wat Suan Dok.*

Near Chiang Mai

Beyond the highway that surrounds Chiang Mai you will find plenty to hold your attention. The most famous sight is Wat Phra That Doi Suthep, the mountaintop temple that overlooks the city.

A GOOD TOUR

Start out early for an excursion into the mountains to **Wat Phra That Doi Suthep** ⑦, a secluded temple reached by a 304-step staircase flanked by fearsome dragons. Beyond is **Phuping Palace** ⑧, the summer palace of the royal family.

Off the highway that rings Chiang Mai is **Wat Chedi Yot** ⑨, built to resemble the temple where the Buddha achieved enlightenment. From Wat Chedi Yot you can walk to the **National Museum** ⑩, where you'll find a fine collection of ceramics. Nearby is the **Chiang Mai Tribal Museum** ⑪, which has exhibits about the hill tribes that live in the region. If you have kids, consider rounding out the day with a drive to the **Elephant Training Centre** ⑫ in the village of Mae Sa.

TIMING

This tour will take a day, especially if you spend time wandering around the museums.

SIGHTS TO SEE

⑪ **Chiang Mai Tribal Museum.** Rachanangkla Park is home to this museum holding more than 1,000 pieces of traditional crafts from the hill tribes living in the region. The varied collection—farming implements, colorful embroidery, weapons, hunting traps, and musical instruments—is one of the finest in the country. ⊠ *Chang Puak Rd.,* ☎ *053/210872.* ⊒ *Admission.* ☉ *Daily 9–4.*

☾ ⑫ **Elephant Training Centre.** Animal shows aren't everybody's idea of fun, but the Elephant Training Centre, about 20 km (12 mi) northwest of Chiang Mai, is actually quite entertaining. The big fellows in the cast seem to enjoy showing off their skills. They certainly delight in the dip

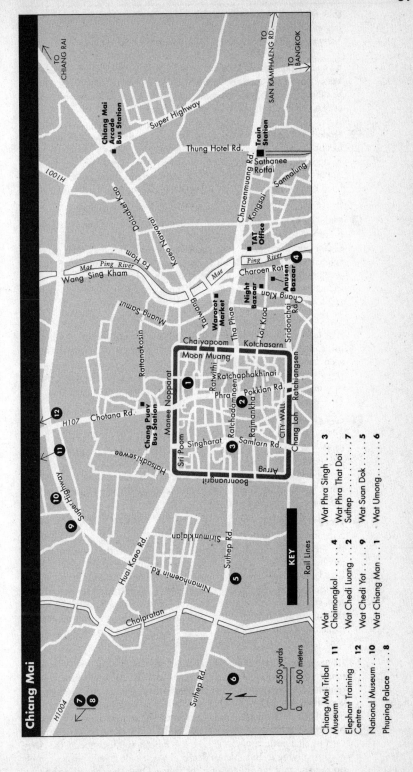

Chiang Mai

TO CHIANG RAI

TO SAN KAMPHAENG RD.

TO BANGKOK

Super Highway

Chiang Mai Arcade Bus Station

Thung Hotel Rd.

Train Station

Sathanee Rotfai

H1001

Daisdet Kao

Kaeo Nawrat

Charoenmuang Rd

Kongsai

Sannalung

To Hom

Mae Ping River

Wang Sing Kham

Mae

Muang Samui

Talwang

Warorot Market

Ping River

TAT Office

Charoen Rat

Night Bazaar

Anusen Bazaar

Chang Klan Rd.

Tha Phae

Loi Kroa

Sridonchai Rd.

Chang Loh Ratchangsen

Rattanakosin

Chaiyapoom

Kotchasarn

Moon Muang

Ratchaphakhinai

Raiwithi

Phra

Ratchadamnoen

Rajmankha

Pokklan Rd.

Manee Nopparat

CITY WALL

Chang Puak Bus Station

Chotana Rd.

H107

Singharat

Samlarn Rd.

Sri Poom

Hatsadhisewee

Boonruangrit

Arrug

Sirimunkiajan

Suthep Rd.

Super Highway H1001

Huai Kaeo Rd.

Nimanhaemin Rd.

Cholpratan

Suthep Rd.

H1004

N

550 yards

0

500 meters

0

KEY

—— Rail Lines

Chiang Mai Tribal Museum **11**

Elephant Training Centre..........**12**

National Museum..........**10**

Phuping Palace **8**

Wat Chaimongkol......**4**

Wat Chedi Luang ...**2**

Wat Chedi Yot.....**9**

Wat Chiang Man.....**1**

Wat Phra Singh **3**

Wat Phra That Doi Suthep..........**7**

Wat Suan Dok.....**5**

Wat Umong........**6**

they take in the river before demonstrating log-rolling routines or giving rides around the grounds. ✉ *Mae Sa, between Mae Rim and Sameng.* ☉ *Daily 8:30–noon.* ☏ *B500.*

NEED A BREAK?

If you're visiting the Elephant Training Centre, stop for lunch at **Mae Sa Valley Resort** (✉ Mae Sa, ☎ 053/291051, FAX 053/290017), which has thatched cottages in beautifully tended gardens. The owner's honey-cooked chicken with chili is particularly good.

⑩ National Museum. This northern Thai-style building contains many statues of Lord Buddha, including a bust that measures 10 ft. There's also a huge Buddha footprint of wood with mother-of-pearl inlay. The upper floor's collection includes a bed with mosquito netting that was used by an early prince of Chiang Mai. *Chiang Mai-Lampang Rd.,* ☎ *053/221308.* ☏ *Admission.* ☉ *Wed.–Sun. 9–4.*

⑧ Phuping Palace. The summer residence of the royal family is a serene mansion that shares an exquisitely landscaped park with the more modest mountain retreats of the crown prince and princess. The palace itself cannot be visited, although the gardens are open on Friday, weekends, and public holidays, unless any of the royal family is in residence (usually in January). Gardening enthusiasts will swoon at the sight of the roses—among the lovely blooms is a new variety created by the king himself.

A rough, unpaved road left of the palace brings you after 4 km (2½ mi) to a village called Doi Pui Meo, where most of the Hmong women seem busy creating finely worked textiles. On the mountainside above the village are two tiny museums documenting hill tribe life and the opium trade. ✉ *Off Huai Kaeo Rd., 6 km (4 mi) past Wat Phra That Doi Suthep.*

⑨ Wat Chedi Yot. Wat Photharam Maha Viharn is more commonly known as Wat Chedi Yot, or Seven-Spired Pagoda. Built in 1455, it is a copy of the Mahabodhi temple in Bodh Gaya, India, where the Buddha achieved enlightenment. The seven spires represent the seven weeks that he subsequently spent there. The sides of the chedi have striking bas-relief sculptures of celestial figures. ✉ *Super Hwy. between Huai Kaeo Rd. and Chang Puak Rd.*

★ ⑦ Wat Phra That Doi Suthep. Perched on the top of 3,542-ft Doi Suthep, a mountain 16 km (10 mi) northwest of Chiang Mai that overlooks the city. You can find songthaews to take you on the 30-minute drive at Chuang Puak Gate or at the Central Department Store on Huai Kaeo Road. When you arrive, you are faced with an arduous but exhilarating climb up the broad staircase leading to the temple compound. The 304-step staircase is flanked by 16th-century tiled balustrades taking the customary form of *nagas* (mythical snakes believed to control the irrigation waters in rice fields). If you find the ascent too daunting, there's also a short ride up the funicular railway.

As in so many chapters of Thai history, an elephant is closely involved in the foundation of Wat Phra That, Northern Thailand's most revered temple and one of only a few enjoying royal patronage. The elephant was dispatched from Chiang Mai carrying religious relics from Wat Suan Dok. Instead of ambling off into the open countryside, it stubbornly climbed up Doi Suthep. When it finally came to rest, and after turning in a pattern of circles given symbolic significance by the party accompanying it, the solemn decision was made to establish a temple on the site that would contain the relics. Over the centuries the temple compound grew into the glittering assembly of chedis, bots, viharns, and frescoed cloisters you see today. The vast terrace, usually smothered with flowers, commands a breathtaking view of Chiang Mai, spread out like an apron on the plain below.

Constructing the temple was quite a feat—until 1935 there was no paved road to the temple. Workers and pilgrims alike had to slog through thick jungle. The road was the result of a vast community project—individual villages throughout the Chiang Mai region contributed the labor, each laying 1,300-ft sections. ⊠ *Off Huai Kaeo Rd., west of Chiang Mai.*

Dining

All the top hotels serve good food, but for the best Thai cuisine go to the restaurants in town. Several good restaurants serving northern Thai cuisine are across from the Rincome Hotel on Nimanhaemin Road, about 1½ km (1 mi) northwest of downtown. Also try the food at the Anusan Market, found near the Night Bazaar.

$ ✕ **Antique House.** Built in 1870, this teak house is one of Chiang
★ Mai's true treasures. It's furnished with the antiques from Chiang Mai's finest shops. If you like the chair you're sitting on or the table in front of you, it's possible to add to your (surprisingly modest) bill an order for a replica from a local workshop. The menu, of course, is authentic northern cuisine. A big surprise is the wine list—small but very interesting, with some real finds for oenophiles. ⊠ *71 Charoen Prathet Rd.,* ☎ *053/276810,* FAX *053/213058. MC.*

$ ✕ **Chiengmai Gymkhana Club.** The son of the author of *Anna and the King of Siam* was among the founders of Chiang Mai's delightfully eccentric Chiengmai Gymkhana Club. Harking back to when it was founded, the club insists on keeping the spelling of the city used back in 1898. Polo isn't played as often now, but a very horsey crowd gathers regularly at the restaurant for lunch and dinner. Visitors are more than welcome. The food is remarkably good, with a variety of local and foreign dishes. Sporty types can enjoy a round of golf on the nine-hole course or a set or two of tennis. ⊠ *349 Chiangmai-Lamphun Rd.,* ☎ *053/241035 or 053/247352. No credit cards.*

$ ✕ **The Gallery.** This riverside restaurant doubles as an art gallery, so you can admire outstanding contemporary works while waiting for your order. It's a very civilized place indeed, filled with choice antiques. There are nightly performances of classical northern music by a small orchestra. If the music isn't your thing, you can escape to a quiet table on one of the terraces descending to the Mae Ping River. Don't miss the *nam phrik ong* (spicy pork curry). ⊠ *25–29 Charoen Rat Rd.,* ☎ *053/248601. AE, DC, MC, V.*

$ ✕ **The Good View.** Of the three terraced restaurants along the Mae Ping River, this one in the middle is the prettiest. It also has the best views, either from the shaded deck outside the dining room or from any of the quiet nooks down toward the water. A broad menu with both Thai and Western dishes should satisfy everyone. ⊠ *13 Charoen Rat Rd.,* ☎ *053/302764. MC, V.*

$ ✕ **Mango Tree Café.** A mango-yellow sign welcomes you to this small restaurant, where you can sip a coffee and leaf through one of the newspapers and magazines or settle in for a full meal. The atmosphere isn't your typical Thai, but the menu is—try the fried fish with chilli sauce or the curried crab. ⊠ *8/2 Loi-Kroh Rd.,* ☎ *053/208292. No credit cards.*

$ ✕ **Nang Nuan.** Although this sprawling restaurant has plenty of tables indoors, it's much more pleasant to dine on the terrace overlooking the Mae Ping River. Because it's 3 km (2 mi) south of the city, you'll need to take a tuk-tuk, but the *tom kha gai* (shrimp soup) and the *yam nua* (beef salad) are worth the trip. Grilled charcoal steaks and fresh seafood (displayed in bubbling tanks) are also on the menu. ✉ *27/2 Ko Klang Rd., Nonghoy,* ☎ *053/281955. AE, DC, MC, V.*

$ ✗ **Riverside.** Housed in a century-old teak house on the bank of the Mae Ping River, this casual restaurant serves Western favorites given some extra zing by the Thai chef. The conversation-laden atmosphere attracts young Thais as well as Westerners, and with lots of beer flowing the food gets only partial attention. Choice tables are on the deck, where you're treated to views of Wat Phra That on the peaks of Doi Suthep in the distance. There's live light jazz and pop music after 7 PM. ✉ *9–11 Charoen Rat Rd.,* ☎ *053/243239. Reservations not accepted. No credit cards.*

$ ✗ **Whole Earth.** On the second floor of an attractive old house in a garden, this longtime favorite serves delicious and healthy foods. It's mostly vegetarian fare, but there are a few meat dishes for the carnivorous, such as *kai tahkhrai* (fried chicken with lemon and garlic). Many of the favorites here, including the tasty eggplant masala, are Indian dishes. The dining room is air-conditioned, and the terrace that surrounds it takes full advantage of any breezes. The service is sometimes slow. ✉ *88 Sridonchai Rd.,* ☎ *053/282463. Reservations not accepted. No credit cards.*

¢ ✗ **Arun Rai.** Chef Khun Paichit smiles when she says that some travelers have been so taken with her food that they return again and again during their stays in Chiang Mai. For more than 30 years she has prepared such traditional northern dishes as frogs' legs fried with ginger, adding from time to time to a menu that has expanded at the same rate as her very popular restaurant. Try the *tabong* (boiled bamboo shoots fried in batter) and *sai ua* (pork sausage with herbs). ✉ *45 Kotchasarn Rd.,* ☎ *053/276947. Reservations not accepted. No credit cards.*

¢ ✗ **Ban Suan.** A short tuk-tuk ride from downtown, this northern-style teak house is nestled in a peaceful garden. The carefully prepared food is typical of the region. Try the hot Chiang Mai sausage, broccoli in oyster sauce, and shrimp-and-vegetable soup. ✉ *51/3 San Kamphaeng Rd.,* ☎ *053/242116. Reservations essential. No credit cards.*

¢ ✗ **By the Pond.** At this lakeside retreat you can hire a rod and reel and fish all day, then enjoy your catch when it's served up in the rustic restaurant. Even if you're no angler this is a peaceful place to withdraw from the hustle and bustle of Chiang Mai. If you decide to stay the night, you can rent a bungalow for B400. The restaurant is near the Chiengmai Gymkhana Club, about 7 km (4 mi) south of the city. ✉ *225 Moo 3, Tambon Nongpheung,* ☎ *01/765–7267. No credit cards.*

¢ ✗ **Hong Tauw Inn.** An intimate atmosphere makes you want to linger here as you sample dishes from Northern Thailand and from the Central Plains. Excellent soups, crispy *pla mee krob* (fried fish with chili), and *nam phrik ong* (minced pork with chili paste and tomatoes) are among the popular dishes. ✉ *95/17–18 Nantawan Arcade, Nimanhaemin Rd.,* ☎ *053/218333. MC, V.*

¢
★ ✗ **Huen Phen.** The small rooms in this restaurant, once a private home, are full of old handicrafts that are typical of the region. Be sure to browse through each of the dining rooms before selecting a table either inside or out among the plants of the garden. Make sure to study the extensive menu, as the choices are endless. The *kaeng hang lae* (northern pork curry) with *kao neeu* (sticky rice) is a specialty. The *larb nua* (spicy ground beef fried with herbs) and deep-fried pork ribs are two more good dishes you won't want to miss. ✉ *112 Rachamongka Rd.,* ☎ *053/277103. MC, V.*

¢
★ ✗ **Kaiwan.** Not many tourists come here, but the food is held in high esteem by locals. The best place to sit is upstairs at one of the tables under the stars. Try the not-so-spicy *kaeng mat sa man* (beef curry) or

the zesty fried fish (*pla tot na phrik*). ⊠ *181 Nimanhaemin Rd. Soi 9*, ☎ *053/221147. MC, V.*

¢ ✕ **Len Pae.** If you've been busy shopping along San Kamphaeng Road and are looking for a relaxing place for lunch, try this restaurant floating on an artificial lake. Gentle breezes off the water keep the temperatures comfortable. The choicest tables are on the piers extending into the lake. The menu is typical northern fare, which means a variety of spicy sausages and fried fish. If you want something less spicy, try one of the Chinese entrées. ⊠ *114 Moo 2 Sanklang, Chiang Mai–San Kamphaeng Rd.,* ☎ *053/338641. No credit cards.*

Lodging

Chiang Mai's top hotels rival those in Bangkok, with prices about half what you'd expect to pay in the capital (although in January and February surcharges close the gap). The west side of Chiang Mai, towards Wat Phra That Doi Suthep, has attracted several of the most expensive hotels; it's a quieter part of the city, but also far from many points of interest. Unlike Bangkok, the luxury hotels do not enjoy a monopoly on river frontage, and some charming and modestly priced guest houses are right on the water. There are also small hotels within the walls of the Old City that are cheap and ideally located for sightseeing.

Some taxi and tuk-tuk drivers will try to get you to change your hotel for one they recommend (which gives them a commission). Remain firm and insist on being taken to your original destination.

$$$$ ★ 🏨 **Regent Chiang Mai.** A true showplace, the Regent Chiang Mai ranks as one of the most beautiful hotels in all of Southeast Asia. The majestic resort sits amid 20 acres of tropical gardens above the lush Mae Rim Valley, looking out over rice paddies to the mountains beyond. The accommodations are in clusters of Lanna-style buildings that reflect the region's architectural heritage. Each suite has an outdoor *sala* (gazebo), ideal for breakfast and cocktails. Rooms of polished teak are furnished with richly colored fabrics and traditional art. The restaurant, which serves beautifully presented Thai dishes, has sweeping views of the valley. ⊠ *Mae Rim-Samoeng Old Rd., 50180,* ☎ *053/298181; 800/545–4000 in the U.S;* FAX *053/298189,* WEB *www.regenthotels.com. 67 suites. 2 restaurants, room service, minibars, cable TV, 2 tennis courts, pool, health club, bar, laundry service, business services. AE, DC, MC, V.*

$$$ 🏨 **Imperial Mae Ping Hotel.** Festooned with lights sweeping down from the building's towering heights, the Imperial Mae Ping Hotel truly sparkles. In the vast courtyard below you can enjoy a delicious buffet dinner, and in the well-tended garden bands drown out any noise from the street. Colorfully dressed women perform traditional dances at the far end of the garden. Inside the massive hotel are three more restaurants serving European, Chinese, and Japanese cuisine. With 371 modern rooms to fill, the hotel caters to those on package tours. ⊠ *153 Sridonchai Rd., 50100,* ☎ *053/270160; 02/261–9460 in Bangkok;* FAX *053/270181,* WEB *www.imperial-hotels.com. 371 rooms. 4 restaurants, coffee shop, room service, minibars, cable TV, pool, massage, bar, beer garden, laundry service, meeting rooms, travel services. AE, DC, MC, V.*

$$–$$$ 🏨 **Royal Chiangmai Golf Resort.** Golfers flock to this luxurious resort in the hills about 25 km (18 mi) outside Chiang Mai. Tired travelers can pamper themselves with massages and other treatments. The luxuriously appointed rooms, in gleaming white wings that embrace a large swimming pool, overlook the nearby mountains. ⊠ *169 Moo 5, Prao Rd., 5000,* ☎ *053/849301; 02/233–7950 in Bangkok;* FAX *053/849310,* WEB *www.royalchiangmai.co.th. 60 rooms. Restaurant, 18-hole golf course, pool, gym, massage, sauna, airport shuttle. AE, MC, V.*

$$ ▥ **Chiang Inn.** Although it's not far from the Night Bazaar, the Chiang Inn is set back from the street so you can escape the noise and the crowds. The rooms are spacious and decorated with handwoven fabrics. The more formal La Grillade serves Thai-influenced French cuisine that has proven popular with local shoppers and business executives. The casual Ron Thong Coffee House serves local and foreign dishes. ✉ *100 Chang Khlan Rd., 50000,* ☎ *053/270070; 02/251–6883 in Bangkok;* FAX *053/274299. 190 rooms. 2 restaurants, minibars, cable TV, pool, nightclub, meeting rooms, travel services. AE, DC, MC, V.*

$$ ▥ **Chiang Mai Orchid Hotel.** With teak pillars lining the lobby, the Chiang Mai Orchid is a grand hotel in the old style. The rooms are tastefully furnished and trimmed with hardwoods. The lavish honeymoon suite is often used by the crown prince. You can dine at either the formal Le Pavillon, which serves French fare, or at Puping, where you can enjoy Chinese favorites. The more informal Mae Rim Café features a buffet. You'll want to stop for a cocktail in the lobby bar or the cozy Opium Den. The hotel is a 10-minute taxi ride from the center of Chiang Mai. ✉ *100–102 Huai Kaeo Rd., 50000,* ☎ *053/222099; 02/245–3973 Bangkok reservations;* FAX *053/221625. 364 rooms. 2 restaurants, coffee shop, room service, minibars, cable TV, pool, hair salon, health club, massage, sauna, 2 bars, laundry service, business services, meeting rooms, travel services. AE, DC, MC, V.*

$$ ▥ **Royal Princess.** This centrally located hotel is ideal if you'd like to step out of the lobby and into the tumult of downtown Chiang Mai. Street vendors are practically at the front door, as the famous Night Bazaar is barely a block away. The rooms are short on natural light, making them a little dreary, but they are clean and comfortable. The staff is well trained and helpful. The cocktail lounge has a pianist in the evenings, and the restaurant serves the best Cantonese fare in Chiang Mai. ✉ *112 Chang Rd., 50000,* ☎ *053/281033; 02/233–1130 in Bangkok;* FAX *053/281044,* WEB *www.dusitgroup.com. 200 rooms. 2 restaurants, room service, minibars, cable TV, pool, massage, meeting rooms, airport shuttle, travel services. AE, DC, MC, V.*

$–$$ ▥ **Paradise Spa Resort.** Nina Boonsirithum graduated from Washington State University with a degree in interior design, and her background shows in the exquisitely attractive layout of this lakeside retreat near Chiang Mai. Ask for one of the special spa rooms, which have huge marble sunken baths and luxurious furnishings. Richly colored fabrics are used throughout, complemented by fine carvings. The airy restaurant has an adjacent antiques shop stocked with items that caught Boonsirithum's expert eye. ✉ *43/1 Moo 6, Tambon Maerim, 50000,* ☎ *053/860463,* FAX *053/860464. 50 rooms. Restaurant, cable TV, bar. MC, V.*

$ ▥ **Gap's House.** This collection of traditional wooden houses resembles a little village within the walls of the Old City. Room 5 is among the best, as it overlooks a tiny vegetable garden. A lively rooster and a bilingual mynah bird add to the rural atmosphere. The rooms are furnished with an odd assortment of antiques, giving the place a well-worn feel. Baths are basic, with cement floors and rudimentary showers. The staff is happy to arrange local excursions. ✉ *4 Ratchadamnoen Rd. Soi 3, 50200,* ☎ *053/278140. 18 rooms. Bar. MC, V.*

$ ★ ▥ **River View Lodge.** Facing a grassy lawn that runs down to the Mae Ping River, this lodge lets you forget the noise of the city. The restful rooms have terra-cotta floors and locally made wood furniture; some have private balconies overlooking the river. Although it couldn't be called luxurious, there's a restful simplicity here that's a far cry from the standard uniformity of most of the city's hotels. The small restaurant has an adequate menu, and the veranda overlooking the pool is a good place for afternoon tea. After dark, it's an easy 10-minute walk to the Night Bazaar. ⊠ *25 Charoen Prathet Rd. Soi 2, 50000,* ☎ *053/271109,* ℻ *053/279019. 36 rooms. Restaurant, pool. AE, DC, MC, V.*

¢ 🏠 **Come-On Place.** The cheerfully inviting name of this bed-and-breakfast sums up its laid-back atmosphere. Most of the simple but well-equipped rooms overlook a shady terrace. The inn is next to Buk Had Park, a patch of green in the southeast corner of the Old City. Continental breakfast is included in rates. ⊠ *15/14 Bumrungburi Rd., 51000,* ☎ *053/278936,* ℻ *053/282541. 14 rooms. Restaurant. MC, V.*

¢ 🏠 **Galare Guest House.** This pleasant guest house on the Mae Ping River
★ has a location that is the envy of many of the city's top hotels—its gardens lead right down to the shore. Even better, it's a short walk to the Night Bazaar. The teak-paneled rooms are simply but adequately furnished and overlook the shady grounds. The terrace restaurant faces the river. The staff is happy to assist with all travel requirements, from bus, train, and plane tickets to visas to Myanmar and Laos. ⊠ *7 Charoenprathet Rd. Soi 2, 50100,* ☎ *053/818887,* ℻ *053/279088. 35 rooms. Restaurant, refrigerators, cable TV MC, V.*

¢ 🏠 **Lai Thai.** This rambling guest house on a busy thoroughfare just out-
★ side the moat is a budget travelers' favorite, so book far ahead. Rooms, some of them cooled with lazily turning fans, are huddled around a courtyard with a delightful swimming pool. The adjacent open-air restaurant is also always buzzing with activity—this is the place to pick up helpful hints from seasoned travelers. The food here is some of the best in the city. The staff is happy to take you on excursions in the area, but the prices are a bit higher than you'll find at nearby travel agencies. ⊠ *111/4–5 Kotchasarn Rd., 50000,* ☎ *053/271725,* ℻ *053/272724. 120 rooms. Restaurant, pool, coin laundry, travel services. MC.*

¢ 🏠 **Montri Hotel.** Next to the Tha Pae Gate, this hotel overlooking the moat, makes up what it lacks in creature comforts with an unrivaled location. It's adjacent to the bars and restaurants on Tha Pae Road and Loy Kroh Road and is an easy walk to the Night Bazaar. Although the rooms lack a view of the moat, they are quiet. ⊠ *2-6 Ratchadamnoen Rd., 50200,* ☎ *053/211070,* ℻ *053/217416. 75 rooms. Restaurant, refrigerators, cable TV, laundry service, airport shuttle, travel services. MC, V.*

¢ 🏠 **River Ping Palace.** The traditional wooden houses that make up this welcoming little guest house are a glimpse of what Chiang Mai was like 50 years ago. Owned by a Frenchman and his Thai wife, the inn has smallish rooms decorated with old furnishings and artifacts—very personal, if a bit fussy. Food is served in the pleasant terrace restaurant. ⊠ *385/2 Charoen Phrathat Rd., 50100,* ☎ *053/274932,* ℻ *053/204281. 5 rooms. Restaurant. MC, V.*

Nightlife

This being Thailand, Chiang Mai has its share of Bangkok-style bars where anything goes. If you don't want to be hassled, there are also dozens of places where you can grab a beer and listen to live music. Many restaurants, such as the Riverside, double as bars later in the evening.

BARS

If you want to mix with the locals, there are plenty of places to go. At the **Cozy Corner** (⊠ 27 Moon Muang Rd., ☎ 053/277964), grab a beer and find a seat in the garden with a waterfall. The covered courtyard at **The Hill** (⊠ 92–93 Bumrungburi Rd., ☎ 053/277968), attracts locals who while away the evening listening to live bands. Thai musicians perform on an artificial hill covered with ferns. A wooden bridge crosses an artificial stream that divides the cavernous space.

Plenty of ex-pats make their home in Chiang Mai, and quite a few bars cater to them. In the Anusara Market is the **Britannia Arms** (✉ Changklan Rd., ☎ 053/271921), which serves a big buffet on Friday nights. The city claims to have Asia's most authentic English pub, called—what else?—**The Pub** (✉ 189 Huai Kaeo Rd., ☎ 053/211550). It's a fun place where you can order a draft beer and play a game of darts. Ex-pats and locals alike favor the **Red Lion** (✉ 123 Loy Kroh Rd., ☎ 053/818847). If you're hungry, you can order lamb chops or fish-and-chips.

DANCE CLUBS
Bubbles (✉ Charoen Prathet Rd., 052/270099) is a lively disco in the Pornping Tower Hotel. In the Chiang Mai Orchid Hotel, **Club 66** (✉ 100–102 Huai Kaeo Rd., ☎ 053/222099), caters to a stylish, sophisticated crowd. The beat goes on late into the evening at **Stairway to Heaven** (✉ 6-8 Loi Kroh Rd., ☎ 053/207124).

KHANTOKE
Khantoke originally described a revolving wooden tray on which food is served, but it has now come to mean an evening's entertainment combining a seemingly endless menu of northern cuisine and presentations of traditional music and dancing. With sticky rice, which you mold into balls with your fingers, you sample delicacies like *kap moo* (spiced pork skin), *nam phrik naw,* (a spicy dip made with onions, cucumber, and chili), and *kang ka* (a chicken and vegetable curry).

Among the best of places offering khantoke is the sumptuously templelike **Khum Khantoke** (✉ Chiang Mai Business Park, 139 Moo 4, Nong Pakrung, ☎ 053/304121). Another popular place is **Kantoke Palace** (✉ 288/19 Chang Klan Rd., ☎ 053/272757). At **Khum Kaew Palace** (✉ 252 Pra Pok Klao Rd., ☎ 053/214315), an authentic northern Thai house, you sit cross-legged on the floor or at long tables. The **Old Chiang Mai Cultural Centre** (✉ 185/3 Wualai Rd., ☎ 053/275097), resembling a hill tribe village, has nightly classical music and dancing after a big dinner.

MUSIC
For live jazz, drop by the casual **Bantorie** (✉ 99/4 Moo 2, Huai Kaeo Rd., ☎ 053/224444). Soft rock is the specialty of the house at **Brasserie** (✉ 37 Charoenraj Rd., ☎ 053/241665). If folk music is more to your taste, then head to **River Ping Terrace** (✉ 154/1 Chiang Mai-Lamphun Rd., ☎ 053/240270).

Shopping
Day-to-day life in Chiang Mai seems to revolve around shopping. The delightful surprise is that you don't have to part with much of your hard-earned money—even the most elaborately crafted silver costs a

fraction of what you'd expect to pay at home. Fine jewelry, weighed and priced at just above the current market value, pewter, leather, and silk are all on display all around the city. The justifiably famous **Night Bazaar,** on Chang Klan Road, is a kind of open-air department store filled with vendors offering everything from inexpensive souvenirs to pricey antiques. In the afternoon and evening traders set up tented stalls along Chan Klang Road and the adjoining streets. You're expected to bargain, so don't be shy. Do, however, remain polite. Many vendors believe the first and last customers of the day bring good luck, so if you're after a real bargain (up to 50% off) start your shopping at 9 AM. Some of the so-called antiques in the Night Bazaar were manufactured last week, but there are some genuine ones still to be found. **Lanna Antiques** (✉ Booth 2 on the 2nd floor) has a good selection.

For two of Chiang Mai's specialties, lacquerware and exquisite paper, take a taxi or songthaew to any of the outlets along the **Golden Mile,** a long stretch of the road that runs east to San Kamphaeng. Large emporiums sell a variety of items, including hand-painted umbrellas made from lacquered paper and tree bark. Whole communities here devote themselves to following their traditional trades. You can watch them rearing silkworms, for instance, to provide the raw product for the looms humming in workshops.

Around 13 km (8 mi) south of the city lies a small version of the Golden Mile—the village of **Hang Don,** where virtually everybody seems to be in the teak trade. One community, called Baan Tawai, has many small workshops devoted to wood carving. If you become attached to a teak table or chair, there are reliable firms there that will arrange for transport.

En Route   About 3 km (2 mi) south of Chiang Mai, between the Chiengmai Gymkhana Club and the main road to Lamphun, is one of the most curious cemeteries in Southeast Asia. It's the Foreign Cemetery, a plot of land given to the expatriate community by King Chulalongkorn in the late 19th century to be held in perpetuity for the internment of foreign residents. The first grave contains the remains of an English soldier who rode alone into Chiang Mai from northern China and died of dysentery before he could relate to the curious locals what he was doing there. A bronze statue of Queen Victoria, empress of much of Asia at that time, watches over his tombstone and those of several Americans, most of them missionaries and teachers.

Doi Inthanon National Park

⑬ *57 km (36 mi) southwest of Chiang Mai.*

Doi Inthanon, Thailand's highest mountain (8,464 ft), rises majestically over a national park of staggering beauty. Many have compared the landscape with that of Canada—only the 30 villages that are home to 3,000 Karen and Hmong people remind you that this is indeed Asia. The reserve is of great interest to nature lovers, especially birders who come to see the 362 species that nest in its thick forests of pines, oaks, and laurels. Red and white rhododendron run riot here, as do other plants found nowhere else in Thailand.

A 48-km (30-mi) toll road winds to the mountain's summit, where the ashes of Chiang Mai's last ruler, King Inthawichayanon, are contained in a stupa that draws hundreds of thousands of pilgrims annually. Hiking trails penetrate deep into the park, which has some of Thailand's highest and most beautiful waterfalls. The Mae Klang Falls is the most accessible—take the turnoff 6 km (3½ mi) past the park entrance.

Lamphun

⑭ *26 km (16 mi) south of Chiang Mai.*

Lamphun claims to be the oldest existing city in Thailand (but so does Nakhon Pathom). Originally called Nakhon Hariphunchai, it was founded in AD 680 by the Chamdhevi dynasty, which ruled the region until 1932. Unlike Chiang Mai, Lamphun has remained a sleepy community that you can easily explore in an afternoon.

The town is known throughout Thailand for the *lamyai,* a sweet cherry-size fruit with a thin shell. In this region it's big business. In the nearby village of Tongkam, the "10,000 baht lamyai tree" nets its owner that sum every year. A good time to visit is in early August, when the Ngam Lamyai festival brings parades, beauty pageants, and a drum-beating competition. Buy yourself a jar of lamyai honey—it's supposed to have great healing and aphrodisiac powers.

Minibus songthaews (B10) go from Chiang Mai to Lamphun. It's also a pleasant day's trip to drive south on Highway 106, a shady road lined by 100-ft rubber trees.

Lamphun's architectural treasures include two monasteries. About 2 km (1 mi) west of the town's center is **Wat Chamthewi,** often called the "topless chedi" because the gold that once covered the spire has been removed. Despite a modern viharn at the side of the complex, the monastery has an ancient weathered look. Suwan Chang Kot, to the right of the entrance, is the most famous of the two chedis, built by King Mahantayot to hold the remains of his mother, the legendary Queen Chamthewi. The five-tier sandstone chedi is square; on each tier are Buddha images that get progressively smaller. All are in the 9th-century Dvaravati style, though many have obviously been restored. The other chedi was probably built in the 10th century, though most of what you see today is the work of 12th-century King Phaya Sapphasit. You'll probably want to take a samlor down the narrow residential street to the complex. Since it is not an area where samlors generally cruise, ask the driver to wait for you. ✉ *Lamphun-San Pa Tong Rd.*

The monastery of **Wat Phra That Hariphunchai** is dazzling. Through the gates, guarded by ornamental lions, is a three-tier, sloping-roof viharn, a replica of the original, which burned down in 1915. Inside, note the large Chiang Saen–style bronze image of the Buddha and the carved *thammas* (Buddhism's universal principals) to the left of the altar. As you leave the viharn, you'll pass what is reputedly the largest bronze gong in the world, cast in 1860. The 165-ft Suwana chedi, covered in copper and topped by a golden spire, dates from 847. A century later, King Athitayarat, the 32nd ruler of Hariphunchai, added a nine-tier umbrella, gilded with 14 pounds of gold. At the back of the compound—where you'll find a shortcut to the center of town—there's another viharn with a standing Buddha, a sala housing four Buddha footprints, and the old museum. ✉ *Inthayongyot Rd.* 🎟 *Admission.* ⊙ *Wed.–Sun. 8:30–4.*

Just outside Wat Phra That Hariphunchai, the **National Museum** has a fine selection of Dvaravati-style stuccowork. There's also an impressive collection of Lanna antiques. ✉ *Inthayongyot Rd.* 🎟 *Admission.* ⊙ *Wed.–Sun. 9–noon and 1–4.*

Dining and Lodging

¢ ✕ **Lamphun Ice.** The odd name of this restaurant seems to come from its origins as an ice cream parlor. The interior has booths and the cool feel of a vintage soda fountain. The Asian food served here is the real thing—try the sensational Indian-style crab curry. ⊠ *Opposite southern gate of Wat Phra That Hariphunchai,* ☎ *053/560909. No credit cards.*

¢ ⌨ **Supamit.** From this hotel's fifth-floor restaurant you'll have fine views of Wat Chamthewi, located on the opposite side of the road. Lamphun's best hotel, Supamit has rooms that are clean and comfortable. After a day touring the city's temples the airy lobby offers a cool and soothing retreat. ⊠ *Lamphun-Rim Ping Rd.,* ☎ *053/534865,* ⅌ *053/534355. 50 rooms. Restaurant, bar. MC, V.*

Pa Sang

⑮ *12 km (7 mi) south of Lamphun, 38 km (19 mi) south of Chiang Mai.*

Women weaving fabrics in traditional designs are the main attraction of this village south of Lamphun. Although in recent years the selection has diminished somewhat, you can find fine cloth by the yard as well as ready-made clothing. Expect to pay B100–B250 for a shirt with a batik pattern, and around B200–B300 for a sarong-style dress.

About 5 km (3 mi) south of Pa Sang is **Wat Phra Bhat Tak Pha,** commonly known as the Temple of Buddha's Footprint. You can climb the 600 steps to the hilltop chedi, but the main attraction here is the two huge imprints representing Lord Buddha's foot, found indented in the floor inside the temple. As you enter, buy a piece of gold leaf to afix in the imprint. ⊠ *Pa Sang-lee Rd.*

Lampang

⑯ *65 km (40 mi) southeast of Lamphun, 91 km (59 mi) southeast of Chiang Mai.*

At the end of the 19th century, when Lampang was a thriving center of the teak trade, the well-to-do city elders gave the city a genteel look by buying a fleet of English-built carriages and a stable of nimble ponies to pull them through the streets. Until then, elephants had been a favored means of transport—a century ago the number of elephants, employed in the nearby teak forests, nearly matched the city's population. The carriages arrived on the first trains to steam into Lampang's fine railroad station, which still looks much the same as it did back then. More than a century later, the odd sight of horse-drawn carriages still greets visitors to Lampang. The brightly painted, flower-bedecked carriages, driven by hardened types in Stetson hats and cowboy boots, look very touristy, but the locals also use them to get around the city. They pay considerably less than the B100 visitors are charged.

Apart from some noteworthy temples, not much else remains of Lampang's prosperous heyday. An ever-dwindling number of fine teak homes can be found among the maze of concrete. Running parallel to the south bank of the Wang River is a narrow street of ancient shops that once belonged to the Chinese merchants who catered to Lampang's prosperous populace. The riverfront promenade is a pleasant place for a stroll; a handful of cafés and restaurants with terraces overlooks the water.

Workers from Burma were employed in the region's rapidly expanding logging business, and these immigrants left their mark on the city's architecture. Especially well preserved is **Wat Sri Chum,** a lovely Burmese temple. Pay particular attention to the viharn, as the eaves are covered with beautiful carvings. Inside you'll find gold-and-black lacquered pillars supporting a carved-wood ceiling. To the right is a bronze Buddha cast in the Burmese style. Red-and-gold panels on the walls depict temple scenes. ⊠ *Sri Chum Rd.*

Near the banks of the River Wang is **Wat Phra Kaeo Don Tao,** dominated by its tall chedi, built on a rectangular base and topped with a rounded spire. More interesting, however, are the Burmese-style shrine and adjacent Thai-style sala. The 18th-century shrine has a multi-tier roof. The interior walls are carved and inlaid with colored stones; the ornately engraved ceiling is painted with enamel. The sala, with the traditional three-tier roof and carved-wood pediments, houses a Sukhothai-style reclining Buddha. Legend has it that the sala was once home to the Emerald Buddha, which now resides in Bangkok. In 1436, when King Sam Fang Kaem was transporting the statue from Chiang Rai to Chiang Mai, his elephant reached Lampang and refused to go farther. The Emerald Buddha is said to have remained here for the next 32 years, until the succeeding king managed to get it to Chiang Mai. ⊠ *Phra Kaeo Rd.*

Wat Phra That Lampang Luang. Near the village of Ko Khang is one of the most venerated temples in the north. It is also one of the most striking. Surrounded by stout laterite defense walls, the temple has the appearance of a fortress—and that's exactly what it was when the legendary Queen Chamthewi founded her capital here in the 8th century. The Burmese captured it two centuries ago, but were ejected by the forces of a Lampang prince (a bullet hole marks the spot where he killed the Burmese commander). The sandy temple compound has much much to hold your interest, including a tiny chapel with a hole in the door that creates an amazing, inverted photographic image of the Wat's central, gold-covered chedi. The temple's ancient viharn has a beautifully carved wooden facade; note the painstaking workmanship of the intricate decorations around the porticoes. A museum has excellent wood carvings, but its treasure is a small emerald Buddha, which some claim was carved from the same stone as its counterpart in Bangkok. ⊠ *15 km (9 mi) south of Lampang.* 🖃 *Admission.* ☉ *Tues.–Sun. 9–4.*

On the main highway between Lampang and Chiang Mai is Thailand's internationally known **Elephant Conservation Center.** So-called training camps are scattered throughout the region, but many of them are little more than overpriced sideshows. This is the real thing: a government-supported research station. Here you'll find the special stables that house the white elephants owned by the king. The 36 "commoner" elephants (the most venerable are over 80) get individual care from more than 40 mahouts, and the younger ones evidently enjoy the routines they have to perform for the tourists—not only the usual log-rolling, but painting pictures (a New York auction of their work raised thousands of dollars for the center). There's even an elephant band (its trumpeter is truly a star). The elephants are bathed every morning at 9:30 and perform at 10 and 11, with an additional 1:30 show on weekends and holidays. You can even take an elephant ride through the center's extensive grounds, and if you fancy becoming a mahout you can take a residential course in elephant management. ⊠ *Baan Tung Kwian,* ☎ *054/228034 or 054/229042.* 🖃 *Admission.* ☉ *Daily 8–4.*

Dining and Lodging

$ ✕ **Riverside.** A random assortment of wooden rooms and terraces gives this place an easygoing charm. Perched above the sluggish Wang River, it's a great place for a casual meal. The moderately priced Thai and European fare is excellent, and on weekends the remarkable chef serves up the best pizza east of Brindisi. Most nights a live band performs, but there are so many quiet corners that you can easily escape the music. There are a handful of rooms on the lower floor if you want to stay over for the authentic American breakfast. ⊠ *328 Tipchang Rd.*, ☎ *054/221861*, ℻ *054/227005. MC, V.*

$ ✕ **Terrace River View.** If you want to escape the tourists at nearby establishments, head directly to this place on the Wang River. Dine beneath massive teak beams and slowly revolving fans on the flagstone terrace. There's regular live music. The food is strictly Thai—attempts to add a few foreign dishes such as spaghetti have not been successful. ⊠ *340 Tipchang Rd.*, ☎ *054/310103. MC.*

¢ ✕ **Cozy Little Place.** Its name aptly describes this warren of small, heavily timbered dining rooms favored by local business executives. The imaginative menu has some milder Chinese dishes to offset the heat of chili-laden Northern Thai specialties. ⊠ *79/17 Phaholyothin Rd.*, ☎ *054/288739. MC, V.*

¢ ✕ **Kelang Golf Club.** You don't have to be a golfer to enjoy a simple meal at Lampang's lovely links, located about 3 km (2 mi) northeast of town. The airy terrace overlooks the club's driving range, so you can admire the skills of the city's well-heeled businessmen as they practice their swings during their lunch breaks. ⊠ *Chiang Rai Rd., Km 3*, ☎ *054/225941. No credit cards.*

$ 🏨 **Lampang River Lodge.** Facing the Wang River, this lodge is nestled in a tropical forest. The simple but comfortable rooms are in Thai-style wooden pavilions near a small lake where you can rent boats. The vast, airy restaurant is often crammed with tour groups, but you shouldn't find a problem securing a quiet corner. To get away from the crowds, totter over the swaying bridge to the riverside bar. The complex is 6 km (4 mi) south of Lampang. ⊠ *330 Mu 11, Tambol Champoo, 52000*, ☎ *054/226922*, ℻ *054/226922. 47 rooms. Restaurant, bar. AE, MC, V.*

¢ 🏨 **Asia Lampang Hotel.** Although this hotel sits on a bustling street, most of the rooms are quiet enough ensure a good night's sleep. Some are newly renovated, so ask to see a few before you decide. The airy terrace is just the place to relax on a warm evening. If you fancy singing along with the locals, there's a delightfully named karaoke room called the Sweety Music Room. ⊠ *229 Boonyawat Rd.*, ☎ *054/ 227844*, ℻ *054/224436. 71 rooms. Restaurant, bar, convention center. MC.*

¢ 🏨 **Lampang Wiengthong Hotel.** One of the city's best hotels, this modern high-rise has a number of quite luxuriously appointed rooms and suites. Its "Drinks Palace" features live music most nights. The Wiengthip coffee shop and Wiengpana restaurant rank among Lampang's smartest eateries. ⊠ *138/109 Phaholyothin Rd.*, ☎ *054/225801*, ℻ *054/ 225803. 235 rooms. Restaurant, coffee shop, pool, piano bar, convention center. AE, MC, V.*

Shopping

Lampang is known for its blue, white, and orange pottery, much of it incorporating the image of a cockerel, the city's emblem. If you're driving you'll find the best bargains at markets a few kilometers south of the city, on the highway to Bangkok, or north of the city on the road to Chiang Mai. There are also several outlets in the city. **Ku Ceramic** (⊠ *167 Mu 6, Phahonyothin Rd.*, ☎ *054/218313*) has a good selection of traditional pottery.

Phrae

❶⓻ *110 km (68 mi) southeast of Lampang, 201 km (125 mi) southeast of Chiang Mai, 118 km (73 mi) southwest of Nan.*

A market town in a narrow valley, Phrae is off the beaten path. The town's recorded history starts in the 12th century, when it was called

Wiang Kosai, the Silk City. It remained an independent kingdom until the Ayutthaya period. Remains of these former times are seen in the crumbling city walls and moat, which separate the Old City from the new commercial sprawl.

On the northeastern edge of town stands **Wat Chom Sawan,** a beautiful monastery designed by a Burmese architect and built during the reign of King Rama V (1868–1910). The bot and viharn are combined to make one giant sweeping structure. Phrae's oldest building is **Wat Luang,** within the old city walls. Although it was founded in the 12th century, renovations and expansions completely obscure so much of the original design that the only original section is a Lanna chedi with primitive elephant statues. A small museum on the grounds contains sacred Buddha images, swords, and texts.

On a hilltop in Tambon Pa Daeng, 10 km (6 mi) southeast of Phrae, stands another ancient temple, **Wat Phra That Cho Hae.** It was built in the late 12th century, and its 108-ft chedi is coated in gold. The chedi is linked to a viharn, a later construction, that contains a series of murals depicting scenes from the Buddha's life. The revered Buddha image is said to increase a woman's fertility. Cho Hae is the name given to the cloth woven by the local people, and in the fourth lunar month (June) the chedi is wrapped in this cloth during the annual fair. About 2 km (1 mi) from Wat Cho Hae is another smaller wat, **Wat Phra That Chom Chang,** whose chedi is said to contain a strand of Lord Buddha's hair.

Phrae is renowned in Northern Thailand for its fine teak houses. There are many to admire all over the city, but none to match what is claimed to be the world's largest teak structure, the **Ban Prathap Chai,** in the hamlet of Tambon Pa Maet near the southern edge of Phrae. Like many such houses, it's actually a reconstruction of several older houses—in this case, nine of them supported on 130 huge centuries-old teak posts. The result is remarkably harmonious. A tour of the rooms open to public view give a fascinating picture of bourgeois life in the region. The space between the teak poles on the ground floor of the building is taken up by stalls selling a variety of handicrafts, including much carved teak. The small admission charge includes a carved elephant key ring—a charming touch.

Lodging

For a quick bite, there is a night market at Pratuchai Gate with numerous stalls offering cheap, tasty food.

$ 🏨 **Mae Yom Palace Thani Hotel.** Phrae's top hotel is scarcely palatial, but has comfortable, well-appointed rooms at a modest price. There are plenty of amenities, including a very pleasant pool and an outdoor bar. The two restaurants serve a comprehensive menu of Thai and European dishes. ⊠ *181/6 Yantrakritson Rd., 54000,* ☎ *054/521028,* F̄A̅X̄ *054/522904. 104 rooms. 2 restaurants, minibars, cable TV, in-room VCRs, pool, Internet, meeting rooms. AE, MC, V.*

¢ 🏨 **Nakorn Phrae Tower.** Although Phrae does not attract many tourists, you'll find all the creature comforts at this high-rise hotel. Enter the modern structure through a traditional Lanna gateway. Rooms are nicely furnished with desks and chairs, and the tiled baths are small and functional. The restaurant serves Thai, Chinese, and Western fare. In the evening stop by for a drink in the lounge or at the small bar. ⊠ *3 Muanghit Rd., 54000,* ☎ *054/521321,* F̄A̅X̄ *054/523503. 139 rooms. Restaurant, bar, lounge, meeting rooms. AE, DC, MC, V.*

Nan

⓲ *270 km (167 mi) southeast of Chiang Rai, 118 km (73 mi) northeast of Phrae.*

Near the border of Laos lies the city of Nan, a provincial capital founded in 1272. According to local legend, the Lord Buddha, passing through Nan valley, spotted an auspicious site for a temple to be built. By the late 13th century Nan was brought into Sukhothai's fold, but it maintained a fairly independent status into the 20th century. Only in the last two decades has a modern road been cut from Phrae to bring this region into closer communication with authorities in Bangkok.

Nan is rich in teak plantations and fertile valleys that produce rice and superb oranges. The town of Nan itself is small; everything is within walking distance. Daily life centers on the morning and evening markets. The Nan River, which flows past the eastern edge of town, draws visitors every October, when traditional boat races are held.

To get a sense of the region's art visit the **National Museum,** housed in the former palace of the Nan royal family. There's a good array of wood and bronze Buddha statues, musical instruments, ceramics, and other works of Lanna art. Everything is captioned in English. ⊠ *Phalong Rd.,* ☎ *054/710561.* ▱ *Admission.* ⊘ *Wed.–Sun. 9–12 and 1–5.*

★ Nan has one of the region's most unusual and beautiful temples, **Wat Pumin** (⊠ Phalong Rd.). The cruciform bot, built in 1596, is small and quite intimate. You climb a flight of steps flanked by two superb nagas, their heads guarding the north entrance and their tails the south. The temple was extensively renovated in 1865 and 1873, and at the end of the 19th-century murals picturing everyday life were added to the inner walls. The images range from the traumas of hell to the joys of courtly life. These are simple murals totally unlike the sophisticated art found in Bangkok's Grand Palace. The bot's central images are also quite unusual—four Sukhothai Buddhas in the vanquishing Mara position, facing the cardinal compass points.

Nan is dotted with other wats. **Wat Hua Wiang Tai** (⊠ Sumonthewarat Rd.) is the gaudiest, with a naga running along the top of the wall and lively murals painted on the viharn's exterior. **Wat Suan Tan** (⊠ Tambon Nai Wiang) has a 15th-century bronze Buddha image. It is the scene for fireworks during the annual Songkran festival. **Wat Ming Muang** (⊠ Suriyaphong Rd.) contains the city pillar. **Wat Chang Kham** (⊠ Suriyaphong Rd.) has a large chedi supported by elephant-shape buttresses.

Lodging

¢ ▥ **Dhevaraj.** The first international hotel in Nan is still the town's choicest lodging. Across from the downtown market, Dhevaraj is a meeting point for locals as much as tourists. The rooms are smartly furnished, with small but modern bathrooms. The courtyard restaurant serves dinner in a romantic setting. For other meals, a coffee shop is open from 6 AM to midnight. ⊠ *T44 Sumonthevaraj Rd., 50000,* ☎ *054/710094,* ℻ *054/710212. 154 rooms. Restaurant, coffee shop. MC, V.*

¢ ▥ **Nan Fah Hotel.** A reminder of the past, this old wooden Chinese hotel is worth a visit, even if you are disinclined to stay in its rather dark rooms. The wide-plank floors are of a bygone age. A balcony overlooking the street is a great place to take in the town. Marvelous antiques are scattered around the hotel, and the delightful owner is happy to sell you some in the shop in the lobby. A live band plays in the restaurant at night. The music does not help if you are trying to sleep in a room above, so ask for one at the back of the hotel. ⊠ *438 Sumon-*

thevaraj Rd., 55000, ☎ 054/772640. 14 rooms. Restaurant, lounge, shop. No credit cards.

Chiang Dao

⑲ *72 km (40 mi) north of Chiang Mai.*

The village of Chiang Dao, north of Chiang Mai, is where you'll find Thailand's most spectacular caves. This complex of cathedral-proportioned caverns penetrate more than 2 km (1 mi) into Doi Chiang Dao, an astonishing 7,500-ft mountain that leaps up from the valley floor. About half the caves have electric lights, but make sure you have a flashlight in your pocket in case there's a power failure. If you want to explore more of the mountain, hire a guide.

Lodging

¢ 🏨 **Rim Doi Resort.** Rim Doi means "on the edge of the mountain," so it's fitting that two extraordinary peaks loom over this peaceful little resort near Chiang Dao. After a day exploring the nearby caves or venturing into the mountains, it's just the place to relax and prepare for the journey farther north. Be careful, as you'll probably be tempted to stay longer than just a night. Just B200 buys you a comfortable bed in a rustic bungalow, while a more stylish room in a modern extension overlooking a placid lake is an unbeatable B350. ⊠ *46 Moo 4, Muang Ghay,* ☎ *053/375028,* 🆑 *053/375029. 40 rooms. Restaurant, café, lake, bar. MC, V.*

Mae Hong Son

270 km (169 mi) northwest of Chiang Mai via Pai, 368 km (230 mi) via Mae Sariang.

Stressed-out Bangkok business executives have transformed this remote, mountain-ringed market town into one of northern Thailand's major resort areas. Some handsome hotels have arisen in recent years to cater for them and their families. Overseas travelers also love the town because of its easy access to some of Thailand's most beautiful countryside.

For a small town, Mae Hong Son has some notable temples, thanks to immigrants from nearby Myanmar, where Burmese architecture and decorative arts were historically more advanced. Nearby are dozens of villages inhabited by the Karen, the so-called "long-neck" people. Fine handicrafts are produced in these hamlets, whose inhabitants trek daily to Mae Hong Son to sell their wares at the lively morning market.

Although Mae Hong Son offers a welcome cool retreat during the sometimes unbearably hot months of March and April, the mountains can be obscured during that part of the year by fires set by farmers to clear their fields. One of the local names for Mae Hong Son translates as "City of the Three Mists." The other two are the clouds that creep through the valleys in the depths of winter and the gray monsoons of the rainy season.

A Good Walk

For a giddy view of Mae Hong Son and the surrounding mountains, take a deep breath and trudge up Doi Kong Mu, a hill on the western edge of town. It's well worth the effort—from here you can watch the sunset blaze against the mountains on the border of Myanmar. There's another shade of gold to admire—a flame-surrounded white-marble Buddha in a hilltop temple called **Wat Phra That Doi Kong Mu** ⑳.

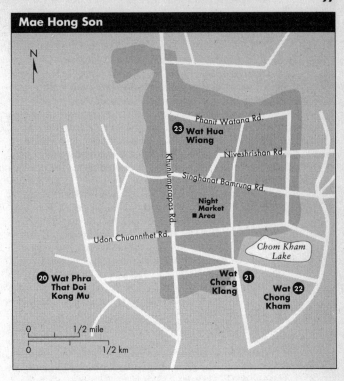

Mae Hong Son

In the center of town, a pair of the region's fine temples sit on the southern edge of a lily-strewn lake called Jong Kham. **Wat Chong Klang** ㉑ and **Wat Chong Kham** ㉒ both overlook the serene lake. A short walk up Panishwatana Road leads you to **Wat Hua Wiang** ㉓, which holds the region's most honored image of the Buddha.

TIMING

Because Mae Hong Son is so compact, this walk should only take a few hours.

Sights to See

㉒ **Wat Chong Kham.** A wonderfully self-satisfied Buddha, the cares of the world far from his arched brow, watches over the temple, which has a fine pulpit carved with incredible precision. ⊠ *Chamnansathit Rd.*

㉑ **Wat Chong Klang.** This temple is worth visiting to see a collection of figurines brought from Burma more than a century ago. The teak-wood carvings depict an astonishing range of Burmese individuals, from peasants to nobles. ⊠ *Chamnansathit Rd.*

㉓ **Wat Hua Wiang.** Mae Hong Son's most celebrated Buddha image— one of the most revered in Northern Thailand—is in this temple. Its origins are clear—note the Burmese-style long earlobes, a sign of the Buddha's omniscience. ⊠ *Panishwatana Rd.*

㉒ **Wat Phra That Doi Kong Mu.** On the top of Doi Kong Mu, this temple has a remarkable view of the surrounding mountains. The temple's two chedis contain the ashes of 19th-century monks. ⊠ *West of Mae Hong Son.*

Dining and Lodging

¢ ✕ **Bai Fern.** Mae Hong Son's main thoroughfare, Khunlum Praphat Road, is lined with inexpensive restaurants serving local cuisine. Bai

Fern is among the best. In the spacious dining room you eat in typical Thai style between massive teak columns and beneath whirling fans. The staff is friendly and helpful, anxious for you to enjoy your meal. They will even adapt spicy dishes to your taste. ⊠ *87 Khunlum Praphat Rd.,* ☎ *053/611374. MC, V.*

$$ 🏨 **Imperial Tara Mae Hong Son.** Set amid mature teak trees, this fine
★ hotel was designed to blend in with the surroundings. Bungalows in landscaped gardens have both front and back porches, giving the teak-floored and bamboo-furnished rooms a light and airy feel. Golden Teak, which serves excellent Thai, Chinese, and European dishes, has a glassed-in section for chilly mornings and evenings. The restaurant and bar face the valley, as does the beautifully landscaped pool area. ⊠ *149 Moo 8 Tambon Pang Moo, 58000,* ☎ *053/611473; 02/261–9000 in Bangkok;* 𝐅𝐀𝐗 *053/611252, 02/261–9546 in Bangkok. 104 rooms. Restaurant, minibars, cable TV, pool, gym, sauna, bar, shop, business center, travel services. AE, DC, MC, V.*

$–$$ 🏨 **Rooks Holiday Hotel.** If you're looking for a quiet retreat, then Rooks Holiday Hotel should not be your top choice. A favorite with tour groups, the resort has a disco that pulsates until the wee hours. Set in attractive tropical gardens that border a large pool, it has rooms with private balconies. ⊠ *114/5–7 Khunlum Praphat Rd., 58000,* ☎ *053/611390,* 𝐅𝐀𝐗 *053/611524. 114 rooms. Restaurant, minibars, cable TV, pool, billiards, nightclub, travel services. AE, DC, MC, V.*

$ 🏨 **Rim Nam Klang Doi.** About 5 km (3 mi) outside Mae Hong Son, this retreat is an especially good value. Some of the cozy rooms overlook the Pai River, while others have views of the tropical landscaped grounds. A minivan shuttles you to town for B100. ⊠ *Ban Huay Dua, 58000,* ☎ *053/224339,* 𝐅𝐀𝐗 *053/612086. 39 rooms. Restaurant, pool. MC, V.*

¢ 🏨 **Jean's Guest House.** There are few frills at this modest bungalow, but the price couldn't be better. Rooms with fans are just B80, while more comfortable ones with air-conditioning and private bathrooms are a reasonable B400. The English-speaking owner makes you feel very much at home and can help you find a guide. ⊠ *6/1 Prachautith Rd., 58000,* ☎ *053/611662. 9 rooms. No credit cards.*

¢ 🏨 **Piya Guest House.** The most comfortable inn in the area, Piya Guest House faces sedate Lake Jong Kham. Ask owner Piya Grongpherpoon for one of the air-conditioned rooms that face the garden. Tables at the terrace restaurant face the lake; those in the dining room share space with a pool table. ⊠ *1 Soi 6, Khunlum Praphat Rd., 58000,* ☎ *053/ 611260,* 𝐅𝐀𝐗 *053/612308. 11 rooms, most with bath. Restaurant. No credit cards.*

Outdoor Activities and Sports

TREKKING

In the 1960s, a few intrepid travelers in northern Thailand started wandering through the countryside and finding rooms at the hill tribe villages. By 1980, tour companies were organizing guided groups and sending them off for three- to seven-day treks. The level of difficulty varies; you might traverse tough, hilly terrain for several hours, or travel by mostly by car and hike just the last few miles. Days are spent walking forest trails between villages, where you can sleep overnight. Accommodations are in huts, where the bed can be a wooden platform with no mattress. Food is likely to be a bowl of sticky rice and stewed vegetables. Travel light, but be sure to wear sturdy hiking shoes and to pack a sweater. Mosquito repellent is a must.

Always use a certified guide. It's important to pick one who's familiar with local dialects and who knows which villages are not overrun with tour groups. It is also imperative that you discuss the route; that

When you pack your MCI Calling Card, it's like packing your loved ones along too.

Your MCI Calling Card is the easy way to stay in touch when you travel. Use it to call to and from over 125 countries. Plus, every time you call, you can earn frequent flier miles. So wherever your travels take you, call home with your MCI Calling Card. It's even easy to get one. Just visit **www.mci.com/worldphone** or **www.mci.com/partners**.

EASY TO CALL WORLDWIDE

1. Just enter the WorldPhone® access number of the country you're calling from.
2. Enter or give the operator your MCI Calling Card number.
3. Enter or give the number you're calling.

Australia ◆	1-800-881-100
China	108-12
Hong Kong	800-96-1121
India	000-127
Japan ◆	00539-121▶
Kenya	080011
Morocco	00-211-0012
South Africa	0800-99-0011

◆ Public phones may require deposit of coin or phone card for dial tone.
▶ Regulation does not permit intra-Japan calls.

EARN FREQUENT FLIER MILES

Find America *with a Compass*

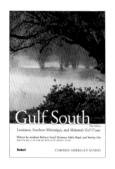
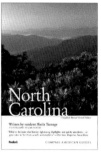
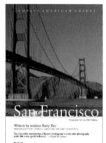

Written by local authors and illustrated throughout
with spectacular color images, Compass American
Guides reveal the character and culture of more than
40 of America's most fascinating destinations. Perfect
for residents who want to explore their own backyards
and for visitors who want an insider's perspective
on the history, heritage, and all there is to see and do.

Fodor's COMPASS AMERICAN GUIDES

At bookstores everywhere.

way you'll know what to expect. You can usually tell whether the guide is knowledgeable and respects the villagers, but question him thoroughly about his experience before you sign up. The best way to select a tour that is right for you is to talk to other travelers. Guides come and go, and what was true six months ago may not be today.

Many people come to Mae Hong Son to visit the villages belonging to the Karen people, whose women often extend their necks by adding more and more brass bands. Most of the Karen people—an estimated 3,000 families—still live in Myanmar. In Thailand there are three villages, all near Mae Hong Son, with a total of 36 families, all of whom are accustomed to posing for photographs. Some visitors find there's an ethical dilemma in visiting these villages, as tourism may perpetuate what some find to be a rather barbaric custom. At the same time, tourist dollars also help to feed these people, many of whom are refugees from the unrest in Mayanmar. With as many as 150 tourists a day during the peak season, a village can make good money by exhibiting their long-neck women.

THE GOLDEN TRIANGLE

Once the capital of an empire, Chiang Rai's reputation now rests on its proximity to the fabled Golden Triangle. The little town may have little to make you want to linger, but it has a wide range of tour operators ready to whisk you off into the countryside. The mighty Mae Khong River, the borders of Myanmar and Laos and dozens of authentic hill tribe villages are all within a few hours.

Chiang Rai

180 km (112 mi) northeast of Chiang Mai, 780 km (485 mi) north of Bangkok.

Once again, an elephant played a central role in the foundation of an important Thai city. Legend has it that a royal elephant ran away from its patron, a 13th-century king named Mengrai, founder of the Lanna kingdom. The beast stopped to rest on the banks of the Mae Kok River. The king regarded this as an auspicious sign and in 1256 built his capital, Chiang Rai, on the site. Little is left from those heady days. Wat Phra Keo once housed the Emerald Buddha that is now in Bangkok's Grand Palace, and a precious Buddha image in the 15th-century Wat Phra Singh has long since disappeared.

Chiang Rai attracts more and more visitors each year, and it's easy to see why. Six hill tribes—the Akha, Yao, Meo, Lisu, Lahu, and Karen tribes all live within Chiang Rai province. Each has different dialects, customs, handicrafts, costumes, and all still venerate animist spirits despite their increasing acquaintance with the outside world. As in Chiang Mai, they make daily journeys to the markets of Chiang Rai. The best of these is a night bazaar, just off Phaholyothin Road, which has a cluster of small restaurants and food vendors.

A Good Walk

Doi Tong, a modest hill on the northeastern edge of Chiang Rai, is a great way to learn the lay of the land. From the grounds of a 13th-century temple called **Wat Doi Tong** ㉔ you have fine view of the Mae Kok River and the mountains beyond. Down the hill you'll soon reach Trairat Road, where you'll find **Wat Phra Keo** ㉕, once home to the famed Emerald Buddha. A copy now resides here. On Singhaklai Road is **Wat Phra Singh** ㉖, known for its restful atmosphere.

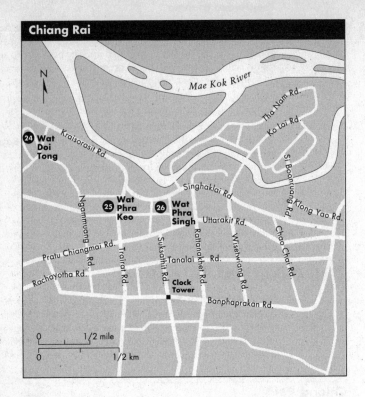

Chiang Rai

TIMING

Chiang Rai has very few sights of note, so a leisurely walk around town will take at most a few hours.

Sights to See

24 Wat Doi Tong. Near the summit of Doi Tong, this temple overlooks the Mae Kok River. The ancient pillar that stands here once symbolized the center of the universe for devout Buddhists. The sunset view is worth the trip. ✉ *Winitchaikul Rd.*

25 Wat Phra Keo. The Emerald Buddha which now sits in Thailand's holiest temple, Wat Phra Keo in Bangkok, is said to have been discovered when lightning split the chedi housing it at this similarly named temple at the foot of the Doi Tong. A Chinese millionaire financed a jade replica in 1991—although it's not the real thing, the statuette is still strikingly beautiful. ✉ *Trairat Rd.*

26 Wat Phra Singh. This 14th-century temple is worth visiting for its viharn, distinguished by some remarkably delicate wood carving and for colorful frescoes depicting the life of Buddha. A sacred Indian Bhoti tree stands in the peaceful temple grounds. ✉ *Singhaklai Rd.*

Dining and Lodging

¢ ✕ **Honarira.** Apart from the Night Bazaar, this restaurant is by far the city's best spot for a casual meal under an umbrella of small trees. The extensive menu is a mix of northern and central Thai dishes, so you might start with some spicy sausages and move on to red curry beef and *pla tod chon* (deep-fried serpent-head fish). ✉ *402/1–2 Banphaprakan Rd.,* ☎ *053/715722. No credit cards.*

$$$–$$$$ 🏨 **Dusit Island Resort.** Sitting on an island in the Mae Kok River, this
★ gleaming white high-rise has all the amenities you'd expect from a world-class hotel. On the premises you'll find the largest outdoor pool in North-

ern Thailand. The complex's three wings all have rooms overlooking the shore. Filled with modern renditions of traditional Thai furnishings, the spacious rooms have unexpected extras like large marble baths. The Peak grills up delicious steaks, while Chinatown stir-fries Cantonese fare. The casual Island Café, where a buffet breakfast is served, serves Thai food all day. All three dining rooms have impressive views. ⊠ *1129 Kraisorasit Rd., 57000,* ☎ *053/715777; 02/238–4790 in Bangkok,* 🅵🅰🆇 *053/ 715801; 02/238–4797 in Bangkok;* 🆆🅴🅱 *http://chiangrai.dusit.com. 176 rooms. 3 restaurants, minibars, cable TV, 2 tennis courts, pool, health club, hair salon, massage, 4 bars, shops, nightclub, meeting rooms, airport shuttle, car rental. AE, DC, MC, V.*

$$ 🏨 **Rimkok Resort.** Because it's across the Mae Kok River, this quiet hotel has more appeal for tour groups than for independent travelers. The main building is designed in modern Thai style with palatial dimensions—a long, wide lobby lined with boutiques leads to a spacious lounge and dining room. Rooms are in wings on either side, and most have views of the river from picture windows. ⊠ *6 Moo 4 Chiang Rai Tathorn Rd., Rimkok Muang, 57000,* ☎ *053/716445; 02/279–0102 in Bangkok;* 🅵🅰🆇 *053/715859. 256 rooms. 4 restaurants, minibars, cable TV, pool, hair salon, bar, nightclub, shops, meeting rooms, car rental. AE, DC, MC, V.*

$ 🏨 **Chiang Rai Inn.** All the accommodations at this Lanna-style hotel look out over a cool, palm-shaded courtyard. Some of the comfortable rooms have sitting areas. The casual restaurant, furnished in cane and bamboo, serves an excellent choice of Northern Thai dishes. ⊠ *661 Uttarakit Rd., 57000,* ☎ *053/712673,* 🅵🅰🆇 *053/711483. 77 rooms. Restaurant. MC, V.*

$ 🏨 **Little Duck Hotel.** The first luxury resort in downtown Chiang Rai, Little Duck combines modern convenience with traditional Lanna design. There are even a few touches of Tibetan arts that make the place eclectic. The rooms are bright and cheery, with light-wood furnishing. Service is brisk and businesslike, as befits a hotel that handles many conventions. The travel desk organizes excursions into the neighboring hills. ⊠ *450 Super Highway Rd., Amphoe, Muang, 57000,* ☎ *053/ 715637; 02/255–5960 in Bangkok;* 🅵🅰🆇 *053/715639. 350 rooms. 2 restaurants, coffee shop, tennis court, pool, meeting rooms, travel services. AE, DC, MC, V.*

$ 🏨 **Wiang Inn.** In the heart of downtown, this low-slung hotel is still the best lodging in Chiang Rai. Spacious rooms are decked out in dark woods and fine fabrics. Outside is a small outdoor pool surrounded by exotic greenery. The Golden Teak restaurant serves Thai, Chinese, and other fare. ⊠ *893 Phaholyothin Rd., 57000,* ☎ *053/711533,* 🅵🅰🆇 *053/ 711877,* 🆆🅴🅱 *www.wianginn.com. 260 rooms. Restaurant, minibars, cable TV, pool, health club, nightclub, travel services. AE, DC, V.*

¢ 🏨 **Ben's Guest House.** This family-run inn has repeatedly won accolades for its first-rate accommodations. The steep-eaved Lanna-style home is at the end of a quiet lane on the western edge of town. Transportation into Chiang Rai is easy to arrange. ⊠ *35/10, San Khon Noi Rd., Soi 4, 57000,* ☎ *053/716775. 22 rooms.*

¢ 🏨 **Golden Triangle Inn.** Don't confuse this cozy guest house with the backpackers hangout at Ban Sop Ruak. This comfortable little place is all too popular—advance reservations are necessary—because of its ideal location in the center of town. Wood-ceiling rooms are cooled by slowly turning fans. The café serves Thai and Western fare, while the terrace bar has a wide range of fruity drinks. Next door is a travel agency that arranges treks into Laos. ⊠ *590 Phaholyothin Rd., 57000,* ☎ *053/711339,* 🅵🅰🆇 *053/713963. 20 rooms. Restaurant, fans, bar, travel services. No credit cards.*

¢ ⊡ **The White House.** The charming Indian-Thai couple who run this
★ attractive inn are justifiably proud of what they regard as their own
home. Rooms are huddled around a courtyard. Nearby is a small pool
and an open-air café. The owners also run an efficient travel service
and a modest business center. ⊠ *789 Phaholyothin Rd., 57000,* ☎ *053/*
713427 or 053/744051, FAX *053/713427. 24 rooms. Restaurant, café,*
pool, business center, travel services. MC.

Outdoor Activities and Sports

If you really want a dramatic journey north, board a long-tail boat at
the border town of Tha Ton, 25 km (18 mi) north of Fang, and ride
the rapids to Chiang Rai. The 100-km (60-mi) trip takes four hours
by high-powered long-tail boat, or two days by raft.

En Route   If you're travelling north from Chiang Rai on Highway 110, watch for
the left-hand turn at Km 32 to **Doi Tung.** The road winds 42 km (25
mi), to the summit, where an astonishing view opens out over the surrounding countryside. The temple here, Wat Phra That Doi Tung,
founded more than a millennium ago, is said to be the repository of
some important relics of the Buddha, including a collarbone. The
shrine attracts pilgrims from as far away as India and China, for whom
its huge Chinese Buddha figure is a vastly important symbol of good
fortune. On the mountain slopes below the temple is the summer home
built for the king's late mother. The fine mansion is closed to the public, but the gardens, an explosion of color in all seasons, is often open.

Chiang Saen

❷⓿ *59 km (37 mi) north of Chiang Rai, 239 km (148 mi) northeast of Chi-*
ang Mai, 935 km (581 mi) north of Bangkok.

On the banks of the Mae Khong River sits Chiang Saen, a one-road
town that in the 12th century was home to the future King Mengrai.
Only fragments of the ancient ramparts survived the incursion by the
Burmese in 1588, and the rest of the citadel was ravaged by fire when
the last of the Burmese were ousted in 1786. The government-financed
excavation project now under way is well worth visiting.

Only two ancient chedis remain standing. Just outside the city walls
is the oldest chedi **Wat Pa Sak,** whose name refers the 300 teak trees
that were planted in the surrounding area. The stepped temple, which
narrows to a spire, is said to enshrine holy relics brought here when
the city was founded. Inside the city walls stands the imposing octagonal **Wat Phra That Luang.** Scholars say it dates from the 14th century.

Next door to Wat Phra That Luang is the **National Museum,** which
houses artifacts from the Lanna period, as well as some Neolithic discoveries. The museum also has a good collection of carvings and traditional handicrafts from the hill tribes. ☎ *053/777102.* ⊡ *Admission.*
⊙ *Wed.–Sun. 9–4.*

Lodging

¢ ⊡ **Chiang Saen Guest House.** One of several guest houses now found
in Chiang Saen, this one was among the first on the scene and is popular as a gathering point for travelers, who trade tales at the riverside
restaurant. Rooms are simply furnished but more than adequate for
the price. The helpful owner is well informed about trips in the area.
⊠ *45 Tambon Wiang, 57150,* ☎ *053/650146. 10 rooms, 3 bungalows.*
No credit cards.

¢ ⊡ **Gin's Guest House.** The best guest house in Chiang Saen is run by a
local schoolteacher. A couple of kilometers north of town, the main house
has attractively furnished, spacious rooms. Less expensive rooms are avail-

able in A-frame buildings in the garden. A simple breakfast is included. ✉ *Sop Ruak Rd., 57150,* ☎ *053/650847. 12 rooms. No credit cards.*

Chiang Khong

㉘ *53 km (33 mi) northeast of Chiang Rai.*

The recently paved road east out of Chiang Saen parallels the Mae Khong River en route to Chiang Khong, a town with magnificent views across the river to Laos. Songthaews ply the route, but you can also hire a speedboat to go down the river, a thrilling three hours of slipping between the rocks and rapids. Not too many tourists make the journey, especially to villages inhabited by the local Hmong and Yao tribes. The rugged scenery along the Mae Khong River that is actually more dramatic than that around the Golden Triangle.

Across the river from Chiang Khong is the Laotian town of **Ban Houie Sai,** where you can find beautiful antique Laotian textiles. Thais are permitted to cross the river, but foreigners require visas. Numerous guest houses in Chiang Khong accommodate overnight visitors. A 15-day visa can be acquired in Chiang Khong from **Ann Tour** (✉ 6/1 Moo 8, Saiklang Rd., ☎ 053/655198).

Lodging

¢ 🏨 **Bamboo.** On the banks of the Mae Khong River, Bamboo has thatched bungalows with hot and cold running water. There's also a pleasant restaurant and lounge. ✉ *71/1 M.1 Huaviang,* ☎ *053/791621. 12 rooms. Restaurant, lounge. No credit cards.*

Ban Sop Ruak

㉙ *8 km (5 mi) north of Chiang Saen.*

Ban Sop Ruak, a village in the heart of the Golden Triangle, was once the domain of the opium warlord Khun Sa. More than a decade ago, government troops forced him back to Burmese territory, but his reputation still draws those eager to see evidence of the man who once held the region under his thumb.

The only evidence of opium that you are likely to see will be at the **Opium Museum** in the center of town. A commentary in English details the growing, harvesting, and smoking of opium. Many of the exhibits, such as carved teak opium boxes and jade and silver pipes, are fascinating. It's open daily from 7 to 6.

Even if you don't stay overnight, pay a visit to the sumptuous **Imperial Golden Triangle Resort,** which has some of the best views over the confluence of the Mae Sai, Mae Ruak, and Mae Khong. Beyond you can see the hills of Myanmar and Laos.

Lodging

$$ 🏨 **Le Meridien Baan Boran Hotel.** This distinctive resort, perched on
★ a hill about 12 km (7 mi) from Chiang Saen, overlooks the confluence of the Mae Ruak and Mae Khong rivers. Rooms are luxuriously furnished in indigenous woods and draped with handmade Thai fabrics. Enjoy the view from the picture windows that open onto your private balcony. The two contrasting restaurants—a formal one indoors, an informal one outside—both serve excellent Thai, Burmese, and Chinese fare. The Opium Den Bar is just the address to put on your postcards home. ✉ *Chiang Saen, 57150,* ☎ *053/784084; 02/476–0022 in Bangkok;* 📠 *053/784090; 02/653–2208 in Bangkok. 106 rooms, 4 suites. 2 restaurants, in-room safes, minibars, cable TV, 2 tennis courts,*

pool, health club, squash, 2 bars, laundry service, meeting rooms, airport shuttle, car rental, travel services. AE, DC, MC, V.

$–$$ 🏨 **Imperial Golden Triangle Resort.** From the superior rooms in this high-eaved, Lanna-style hotel you are treated to magnificent views of three rivers rushing together. The smart restaurant, the Border View, lives up to its name, but the best way to enjoy the panorama is to soak it up with a glass of Mae Khong whisky on the terrace. Classical Thai dance is performed in the evening. ✉ 222 Ban Sop Ruak, ☎ 053/784001; 02/261–9000 Bangkok reservations; 🅵🅰🆇 053/784006 or 02/261–9518, 🆆🅴🅱 www.imperialhotels.com. 74 rooms. 2 restaurants, minibars, cable TV, pool, travel services. AE, DC, MC, V.

Mae Sai

③⓪   25 km (15 mi) west of Ban Sop Ruak, 60 km (36 mi) north of Chiang Rai.

From Ban Sop Ruak you can travel west on a dusty road to Mae Sai, a town that straddles the Mae Sai River. At this market town the merchants trade goods with the Burmese. For the best view across the river into Burma, climb up to **Wat Phra That Doi Wao**—the 207-step staircase starts from behind the Top North Hotel.

Foreigners may cross the river to visit **Tha Kee Lek** on a one-day visa, obtainable at the bridge for $10. It's a smaller version of Mae Sai, selling the same goods. For $30 you can get a three-night visa that lets you travel north to **Kengtung,** a quaint town with colonial-era structures built by the British alongside old Buddhist temples. The 63-km (39-mi) trip on the unpaved road takes four to five hours in the dry season and up to eight the rest of the year.

Dining and Lodging

$ ✕ **Rabiang Kaew.** Set back from the main road by a wooden bridge, this restaurant built in the northern style has an unmistakable charm. Antiques adorning the dining room add to its rustic style. The Thai fare is tasty and expertly prepared. ✉ 356/1 Phaholyothin Rd., ☎ 053/731172. MC, V.

$ 🏨 **Wang Thong.** This riverside hotel was originally intended to cater for business executives trading across the nearby Thai-Burmese border, but now the guests are mostly travelers. Choose a room high up on the river side so you can spend an idle hour or two watching the flowing waters and the flowing pedestrian traffic across the bridge. Its rooms are modern and functional. The restaurant offers only average fare. ✉ 299 Phaholyothin Rd., 57130, ☎ 053/733388, 🅵🅰🆇 053/733399. 150 rooms. Restaurant, coffee shop, cable TV, in-room VCRs, pool, bar, pub, dance club, laundry service, business services. MC, V.

¢   🏨 **Mae Sai Guest House.** Backpackers rank this riverside guest house, about 1 km (½ mi) west of the bridge, as the best in Mae Sai. It's certainly among the cheapest, with a bungalow without air-conditioning costing just B80. A small garden area surrounds the main building, which houses a casual dining room. ✉ 688 Wiengpangkam, 57130, ☎ 053/732021. 20 bungalows. No credit cards.

¢   🏨 **Northern Guest House.** When the Mae Sai Guest House is full, this is a good second choice. The rooms are small (there's just enough room for a bed) but clean. A few have their own bath. The veranda-style dining room is pleasant in the evenings, as the river flows at the edge of the garden. ✉ 402 Tumphajom Rd., 57130, ☎ 053/731537. 26 cottages, some with bath. Dining room. No credit cards.

Shopping

Thais take household goods and consumer products across the river, where the Burmese trade them for sandalwood, jade, and rubies. Though you may want to see Myanmar, the prices and quality of the goods will not be better than in Mae Sai. Near the bridge, **Mengrai Antique** (⊠ Phaholyothin Rd., ☎ 053/731423) has a matchless reputation.

Rubies aren't the only red gems here. Mae Sai is also justifiably proud of its sweet strawberries, which ripen in December or January.

NORTHERN THAILAND A TO Z

To research prices, get advice from other travelers, and book travel arrangements, visit www.fodors.com.

AIR TRAVEL TO AND FROM NORTHERN THAILAND

In peak season, flights to Chiang Mai are heavily booked. Bangkok Airways flies daily from Bangkok, with a stopover in Sukhothai. Thai Airways has almost hourly flights from 7 AM to 9 PM from Bangkok (70 minutes; B2,100–B2,900), and direct daily flights from Phuket. Thai Airways International flies twice weekly to Kunming in China, and other international carriers fly to Chiang Mai from Singapore, Kuala Lumpur, Taipei, the Burmese cities of Yangon and Mandalay, and the Laotian cities of Vientiane and Luangprabang.

Thai Airways has five daily flights from Bangkok to Chiang Rai, two a day from Bangkok to Lampang, and a daily flight from Bangkok to Mae Hong Son. It also has flights daily between Chiang Mai and Mae Hong Son. In March and April, smoke from slash-and-burn fires often prevents planes from landing at the airport in Mae Hong Son.
➤ CARRIERS: **Air Mandalay** (⊠ Doi Ping Mansion, 148 Charoen Prathet Rd., Chiang Mai, ☎ 053/276884). **Bangkok Airways** (⊠ Chiang Mai International Airport, Chiang Mai, ☎ 053/281519). **Lao Aviation** (⊠ 240 Prapokklao Rd., Chiang Mai, ☎ 053/418258). **Silk Air** (⊠ Chiang Mai International Airport, Chiang Mai, ☎ 053/276459). **Thai Airways** (⊠ 240 Prapokklao Rd., Chiang Mai, ☎ 053/211044).

AIRPORTS AND TRANSFERS

Chiang Mai International Airport is about 10 minutes from downtown, a B80 taxi ride. Chiang Rai International Airport is east of the city. Lampang Airport is just south of downtown, while Mae Hong Son Airport is along the town's northern edge.
➤ AIRPORT INFORMATION: **Chiang Mai International Airport** (☎ 053/270222). **Chiang Rai International Airport** (☎ 053/793048). **Lampang Airport** (☎ 054/226258). **Mae Hong Son Airport** (☎ 053/612057).

BOAT AND FERRY TRAVEL

At Tha Thon, a town north of Fang, buy a B160 ticket for the long-tail boat departing at 12:30 PM. These public boats hold about a dozen passengers. You may hire your own boat for about B1,600. The trip down the Mae Nam Kok River to Chiang Rai takes about five hours, going through rapids and passing a few hill tribe villages. Bring bottled water, an inflatable cushion, and (most importantly) a sun hat. The more adventurous can travel by unmotorized raft (best during October and November, when the water flows quickly), staying overnight in villages on the three-day journey.

BUS TRAVEL TO AND FROM NORTHERN THAILAND

So-called VIP buses ply the route between Bangkok and Chiang Mai, stopping at Lampang on the way. The privately operated coaches depart Bangkok's Northern Bus Terminal at Mo Chit almost hourly. For around B400–B500 you get a very comfortable 10-hour ride in a modern bus with reclining seats, blankets and pillows, television, on-board refreshments—a lunch or dinner is even included in the ticket price. You can take cheaper buses, but the faster service is well worth the extra few bahts.

Destinations in Chiang Rai and the Golden Triangle are serviced by buses that leave regularly from Chiang Mai's two terminals. Chiang Mai's Arcade Bus Terminal serves Bangkok, Mae Hong Son, and destinations within Chiang Rai province. Chiang Phuak Bus Terminal serves Lamphun, Fang, Tha Ton, and destinations within Chiang Mai province. From Lampang, air-conditioned buses leave for Lamphun, Phrae, and Nan.

The easiest way to reach Lamphun from Chiang Mai is to take the minibuses that leave every 20 minutes from across the Tourism Authority of Thailand office on Lamphun Road. Both air-conditioned and non-air-conditioned buses connect Lampang to cities in the north as well as to Bangkok. Lampang's bus station is 2 km (1 mi) south of the city, just off the main highway to Bangkok.

➤ Bus Stations: **Arcade Bus Terminal** (✉ Super Hwy. and Kaew Nawarath Rd., Chiang Mai, ☎ 053/274638 or 053/242664). **Chiang Phuak Bus Terminal** (✉ Rattanakosin Rd., Chiang Mai, ☎ 053/211586). **Chiang Rai Bus Terminal** (✉ Prasopsook Rd., Chiang Rai, ☎ 053/711224).

CAR RENTALS

Two major car-rental agencies in Chiang Mai are Avis and Hertz. In Chiang Rai, the most prominent companies are Avis, National, and Budget. Budget has a good range of four-wheel-drive vehicles for trips off the beaten path. Avis also has an office at Mae Hong Son airport.

➤ Agencies: **Avis** (✉ Chiang Mai International Airport, ☎ 053/201574; ✉ Chiang Rai International Airport ☎ 053/793827; ✉ Mae Hong Son, ☎ 053/620457). **Budget** (✉ Chiang Mai, ☎ 053/202871; ✉ Chiang Rai, ☎ 053/740442). **Hertz** (✉ 90 Sridonchai Rd., Chiang Mai, ☎ 053/279474). **National** (✉ Chiang Rai International Airport, ☎ 053/793683).

CAR TRAVEL

The roads south of Chiang Mai or between Chiang Mai and Chiang Rai are no problem for most drivers. Even the Mae Rim route north of Chiang Mai is perfectly drivable. The road to Mae Hong Son from Chiang Mai, however, has more than 1,200 curves, so make sure your rental car has power steering. The most comfortable way to travel the route and enjoy the breathtaking mountain scenery is to let somebody else do the driving. The northern route through Pai (4 hours) is a more attractive trip; the southern route through Mae Sariang is easier driving but takes about two hours longer.

EMERGENCIES
CHIANG MAI
➤ Emergency Numbers: **Police** (☎ 191). **Tourist Police** (✉ 105/1 Chiang Mai–Lamphun Rd., ☎ 053/248130).
➤ Hospital: **Lanna Hospital** (✉ 103 Super Hwy., ☎ 053/357234).

CHIANG RAI
➤ Emergency Number: **Police** (☎ 053/711444).
➤ Hospital: **Overbrooke Hospital** (✉ Singhaklai Rd., ☎ 053/711366).

MAE HONG SON
➤ Emergency Number: **Tourist Police** (✉ Rajadrama Phithak Rd., ☎ 053/611812).

➤ HOSPITAL: **Srisangwarn Hospital** (✉ Singhanat Bamrung Rd., ☎ 053/611378).

HEALTH
Malaria and other mosquito-borne diseases are virtually unknown in the urban centers in the north, but if you're traveling in the jungle during the rainy season that stretches from May to August you might want to take antimalarials for your own peace of mind.

Hospitals are found in every major city. Even the simplest village clinic is clean and well equipped, so you need not fear of contaminated surgical implements or hypodermic needles. Doctors almost invariably speak English.

INTERNET
Internet cafés are on virtually every street corner in Chiang Mai and Chiang Rai, and you'll have no trouble locating one in the region's smaller towns. Charges vary enormously, ranging from B15 an hour to B2 a minute. Sometimes a half hour's Internet use includes a free cup of coffee. Rates in hotel business centers are much higher than in Internet cafés.

MAIL AND SHIPPING
Post offices are normally open weekdays 8:30 to 4:30 and for a few hours on Saturday morning. Chiang Mai's main post office is also open Sundays from 9 to noon. Post office employees are most often invariably friendly and helpful, proudly covering your letters with colorful pictorial stamps.
➤ POST OFFICES: **Chiang Mai** (✉ 402 Charoenmuang Rd., ☎ 053/241070). **Chiang Rai** (✉ 21 Uttarakit Rd., ☎ 053/711444). **Lampang** (✉ 61 Takrawnoi Rd., ☎ 054/224069).

MONEY MATTERS
Banks are swift and professional in all the region's major cities, and you can expect friendly assistance in English. ATMs are everywhere to be found and are clearly marked, as Thais have a predilection for machine banking. Instructions for using the machines are in English.

TAXIS AND TUK-TUKS
Most trips in a tuk-tuk within Chiang Mai should cost less than B30. Songthaews trundle around the city on fixed routes, but will deliver you to any destination for an extra B20. Settle the fare before you get in—if your Thai is limited, just hold up the relevant number of fingers. If you hold up three and your gesture evokes the same response from the driver, you'll be paying B30. Drivers of taxis and songthaews are scrupulously honest, at least in Chiang Mai.

TOURS OPERATORS
Every other storefront in Chiang Mai seems to be a tour agency, so you'd be wise to pick up a list of agencies approved by the Tourism Authority of Thailand before choosing one. Prices vary quite a bit, so shop around, and carefully examine the offerings. Each hotel also has its own travel desk with ties to a tour operator. The prices are often higher, as the hotels add a surcharge.

Chiang Mai's Trekking Club is an association of 87 licensed guides with enough experience between them to manage the most demanding customer. "Tell us what you want and we can arrange it" is the club's boast. The club has its own café where you can meet the guides over a drink.

If you want to go beyond getting your money's worth, try Dapa Tours, a nonprofit company run by Akha people to raise money for their villages. Summit Tour and Trekking and Top North also offer good tours at reasonable prices. World Travel Service is another reliable operator.

The major hotels in Chiang Rai and the Golden Triangle Resort in Chiang Saen organize minibus tours of the region. Their travel desks will also arrange treks to the hill tribe villages. Should you prefer to deal directly with a tour agency, try Golden Triangle Tours.

Since it is the guide who sets the tone for the trip, arrange to meet yours before you actually sign on the dotted line. This is particularly important if you are planning a longer trek to the hill tribe villages. Make sure the guide knows the local dialects and will bring you to villages that haven't seen dozens of tour groups in the past week.

➤ CONTACTS: **Dapa Tours** (✉ 115 Moo 2, Rimkok Rd., Chiang Rai, ☎ 053/711354). **Golden Triangle Tours** (✉ 590 Phaholyothin Rd., Chiang Rai, ☎ 053/711339). **Summit Tour and Trekking** (✉ Thai Charoen Hotel, Tapas Rd., Chiang Mai, ☎ 053/233351). **Top North** (✉ 15 Soi 2, Moon Muang Rd., Chiang Mai, ☎ 053/278532). **Trekking Club** (✉ 41/6 Loi Kroh Rd., Soi 6, Chiang Mai, ☎ 053/818519). **World Travel Service** (✉ Rincome Hotel, Huai Kaeo Rd., Chiang Mai, ☎ 053/221044).

TRAIN TRAVEL

The State Railway links Chiang Mai to Bangkok and points south. As the uninteresting trip from Bangkok takes about 13 hours, overnight sleepers are the best choice. The overnight trains are invariably well maintained, with clean sheets on the rows of two-tier bunks. Parting with an few extra baht for a first-class compartment is strongly recommended. In second-class, you could find yourself kept awake all-night by revelers.

Trains for the north depart from Bangkok's Hualamphong Railway Station and arrive in the Chiang Mai Railway Station. Overnight sleepers leave Hualamphong at 3 PM, 6 PM, 8 PM, and 10 PM, arriving at 5:35 AM, 7:20 AM, 9:05 AM, and 1:05 PM. Return trains leave at 2:50 PM, 4:25 PM, 5:25 PM, and 11:30 PM and arrive in Bangkok at 5:55 AM, 6:25 AM, 6:50 AM, and 2:55 PM. The second-class carriages (the fare is B421–B681) are reasonably comfortable. First-class carriages (B1,193) are recommended if you value a good night's sleep. The Nakornping Special Express (no first-class coaches) leaves Bangkok at 7:40 PM and arrives in Chiang Mai at 8:25 AM. The return trip departs at 9:05 PM and arrives in Bangkok at 9:40 AM.

Most Bangkok–Chiang Mai trains stop at Lampang and at Lamphun, where a bicycle samlor can take you the 3 km (2 mi) into town for B30. The train to Lampang from Chiang Mai takes approximately 2½ hours; from Bangkok, it takes 11 hours.

➤ TRAIN STATION: **Chiang Mai Station** (✉ Charoenmuang Rd., ☎ 053/245563).

VISITOR INFORMATION

In Chiang Mai you'll find an office of the Tourist Authority of Thailand on Chiang Mai-Lamphun Road. It's in a small building on the eastern bank of the Mae Ping River, opposite the New Bridge. For information in Chiang Rai try the Tourist Information Centre on Singhakhlai Road.

➤ TOURIST INFORMATION: **Tourist Authority of Thailand** (✉ 105/1 Chiang Mai-Lamphun Rd., Chiang Mai, ☎ 053/248604). **Tourist Information Centre** (✉ Singhakhlai Rd., Chiang Rai, ☎ 053/711433).

5 ISAN

In the northeastern reaches of Thailand you'll find more than the centuries-old ruins of Khmer strongholds. Some of the country's most pristine nature reserves, including Phu Kra Dueng National Park and Khao Yai National Park, are also found in this little-explored region. Best of all, you'll encounter a way of life that is essentially unchanged from many years ago.

Updated by
Robert Tilley

TEAMS OF SNORTING WATER BUFFALO yoked to wooden plows are a common sight in the northeastern reaches of Thailand. This is the country's rice belt, where subsistence farmers work the fields so diligently that they can provide for not only their country's needs but also for those of neighboring countries. These fertile fields, which cover an area bigger than Portugal, are the heart (and many say, the soul) of Thailand.

Tour buses are rare on the roads of the sprawling northeast plateau. Consequently, the few travelers you'll see here are in search of the relatively undisturbed culture or remnants of its fascinating history. The region's chief attractions are its Khmer ruins, most of which have been only partially restored. Others come for its pristine nature reserves, such as Phu Kra Dueng National Park and Khao Yai National Park. Still others come to see the Mae Khong River, which borders the region to the north and east.

The good news is that even on a short trip you can get a sense of the region. If you are short on time, you may want to limit your visit to Nakhon Ratchasima, a four-hour journey by train from Bangkok. The town can serve as a base for trips to the nearby Khmer ruins at Phimae. Surin and Si Saket, a little farther away, are also good bases from which to visit more ruins.

Comprising about a third of Thailand's total area, Isan is nevertheless the country's poorest region. Life here is difficult, depending for the most part on the fickleness of the monsoons. The people of the Northeast, burned by the scorching sun and drenched by the torrential rains, are straightforward and direct, passionate and obstinate. Their food is hot and spicy, their festivals are robust, and their regional language is very similar to that of Laos. The new bridge over the Mae Kong River at Nong Khai has stimulated trade between Thailand and Laos, and you'll find interesting goods there and at Mukdahan. The handmade lace and tie-dyed cottons may tempt you, as may such oddities as large washbowls made of aluminum recycled from U.S. aircraft shot down during the Vietnam War. Nong Khai is also a good source for silver. For silk, try Udon Thani and its nearby silk-weaving villages.

Foreigners can cross into Laos at Nong Khai, Nakhon Phanom, and Mukdahan. They require Laotian visas costing $30, which can be obtained from the Laotian Embassy in Bangkok, the consulate in Khon Kaen, or directly at the Friendship Bridge. Some hotels and guest houses in Nong Khai can also obtain visas for an added fee.

Pleasures and Pastimes

Architecture

Toward present-day Laos and Cambodia, the Khmer influence is evident in the occasional *phrasat,* or tower, that dots the region. The phrasat wasn't a royal residence, but rather a retreat for those traveling from the Khmer temple of Angkor in present-day Cambodia. A few have been restored, but many are ruins redolent of their rich past.

Dining

The cuisine of Isan, the country's easternmost region, is nationally famous. Much is made from a limited range of staples that can be grown in the region's extreme climate—hot and dry until heavy rains flood the fields from May through October. The region is poor and the people have learned to make a little go a long way, but, as in other such regions, necessity has proved to be a virtue.

Always on the table is the glutinous *khao niaw* (sticky rice), which is preferred to the more refined *khao suay* (steamed rice). An Isan cook is also more generous with the spices, and herbs like basil and mint are liberally added to meat dishes. An especially tasty dish is *nua namtok,* which is sliced beef lightly grilled and garnished with shallots, dried chilies, lemon juice, and fresh mint leaves. Pork is popular, eaten in a style called *moo pan* (beaten flat and roasted over charcoal) and another called *moo yor* (ground and wrapped in a banana leaf).

Each province claims to have the best *kai yang* (roast chicken), but Si Saket and Udon Thani brag the loudest. Especially popular in Korat is *sai krog Isan,* a sausage filled with minced pork, garlic, and rice. It is usually cooked and eaten with sliced ginger, dry peanuts, and grilled chilies. But be warned—it is *very* spicy. The locals douse just about everything with *balah,* a vile-smelling but tasty fermented fish sauce that is certainly worth trying.

CATEGORY	COST*
$$$$	over B400 (over US$10)
$$$	B300–B400 (US$7.50–$10)
$$	B200–B300 (US$5–$7.50)
$	B100–B200 (US$2.50–5)
¢	under B100 (under US$2.50)

*per person, for a main course at dinner

Lodging

Because relatively few tourists visit Isan, most hotels and guest houses cater chiefly to a business clientele. There are some top-class hotels in larger towns like Nakhon Ratchasima, Khon Kaen, and Udon Thani, but most accommodations are much more modest. As elsewhere in Thailand, standards of cleanliness are high and even the most basic room will invariably have fresh linen and towels.

Isan is a bargain—even the most expensive hotels charge less than $60 a night. Remember that such refinements as room telephones, televisions, and even hot water can be rare outside the cities.

CATEGORY	COST*
$$$$	over B6,000 (over US$150)
$$$	B4,000–B6,000 (US$100–$150)
$$	B2,000–B4,000 (US$50–$100)
$	B1,000–B2,000 (under US$50)
¢	under B1,000 (under US$25)

*All prices are for a standard double room, excluding tax.

Natural Wonders

Two of the most popular national parks are found in the Isan. Misty Phu Kra Dueng National Park, in mountainous Loei province, is where you'll find a profusion of wildflowers in the spring. Khao Yai National Park, southwest of Korat, is so expansive that it extends into four provinces. Another favorite is Ban Phue, northwest of Udon Thani, a 1,200-acre park covered with rocks of all sizes, some shaped into Buddhist and Hindu mythical figures.

Shopping

Villagers in the country's northeastern reaches have a rich tradition of handicrafts. Nakhon Ratchasima has a night market offering a big variety of local handicrafts. The village of Renu Nakhon produces cheerful quilted blankets and intricately patterned ceramics. Pottery made with rust-color clay is found in the village of Ban Kwian. Straw baskets are woven at Ban Butom, and Ban Choke produces fine silver bracelets and necklaces. Along the Mae Khong River you'll find markets, like the one in Mukdahan, that sell crafts brought over from Laos; look for fine handmade embroidery and lace. The villagers of Chonnabot weave high-quality mudmee silk, as does those who live around Si Chiang. More silk comes from Chiang Khan and from villages south of Nakhon Ratchasima.

Exploring the Central Plains and Isan

In the best of all possible worlds you'd spend at least two weeks in this region, gazing down from its mysterious temples, strolling through the strongholds of long-gone civilizations, and wandering along the banks of the meandering Mae Khong River. You would browse in the markets and explore the villages. But on a trip of any length, you're sure to discover classic architecture of southern Isan.

Great Itineraries

Numbers in the text correspond to numbers in the margin and on the Isan map.

IF YOU HAVE 3 DAYS

From Bangkok, take an early morning flight to ☷ **Nakhon Ratchasima** ①, a city also known as Korat. Visit Prasat Hin Phimae, the late 11th-century Khmer sanctuary. In the evening, be sure to explore the Night Bazaar. On the next day take a car or bus to Prasat Hin Khao Phanom Rung, a supreme example of 12th-century Khmer architecture. On your third day, return to Bangkok.

IF YOU HAVE 5 DAYS

Take the overnight sleeper train to ☷ **Nong Khai** ⑭, which many people use as a gateway to Laos and its sleepy capital, Vientiane. On the next day travel south to **Udon Thani** ⑩, then go east to Ban Chiang, where archaeological finds suggest a civilization more than 7,000 years old. Continue on to ☷ **Nakhon Phanom** ⑧, on the banks of the Mae Khong River, leaving early on Day Three for **That Phanom** ⑦, home of northeast Thailand's most revered shrine. Continue south to ☷ **Mukdahan** ⑥, also on the Mae Khong River, for great shopping. Spend the night here or three hours south in ☷ **Ubon Ratchathani** ⑤, southern Isan's largest city, where you can visit two ancient temples. On the fourth day, travel west from Ubon to **Si Saket** ④, then turn south to Prasat Hin Wat Sra Kamphang Yai. Continue on to Prasat Sikhoraphum, a five-prang Khmer pagoda built in the 12th century. End the day at ☷ **Surin** ③, famous for its annual elephant roundup in the third week of November. On Day Five, push on to the restored hilltop sanctuary of Prasat Hin Khao Phanom Rung, a supreme example of 12th-century Khmer art.

When to Tour Isan

The dry months between November and March are also the coolest and therefore the best time to visit. After March, this central area of Thailand becomes almost unbearably hot. It is only slightly cooled by the rains that fall between June and early October.

NAKHON RATCHASIMA AND ENVIRONS

Nakhon Ratchasima

❶ *259 km (160 mi) northeast of Bangkok.*

Considered the gateway to the Northeast, Nakhon Ratchasima is the largest city in Isan and the second largest in Thailand. Most visitors

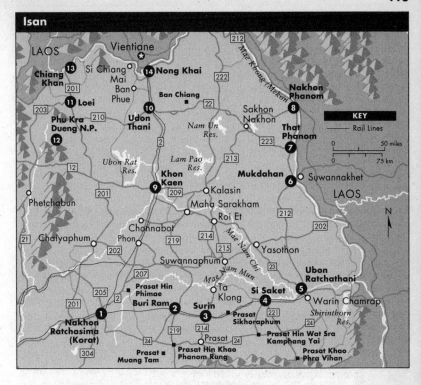

use the city, which is often called Korat, as a base for visiting Khmer treasures like Prasat Hin Khao Phanom Rung and Prasat Hin Phimae. It's also near **Khao Yai National Park,** a nature reserve that covers 2,168 square km (833 square mi) in four provinces. It's a frequent destination for Thais needing a break from Bangkok.

★ Along with nearby Prasat Hin Khao Phanom Rung, **Prasat Hin Phimae** is one of the great Khmer structures in Isan. Built sometime in the late 11th or early 12th century, it has been carefully restored. To enter the prasat through the two layers—the external sandstone wall and the gallery—is to step back eight centuries. By the time you reach the inner sanctuary, you're swept up in the creation and destruction of the Brahman gods engraved on the lintels. A quartet of *gopuras* (gate towers) guard the entrances, with the main one facing south toward Angkor. The central white sandstone prang, towering more than 60 ft, is flanked by two smaller buildings, one in laterite, the other in red sandstone. The combination of pink and white is exquisite, especially in the light of early morning and late afternoon. The principal prasat is surrounded by four porches, whose external lintels depict Hindu gods and scenes from the Ramayana. Inside, the lintels portray the religious art of Mahayana Buddhism.

The excellent museum was founded with the support of Princess Maha Chakri Sirindhorn. Its two floors contain priceless treasures from the Dvaravati and Khmer civilizations—notably great works of Khmer sculpture. The museum's masterpiece is a stone statue of King Jayavarman VII of Anghor Thom, found at Prasat Hin Phimae. ⊠ *Tha Songkran Rd.,* ☎ *044/471167.* 🖼 *Admission.* ☉ *Tues.–Sun. 9–4.*

From Prasat Hin Phimae, take a 2-km (1-mi) excursion to the village of **Sai Ngam,** home of the world's largest banyan tree. It's said to be 3,000 years old, which is easy to believe if you examine its mass of intertwined trunks. Its shade makes it a favorite picnic spot for Thai families.

Lodging

$–$$ ⊞ **Hermitage Resort & Spa.** The hotel's name is misleading—it sounds like a secluded retreat, but it's very much in the center of town. The high-rise is set in a garden, so you might just feel you are out in the country. Rooms, some of them with attractive oriel windows, are tastefully furnished with flowing fabrics and indigenous woods. At the health club you can work out, then reward yourself with a traditional Thai massage at the spa. ⊠ *725/2 Thaosura Rd., 3000,* ☎ *044/247444,* FAX *044/247463,* WEB *www.hermitagekorat.com. 139 rooms. Restaurant, coffee shop, room service, minibars, cable TV, pool, aerobics, gym, health club, massage, sauna, bar, shops, business center, travel services. AE, DC, MC, V.*

$–$$ ⊞ **Royal Princess.** Regal it's not, but this gleaming showplace does have finely furnished guest rooms decorated in restful pastel shades. The expansive lobby gives way to a comfortable lounge. The coffee shop overlooks a small garden and pool, which offers some relief from the glare of the noonday sun reflecting off the hotel's white concrete walls. The formal restaurant serves the best Cantonese food in town. ⊠ *1/37 Surenarai Rd., 3000,* ☎ *044/256629,* FAX *044/256601,* WEB *korat.royalprincess.com. 186 rooms. Restaurant, coffee shop, minibars, cable TV, 2 tennis courts, pool, health club, laundry service, business services, meeting rooms, travel services. AE, DC, MC, V.*

$ ⊞ **Chamsurang.** In the heart of town, this lodging is minutes away from the Night Bazaar. It's an older hotel, but the lobby and rooms have been smartened up for modern times. The English-speaking staff is very friendly and helpful. The restaurant serves Thai dishes, including Isan specialties. ⊠ *2701/2 Mahadthai Rd., 30000,* ☎ *044/257088,* FAX *044/252897. 157 rooms. Restaurant, refrigerators, cable TV, pool, laundry service. MC, V.*

$ ⊞ **Ratchapruk Grand Hotel.** This modern high-rise has all the comforts and conveniences business travelers expect. The light and airy rooms, decorated mostly in primrose accented with pale woods, are a delight for the eye. The hotel's Sha Sha disco and karaoke bar are a magnet for the city's young and trendy crowd. ⊠ *311 Mittraphat Rd., 3000,* ☎ *044/261277. 159 rooms. Restaurant, minibars, cable TV, pool, gym, bar, laundry service, meeting rooms, travel services. AE, DC, MC, V.*

$ ⊞ **Rooks Korat.** Even if you're not an avid golfer, you might enjoy this country club about 28 km (17 mi) southwest of Nakhon Ratchasima. The cozy, comfortable rooms have private patios that overlook the par-72 golf course. The terrace beside the pool is a pleasant spot for dinner—try the excellent crispy free-range chicken. ⊠ *Km 22, Korat–Pakthonchai Rd., Ban Laemluak, 30000,* ☎ *01/212–0254,* FAX *01/222–1371. 62 rooms. Restaurant, golf course, pool. MC, V.*

$ ⊞ **Sima Thani Hotel.** This long-established business hotel has a regular clientele of corporate executives from Bangkok, but it also draws travelers intent on exploring this fascinating region. Rooms are quite comfortable, furnished with extras like desks and easy chairs. If you get a hankering for a midnight snack, the coffee shop is open 24 hours. Best of all is the extensive evening buffet, with musicians and dancers wandering about the open-air terrace. The hotel's only disadvantage, however, is its out-of-town location. ⊠ *Mittraphap Rd., Tambon Nai Muang, 30000,* ☎ *044/243812,* FAX *044/251109. 135 rooms. Restaurant, coffee shop, minibars, cable TV, pool, gym, health club, massage, billiards, piano bar, laundry service, meeting rooms, travel services. AE, DC, MC, V.*

Shopping

Between 6 and 9 PM head to Nakhon Ratchasima's **Night Bazaar,** on Manat Road in the center of town. A block-long street is taken over by food stands and vendor stalls and is crowded with locals. Another huge local bazaar for clothes and general merchandise is fun to explore during the day. It's near the Night Bazaar on Chomsuranyart Road.

A side trip to **Pak Thongchai Silk and Cultural Centre,** 32 km (20 mi) south of Korat, offers a chance to see how locals make silk, from the raising of silkworms to the spinning of thread and the weaving of fabric. You can buy silk at some 70 factories in the area. For ceramics, drive out to the village of **Ban Dan Kwian,** 15 km (10 mi) southwest of Nakhon Ratchasima. The rust-color clay here is used for reproductions of classic designs.

Buri Ram

❷ *90 km (56 mi) east of Nakhon Ratchasima.*

The provincial capital of Buri Ram, between Nakhon Ratchasima and Surin, is a good gateway for those visiting the nearby Khmer prasats.

★ The restored hilltop shrine of **Prasat Hin Khao Phanom Rung,** 7 km (4½ mi) from the village, is a supreme example of Khmer art. Built in the 12th century under King Suriyaworamann II, one of the great Khmer rulers, it was restored in the 1980s at a cost of $2 million. It's one of the few Khmer sanctuaries without later Thai Buddhist additions. The approach to the prasat sets your heart thumping—you cross an imposing bridge and climb majestic staircases to the top, where you are greeted by a magnificent reclining Vishnu lintel. This architectural treasure hit the headlines some 30 years ago. It mysteriously disappeared in the 1960s, then reappeared at the Chicago Art Institute. After 16 years of protests it was finally returned to its rightful place. Step under the lintel and through the portal into the double-walled sanctuary. Intricate carvings in a style similar to those found in Lopburi cover the interior walls, and in the center of the prasat stands the great throne room dedicated to Lord Shiva.

Scattered around the area are other Khmer prasats in various stages of decay, many of them overgrown by vegetation. One of these has been rescued by Thailand's Department of Fine Arts. **Prasat Muang Tam,** estimated to be 100 years older than its neighbor, started off as a 10th-century Hindu sanctuary. Its main building symbolically represents the universe, with lesser towers emanating from the center. Today four towers remain, all containing carvings of Shiva and his consort Uma, Varuna on a swan, Krishna with cows, and Indra on the elephant Erawan. The complex is flanked by ceremonial ponds, with five-headed nagas lying alongside.

Surin

❸ *98 km (60 mi) east of Buri Ram, 198 km (119 mi) east of Nakhon Ratchasikma.*

Surin is famous for its annual Elephant Roundup, held the third week of November. The impressive show includes elephants performing tricks while their mahouts reenact scenes of capturing them in the wild. The main show starts at 7:30 AM. The town is packed with visitors at roundup time, so make sure you have a hotel reservation if you plan to join them.

If you want to see elephants the rest of the year, head to Ta Klang, a village 60 km (37 mi) north of Surin. The village is home of the Suay people, who migrated from southern Cambodia several centuries ago. Until recently, groups of Suay would venture into Cambodia to capture wild elephants and train them for the logging industry. But as elephants have been replaced by heavy machinery, the animals and their mahouts have become little more than tourist attractions. In Ta Klang you'll find an **Elephant Study Centre.** It includes a clinic to treat sick animals and spare them the journey to the elephant hospital in Lampang. Healthy animals give shows of their skills in public performances every Saturday morning, from 9:30 to 11.

On the road between Si Saket and Surin is **Prasat Sikhoraphum,** a five-prang Khmer pagoda built in the 12th century. The central structure has engraved lintels depicting Shiva, as well as carvings of Brahma, Vishnu, and Ganesha. ⊠ *40 km (24 mi) east of Surin.* ☎ *Admission.*

Lodging

¢ 🏨 **Phet Kasem Hotel.** The elephant grounds are within walking distance of this longtime favorite. Rooms are furnished with indigenous woods and colorful Thai fabrics. Its billiards room, bar, and cocktail lounge are a center of local nightlife. ⊠ *104 Jitbamroong Rd., 32000,* ☎ *044/511274,* 🖷 *044/511041. 162 rooms. Restaurant, minibars, cable TV, billiards, bar, lobby lounge, nightclub, meeting rooms, travel services. AE, MC, V.*

¢ 🏨 **Pirom Guest House.** This is a jewel of a place, a comfy little inn with incredibly reasonable rates. Owner Kun Pirom is a wealth of information about Surin and its elephants. ⊠ *242 Krungsrinai Rd., 32000,* ☎ *044/515140. 6 rooms. Breakfast room. No credit cards.*

¢ 🏨 **Thong Tarin Hotel.** Ask for a corner room at the town's most stylish hotel—they're larger and have commanding views. There's a fresh and airy feel to this hotel, from the polished marble in the lobby and reception areas to the pastel shades of the guest room decor. The Darling Cocktail Lounge attracts local swells every evening, and the disco swings on weekends. The very reasonable rate, which includes an American breakfast, leaps during the Elephant Round Up week. ⊠ *60 Sirirat Rd., 32000,* ☎ *045/514281,* 🖷 *045/511580. 195 rooms. Restaurant, coffee shop, minibars, cable TV, sauna, nightclub, meeting rooms, travel services. AE, MC, V.*

Shopping

About 15 km (10 mi) north of Surin a small road leads to **Ban Choke,** a village famous for its excellent silk. Silver jewelry is now fashioned there as well. You can find bargains for bracelets and necklaces with a minimal amount of negotiation. You can detour south to **Ban Butom,** 12 km (7 mi) from Surin, where villagers weave the straw baskets sold in Bangkok. They'll be happy to demonstrate their techniques and sell their wares.

Si Saket

❹ *312 km (187 mi) east of Nakhon Ratchasima, 61 km (36 mi) west of Ubon Ratchathani.*

With the exception of a newly constructed temple that is said to be one of the grandest in the northeastern part of the country, the town of Si Saket is best known more for its pickled garlic and onion. But in early March, when the lamduan flower blooms, the town comes alive in a riot of yellows and reds. Locals celebrate with a three-day festival.

Prasat Hin Wat Sra Kamphang Yai, just outside Ban Sa Kamphang, is in better condition than many of the region's other Khmer sanctuaries. It has been carefully restored, even down to the items that have been lost or stolen over the last 900 years. Particularly spectacular are the lintels of the middle stupa, which depict the Hindu god Indra riding his elephant Erawan. The main gate, inscribed with Khom letters, is thought to be from the 10th century, built during the reign of King Suriyaworamann. The temple behind the prasat is a Thai addition, its walls covered with pictures illustrating Thai proverbs. ⊠ *40 km (25 mi) south of Si Saket.* ▣ *Admission.*

★ The spectacular ruins of **Prasat Khao Phra Vihanalong** are officially in Cambodia, now that the World Court resolved that country's bitter territorial dispute with Thailand. Until 1999 the temple was closed to visitors, as thick jungle bars the way from Cambodia. But the lure of tourist dollars led that country to work together with its former rival. The only practical route to the temple is through Thailand, so you'll have to show your passport at a checkpoint. The 12th-century compound, a jumble of red laterite, runs for more than 1 km (½ mi) along a steep escarpment that plunges into a thick rain forest. It's a long climb to the top, but the effort is rewarded by a truly breathtaking view of the jungle beyond. Tour operators in Ubon Ratchathani and Si Saket offer trips to the ruins, and it's certainly worth the expense. ⊠ *125 km (86 mi) southeast of Si Saket.* ▣ *Admission.*

Lodging

$$$$ 🏠 **Manee's Retreat.** In the center of a small village surrounded by rice
★ fields, this stylish wooden house perched atop 9-ft stilts lets you experience the Thailand that eludes most tourists. There are only two rooms, making this place ideal for a family or for two couples traveling together. You can dine on traditional Thai food on the spacious balcony, but most people opt for eating under the house, joined by locals who come to check out the foreigners. Daily activities designed to fit your interests are arranged by Manee, a charming lady who speaks fluent English. Activities include a trip to the Khmer ruins, a visit to the elephant camp at Surin, and a visit to a local village. You can even try your hand at planting rice. ⊠ *Ban Nong Wa, Moo 13/29, Klueg Kwang, Huey Tap Tan, 33120,* ☎ *01/834–5353. 2 rooms. No credit cards.*

Ubon Ratchathani

⑤ *227 km (141 mi) east of Surin, 167 km (100 mi) south of Mukdahan.*

Eastern Isan's largest city, Ubon Ratchathani is known as the "Royal City of the Lotus." It's the gateway to the so-called "Emerald Triangle," the verdant region where Thailand, Laos, and Cambodia meet. In the northern reaches of Ubon Ratchathani you'll find the Indian-style pagoda **Wat Nong Bua,** a copy of the famous one in India where the Buddha attained enlightenment more then 2,500 years ago. The rectangular white chedi is breathtaking. Another nice temple is **Wat Maha Wanaram,** which houses a revered Buddha image named Phra Chao Yai Impang, believed to have magical powers. Check out the wax float at the rear of the chedi, used in the Ubon Ratchathani Candle Procession held here in late July. Huge beeswax sculptures of Buddhist-inspired mythical figures are paraded through town.

Locals love the food stalls of **Haad Wat Tai,** an island in the middle of the Mun River. It's connected to the shore by a rope bridge that sends shivers of apprehension through those who cross. Try such favorites as *pla chon* (a fish whose name is often translated as "snakehead mullet") or the ubiquitous *kai yang* (roast chicken).

Lodging

$ 🏠 **Laithong Hotel.** Locally made crafts and colorful textiles make the rooms at this comfortable hotel stand out. This is one of the few places in the area in which you can experience a *phalaeng*, the traditional Isan meal served as you recline on cushions arranged on the floor. You'll be offered a raised bamboo tray with at least half a dozen specialties of the region. If that's too exotic, the Ruen Thong restaurant serves international dishes. There's also a pub where you can relax with a beer. ⊠ *50 Pichit Rangsan Rd.*, ☎ *045/264271*, FAX *045/264270. 124 rooms. Restaurant, coffee shop, minibars, cable TV, massage, piano bar, pub, nightclub, airport shuttle. MC, V.

¢ 🖬 **Rajthani Hotel.** A modest hotel used by business travelers, Rajthani Hotel is located in the center of the city. The rooms are simply furnished, and the baths have plenty of hot water. The clerks at the reception desk are friendly, but unable to provide much information about the area. ⊠ *297 Khuan Thani Rd., 34000*, ☎ *045/244388*, FAX *045/243561. 100 rooms. Restaurant. No credit cards.*

¢ 🖬 **Sri Kamol Hotel.** A five-minute walk from the Night Market, this downtown hotel wins points for its location. The hotel's best feature, however, is the friendliness of its young staff. ⊠ *26 Ubonsak Rd., 34000*, ☎ *045/241501*, FAX *045/243793. 82 rooms. Restaurant, refrigerators, cable TV. No credit cards.*

ALONG THE MAE KHONG

Mukdahan

❻ *167 km (100 mi) south of Ubon Ratchathani, 40 km (24 mi) south of Phra That Phanom.*

Thailand's newest provincial capital, Mukdahan is across the Mae Khong River from the Laotian town of Suwannakhet. All along the river you'll find vendors selling goods imported from Laos—a fascinating array of detailed embroidery, delicate lace, lacquered trays and bowls, and a wide array of souvenirs. When you're not shopping, sample some Thai and Laotian delicacies from one of the numerous waterfront food stalls. If you have secured a visa you can cross the Mae Khong.

Lodging

¢ 🖬 **Mukdahan Grand Hotel.** A modern concrete building, the Mukdahan Grand Hotel is the town's best lodging. Although the employees speak very little English, they are friendly and helpful. Rooms are plain, but adequately furnished with twin- or king-size beds and a table and chair. The restaurant serves a buffet breakfast that is included in the room rate, as well as Thai and Western dishes for lunch and dinner. ⊠ *70 Songnang Sanid Rd., 49000*, ☎ *042/612020*, FAX *042/ 612021. 200 rooms. Restaurant, refrigerators, cable TV. AE, MC, V.*

That Phanom

❼ *40 km (24 mi) north of Mukdahan, 50 km (31 mi) south of Nakhon Phanom.*

North of Mukdahan is the village of That Phanom, site of northeast Thailand's most revered shrine. No one knows just when **Phra That Phanom** was built, though archaeologists believe its foundations were in place by the 5th century. The temple has been rebuilt several times—its chedi now stands 171 ft high, with a decorative tip of gold that weighs more than 20 lbs. A small museum houses the shrine's ancient bells and artifacts. Droves of devotees attend an annual festival, usually held in February. The normally sleepy town comes to life as thousands fill the narrow streets.

About 10 km (6 mi) north is the small village of **Renu Nakhon,** which has along its main street a row of workshops similar to those that line San Kamphaeng Road near Chiang Mai. The artisans sell an extensive range of products, including clothing made of cotton and silk, quilted blankets, and colorful ceramics.

Nakhon Phanom

❽ *50 km (31 mi) noth of That Phanom, 252 km (156 mi) east of Udon Thani.*

Along the border of Laos you'll find Nakhon Phanom, a sleepy market town on the banks of the Mae Khong. Foreigners are allowed to cross the Mae Khong into Laos on one of the regularly scheduled ferries if they have a visa.

Lodging

¢ ▣ **Mae Nam Khong Grand View.** The views of the Mae Khong River are certainly grand at the town's leading hotel. The high-rise is bland, but the rooms are comfortable and clean. The restaurant serves Thai and Western dishes, and a live band plays in the nightclub on weekends. ✉ *527 Sunthon–Wichit Rd.,* ☎ *042/513564,* 𝔽𝔸𝕏 *042/511037. 116 rooms. Restaurant, minibars, cable TV, bar, nightclub. AE, MC, V.*

Khon Kaen

❾ *190 km (118 mi) northeast of Nakhon Ratchasima, 115 km (69 mi) south of Udon Thani.*

Thailand's third-largest city, Khon Kaen has seen rapid growth due to the government's efforts to bolster the economy of the northeastern region. Khon Kaen has long been renowned for its mudmee silk, celebrated each December with a huge festival. At **Chonnabot,** 50 km (30 mi) to the south, you can see the silk being processed, from its cocoon stage through its spinning and dying to its weaving on hand looms.

About 50 (30 mi) north of Khon Kaen is a small village called **Ban Kok Sa-Nga** where virtually every household is dependent on raising king cobras. The practice was started by a local medicine man some 50 years ago, but is now under the strict control of the Thai Tourism Authority. An official king cobra breeding center has been established on the grounds of the local temple. Many families, though, still raise the snakes in cages beneath their homes. (Many of the creatures do escape, so an overnight stay here is not recommended.) The cobras are displayed daily 7–5 (admission). Bus number 501 runs every half hour from Khon Kaen bus station to Ban Kok Sa-Nga.

About 80 km (50 mi) west of Khon Kaen is **Phuwiang National Park,** where the world's oldest fossils of carnivorous dinosaurs, the Siam Mityrennous Esannensil, were discovered. There are dinosaur museums at the park entrance, at Phu Pratu Teema, as well as in the nearby village of Kok Sanambin.

Lodging

$$ ▣ **Bungalow Thongwong.** For home comforts and informative tours of Ban Chiang and other places of local interest, you couldn't do better than stay with this hospitable couple at their bungalow halfway between Udon Thani and Khon Kaen. They are a wealth of information about the region, and can introduce you to all aspects of local life and culture. The newly built bungalow has two separate units, with individual sitting rooms and kitchens. Guests can also enjoy marvelous Thai home cooking at the family's table. The daily room rate includes all meals, airport transfers, and a car and driver to Ban Chiang, Khon Kaen,

Udon Thani, and other points of interest. ✉ *214 Moo 2, Non Sa-At, 41240,* ☎ *042/391205,* 🕸 *www.thaihomestay.co.uk. 2 suites. Kitchens. No credit cards.*

$ 🏨 **Sofitel Raja Orchid.** Khon Kaen's skyline is dominated by the gleaming 25-story facade of the Sofitel Raja Orchid, one of Isan's most luxurious hotels. Everything about it is first-rate—the rooms are elegant, furnished with indigenous woods and handwoven silks. If you're looking to splurge, there's always the 6,500-square-ft royal suite, which has its own helipad. The hotel is the center of Khon Kaen's nightlife, with Isan's largest karaoke bar, Studio 1, and a disco, the Funhouse, that really lives up to its name. German visitors marvel at Thailand's first microbrewery, the Kronen Brauhaus, where you can even order bratwurst. ✉ *9/9 Prachasumran Rd., 44000,* ☎ *043/322155; 800/221–4542 in U.S.;* 📠 *043/322150,* 🕸 *www.sofitel.com. 293 rooms. 5 restaurants, café, room service, minibars, cable TV, pool, aerobics, gym, health club, sauna, 3 bars, dance club, dry cleaning, laundry service, concierge, business services, meeting rooms, car rental, helipad, travel services. AE, DC, MC, V.*

¢ 🏨 **Roma Hotel.** An inexpensive lodging near the bus station, Roma Hotel has large, sparsely furnished rooms and baths with plenty of hot water. Air-conditioned rooms are better maintained than the fan-cooled ones. The staff is friendly. ✉ *50/2 Klangmuang Rd., 40000,* ☎ *043/237766,* 📠 *043/243458. 46 rooms. Restaurant, coffee shop. MC, V.*

Shopping

If you don't have time to make the trip to nearby Chonnabot, visit **Rin Thai Silk** (✉ 412 Namuang Rd., ☎ 043/220705 or 043/221042), an emporium that carries mudmee silks and cottons, both new and old. There are also ready-to-wear items at reasonable prices.

Udon Thani

⑩ *115 km (69 mi) north of Khon Kaen, 51 km (32 mi) south of Nong Khai.*

As the site of a major U.S. Air Force base during the Vietnam War, Udon Thani quickly grew in size and importance. There are still traces of the massive U.S. presence in the hostess bars, hamburger joints, and shopping malls. The independent Thais have managed to keep their hold on the city, and made it famous for their version of *kai yang,* or roast chicken that you can try at stalls on virtually every street. There's also an interesting city museum at the **Udon Cultural Centre** (✉ Tahaan Rd.). This exhibition space at Udon Teacher's College displays photographs and other items that depict the daily life of people in the region.

The chief attraction near Udon Thani is **Ban Chiang,** about 60 km (36 mi) east of Udon Thani. At this Bronze Age settlement, archaeologists have found evidence to suggest a civilization thrived here more than 7,000 years ago. The United Nations declared it a World Heritage Site in 1992. The peculiar pottery—red-on-cream with swirling geometric spirals—indicates that this civilization was ahead of its time in cultural development. Even more intriguing are that copper bells and glass beads are found here, many of which are similar to some found in North and Central America. This poses the question: did Asians trade with Americans 7,000 years ago, or even migrate halfway around the world? You can reach Ban Chiang from Udon Thani on the local bus, or take a car and driver for about B600.

Dining and Lodging

$ ✕ **Steve's Bar and Restaurant.** If you're yearning for some familiar fare, this is the place to find it. You'll also run into American ex-pats hobnobbing at the bar. (At least one regular is whispered to be an ex-CIA operative.) A lounge area is stocked with English-language newspapers and periodicals. The kitchen serves up staples like steak and kidney pie. ⊠ *254/26 Prajaksilapakom Rd.,* ☎ *042/244523. No credit cards.*

$–$$ 🏨 **Charoensri Grand Royal.** Just to make sure you get the message, the city's top hotel calls itself both grand and royal. It's certainly luxurious, with softly carpeted rooms furnished in pale woods and decorated in restful pastels. The two restaurants serve Thai, Chinese, and Western food, and there's a variety of beers on tap in the pleasant beer garden. ⊠ *277/1 Prachak Rd., 41000,* ☎ *042/343555,* ℻ *042/343550. 260 rooms. 2 restaurants, room service, minibars, cable TV, pool, gym, health club, sauna, piano, bar, beer garden, convention center, meeting rooms, car rental, travel services. AE, DC, MC, V.*

Shopping

If you're here for textiles, there's a busy community of silk weavers at the village of **Ban Na Kha,** about 14 km (8 mi) north on the Nong Khai Road.

OFF THE BEATEN PATH

BAN PHUE – One hour by bus northwest of Udon Thani is a 1,200-acre mountainside retreat near the village of Ban Phue. It's littered with rocks of all sizes, some in shapes that the faithful say resemble Buddhist and Hindu images. Wat Phra Buddha Baht Bua Bok, at the peak, is named after the replica of the Buddha's footprint at its base. The 131-ft pagoda is in the style of the revered Wat That Phanom, farther to the east. Take the path to the right of the temple and you'll reach a cave with a series of silhouette paintings thought to be 4,000 years old.

Loei

⓫ *152 km (90 mi) west of Udon Thani, 43 km (26 mi) south of Chiang Khan.*

The capital of the province, Loei is a quiet town that makes a good base from which to explore Phu Kra Dueng National Park and the other sights in the region. The local tourist office provides maps and brochures. It's located in the town's own park, a shady retreat containing two tiny shrines (one of them Chinese) said to be inhabited by a spirit so powerful that the king himself inaugurated the site.

Lodging

$$ 🏨 **Phu Pha Nam Resort.** With the exception of the rustic tiled floors of its pavilion-style restaurant and a stone walls of the billiards room, this entire hotel seems to be constructed of richly colored teak. You'll sleep on carved teak beds in teak-floor rooms, all of which have sitting areas with picture windows framing views of the nearby hills. The resort is set on a 52-acre estate about 70 km (42 mi) south of Loei. ⊠ *252 Moo 1, Koakngam Amphur Dansai, 42120,* ☎ *042/892055,* ℻ *042/892057,* 🌐 *www.phuphanamresort.com. 49 rooms. AE, DC, MC, V.*

$–$$ 🏨 **Loei Palace.** The sinuous white facade of the massive Loei Palace dominates the city's skyline. Surrounded by well-tended gardens, the pool is a welcome sight after a day exploring the mountains. The excellent restaurant, serving Thai, Chinese, and other dishes, reassures you that sophisticated cuisine is still to be found in this remote region. An interesting outing is to the Chateau de Loei, Thailand's top vineyard. ⊠ *Loei-Naduang Rd., 42000,* ☎ *042/815668,* ℻ *042/815675,* 🌐 *www.amari.com. 161 rooms. Restaurant, café, minibars, cable TV, pool, gym, massage, bar, laundry service, business services, meeting rooms, travel services. AE, DC, MC, V.*

Phu Kra Dueng National Park

⑫ *70 km (42 mi) south of Loei.*

Loei province's main attraction is Phu Kra Dueng National Park, a lone, steep-sided mountain crowned by a 60-square-km (23-square-mi) plateau. Because the top is nearly a mile above sea level, it's wonderfully cool. The profusion of flowers during March and April is brilliant. You reach the plateau by a 9-km (5½-mi) hike through lightly forested fields of daisies, violets, orchids, and rhododendrons. Once you're there, well-marked trails lead to scenic overlooks at the edge of the escarpment. The park is closed during the rainy season, which runs from July to October.

Chiang Khan

⑬ *235 km (146 mi) east of Nong Khai, 43 km (26 mi) north of Loei.*

Travel north of Loei and soon you'll come to Chiang Khan, a village set on the banks of the Mae Khong. Because of the old wooden houses along the river, the community retains much of its rural charm. On the eastern edge of town are scores of restaurants with seating areas facing the river and Laos. Downriver, a series of rapids tests the skill of boatmen. From Chiang Khan the road turns south to Loei, the provincial capital, a major stop on bus routes in all directions.

Lodging

¢ 🏨 **Chiang Khan Hill Resort.** On the banks of the Mae Khong, this re-
★ sort commands a marvelous view of a series of rapids. You can also see across to the Laotian countryside, making this resort worth a trip in its own right. Rooms are in octagonal bungalows, the choicest being the ones overlooking the water. Comfortable chairs are set by the windows so you can enjoy the view. There's an excellent open-air restaurant where the deep-fried shrimp cakes are crispy and delicious and the *somtan* (relish) tingles with lime. The chicken dishes are made from free-range birds. ✉ *Kaeng Khut Khu, 28/2 Mu 4,* ☎ *042/821285,* ℻ *042/821414. 40 rooms. Restaurant, refrigerators. MC, V.*

Nong Khai

⑭ *51 km (32 mi) north of Udon Thani, 60 km (36 mi) east of Chiang Khan.*

Nong Khai is literally the end of the line—it's the country's northernmost railhead and bus terminus. To the east and west the mighty Mae Khong meanders through largely uncharted territory, while across the river to the north lies Laos. The French influence that is still evident in the Laotian capital of Vientiane can also be seen in Nong Khai. The architecture of the town has noticeable Gallic touches, particularly the governor's residence on Meechai Road. Running parallel to Meechai Road is Rim Khong Road, lined by small guest houses and restaurants. Laotian goods, mostly textiles, are cheap and plentiful at Nong Khai's lively night market.

One of the main draws to Nong Khai is access to Laos via the **Friendship Bridge.** The kilometer-long bridge, which opened in 1992, has brought Nong Khai and its province a boost in tourist traffic, which means you can find accommodations here that rival those of bigger towns. To cross into to Laos, you must buy a visa for $30. From the Laotian side it's a 25-km (15-mi) samlor ride to the immensely charming capital city of Laos, sleepy little Vientiane.

Wat Pho Chai, the best-known temple, houses a gold image of the Buddha, Luang Pho Phra Sai, that was lost for many centuries in the muddy bottom of the Mae Khong. Its rediscovery, part of the local lore, is told in pictures on the temple's walls. Thailand's strangest temple grounds are just 5 km (3 mi) west of town on the Nong Khai–Phon Pisai Road at **Wat Khaek** (also called Sala Kaew Koo). The temple's gardens, created by an ecumenically minded monk, have an extraordinary collection of immense and immensely bizarre statues representing gods, goddesses, demons, and devils from many of the world's faiths, though the emphasis is on Hindu gods.

Lodging

$–$$ ☷ **Mae Khong Royal.** The main attraction of this Western-style lodging is its large pool, which is a godsend in the hot summer season. The nearby terrace, cooled by breezes off the Mae Khong River, is also pleasant. Rooms have great views of the Friendship Bridge and across to Laos. The hotel's only disadvantage is its isolated location about 2 km (1 mi) outside the town. ⊠ *222 Jommanee Beach, 43000,* ☎ *042/411022; 02/272–0087 in Bangkok;* ℻ *042/421280; 02/272–0090 in Bangkok. 177 rooms. Restaurant, coffee shop, room service, minibars, cable TV, miniature golf, 2 tennis courts, pool, billiards, bar, beer garden, dance club, shop, laundry service, meeting rooms, travel services. AE, DC, MC, V.*

¢ ☷ **Maekhong Guest House.** At this rambling collection of Thai-style buildings, meals are served on a wooden terrace perched on the banks of the river. One of the pleasures of an evening here is to sit at the balustrade and watch the fishermen haul in their nets. Most of the rooms are spartan, but a quartet of "VIP rooms" in a wooden annex overlooking the river are much nicer. On the premises you'll find a reasonably priced Internet café. ⊠ *519 Rimkhong Rd., 43000,* ☎ *042/460689,* ℡ *www.maekhongguesthouse.com. 40 rooms. Restaurant, Internet, travel services. No credit cards.*

¢ ☷ **Pantawee Resort.** It's not really a resort, but this spacious complex on the banks of the Mae Khong River is certainly comfortable. It's also ideally located just west of the Friendship Bridge. Many of the inexpensive rooms have sweeping views of the river—ask for Number 5, which has a private terrace with access to the waterside restaurant and café. The resort is a 15-minute bus ride to town. ⊠ *210 Jommanee Soi 5, 43000,* ☎ *042/411008,* ℻ *042/420059. 36 rooms. 2 restaurants, café, refrigerators, cable TV, Internet, travel services. AE, DC, MC, V.*

Shopping

Village Weaver Handicrafts, next to Wat Pho Chai, employs 350 families in the production of indigo-dyed mudmee cotton.

En Route You can take a marvelous scenic trip on the old dirt road west along the Mae Khong. Take your own wheels or travel by bus to **Si Chiang Mai,** 50 km (31 mi) from Nong Khai. This sleepy backwater is famous for producing spring-roll wrappers—you'll see the white translucent rice flour everywhere, spread out on mats to dry. Just out of Si Chiang Mai at road marker 83 you come to Wat Hin Maak Peng, a meditation temple run by *mae chee* (Buddhist nuns).

ISAN A TO Z

To research prices, get advice from other travelers, and book travel arrangements, visit www.fodors.com.

AIR TRAVEL

All air traffic to Isan radiates from Bangkok. There are several Thai Airways flights each day from Bangkok to Khon Kaen, Udon Thani, Buri Ram, Nakhon Phanom, Ubon Ratchathani, and Nakhon Ratchasima. There are buses and taxis at all airports.

➤ CARRIER: **Thai Airways** (✉ Sofitel Raja Orchid, 9/9 Prachasumran Rd., Khon Kaen, ☎ 043/227701; ✉ Manat Rd., Nakhon Ratchasima, ☎ 044/255542).

AIRPORTS
There are airports at Buri Ram, Khon Kaen, Nakhon Phanom, Nakhon Ratchasima, Ubon Ratchathani and Udon Thani. With the exception of Nakhon Ratchasima, which is 30 km (18 mi) from town, all airports are close to downtown.

BUS TRAVEL
Most of the towns in Isan are served by buses from Bangkok's Northern Bus Terminal. Nakhon Ratchasima is a major transport hub, with direct bus services to Bangkok, Pattaya, Rayong, Chiang Rai, Chiang Mai, and Phitsanulok.

From Phitsanulok, buses originating in Bangkok and Chiang Mai operate daily services to Loei, Khon Kaen, Nong Khai, and Udon Thani.

In general, buses are a bit cheaper than trains. Remember that many towns do not have formal bus terminals, but rather a spot along a main road where most buses stop.

Nakhon Ratchasima has two bus stations—the newer terminal in the city center and the older one north of Mittraphat Road. Buses to and from Bangkok use the new terminal, while buses to other destination in Isan depart from the older terminal.

Khon Kaen also has two bus stations. The one at the corner of Ammart Road and Klangmuang Road is for long-distance buses. The other, on Prachasamosorn Road between Namuang Road and Thaprarak Road, is for shorter trips.
➤ BUS STATIONS: **Khon Kaen** (✉ Ammart Rd. and Klangmuang Rd., ☎ 043/236574; ✉ Prachasamosorn Rd., ☎ no phone). **Nakhon Ratchasima** (✉ North of Mittraphat Rd., ☎ 044/242899; ✉ South of Mittraphat Rd., ☎ 044/245443).

CAR RENTALS
International chains Avis and Budget are well represented at airports throughout the region. Avis is found in Khon Kaen and Udon Thani, while Budget is at Khon Kaen, Nakhon Ratchasima, Ubon Ratchathani, and Udon Thani.

In Nakhon Ratchasima, local agency L.A. Trans Services will deliver a car to your hotel.
➤ AGENCIES: **Avis** (✉ Khon Kaen Airport, ☎ 043/344313; ✉ Udon Thani Airport, ☎ 042/244770). **Budget** (✉ Khon Kaen Airport, ☎ 043/345460; ✉ Nakhon Ratchasima Airport, ☎ 044/341654; ✉ Ubon Ratchathani Airport, ☎ 045/240507; ✉ Udon Thani Airport, ☎ 042/246805). **L.A. Trans Services** (✉ Nakhon Ratchasima, ☎ 044/267680).

CAR TRAVEL
The region's roads are well maintained, particularly those along the east–west route connecting Phitsanulok and Ubon Ratchathani and the north–south route of Nong Khai and Nakhon Ratchasima. The two routes intersect at Khon Kaen. You should experience no difficulty finding their way around on those roads; if you plan to explore further afield remember that few road signs are in English.

EMERGENCIES

➤ IN KHON KAEN: **General Emergencies** (☎ 191). **Police** (☎ 043/221162). **Khon Kaen Hospital** (✉ Chatu Phadung Rd., ☎ 043/236005).
➤ IN NAKHON RATCHASIMA: **General Emergencies** (☎ 191). **Police** (☎ 044/242010). **Maharat Hospital** (✉ Chang Phuak Rd., ☎ 044/254990).
➤ IN NONG KHAI: **Police** (☎ 042/411020). **Nong Khai Provincial Hospital** (✉ Meechai Rd., ☎ 042/411504).
➤ IN UBON RATCHATHANI: **Police** (☎ 045/254216). **Rom Gao Hospital** (✉ Auparat Rd., ☎ 045/254053).

HEALTH

The same precautions apply in Isan as in the rest of Thailand. Urban areas are free of malaria, but if you are traveling along the Mae Khong river or in the National Parks in the rainy season you're well advised to pack sprays and creams and sleep under mosquito nets.

MAIL AND SHIPPING

Post office employees are invariably friendly and helpful. Any hotel catering for international travelers will be happy to mail your letters.
➤ POST OFFICES: **Khon Kaen** (✉ 257/2 Klangmuang Rd.). **Loei** (✉ 137 Charoenrat Rd.). **Nakhon Ratchasima** (✉ Mukmontri and Mittraphap Rds.). **Nong Khai** (✉ 1167/23 Meechai Rd.). **Ubon Ratchathani** (✉ 17 Srinarong Rd.). **Udon Thani** (✉ Mukmontri and Wattana Rds.).

MONEY MATTERS

You'll have no difficulty at all finding banks with ATMs in all larger towns. They're easily identifiable by a blue-on-white sign. In smaller towns and villages you might have to seek out the foreign exchange counter of a local bank. Banks large and small will exchange foreign currency, particularly dollars, and cash traveler's checks. There's usually a nominal fee.

TOUR OPERATORS

For tours along the Mae Khong River east and west of Nong Khai, contact Holiday Puyfay Tour at the Pantawee Resort in Nong Khai. Ask for tour coordinator Komol Senjantchai. Central and eastern Isan are well covered by Kannika Tours, Prayoon Transport Tours, and Thorsaeng Travel in Udon Thani and B.B. Tour in Khon Kaen.
➤ TOUR COMPANIES: **B.B. Tour** (✉ 95-97 Ruenrom Rd., Khon Kaen, ☎ 043/320432). **Holiday Puyfay Tour** (Pantawee Resort, 210 Jommanee Soi 5, Nong Khai, ☎ 042/411008). **Kannika Tour** (✉ 36/9 Sisutha Rd., Udon Thani, ☎ 042/240443). **Prayoon Transport Tour** (✉ 546/1 Phosi Rd., Udon Thani, ☎ 042/221048). **Thorsaeng Travel** (✉ 546/1 Phosi Rd., Udon Thani, ☎ 042/221048).

TRAIN TRAVEL

The Northeastern Line runs frequent service from Bangkok to Isan (there are 26 trains a day from Bangkok to Nakhon Ratchasima alone). All trains go via Don Muang airport and Ayutthaya to Kaeng Khoi Junction, where the line splits. One track goes to Nakhon Ratchasima, continuing east to Buri Ram, Surin, and Si Saket before terminating at Ubon Ratchathani; the other line goes north, stopping at Bua Yai, Khon Kaen, and Udon Thani before arriving at Nong Khai.

Both routes have daytime express and local trains and an overnight express train with sleeping cars. The Ubon Ratchathani sleeper leaves Bangkok at 9 PM to arrive at 7:05 AM and departs from Ubon Ratchathani at 7 PM to arrive in Bangkok at 5:20 AM. The Nong Khai sleeper departs from Bangkok at 7 PM to arrive at 7:10 AM and on the return trip leaves Nong Khai at 6:35 PM to be back in Bangkok at 6:10 AM.

➤ TRAIN STATIONS: **Khon Kaen** (✉ Darunsamran Rd., ☏ 043/221112). **Nakhon Ratchasima** (✉ Mukkamontri Rd., ☏ 044/242044).

VISITOR INFORMATION

The Tourist Authority of Thailand has developed a highly organized network of offices to promote tourism in this long-neglected part of Thailand. The program centers on the geographical and logistical hub of Khon Kaen. Here you can obtain a sackful of information brochures and maps.

➤ TOURIST INFORMATION: **Khon Kaen** (✉ 15/5 Prachasamosorn Rd., ☏ 045/243770). **Nakhon Phanom** (✉ 184/1 Soontornvit Rd., ☏ 042/513490). **Nakhon Ratchasima** (✉ 2102–2104 Mittraphap Rd., ☏ 044/213666). **Ubon Ratchathani** (✉ 264/1 Khuan Thani Rd., ☏ 045/243770). **Udon Thani** (✉ 16/5 Mukmontri Rd., ☏ 042/325406).

6 THE SOUTHERN BEACHES

Hidden coves disturbed only by sea kayakers, sweeping bays perfect for sailing, and beaches blanketed with hundreds of sun-worshippers from around the world—this is what you'll find along Thailand's sandy coastline. Accommodations run the gamut here. You can choose a luxurious air-conditioned resort or sleep outside under the stars.

Updated by
Robert Tilley

T**HE MILES OF SANDY BEACHES** in Southern Thailand are pure hedonism. Everything is here for those in search of sun and surf. Water sports abound, ranging from sea kayaking around the otherworldly rock formations to sailing the waters of crystal-clear bays. Accommodations range from luxury resorts with every amenity to simple thatched bungalows a stone's throw from the ocean. And the food will delight the palate, with exotic fruits for breakfast and bountiful seafood grilled to perfection in the evening.

What you'll have to search for, however, is a little privacy. The southern tip of Thailand is crowded with sun-seekers that literally blanket the best beaches. In their wake high-rise hotels and low-budget eateries serving hamburgers and pizza have cropped up. There are still stretches of shore that are deserted, but you'll have to get far off the beaten track to find them.

Pleasures and Pastimes

Beaches

The curving beaches on the island of Phuket, some small and intimate, some large and sweeping, are made for sun-soaked idleness. If the crowds are too intense, across the bay you'll find the less traveled beaches of Krabi, many overhung by dramatic limestone cliffs. Along the Gulf of Thailand, beaches come in all shapes and sizes. You can relax by the shore in genteel surroundings at Cha-Am and Hua Hin. If you seek idyllic beaches, go south of Hua Hin or Ko Samet. Some lotus-eaters will tell you that nothing can beat the beaches of Ko Samui and its neighboring islands.

Dining

In the south of Thailand, the food can get very spicy; they say the hottest curries come from the country's southernmost region. Around the beach resorts seafood is king, usually lightly sautéed in oil and garlic or spiced up with chilies. Grilled king prawns melt in your mouth. A dish like *her thalee kanom khrok,* seafood cooked in coconut milk to which spices, including lemongrass, are added, is one of the joys of visiting the south. Crabs are a real treat on Phuket. Around Surat Thani the oysters are famous; they are farmed on bamboo poles in river estuaries. Another east coast specialty is salted eggs: coated in a mixture of salt and earth from anthills, they're then rolled in the ashes of rice husks. In August, head to Surat Thani to sample the luscious fruit from the rambutan tree.

CATEGORY	COST*
$$$$	over B400 (over US$10)
$$$	B300–B400 (US$7.50–$10)
$$	B200–B300 (US$5–$7.50)
$	B100–B200 (US$2.50–5)
¢	under B100 (under US$2.50)

per person, for a main course at dinner

Lodging

One thing that makes the country's beach resorts so attractive to travelers from around the world is the wide range of accommodations. There are hotels and guest houses for every budget, from the height of luxury to the most modest of digs. Phuket is the most popular resort in the resort region, and has the high prices to prove it. Krabi is quickly catching up. The small island of Ko Phi Phi has a score of little bungalow resorts and a couple of luxury resorts.

On the Gulf of Thailand, Ko Samui is extremely popular, as is Pattaya. Other towns along the coast are more modest, with mostly simple bungalows and small restaurants.

Rates fluctuate widely—in holiday periods they can more than double. Always double-check your rate when you book.

CATEGORY	COST*
$$$$	over B6,000 (over US$150)
$$$	B4,000–B6,000 (US$100–$150)
$$	B2,000–B4,000 (US$50–$100)
$	B1,000–B2,000 (under US$50)
¢	under B1,000 (under US$25)

All prices are for a standard double room, excluding tax.

Scuba and Snorkeling

The Similan Islands in the Andaman Sea and the Angthong National Park in the Gulf of Thailand, each protected by the government, are superb dive sites where visibility ranges from 60 to 120 ft. Ask at your hotel about taking an overnight dive trip, or investigate a three- to four-day live-aboard cruise. Be sure to wear something to protect your feet when swimming or wading among coral reefs. Better still, don't touch coral at all. Irreparable damage is being caused to Thailand's coral reefs by inconsiderate divers and swimmers.

Exploring the Southern Beaches

You don't have to travel far from Bangkok to find exhilarating beaches. Head south on the west coast of the Gulf of Thailand to Cha-Am and Hua Hin, two courtly resorts, or try the eastern coast for gaudy Pattaya. Continue south and you hit isolated beaches on Ko Samet and Ko Chang.

Along the narrow peninsula that stretches south of Bangkok all the way to the Malaysian border there are scores of beaches worth exploring. All are reachable from the town of Surat Thani, about 11 hours by train south of Bangkok. Phuket, an island in the Andaman Sea, was first to be developed. Its expanding popularity has caused tourists to try the beaches of Krabi on the mainland and Ko Phi Phi and other islands in between. Ko Samui, in the Gulf of Thailand, has rapidly grown in recent years to compete with Phuket as an alternative resort area, but it is still less developed.

Great Itineraries

It's unlikely that any traveler, however intrepid, would wander down the peninsula exploring the towns along the coast. Visitors usually settle in at one resort for as many days as they have set aside. Should you wish to cover both coasts, there is a six-hour land/boat service between Phuket and Ko Samui, and both Thai Airways and Bangkok Airways have daily direct flights between the islands. You can travel from Bangkok to the beaches along the northern part of the Gulf of Thailand in a few hours. Getting to the southernmost resorts takes time. By land, count on a good 12 to 14 hours (usually through the night), or by air (including airport transfers), half a day.

IF YOU HAVE 2 DAYS

Drive south of Bangkok to 🏠 **Hua Hin** ⑤ on the western edge of the Gulf of Thailand. Spend two days soaking up the rays. If you're more in the mood for a party, the resort town of 🏠 **Pattaya** ① is on the gulf's eastern shore.

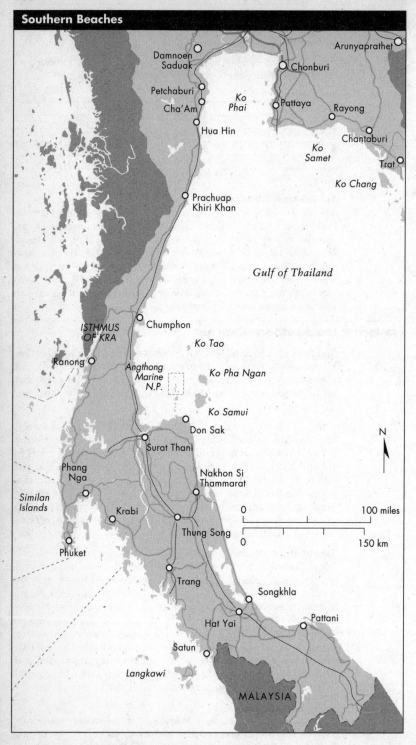

IF YOU HAVE 5 DAYS
Fly from Bangkok to **Ko Samui** ⑧–⑭. A tour of the little island can easily be accomplished in less than a day. For those who are restless lying on beaches, spend an afternoon scuba diving to the Angthong Marine National Park. More adventurous types can take a long-tail boat to 🏕 **Ko Pha Ngan** ⑮ for a night or two, then proceed to **Ko Tao** ⑯. From Ko Tao, take the ferry over to **Chumphon** ⑥ on the mainland and pick up the train for Bangkok.

IF YOU HAVE 7 DAYS
Take an overnight train down to **Surat Thani** ⑦. When you arrive the next day you can you can head to 🏕 **Phang Nga Bay** ⑱. Here you can see the limestone rocks that tower out of the sea. Look familiar? It's where they filmed the James Bond movie *The Man with the Golden Gun*. On your fourth day head south to 🏕 **Phuket** ⑱–㉚, an island that can be reached via a causeway. You can see most of the sights of Phuket in a day, but if you want to see every beach you'd need considerably more time. However, you may want to make some day trips. On your sixth day head to **Ko Phi Phi** ㉛ for some snorkeling. On your last day relax on the beach, then fly back to Bangkok.

When to Tour the Southern Beaches

The west coast along the Andaman Sea has two seasons. During the monsoon season from May through October, when high seas can make beaches unsafe for swimming, hotel prices are considerably lower. The peak season is the dry period from November through April. Ko Samui and the islands in the southern Gulf of Thailand have a different weather pattern: the monsoon runs from late October through December. With the exception of the week from Christmas to New Year's Eve, prices can be halved during this period. Peak season runs from January through early July.

THE EASTERN GULF

As the capital becomes more and more congested, the Eastern Gulf is growing rapidly. The coast has long been a favorite escape from the heat and humidity of Bangkok, but some of the closer beaches have become so crowded that people now continue down the coast to quieter shores. Not all the towns along the way are attractive—Pattaya is particularly seedy—but most have lovely beaches. There are few cultural sights along the way, but you can stop for seafood at the many nearby fishing villages.

Numbers in the text correspond to numbers in the margin and on The Eastern Gulf map.

Pattaya

❶ *147 km (88 mi) southeast of Bangkok.*

Five decades ago, Pattaya was a fishing village sitting beside an unspoiled harbor. Discovered by affluent Bangkok residents, it became a weekend playground, replacing resorts farther south as a vacation destination. Then came the Vietnam War, with thousands of American soldiers stationed at nearby air and naval bases. They piled into Pattaya, and the resort grew with the unrestrained fervor of any boomtown.

But the boom eventually went bust. Today, after quite a few years in the doldrums, Pattaya is regaining a bit of its popularity. Pattaya still has the many hostess bars catering to foreign men, but there are plenty of attractions that appeal to families. Water quality in the bay is improving with the introduction of modern water- and sewage-treatment

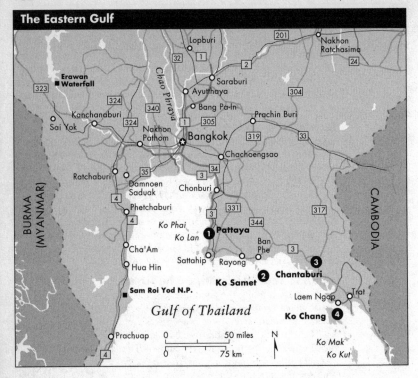

plants. And the overcrowded highway from Bangkok has been expanded, making the trip here easier during the week. On weekends, however, the road still remains congested; the two-hour trip often takes four.

Pattaya can be divided into three sections: the northernmost section, Naklua Beach, has bars and restaurants that cater to foreigners, including some backpackers. On a small promontory south of the Dusit Resort Hotel is the curving bay of Pattaya, along which runs Beach Road, lined with palm trees on the beach side and modern resort hotels on the other. At the southern end of the bay is the fun part of town—bars, nightclubs, restaurants, and open-front cafés dominate Sunset Avenue and the adjoining streets.

In addition to its obvious attraction for adults, Pattaya also has plenty of activities designed for families. Children love the **Elephant Kraal,** where 32 pachyderms display their skills in a two-hour show. There are demonstrations of everything from their part in ceremonial rites to their usefulness in construction. Everything is staged, but it's always fun to see elephants at work and at play. Although it's a bit unsettling to see these gentle giants languishing in the city, their mahouts now have little other choice in making a living. For tickets, go to the Tropicana Hotel on Pattaya 2 Road. ⊠ *5 km (3 mi) from Pattaya,* ☎ *038/ 249818.* ⊠ *Admission.* ☉ *Daily shows at 2:30* PM.

Also popular with kids is the **Pattaya Monkey Training Centre.** The pig-tailed monkeys, who live about 40 years, are adept at harvesting coconuts, a skill they are taught over the course of a year. They are also taught a few other entertaining tricks that bring a smile to the face of even the most jaded traveler. ⊠ *Km 151, Soi Chaiyapruk, Sukhumvit Rd.,* ☎ *038/ 756367.* ⊠ *Admission.* ☉ *Daily shows at 9, 11, noon, 1, 2, and 5.*

☺ If you want to see elephants and monkeys in one trip, **Nong Nuch Village** has a small zoo. Two restaurants serve refreshments that you can enjoy beneath a coconut tree. Despite its touristy nature, the village is a pleasant place to kick back, particularly if you're traveling with children. Hotels will arrange transportation for morning and afternoon visits, as it is 15 km (9 mi) south of Pattaya. ⊠ *163 Sukhumvit Hwy., Bang Saray,* ☎ *038/709358.* ☜ *Admission.* ☉ *Daily 9–5:30; folklore show daily 9:45, 10:30, and 3.*

The **Million Years Stone Park and Crocodile Farm** has gigantic rocks in grotesque shapes that decorate a large garden. A man-catching-crocodile show draws the crowds every hour. ⊠ *22/1 Mu, Nongplalai, Banglamung,* ☎ *038/422957.* ☜ *Admission.* ☉ *Daily 11–5.*

The **Bottle Museum** is actually quite special. Pieter Beg de Leif, a Dutchman, has devoted many hours each day over the last 17 years to creating more than 300 miniatures—tiny replicas of famous buildings and ships—in bottles. ⊠ *79/15 Moo 9, Sukhumvit Rd.,* ☎ *038/422957.* ☜ *Admission.* ☉ *Daily 10–8.*

Dining and Lodging

$$ ✕ **Bruno's.** This restaurant, which replaced a Pattaya institution called Dolf Riks, is well on its way to being an institution itself. It has preserved the warm, friendly atmosphere; you can still chat at the bar or head to the dining room for top-quality food. The difference is in the cuisine. Dolf Riks was Indonesian-influenced, while Bruno's leans toward Swiss recipes. ⊠ *463/28 Sri Nakorn Centre (on cul-de-sac beside Pattaya Bowl),* ☎ *038/361073. AE, DC, MC, V.*

$$ ✕ **Peppermill Restaurant.** This distinctly French restaurant takes a classical approach to dining, with an emphasis on flambéed dishes. Should you prefer that your meal not arrive in flames, entrées such as fresh crab in a white-wine sauce and poached fillet of sole with a lobster tail don't disappoint. Dinner is a special occasion here, particularly if complemented by a bottle of wine from the respectable cellar. You'll find the place tucked away next to the P. K. Villa hotel. ⊠ *16 Beach Rd.,* ☎ *038/428248. AE, DC, MC, V. No lunch.*

$$ ✕ **Pic Kichen.** In this series of classic teak pavilions you can dine on a wide range of Thai dishes such as the delicious deep-fried crab claws and spicy eggplant salad. The food can be made hot or mild. If you are averse to chilies, try the ginger-scented white snapper. ⊠ *Soi 5, Beach Rd.,* ☎ *038/428387. AE, DC, MC, V.*

$$ ✕ **Tak Nak Nam.** This floating restaurant in a pavilion on the edge of a small lake has an extensive menu of both Chinese and Thai dishes. Live classical and folk music plays while you dine on such specialties as steamed crab in coconut milk and blackened chicken with Chinese herbs. ⊠ *252 Pattaya Central Rd., next to Pattaya Resort Hotel,* ☎ *038/429059. MC, V.*

$ ✕ **Nang Nual.** At the southern end of Pattaya Beach Road is Nang Nual, one of the city's better places for seafood. A huge array of freshly caught fish is laid out on blocks of ice as you enter. Point to what you want and explain how you'd like it cooked (most people ask for it to be grilled). For carnivores, the huge steaks are an expensive treat. A menu filled with photographs of the entrées overcomes the language barrier. There's a dining room upstairs, but ask for a table on the terrace overlooking the ocean. A newer branch is across from Jomtien Beach, near the Sigma Resort. ⊠ *214–10 S. Pattaya Beach Rd.,* ☎ *038/428478;* ⊠ *1 25/24-26Moo 1 2 Jomtien Beach Rd.,* ☎ *038/231548. AE, MC, V.*

$ ✕ **Sportsman Inn.** If you can't go another day without steak and kidney pie, bangers and mash, or fish-and-chips, this is the place. It's the best spot in Pattaya for well-prepared pub grub, as testified to by the many expats who get their daily sustenance here. ✉ *Soi Yod Sak (Soi 8),* ☎ *038/361548. No credit cards.*

$ ✕ **Vientiane Restaurant.** Named after the capital of Laos, this restaurant serves both Laotian and Thai cuisine. The dishes from Thailand's northeastern province of Isan, similar in style to those to Laos, are your best bet. If it's a pleasant evening, ask for a table outside on the terrace. The restaurant is located near the Marriott Resort. ✉ *Pattaya 2 Rd.,* ☎ *038/411298. MC, V.*

$$$$ 🏨 **Royal Cliff Beach Hotel.** Pattaya's most lavish resort, the Royal Cliff Beach Hotel is perched high on a bluff jutting into the gulf. This self-contained resort is actually a cluster of four gleaming white hotels. Most rooms gaze down at the shore. The lavish suites in the Royal Wing (about double the price of standard rooms) have extras like butler service and breakfast served in your rooms. The Royal Cliff Terrace has two-bedroom suites perfect for families. There are several swimming pools, each with a view. The resort is about 1½ km (1 mi) south of town. ✉ *Jomtien Beach,* ☎ *038/250421; 02/282–0999 in Bangkok;* ℻ *038/250141,* 🌐 *www.royalcliff.com. 952 rooms, 162 suites. 4 restaurants, miniature golf, 2 tennis courts, 3 pools, sauna, 2 beaches, windsurfing, boating, jogging, squash, bar, shops. AE, DC, MC, V.*

$$$ 🏨 **Dusit Resort.** At the northern end of Pattaya Beach, this large hotel
★ has superb views. The beautifully kept grounds, with a lap pool and a free-form pool with a swim-up bar, are on the tip of a promontory pushing into the ocean. The rooms have comfortable sitting areas and private balconies. For a bit more you can book one of the the larger "landmark rooms," which have elegant touches like wood trim. At the Empress, which serves sophisticated Cantonese fare, you can dine as you enjoy views of Pattaya Bay. This retreat is only a short songthaew ride from Pattaya attractions. ✉ *240/2 Pattaya Beach Rd. 20260,* ☎ *038/425611; 02/236–0450 in Bangkok,* ℻ *038/428239;* 🌐 *pattaya.dusit.com. 500 rooms, 28 suites. 4 restaurants, 3 tennis courts, 2 pools, health club, massage, sauna, windsurfing, boating, Ping-Pong, squash, bar, shops. AE, DC, MC, V.*

$$$ 🏨 **Pattaya Marriott Resort & Spa.** Located a block from the beach, this traditional-style hotel has a large lobby that opens out onto a tropical garden. Towering trees line the path to the shimmering pool. The rooms are large enough for a coffee table and two chairs. Your private balcony overlooks the ocean. Next door is the Royal Garden Plaza, so you're steps away from some of the town's best shopping. ✉ *218 Beach Rd., Chonburi 20260,* ☎ *038/412120; 02/477–0767 in Bangkok;* ℻ *038/429926,* 🌐 *www.marriotthotels.com. 300 rooms. 2 restaurants, 4 tennis courts, pool, health club, hair salon, bar, business services, meeting rooms, travel services. AE, DC, MC, V.*

$$ 🏨 **Montien.** Although it couldn't be described as plush, this centrally located hotel has a laid-back atmosphere that many people prefer. With its generous off-season discounts, the Montien is one of the best values in town. Across from the beach, it is designed to take advantage of the sea breezes. The Garden Restaurant has a dance floor and stage for entertainment. ✉ *Pattaya Beach Rd., Chonburi 20260,* ☎ *038/361340; 02/233–7060 in Bangkok;* ℻ *038/423155,* 🌐 *www.montien.com. 320 rooms. 2 restaurants, coffee shop, snack bar, 2 tennis courts, pool, bar, meeting rooms. AE, DC, MC, V.*

¢ 🏨 **Chris Guest House.** With clean, comfortable rooms at a price far below most lodgings in Pattaya, this hotel is a top choice in the budget category. Its friendly atmosphere means many guests return time and time again. On the ground floor there's an open-air restaurant where old roués gather around a table presided over by the English owner. Although it's on a soi only half a block from the crowds along Pattaya Beach Road, the hotel somehow manages to feel secluded. ✉ *185 Soi*

13, Pattaya Beach Rd., Chonburi 20260, ☎ 038/429586, ℻ 038/423653. 15 rooms. Restaurant, bar. No credit cards.

¢ 🖼 **Palm Lodge.** This was once a very basic hotel, but its location—in the middle of town yet surprisingly tranquil—prompted the owners to make some improvements. Now you'll find modern rooms with such amenities as cable TV and minibars. The pool is small, but set in a shady garden. Besides, the beach is just across the road. ⊠ *Mu 9, Beach Rd., Chonburi 20260, ☎ 038/428780, ℻ 038/421779. 80 rooms. Coffee shop, minibars, cable TV, pool, laundry service. MC, V.*

Nightlife and the Arts

Entertainment in Pattaya revolves around its nightlife. Scattered throughout town are hundreds of beer bars, which are low-key places where the girls merely want to keep you buying drinks. The raunchy go-go bars are mostly found on the southern end of town. Gay bars are located in the sois between Pattaya Beach Road and Pattaya 2 Road called Pattayaland.

Many establishments stay open until 2 AM, but crackdowns have curtailed all-night revelry. Be careful wandering around after dark, as gangs have been known to roam the streets. Take a taxi.

In the Pattaya Marriott Resort & Spa, **Shenanigans** (⊠ 218 Beach Rd., ☎ 038/710641) tries hard to conjure up an Irish pub by serving favorite brews like Guinness. A large-screen TV makes this a favorite for sports fans. For live music, try **Tony's** (⊠ Walking Street Rd., South Pattaya, ☎ 038/425795). Grab a beer and head to the outdoor terrace.

The gay bar on the terrace at **Le Café Royale** (⊠ 325/102-109 Pattayaland Soi 3, ☎ 038/423515) is a good place to go for drinks early in the evening. You can also get the scoop on the most happening clubs here.

Outdoor Activities and Sports

BUNGEE JUMPING

If you like a thrill, try **Kiwi Thai Bungee Jump** (⊠ Off the main road to Jomtien Beach, ☎ 038/250319). You are hoisted up to a platform 150 ft in the air.

GOLF

The **Laem Chabang International Country Club** (⊠ 106/8 Moo 4 Beung, Srirach, Chonburi, ☎ 038/372273) has lovingly maintained links near Pattaya. The greens fee is B1,500, plus B200 for a caddie. Thailand's longest fairway is at the **Royal Thai Navy Course** (⊠ Phiu Ta Luang Golf Course, Sattahip, Chonburi, ☎ 02/466–1180). It's located about 30 km (18 mi) from Pattaya. Bordered by dense vegetation, it's considered one of the country's most difficult courses. The **Siam Country Club** (⊠ 50 Moo 9 T. Poeng A., Banglamung, Chonburi, ☎ 038/418002), close to Pattaya, offers a challenging course with wide fairways lined by wooded hills.

WATER SPORTS

All kinds of water sports are available, including windsurfing (B200 per hr), waterskiing (B1,000 per hr), and sailing on a catamaran (B500 per hr). Private entrepreneurs offer these activities all along the beach. Be on the lookout for unscrupulous operators who rent a defective machine and hold the customer responsible for its repair or loss. The water near the shore is too polluted for diving and snorkeling.

En Route Take highway H3 south for about 20 km (12 mi) and turn right to reach **Bang Saray.** The fishing village has two narrow streets running parallel to the bay. Fully equipped game-fishing crafts are tied to the jetty, and photos to prove fishermen's stories are posted in the area's two hotel bars, Fisherman's Lodge and Fisherman's Inn. It costs about

B2,500 per day to charter one of the faster boats. If you just want to soak up the scene, stop next to the main jetty at the Ruam Talay Restaurant. Highway H332 passes through countryside full of coconut groves and tapioca plantations before it reaches **Rayong** (50 km/31 mi east of Sattahip), a booming market town famous for *nam plaa*, the fermented fish sauce Thais use to flavor their food.

Ko Samet

❷ *30 mins by ferry from Ban Phe, which is 223 km (139 mi) southeast of Bangkok.*

East of Pattaya is the small village of Ban Phe, whose beaches attract Thai families. This is the jumping-off point for trips to Ko Samet. Two ferries make the crossing, one going to Na Duan on the north shore, the other to An Vong Duan halfway down the eastern shore. All the island's beaches are an easy walk from either of these villages. Indeed, from the southern tip to the north is a comfortable three-hour walk.

Ko Samet is known for its sugary beaches. The island's other name is Ko Kaeo Phitsadan (Island with Sand Like Crushed Crystal), so it isn't surprising that its fine sand is in great demand by glassmakers. The island has many bungalows and cottages, with and without electricity. Make sure that yours has mosquito netting: come dusk, Ko Samet's mosquitoes take a fancy to tourists. Restaurants that set up along the beach in the late afternoon let you linger there a little longer. Seafood is the best choice but there's something for everyone. While you dine, the tide will inch its way up to your table in the sand, and your feet could be wet before you leave.

Lodging

$ 🏨 **Samed Cliff Resort.** This little cluster of bungalows has all the amenities you need—air-conditioning, hot water, even televisions and small refrigerators. The rooms are simply furnished, but clean and comfortable. Out front is a small beach with white sand and calm surf. The restaurant serves Thai food, as well as a few other dishes. For dinner venture out to one of the grills set up on the beach. This place is popular, so make reservations in advance. ✉ *Nanai Beach,* ☎ *016/457115; 02/635–0800 in Bangkok. 30 bungalows. Restaurant, pool. No credit cards.*

Chantaburi

❸ *100 km (62 mi) east of Rayong, 180 km (108 mi) east of Pattaya.*

Buses from Rayong and Ban Phe make the 90-minute journey to the pleasant provincial town of Chantaburi. It is a four-hour bus journey from Bangkok's Eastern Bus Terminal. The gem mines are mostly closed, but Chantaburi is still renowned as a center for gems. Rubies and sapphires still rule, but stones from all corners of the world are found in the town's shops. On Gem Street, in the center of town, you'll see traders sorting through gems and making deals worth hundreds of thousands of baht. The street becomes a gem market on Fridays and Saturdays with buyers and sellers from all over the world.

The province of Chantaburi has few beach resorts of note, and those cater mostly to Thais. Laem Sadet, 18 km (11 mi) from Chantaburi, is the most popular, and its accommodations range from small bungalows to low-rise hotels. Chantaburi is once again becoming a gateway to western Cambodia as Thailand's neighbor opens its borders.

Lodging

¢ 🏨 **KP Grand Hotel.** Although this high-rise hotel has little that could be called charming, it does have modern facilities. It's on the eastern side of town, within easy walking distance of Gem Street. Rooms include a buffet breakfast. ⊠ 35/200–201 Theerat Rd., 22000, ☎ 039/ 323201, FAX 039/323214, WEB www.chanthaburihotel.com. 202 rooms. 3 restaurants, pool, health club, bar, meeting rooms. AE, MC, V.

En Route Beyond Chantaburi lies Trat, Thailand's easternmost province. Hemmed in by the Khao Banthat mountain range, the region is waiting to be discovered by tourists. The provincial capital, **Trat**, two hours plus from Chantaburi, is a small market town. For travelers, it is where buses arrive from and depart for Bangkok, and where songthaews leave for the 20-minute trip to Laem Ngop, the port for ferries to Ko Chang.

Ko Chang

★ ❹ 1 hr by ferry from Laem Ngop, which is 15 km (9 mi) southwest of Trat; Trat is 400 km (250 mi) southeast of Bangkok.

Ko Chang made the front pages of the national newspapers in 2002, when people began to question who will develop Thailand's second-largest island. Chances are that the island will become another Ko Samui. Travelers who have enjoyed the solitude—not to mention inexpensive lodging—Ko Chang has offered for years may have to start looking elsewhere.

Ko Chang, or Elephant Island, is the largest and most developed of the 52 islands that make up Mu Ko Chang National Park. Many of these islands are not much more than sandbars protruding from the sea. Undiscovered by tourists, they have not yet been ruined by the commercialism found in Pattaya, Phuket, and Ko Samui. Most of the tourists who make the trip here are looking for unspoiled surroundings and inexpensive lodgings.

Ko Chang's best beaches are found on the western shore. Haad Sai Khao (White Sand Beach) attracts mostly backpackers, who pay B100 a night for lodging in huts along the narrow strip of sand. Haad Khlong Phrao is next, with a long, curving beach of pale golden sand. Accommodations here are spaced farther apart and tend to be more expensive. At the end of the only road on the island is Haad Kai Bae. The beach, with both sand and pebbles, has a very gentle drop-off, making it safe for nonswimmers.

A couple of islands not far from shore have unforgettable views. One of the most beautiful islands in the archipelago is tiny **Ko Wai,** three hours by ferry from Laem Ngop. It has idyllic beaches, tropical flora, and fantastic coral reefs. **Ko Ngam,** almost as small as Ko Wai, is shaped like a butterfly and has waters of different hues. **Ko Mak,** a little larger than the other islands, has a small village where you'll find a few bungalows for rent. **Ko Kut,** the second-largest island in the archipelago, is the most mountainous.

Lodging

$$ 🏠 **Kai Bae Hut Bungalows.** Accommodations here run the gamut from
★ tiny bungalows with few amenities to much larger ones with air-conditioning and private baths. All the lodgings face the beach. Because the resort is near the center of Kae Bae Beach, you can wander over to nearby restaurants for a meal. ⊠ Kai Bae Beach, Trat 23120, ☎ no phone. 25 rooms. Restaurant, dive shop. No credit cards.

$$ 🏠 **Ko Chang Resort.** One of the first comfortable lodgings to be built on Ko Chang, this self-contained complex sits on the edge of the bay. Getting here is easy, as the resort has its own boat service to the island. Rustic bungalows are huddled around a reception lounge and dining room. The rate for the air-conditioned units is fairly steep, however.

⊠ *Klong Prao Beach, Trat 23120,* ☎ *039/538055; 02/277–0482 in Bangkok;* ℻ *02/276–6929 in Bangkok,* 🖥 *www.kohchangresort.20m. com. 45 rooms. Restaurant. MC, V.*

$$ 🏨 **Sea View Resort.** In this resort you choose between thatched bungalows just beyond the sands of Kai Bae Beach or larger bungalows with air-conditioning and private baths on a slight rise a little farther from the beach. The resort is at the far end of the beach, making it quieter than most of the others. There is an attractive terrace restaurant not far from the gentle waves. ⊠ *Kai Bae Beach, Trat 23120,* ☎ *039/529022; 02/256–7168 in Bangkok;* ℻ *02/276–6929 in Bangkok. 32 rooms. Restaurant. MC, V.*

THE WESTERN GULF

In the 1920s King Rama VII built a palace on the western shore of the Gulf of Thailand at the town of Hua Hin. When the royal entourage traveled here from Bangkok, high society inevitably followed. Those were Hua Hin's glory days. After World War II when Pattaya's star shone brightly, Hua Hin grew dimmer. But Pattaya's seedy reputation has made visitors reconsider Hua Hin and neighboring Cha-Am. After a building boom in the 1990s, the coastline below Hua Hin is now dotted with high-rise hotels and sprawling condominiums.

To the south lies Ko Samui, the world's coconut capital. Discovered by backpackers several years ago, the island is regarded by many as a low-key alternative to Phuket. It's true that there are far fewer hotels, restaurants, and bars, but the island can get pretty lively in the evenings.

Ko Pha Ngan, north of Ko Samui, not yet discovered by most tourists, is still one of the world's most idyllic places. Ko Tao, north of Ko Pha Ngan, has some of the country's best snorkeling. The tiny islets of the Angthong Marine National Park, east of Ko Samui, are also superb for snorkeling.

Numbers in the text correspond to numbers in the margin and on The Western Gulf map and the Ko Samui map.

Hua Hin

⑤   *189 km (118 mi) south of Bangkok.*

The king and queen spend the month of April at the royal summer palace, found on the northern boundary of Hua Hin. The palace was completed in 1928 by King Rama VII, who named it Klai Kangwol, which means "Far From Worries." Four years later, while he was staying at Klai Kangwol, the army seized control in Bangkok and demanded that he relinquish absolute power in favor of a constitutional monarchy. He agreed, although the generals later apologized for their lack of courtesy.

When the upper classes from the capital followed the royal family to Hua Hin, they needed somewhere to stay. The Royal Hua Hin Railway Hotel was constructed to give these weary travelers somewhere to rest their heads. Near the intersection of Damnernkasem and Naresdamri roads you can still see the hotel, now called the **Sofitel Central Hua Hin Resort.** The magnificent Victorian-style colonial building was a stand-in for the hotel in Phnom Penh in the film *The Killing Fields.* Be sure to wander through its well-tended gardens and along the lovely verandas.

The highway to the southern provinces passes through the center of Hua Hin. Shops and cafés are found on either side. A congested street of market stalls runs parallel to it. The **Chatchai Street Market** is fun

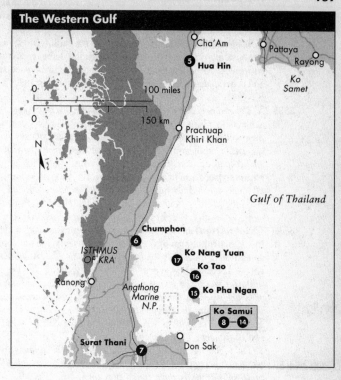

The Western Gulf

to explore. In the morning vendors sell meats and vegetables; beginning in the early evening, everything from food to trinkets is for sale.

If you look south along the coast, you'll see a small headland called **Khao Takiab.** You can reach it by songthaew, but the best way to get there is to hire a pony and trot along the beach. At the end of the 7-km (4-mi) journey you can walk past a large statue of the Buddha to a small Buddhist monastery—the views are worth the climb. Try to rent a fishing boat at the base of Khao Takiab to sail to the small island of Ko Singto, where you are guaranteed to catch a fish you'll describe to your friends back home.

You'll pass rice fields, sugar palms, pineapple plantations, and crab farms as you make your way to **Khao Sam Roi Yod National Park,** about 40 km (25 mi) south of Hua Hin. The park, difficult to reach without your own transportation, is a great place to spot wildlife. Try either of the two nature trails that wind through the park. Often spotted are monitor lizards and barking deer. With a little luck you'll see the dusky langur, a type of monkey also known as the spectacled langur because of the white circles around its eyes.

Dining and Lodging

$$ ✕ **Sang Thai.** For interesting seafood dishes—from grilled prawns with bean noodles to fried grouper with chili and tamarind juice—this open-air restaurant down by the wharf can't be beat. It's popular with Thais, which is always a good sign. Don't miss the *kang* (mantis prawns). Ignore the ramshackle surroundings and floating debris in the water. ⊠ *Naresdamri Rd.,* ☎ *032/512144. AE, DC, MC, V.*

$ ✕ **Fisherman's Seafood Restaurant.** Enjoy excellently prepared clams, crabs, lobsters, mussels, and delicious sea tiger prawns at this restaurant in the Royal Garden Resort. Depending on your taste, these can be cooked with Thai spices (such as garlic and peppers) or simply grilled. As in most

Thai restaurants it's better to order several dishes and share them. ⊠ *107/1 Phetkasem Rd.,* ☎ *032/511881. AE, DC, MC, V.*

$ ✕ **Taj-Mahal.** Thailand is not known for Indian food, but there a few outstanding restaurants serving traditional dishes from the Indian subcontinent. Although not as spicy as you might be used to, the curries and other dishes are quite tasty. ⊠ *31/1 Naresdamri Rd.,* ☎ *032/512613. No credit cards.*

$$$$ 🏨 **Chiva-Som.** Named the world's best health resort by one travel magazine, Chiva-Som has not been toppled from its lofty position, even with the proliferation of spas in Hua Hin. The resort focuses on holistic healing and a wholesome diet, but the setting on the beach will do you a world of good, too. The tasteful and comfortable lodgings have lots of natural woods and private terraces overlooking the ocean. Rates include all meals and a daily massage. ⊠ *73/4 Petchkasem Rd., 77110,* ☎ *032/ 536536; 02/381–4459 in Bangkok;* FAX *032/381154,* WEB *www.chivasom. com. 57 rooms. Restaurant, pool, massage, spa. AE, DC, MC, V.*

$$$$ 🏨 **Sofitel Hua Hin Resort.** Even if you don't stay at this local landmark, ★ its old-world charm makes it worth a visit. Wide verandas open onto splendid gardens that lead down to the beach. More than two dozen gardeners take their work very seriously, caring for the topiaries that look like shadows at night. The lounges on either side of the reception area are open to let in sea breezes. The best rooms are those on the second floor, as they have unforgettable views of the ocean. Come during the low season, when rates are almost half of what they are the rest of the year. ⊠ *1 Damnernkasem Rd., 77110,* ☎ *032/512021; 02/ 541–0123 in Bangkok;* FAX *032/511014,* WEB *www.sofitel.com. 214 rooms. 2 restaurants, coffee shop, 4 tennis courts, pool, snorkeling, boating, bar, nightclub, meeting rooms. AE, DC, MC, V.*

$$$–$$$$ 🏨 **Dusit Resort & Polo Club.** Although this resort opened more than a ★ decade ago, the polo grounds and riding stables have yet to be added, but you could certainly picture a few of the guests playing the game. The spacious lobby serves as a lounge for afternoon tea and evening cocktails, sipped to the soft tunes of traditional music. Just past an ornamental lily pond is the swimming pool complete with bubbling fountains, and beyond that is the beach. All rooms have private balconies, most with a sea view. There's shuttle service to Hua Hin and car service to Bangkok. ⊠ *1349 Petchkasem Rd., Cha-Am, Petchburi 76120,* ☎ *032/520009; 02/636–3333 in Bangkok;* WEB *www.dusit. com. 298 rooms, 10 suites. 5 restaurants, 2 bars, in-room safes, 5 tennis courts, pool, wading pool, gym, steam room, boating, parasailing, waterskiing, squash, meeting rooms. AE, DC, MC, V.*

$$$ 🏨 **Hilton Hua Hin Resort & Spa.** Towering over Hua Hin, this 17-story hotel is popular with European tour groups. Its rooms are spacious, modern, and functional. The lagoonlike pool dominates the garden, and the small sandy beach shares its limited space with vendors and tourists from other hotels. ⊠ *33 Naresdamri Rd., 77110,* ☎ *032/ 511612; 02/253–0123 in Bangkok;* FAX *032/511135,* WEB *www. huahinhilton.com. 297 rooms. 3 restaurants, 2 tennis courts, pool, health club, squash, nightclub, meeting rooms. AE, DC, MC, V.*

$$$ 🏨 **Hua Hin Marriott Resort & Spa.** Adjacent to the Sofitel Hua Hin Resort, this hotel has accommodations and service equal to those of its neighbor. The modern facility doesn't have the colonial ambience, so the rates are a few hundred baht less. Rooms are comfortable, if uninspired. Among the four restaurants is the Salathai, which is less elegant than the similarly named restaurant at the Sofitel, but serves better food. ⊠ *107/1 Phetkasem Rd., 77110,* ☎ *032/511881; 02/476–0021 in Bangkok;* FAX *032/512422,* WEB *www.marriotthotels.com/hhqmc. 215 rooms. 4 restaurants, coffee shop, 4 tennis courts, pool, snorkeling, boating, bar, nightclub, playground. AE, DC, MC, V.*

$$ 🏨 **Regent Cha-Am.** Taking a swim couldn't be easier than at the Regent Cha-Am, which has a quartet of pools spread among the dozens of bungalows facing the beach. The Lom Fang restaurant, overlooking a lake, grills up excellent fish accompanied by a spiced curry-and-lime sauce. The more formal restaurant, the Tapien Thong Grill Room, serves seafood and steak. In the evening, live musicians sing your favorite pop songs in Thai. The hotel has its own car service from Bangkok. ⊠ *849/21 Cha-Am Beach, Petchburi,* ☎ *032/451240; 02/ 251–0305 in Bangkok;* FAX *032/471491; 02/253–5143 in Bangkok;* WEB *www.regent-chaam.com. 630 rooms, 30 suites. 5 restaurants, coffee shop, 4 pools, snorkeling, boating, nightclub. AE, DC, MC, V.*

$ 🏨 **Jed Pee Nong.** On one of the town's main streets, this lodging has bungalows in a quiet courtyard. Rooms have huge beds and not much else, but the price couldn't be better. The terrace restaurant facing the street stays open late. It's a popular spot from which to watch the parade passing by. ⊠ *17 Damnernkasem Rd., 77110,* ☎ *032/512381. 44 rooms. Restaurant, coffee shop. MC, V.*

$ 🏨 **Pran Buri Seaview Beach Resort.** A string of small bungalows facing the beach make the best accommodations at this laid-back resort. Others lack the lovely views. Although simply furnished, the rooms all have their own private terraces. The main lodge contains a bar and dining room, where Thai, Chinese, and other dishes are served. ⊠ *9 Parknampran Beach, Prachuapkhirikhan 77220,* ☎ *032/631765. 60 rooms. Restaurant, minibars, 2 tennis courts, pool, health club, snorkeling, boating, bar, meeting rooms. AE, DC, MC, V.*

$ 🏨 **Sirin.** About a block from the beach, this hotel has comfortable rooms that have plenty of light streaming in through the wide windows. There's a dining room (which doubles as a lounge), but there are plenty of other restaurants nearby. ⊠ *18 Damnernkasem Rd., 77110,* ☎ *032/511150 or 032/512045,* FAX *032/513571. 35 rooms. Restaurant. AE, DC, MC, V.*

¢ 🏨 **All Nations.** Of the backpacker hangouts in Hua Hin, All Nations is the best. Local expats come by for breakfast, so you can get plenty of advice about traveling in the area. Rooms are clean, although none have private baths. The owner has set up a computer you can use for a small fee. ⊠ *10–10/1 Dechanuchit Rd., 77110,* ☎ *032/512747. 11 rooms with shared bath. Restaurant, bar. No credit cards.*

Outdoor Activities and Sports

Across the tracks from the quaint wooden railway station is the well-respected **Royal Hua Hin Golf Course** (⊠ Damnernkasem Rd., Prachuapkhirikhan, ☎ 032/512475). You can play for B800, plus B200 for a caddie. There's a lounge for refreshments.

En Route The charming fishing village of **Wang Daeng** is typical of coastal Thailand 20 years ago. The countryside to the south of the village is magnificent, with jungle-clad hills and a curving shoreline. Try to get as far south as the picturesque fishing village of **Ao Noi.** Beyond that is the pleasant, sleepy town of **Prachuap,** which has staggering views from the hills behind its bay.

Chumphon

❻ *400 km (240 mi) south of Bangkok, 211 km (131 mi) south of Hua Hin.*

Chumphon is regarded as the gateway to the south, since trains and buses connect it to Bangkok in the north, to Surat Thani and Phuket to the south, and to Ranong to the southwest. Ferries to Ko Tao dock at Pak Nam at the mouth of the Chumphon River, 11 km (7 mi) southeast of town. Most of the city's boat services run a free shuttle to the docks.

If you are overnighting here or have a couple of hours to spare before catching a bus, visit the night market. If you have more time, just north of Chumphon there's an excellent beach, **Ao Thong Wua Laen.** You can catch a songthaew on the street across from the bus station. The curving beach is 3 km (2 mi) of white-yellow sand with a horizon dotted by small islands that make up one of the world's strangest bird sanctuaries. Vast flocks of swifts breed here, and their nests are harvested for the bird's nest soup served up in the best Chinese restaurants of Southeast Asia. It's such a lucrative business that the concessionaires patrol their properties with armed guards.

Lodging

$–$$ ⊞ **Chumphon Cabana Beach Resort.** This friendly resort at the south end of Chumphon's Thong Wua Beach is a great place to stay if you want to make brief visits to Ko Samui and other nearby islands. The hotel wins top marks for its ecology-friendly program, essentially designed to save water and power and keep the beach free of the litter that too often disfigures Thai resorts. Accommodations are in bamboo-wall bungalows hidden in the lush foliage and rooms with with private balconies in several low-rise buildings. Furnishings are simple but tasteful. ✉ *69 Moo 8, Saplee, Pathui, 86230,* ☏ *077/560245,* 🖷 *077/560247. 140 rooms. Restaurant, dive shop, meeting rooms. MC, V.*

¢   ⊞ **Marokot.** This is not the most luxurious hotel in Chumphon, but the rooms are comfortable and the baths have plenty of hot water. The hotel is a short walk from the night market. Best of all, the rate is among the lowest in town. ✉ *102–112 Thannon Songkla, 86000,* ☏ *077/503628,* 🖷 *077/570196. 46 rooms. No credit cards.*

Surat Thani

❼ *200 km (124 mi) south of Chumphon.*

Surat Thani is the main embarkation point for boats bound for Ko Samui. Although it's not a particularly attractive city, don't despair if you have to stay overnight while waiting for your ferry. There are some good restaurants and a handsome hotel. There's also the possibility of an entertaining excursion to one of Thailand's most unusual educational establishments, the **Monkey Training College** (Km 91, Hwy 401, ☏ 077/273378). Here, under almost scholastic conditions, monkeys are trained to climb high palms and collect the coconuts which are still an important part of the local economy. The simian school is a half-hour songthaew ride east of Surat Thani.

Lodging

$ ⊞ **Wang Tai Hotel.** If you find yourself searching for a place to stay in Surat Thani this modern high-rise offers everything to prepare you for the onward journey. Rooms here overlook the Tapi River. The local tourist office is conveniently located just a few blocks away. The hotel's two restaurants are among the best in Surat Thani, with a predominantly Thai and Chinese menu. The dim sum is excellent. ✉ *1 Talad Mai Rd., 84000,* ☏ *077/283020; 02/253–7947 in Bangkok;* 🖷 *077/281007. 230 rooms. 2 restaurants, coffee shop, room service, minibars, cable TV, pool, lounge, laundry service, travel services. AE, MC, V.*

Ko Samui

20 km (12 mi) by boat east of Don Sak.

Ko Samui is half the size of Phuket, so you could easily see it all in a day. But most people come for the sun and surf, so they head straight to their hotel and never venture out. The island's best beaches, with glistening white sand, are on the east coast; the others are often a bit

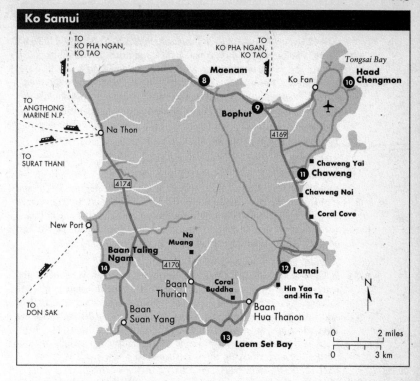

rocky. The water surrounding Ko Samui is already murkier than a few years ago, but the sea surrounding the nearby islands is still crystal clear.

The car ferry from Don Sak on the mainland arrives at New Port, south of the main town of Na Thon. Compared with the other sleepy island villages, Na Thon is a bustling town. There are plenty of shops and restaurants if you find yourself here for a few hours waiting for ferries from the mainland town of Surat Thani or the islands of Ko Pha Ngan or Ko Tao. There's also a hotel, but few people stay in town.

Maenam

8 *10 km (6 mi) northeast of Na Thon.*

On the north coast east of Na Thon, the first major tourist area is Maenam. Its long, curving beach is shaded by coconut trees. The gentle waters are great for swimming. Inexpensive guest houses and one luxurious resort share the 5-km (3-mi) stretch of sand.

You should take one full day for a trip out to the 40 islets that make up the **Angthong Marine National Park,** which covers some 250 square km (90 square mi). The water, the multicolor coral, and the underwater life are amazing, and the rocky islets form weird and wonderful shapes. Boats leave Na Thon daily at 8:30 AM for snorkeling and scuba diving; the cost is B250 and the trip takes about one hour.

LODGING

$$$–$$$$ 🏨 **Santiburi.** The villas on this beachfront estate make you feel as if you're
★ staying at a billionaire's holiday hideaway. The carefully chosen furnishings in the teak-floor rooms are casual, yet elegant. The "less is more" philosophy extends to the huge bathrooms, which have shiny black tiles. Floor-to-ceiling glass in the French windows flood the living areas with light. The main building, a classical pavilion overlooking the oval swimming pool, has European and Thai restaurants. The private beach is ideal

for water sports and has a jetty for the hotel's own cruise ship, a 60-year-old junk. ⊠ *12/12 Moo 1, Tambol Maenam, Ko Samui 84330,* ☎ *077/425031; 02/636–3333 in Bangkok; 800/223–5652 in the U.S.;* FAX *077/425040,* WEB *www.dusit.com. 71 villas and suites. 2 restaurants, snack bar, room service, in-room safes, minibars, cable TV, in-room VCRs, 2 tennis courts, pool, health club, hair salon, massage, spa, beach, windsurfing, boating, squash, 2 bars, shop, baby-sitting, dry cleaning, laundry service, Internet, car rental, travel services. AE, DC, MC, V.*

Bophut

⑨ *11 km (7 mi) east of Na Thon.*

A small headland separates Maenam from the low-key community of Bophut. The beach is quite narrow, but more than wide enough for sunbathing. During the rainy season the runoff waters make the sea slightly muddy, but otherwise the waters are like glass. Lodgings here range from backpacker hangouts to fancier places, and a line of pleasant restaurants faces the seafront. Here high-speed boats to Ko Tao depart every morning at about 8:30.

DINING AND LODGING

$–$$ ✕ **La Sirene.** For elegant French cooking, try this small bistro on the waterfront. A four-course tasting menu begins with homemade pâté followed by medallions of beef or pork in a mustard sauce, then a salad, and then dessert—all for less than B500. À la carte dishes, including Thai selections, are also served up by the owner, who moved here from Nice. A few tables are in the dining room, but the real delight is to sit on the deck overlooking the boats moored a few yards offshore. ⊠ *65/1 Bophut Beach,* ☎ *077/425301. No credit cards.*

$ ✕ **Happy Elephant.** Owner Khun Sasothon displays the day's freshest seafood on ice in front of his restaurant. Choose your favorite and specify how you'd like it cooked. After a drink at the bar, sit outside on the deck perched above the beach and dine under the stars. You can spot the twinkling lights of Ko Pha Ngan across the ocean. Other dishes are also delicious—the *tom yam pla nam sai* (spicy soup with fish) is strongly recommended. ⊠ *79/1 Moo 1,* ☎ *077/245347. No credit cards.*

$ ✕🏨 **Peace Bungalows.** The Pupaiboon family runs this collection of bungalows near the main street of Bophut. All are clean and well-maintained. The expansive lawn shaded by coconut palms leads down to the beach. The lodging has one of the better hotel restaurants on the island, serving zesty local fare as well as international favorites. ⊠ *Bophut Beach, 84320,* ☎ *077/425357,* FAX *077/425343. 36 rooms. Restaurant fans; no air-conditioning in some rooms. MC, V.*

Haad Chengmon

⑩ *20 km (12½ mi) east of Na Thon.*

Continue east along the north coast to Haad Chengmon (*haad* means "beach"). This is the end of the road for the few songthaews that take this route, and few tourists venture this far. Several guest houses and a few resorts are scattered along the shore, but they don't disturb the peace and tranquillity.

Near the northeastern tip of Ko Samui is **Ko Fan,** a little island with a huge sitting Buddha image covered in moss. Try to visit at sunset, when the light off the water shows the statue at its best.

LODGING

$$$$ 🏨 **Imperial Boathouse.** A fleet of 34 converted rice barges provides the luxurious accommodation at this extraordinary property. You don't have to leave dry land, however. The big, bulbous boats are beached like a school of hapless whales not far from the sea. Their incongruous appearance disguises superb amenities; there's an upper deck with a bar, and below you'll find a sitting area, bedroom, and large bath with a grand oval tub. Landlubbers can elect to stay in conventional hotel rooms. They're less expensive, but have no sea view. ⊠ *83 Moo 5, Chengmon Beach, 84140,* ☎ *077/425460; 02/254–0023 in Bangkok;* FAX *077/421462. 34 boat suites, 176 rooms. 2 restaurants, room service, in-room safes, minibars, cable TV, 4 tennis courts, pool, windsurfing, boating, bar, laundry, travel services. AE, DC, MC, V.*

$$$$ 🏨 **Tongsai Bay.** The owners of this splendid all-suites resort managed to build it without sacrificing even one of the tropical trees that give the place a refreshing sense of utter seclusion. Coconut trees pierce through the terraces of some villas and the airy restaurant. The suites, contained in luxurious wooden bungalows, have large private terraces with built-in tubs. Furnishings are nothing short of stunning, with individual touches such as fresh flowers to make you feel more than welcome. ⊠ *84, Moo 5,* ☎ *077/425015,* FAX *077/425462,* WEB *www.tongsaibay.co. th. 83 rooms. Restaurant, room service, in-room safes, minibars, cable TV, 2 tennis courts, pool, gym, beach, bar, laundry service, meeting rooms. AE, MC, V.*

Chaweng

⓫ *20 km (12½ mi) east of Na Thon.*

Ko Samui's most popular beach is Chaweng, a fine stretch of glistening white sand, divided into two main sections—Chaweng Yai (yai means "big") and Chaweng Noi (noi means "little"). Travelers in search of sun flock here, especially during high season. But despite the crowds, Chaweng is no Pattaya or Patong. The mood is very laid back.

Chaweng Yai is divided by a coral reef into two sections—the secluded northern half is popular with backpackers, while the noisy southern half is packed with tourists that flock to the big resorts. Many of the women, young and old, wear little to the beach (locals find it offensive when women shed their tops, although they usually say nothing). Chaweng Noi is not as developed. The salt air has yet to be tainted by the odor of suntan oil, but there are already hotels here, and more are on the way.

South of Chaweng is **Coral Cove,** popular with scuba divers. It's not as idyllic as it once was, because unthinking travelers have trampled the beautiful coral while wading through the water (and worse, many have broken off pieces to take home as souvenirs). To see the lovely formations that still exist a little farther from shore, get a snorkel and swim over the reef—just be careful not to inflict further damage on the reef.

DINING AND LODGING

$ ✕ **Nakorntorung.** There are prettier places to dine than on the plastic-topped tables of this open-air restaurant, but it is hard to find better seafood, curries, and soups. That's why locals flock here, as well as a few travelers who recognize good food and are not put off by the slow service. The restaurant is on the main street in the southern part of town, diagonally across from the Beachcomber Resort. ⊠ *2 Chaweng Beach Rd.,* ☎ *077/422500. No credit cards.*

$$$$ 🏨 **Amari Palm Beach Resort.** This luxurious resort at the north end of Chaweng is set on a beach that is too shallow for swimming. This is an advantage, as it keeps the crowds away. The bungalows all have gleaming wood floors and sumptuous teak furnishings. The huge beds are raised on platforms that make you feel like royalty. The dining room, which serves mostly Western fare, is one floor up to take advantage of the view. A Thai restaurant is in a wood-paneled room in the rear. ⊠

14/3 Moo 2, 84140, ☏ *077/422015; 02/255–4588 in Bangkok;* FAX *077/ 422394,* WEB *www.amari.com. 104 rooms. 2 restaurants, room service, in-room safes, minibars, cable TV, 2 tennis courts, 2 pools, hair salon, beach, dive shop, windsurfing, boating, squash, bar, shop, baby-sitting, laundry service, concierge, Internet, business services, airport shuttle, travel services. AE, DC, MC, V.*

$$$$ 🏨 **Poppies.** More than 80 employees are on hand to pamper guests at this romantic beachfront resort at the southern end of Chaweng. The cottages each have a living room with a sofa bed, making them perfect for families. The floors and trim are of handsome teak, and silk upholstery gives the place a decadent feel. Baths have sunken tubs and showers made of marble. The restaurant, between the pool and the beach, serves seafood under the stars or in the dining room. ✉ *South Chaweng Beach, Box 1, Ko Samui 84320,* ☏ *077/422419,* FAX *077/422420,* WEB *www.poppies.net/samui/htm. 26 cottages. Restaurant, room service, minibars, cable TV, pool, beach, windsurfing, bar, laundry service. AE, MC, V.*

$$$–$$$$ 🏨 **Central Samui Beach Resort.** A three-tiered swimming pool is one of the many unusual features of this resort hotel on the beach at Chaweng Noi. The villas, designed in airy style typical of the south, have views either of the gardens or the sea. The large and airy rooms, furnished in rich teak, are all air-conditioned but have a traditional look because of the lazily turning ceiling fans. Dining possibilities include an excellent Japanese restaurant, as well as two others serving Thai and Chinese dishes. ✉ *111, Moo 2, Chaweng Noi Beach, Ko Samui 84140,* ☏ *077/424020,* FAX *077/424022,* WEB *www.centralhotelsresorts. com. 100 villas. 4 restaurants, coffee shop, room service, minibars, cable TV, 2 tennis courts, pool, hot tub, massage, sauna, beach, snorkeling, windsurfing, boating, fishing, badminton, Ping-Pong, bar, baby-sitting, playground, laundry service, Internet, business services, airport shuttle, car rental. AE, DC, MC, V.*

$$$–$$$$ 🏨 **Tamarind Retreat.** If you want to get away from it all without giving up your creature comforts, then this is your address. The beautifully furnished villas have no televisions or telephones to remind you of the outside world. This lovely resort is the Garden of Eden, without the nettles. Even the spa is sandwiched between two huge boulders, and one villa is set against a granite cliff. In the open-air bath of another villa you shower beneath a tamarind tree. The only drawback is that the nearest swimming beach is 20 minutes away. ✉ *265/7 Thong Takia, 84310,* ☏ *077/424221,* FAX *077/424311,* WEB *www. tamarindretreat.com. 8 villas. Kitchenettes, massage, sauna, spa. No credit cards.*

$$–$$$ 🏨 **Chaweng Regent Beach Resort.** Some of the suites in this resort hotel are on two levels, with fine views from upper terraces. The bungalows are scattered through the tropical gardens, connected to the reception area by elevated walkways. Rooms have teak and marble floors and are furnished with stylish cane furniture. One of the two restaurants, the Red Snapper, serves exclusively Tex-Mex specialties. ✉ *155/4 Chaweng Beach, 84320,* ☏ *077/422389; 02/530–7866-70 in Bangkok;* FAX *077/422222,* WEB *www.chawengregent.com. 45 rooms. 2 restaurants, patisserie, room service, in-room safes, minibars, cable TV, in-room VCRs, 2 pools, gym, health club, hair salon, hot tub, massage, sauna, spa, beach, dive shop, snorkeling, windsurfing, boating, billiards, Ping-Pong, volleyball, 2 bars, shop, baby-sitting, laundry service, car rental, travel services. AE, DC, MC, V.*

$$–$$$ 🏨 **Imperial Samui.** A landscaped terrace leads directly down to a private beach at this stylish resort at the less crowded southern end of Chaweng Noi. It's appealing to the outdoors enthusiast, as it offers every kind of beach activity imaginable. One of the two pools is filled with salt water, a rare luxury on Ko Samui. The elegant Le Jamjuree restaurant serves elaborate royal Thai dishes. A second restaurant, the less formal Le Tara, opens onto the beach. The rooms, some of them on two levels, have polished teak floors and are richly furnished with dark woods and shimmering fabrics. ⊠ *86 Moo 3, Chaweng Noi Beach, Ko Samui 84140,* ☎ *077/421390,* FAX *02/253–3190 in Bangkok,* WEB *www.imperial-hotels.com. 140 rooms, 15 suites. 2 restaurants, in-room safes, minibars, cable TV, 2 tennis courts, 2 pools, beach, windsurfing, boating, badminton, basketball, billiards, Ping-Pong, bar, laundry service. AE, DC, MC, V.*

$$ 🏨 **Baan Talay Resort.** Huddled around a shimmering pool, these two dozen bungalows are a laid-back place to stay. They are just a stone's throw from the beach. The open-front restaurant and bar, both facing the surf, are a great place to unwind after a day of water sports. ⊠ *Chaweng Beach Rd., 84140,* ☎ *077/413555,* FAX *077/413371. 24 rooms. Restaurant, minibars, cable TV, pool. AE, MC, V.*

$$ 🏨 **Chaweng Cabana Resort.** Ask for one of the thatched bungalows at this stylish resort at the south end of Chaweng Beach—the sea is just a few steps away. Others look out over the pool or the tropical gardens. The expansive grounds guarantee privacy, yet the town's nightlife is 10 minutes away. Rooms are attractively furnished in rattan. ⊠ *Chaweng Beach Rd., 84140,* ☎ *077/422377,* FAX *077/422605,* WEB *www.chawengcabana.com. 42 rooms. Restaurant, minibars, cable TV, pool, massage, bar, laundry service, Internet, airport shuttle, travel services. MC, V.*

$–$$ 🏨 **Fair House Beach Resort.** This former bungalow colony has been transformed into a modern beachfront hotel. Furnishings are simple but adequate. The open-front dining room and the adjacent swimming pool have broad sea views. ⊠ *124/1-2 Chaweng Noi, 84140,* ☎ *077/ 422255,* FAX *077/422373. 130 rooms. Restaurant, minibars, cable TV, pool, windsurfing, bar, laundry service. MC, V.*

$ 🏨 **Baan Suan Sook.** Children love this family-run resort because it is overrun with pets of every description, from cats to chickens to a lizard or two. The red-roof bungalows are lined up on a slope above the beach. Most of the modern rooms have views of the sea or the mountains. The lakeside restaurant has a small but adequate menu of local and international dishes. ⊠ *147/7 Chaweng Beach, 84140,* ☎ *077/422835. 24 rooms. Restaurant, refrigerators, cable TV. No credit cards.*

$ 🏨 **Montien House.** Two rows of bungalows line the path leading to the beach at this comfortable little resort. Each modest bungalow has a private patio surrounded by tropical foliage. Rooms are furnished in a spare style, which is nonetheless quite cozy. The management is attentive and helpful. ⊠ *5 Moo 2, Ko Samui 84320,* ☎ *077/422169,* FAX *077/422145. 25 rooms. Restaurant, bar. MC, V.*

$ 🏨 **O. P. Bungalow.** Among the inexpensive bungalow colonies that line Chaweng Beach, this efficiently run hideaway is among the best. Here you'll find tile-floor rooms with private baths that have plenty of hot water. Room 502, very close to the beach, is the best. An open-air coffee shop facing the beach has reasonably priced Thai and Chinese food. ⊠ *111 Chaweng Beach Rd., 84320,* ☎ *077/422424,* FAX *077/422425. 38 rooms. Restaurant. No credit cards.*

NIGHTLIFE

There's plenty of places to go in the evening in Chaweng. The popular **Reggae Pub** (⊠ *Chaweng,* ☎ *077/422331*) is a longtime favorite. It has many bars and dance floors.

Lamai

⑫ *18 km (11 mi) southeast of Na Thon.*

A rocky headland separates Chaweng from Ko Samui's second-most-popular beach, Lamai. It lacks the glistening white sand of Chaweng, but its clear water and rocky pools made it the first area to be developed on the island. Lamai has more of a steeply shelving shoreline than Chaweng, so few families come here, but it does make the swimming better. It's not as congested as Chaweng, though there are plenty of restaurants and bars and enough shops to stir your acquisitive instincts.

Every visitor to Ko Samui makes a pilgrimage to Lamai for yet another reason: at the point marking the end of Lamai beach stand two rocks, named **Hin Yaa** (Grandmother Rock) and **Hin Ta** (Grandfather Rock). Erosion has shaped the rocks to resemble weathered and wrinkled private parts. It's nature at its most whimsical.

About 4 km (2½ mi) from Lamai, at the small Chinese fishing village of Baan Hua Thanon, the road that forks inland toward Na Thon leads to the **Coral Buddha,** a natural formation carved by years of erosion. Beyond the Coral Buddha, toward Na Thon, lies the village of Baan Thurian, famous for its durian trees, where a track to the right climbs up into jungle-clad hills to the island's best waterfall, **Na Muang.** The 105-ft falls are spectacular—especially just after the rainy season—as they tumble from a limestone cliff into a small pool. You are cooled by the spray and warmed by the sun. For a thrill, swim through the curtain of falling water; you can sit on a ledge at the back to catch your breath.

LODGING

$$ 🏨 **Pavilion.** Just far enough from Lamai, the Pavilion offers a little respite from the downtown hustle and bustle. Rooms are in its main building and in much more attractive octagonal thatched bungalows. The restaurant serves tasty seafood. The beachside pool is a refreshing alternative to the often overcrowded sands. ✉ *122/24, Moo 3, Ko Samui 84310,* ☎ *077/424420,* ℻ *077/424029. 56 rooms. Restaurant, in-room safes, minibars, cable TV, pool, laundry service. MC, V.*

$ 🏨 **Aloha Resort.** Ask for a room with a view of the ocean at this beachfront resort—many overlook the parking lot. All have private terraces or balconies. The rooms are divided between those in the main building and those in attractive bungalows. The popular restaurant, Mai Thai, serves Thai, Chinese and European food, while the more casual Captain's Kitchen has a nightly barbecue. ✉ *128 Moo 3, 84130,* ☎ *077/424014,* ℻ *077/424419,* 🕸 *www.samui-hotels.com. 80 rooms. 2 restaurants, room service, minibars, cable TV, pool, beach, bar, laundry service, baby-sitting, airport shuttle. AE, MC, V.*

$ 🏨 **Samui Park Resort.** Although set back from the beach, most rooms at this resort have private balconies with views of the sea and the famous landmarks Hin Yaa and Hin Ta. Restaurants and shops are a short walk away. The carpeted rooms are conventionally but comfortably furnished. ✉ *26/1 Moo 3, 84310,* ☎ *077/424008,* ℻ *077/424435. 61 rooms. Restaurant, minibars, cable TV, pool, bar. AE, MC, V.*

Laem Set Bay

⑬ *17½ km (11 mi) south of Na Thon.*

This small rocky cape on the southeastern tip of the island is far from the crowds. It's a good 3 km (2 mi) off the main road, so without your own transport it's hard to reach. You may want to visit the nearby **Samui Butterfly Garden,** 2 acres of meandering walks enclosed by nets that take you through kaleidoscopic clouds of butterflies. It's open daily 10 to 4.

$$$–$$$$ ✕🏠 **Laem Set Inn.** This idyllic retreat on Laem Set Bay is made up of a cluster of restored traditional houses. The top-priced Kho-Tan suite is an old rosewood house overlooking the sea. To ensure your complete privacy, it has its own pool. Another suite was made from an old post office in Ko Samui, while the restaurant was fashioned out of four teak houses. Cheaper accommodations are in small, thatched cottages with woven bamboo walls. There are cozy lofts for children. A coral-sand beach completes the picture. ✉ *110 Moo 2, Hua Thanon, 84310,* ☎ *077/424393,* 𝔉𝔸𝔛 *077/424394,* 𝔚𝔈𝔅 *www.laemset.com. 4 rooms, 3 suites, 9 cottages. Restaurant, in-room safes, minibars, pool, beach, snorkeling, boating, bicycles, Internet. MC, V.*

Baan Taling Ngam

⑭ *3 km (2 mi) south of New Port.*

The southern and western coasts are less developed, and with good reason—their beaches are not so golden, the water not so clear, and the breezes not so fresh. But there is one very good reason for coming here, and that is a luxury hotel on a pretty stretch of shore with magnificent views.

$$$$ ✕🏠 **Le Royal Meridien Baan Taling Ngam.** Its name means "home on a beautiful cliff," but that doesn't come close to summing up the stunning location of this luxurious hotel. Most of the rooms are built into the 200-ft cliff. Coolly contemporary furnishings are complemented by the generous use of wood paneling. The swimming pool is a magnificent trompe l'oeil, looking as if it's part of the ocean far below. There's a second pool by the beach. You can dine on Thai and European fare at the Lom Talay; seafood is served at the more casual Promenade. ✉ *295 Moo 3, Ko Samui 84140,* ☎ *077/423019; 0800/40–40–40 in U.K.; 800/543–4300 in U.S.;* 𝔉𝔸𝔛 *077/423220,* 𝔚𝔈𝔅 *www.lemeridien-hotels.com. 42 rooms, 7 suites, 33 villas. 2 restaurants, room service, minibars, cable TV, 2 tennis courts, 2 pools, health club, bar, travel services. AE, DC, MC, V.*

Ko Pha Ngan

⑮ *12 km (7 mi) by boat north of Ko Samui.*

Since Ko Samui is no longer off the beaten track, travelers looking for simple pleasures now head for Ko Pha Ngan. A decade ago, the few wanderers stayed in fishermen's houses or slung hammocks on the beach. Simple bungalow colonies have sprung up on most of the best beaches, and investors are buying up beach property with plans for sprawling resorts. For now, though, the lack of transportation around the island limits Ko Pha Ngan's transformation. It remains one of the world's most idyllic places.

Since the island's unpaved roads twist and turn, it's easier to beach-hop. If you want to find the beach that most appeals to you, take a ferry trip around the island—it takes about nine hours and stops in many places along the way. The southeast tip of the island is divided by a long promontory into **Haad Rin West** and **Haad Rin East,** popular areas sometimes referred to as the backpackers' ghetto. Once a month Haad Rin East gets seriously crowded when throngs of young people gather on the beach for an all-night "Full Moon" party. If you're under 30 you might just get swept up in the mood. Boats from Thong Sala, the major town, take about 40 minutes to reach Haad Rin East.

★ If Haad Rin is too crowded, take a boat up the east coast to **Haad Tong Nai Pan,** a horseshoe bay divided by a small promontory. On the beach of the southern half are several guest houses and a couple of small restaurants. The northern part of the bay is called Tong Nai Pan Noi, where a glistening crescent of sand curves around the turquoise waters. Coconut trees behind the beach hide the homes of the villagers.

Dining and Lodging

$ ✕ **Pannoi's.** The owner of this local restaurant goes fishing every evening to catch the next day's fare. The guests, mostly barefoot and shirtless, sit at rough-hewn wood tables set in the sand. A meal may consist of a plateful of tender barbecued prawns with garlic and pepper and succulent *ma pla* (much like snapper). ⊠ *Haad Tong Nai Pan Noi,* ☎ *no phone. No credit cards.*

$ ✕☷ **Panviman Resort.** The big attraction at this friendly resort is its
★   two restaurants, the best of which is a circular Thai-style dining area that is open to the ocean breezes. It serves excellent Thai food. The no-frills accommodations are in thatched cottages and stone-and-stucco bungalows, some cooled by fan and others by air-conditioning. ⊠ *Haad Tong Nai Pan, 84280,* ☎ *077/377048,* FAX *02/587–8493 in Bangkok. 15 rooms, 10 bungalows, 15 cottages. 2 restaurants, refrigerators, billiards, bar, laundry. MC, V.*

$ ☷ **Pha Ngan Chai Hotel.** The pink-and-white facade of this modern hotel wouldn't be out of place on any beach in the world, but you only have to call for the menu in the no-nonsense restaurant to know you're in Thailand. The seafood is bought directly from a local fisherman, and it's prepared in true Thai style. Rooms are undistinguished, but they're comfortable enough and have every amenity. If you're intrigued by the sight of tiny Tae Nai island from your window, the hotel will be happy to organize a day trip. ⊠ *44/65 Moo 1, Thonsala, 84280,* ☎ *077/ 377598,* FAX *077/377560. 60 rooms. Restaurant, refrigerators, pool. AE, MC, V.*

¢   ☷ **Tong Tapan Resort.** These small thatched cottages on stilts are perched on the side of the hill. They are popular with international backpackers. ⊠ *North end of Haad Tong Nai Pan Noi, 84280,* ☎ *no phone. 22 rooms. No air-conditioning. No credit cards.*

Ko Tao

⑯   *47 km (29 mi) by boat north of Ko Pha Ngan.*

Only a few years ago, the tiny island of Ko Tao was compared to the one inhabited by Robinson Crusoe. Today it is inundated with backpackers. It's on the scheduled route of ferries out of Ko Pha Ngan and Ko Samui, and two boats a day make the three-hour (express service) or six-hour (regular service) run from Chumphon on the mainland.

The islanders used to make their living from harvesting coconuts, but tourism is taking over despite the rugged interior and relatively few beaches. More than two dozen small bungalow colonies offer basic accommodation. Since the peace and quiet has gone, the main reason to come here is the underwater world. Speedboats leave at 8:30 AM from Bophut pier on Ko Samui, taking snorkelers on day trips to Ko Tao and neighboring Ko Nang Yuan.

Most of the bungalows on Ko Tao are on Haad Sai Ri, a sweeping crescent beach north of Ban Mae Hut, the village where the ferries dock. The Ko Tao Tourism Centre there can find reasonably priced rooms at short notice.

Lodging

$ ☷ **Ko Tao Cottage Resort.** Of all the bungalow colonies on Ko Tao, this cluster of thatched cottages overlooking the sea at Chalok Kao is one of the best. The simply but adequately furnished rooms all have small private terraces. The open-sided restaurant overlooks the beach. It serves Thai, Chinese and Western food. Aperitifs are served in the aptly named "Last Paradise Bar." ⊠ *19/1 Moo 3, Chalok Baan Kao, 84280,* ☏ *077/456198,* FAX *077/456133. 40 rooms. Restaurant, minibars, cable TV, laundry service. No credit cards.*

Ko Nang Yuan

⑰ *15 mins by boat north of Ko Tao.*

This tiny island—or rather three islands linked by a sandbar—is where you'll find some excellent snorkeling. Just north of Ko Tao, it tends to be flooded with visitors arriving on the 10 AM ferry.

Lodging

$–$$ **Ko Nang Yuan Dive Resort.** The only people who stay on Ko Nang Yuan after the ferry departs are the guests at this lone resort. Most rooms have fans, but the more luxurious ones treat you to air-conditioning. There's a full-fledged dive shop, making this a good place for everyone from beginners to pros. ⊠ *Ko Nang Yuan,* ☏ *01/229–5085,* FAX *01/229–5212,* WEB *www.koh-nang-yuan.com. 12 rooms. Restaurant, refrigerators, dive shop, bar. MC, V.*

KO PHUKET

Backpackers discovered Ko Phuket in the early 1970s. Word quickly spread about its white, sandy beaches and cliff-sheltered coves, its plunging waterfalls and impressive mountains, its cloudless days and fiery sunsets. Entrepreneurs built massive resorts, first at Patong, then spreading out around the island. Charter companies continue to fly in planeloads of sun-seeking tourists. During peak season, the island's 20,000 hotel rooms are jammed to capacity, so hotels add a "peak surcharge" to room rates. Most deserted bays and secluded havens now have at least one hotel, and more are being built despite a shortage of staff and an overburdened infrastructure.

Ko Phuket is linked to the mainland by a causeway. Its indented coastline and hilly interior make the island seem larger than its 48-km (30-mi) length and 21-km (13-mi) breadth. Before tourism, Ko Phuket was already making fortunes out of tin mining (it is still Thailand's largest tin producer) and rubber plantations. Although the west coast, with its glittering sand beaches, is committed to tourism, other parts of the island are largely untainted by the influx of foreigners.

Numbers in the text correspond to numbers in the margin and on the Ko Phuket map.

Phuket Town

⑱ *862 km (539 mi) south of Bangkok.*

About one-third of the island's population lives in Phuket Town, the provincial capital. The town is a bit drab, with modern concrete buildings replacing much of the old colonial-style architecture. This may explain why very few tourists linger here. But if you find yourself in town for a few hours, the tables lining the sidewalk in front of the Thavorn Hotel are a great place to do a little people-watching while sipping a cold beer.

Traveling east along Rasda Road, an immediate right puts you on Phuket Road, where you'll find the tourist office. Heading west on Rasda Road you come to Ranong Road, where there's an aromatic local market filled with fruits, vegetables, spices, and meats. On the next block of

Ranong Road is the songthaew terminal, where minibuses depart for the most popular beaches.

If you want to get your bearings, there's a fine view of Phuket Town and the island's interior from the top of **Khao Rang,** a hill northwest of town.

About 5 km (3 mi) north of Phuket Town is the **Thai Cultural Village,** a 500-seat amphitheater that presents various aspects of southern culture. Here you can see classical dance, shadow puppet shows, Thai boxing exhibitions, sword fighting, and an "elephants-at-work" show. ⊠ *Thepkasati Rd.,* ☎ *076/214860.* ⊡ *Admission.* ⊙ *Shows at 10:15, 11, 4:45, 5:30.*

Dominating a major crossroads is the **Heroines Monument,** a monument to a pair of women who rallied the locals and repelled Burmese invaders in 1785. Ask your guide for the full story—the people of Phuket hold these two women in great esteem. ⊠ *12 km (7 mi) north of Phuket Town.*

The **National Museum,** opposite the Heroines Monument, has an interesting exhibition of the island's culture and history, including its encounter with the Burmese and their defeat by the island's two heroines. ⊠ *12 km (7 mi) north of Phuket Town,* ☎ *076/311426.* ⊡ *Admission.* ⊙ *Wed.–Sun. 10–4.*

About 9 km (5 mi) south of Phuket Town lies the town of **Makham Bay,** where you can catch the ferryboat to the Phi Phi Islands and Krabi.

Lodging

$$ ⬚ **Metropole.** The grand old Metropole—the town's first luxury hotel—has a shuttle service to the closest beaches, so you can stay in town and commute to the sea. The advantages are not only cheaper accommodation, but the opportunity to visit more than just one beach. A sparkling marble lobby greets you as you enter. A spacious lounge is a cool retreat during the day, and a karaoke bar is fun at night. The hotel's handsome Chinese restaurant serves great dim-sum. For Western food, try the Metropole Café. Rooms are bright, with picture windows that let in a lot of sun. ⊠ *1 Soi Surin, Montri Rd., 83000,* ☎ *076/214022,* ℻ *076/215990. 248 rooms. 2 restaurants, refrigerators, cable TV, pool, gym, health club, hair salon, massage, baby-sitting, laundry service, business services, meeting rooms, airport shuttle, car rental, travel services. AE, DC, MC, V.*

$$ ⬚ **Pearl Hotel.** Like the Metropole, the slightly less lustrous Pearl arranges day trips to nearby beaches, so it's a very inexpensive way to see the island's attractions. The top-floor Chinese restaurant has the lovely views that the guest rooms lack. The ground-floor café doubles as an after-dark nightclub with with a team of women singers. Tucked away behind the lobby is a secluded courtyard pool. ⊠ *42 Montri Rd., 83000,* ☎ *076/211044,* ℻ *076/212911. 250 rooms. 3 restaurants, café, minibars, cable TV, pool, massage, laundry service, Internet, convention center, airport shuttle, car rental, travel services. AE, MC, V.*

Khan Phra Thaeo National Park

⑲ *19 km (12 mi) north of Phuket Town.*

Turning inland from Ban Po on the small, partially unpaved road heading for Thalang, you'll traverse Khan Phra Tharo National Park, the last remaining virgin forest on Phuket. Here you'll find a rich variety of animals that would otherwise become extinct in fast-growing Phuket. Keep an eye out for barking deer, mouse deer, and even gibbons.

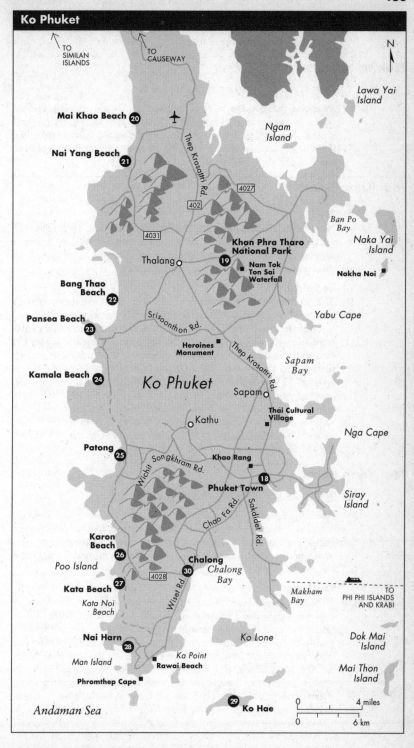

Ko Phuket

TO SIMILAN ISLANDS

TO CAUSEWAY

N

Lawa Yai Island

Ngam Island

Mai Khao Beach 20

Nai Yang Beach 21

Thep Krasattri Rd.

4027

402

4031

Ban Po Bay

Naka Yai Island

Khan Phra Tharo National Park 19

Thalang

■ Nam Tok Ton Sai Waterfall

Nakha Noi ■

Bang Thao Beach 22

Pansea Beach 23

Srisoonthon Rd.

Yabu Cape

Thep Krasattri Rd.

■ **Heroines Monument**

Ko Phuket

Sapam Bay

Kamala Beach 24

Sapam

Nga Cape

Kathu

■ **Thai Cultural Village**

Patong 25

Songkhram Rd.

Wichit

Khao Rang ■

18

Phuket Town

Chao Fa Rd.

Sakdidet Rd.

Siray Island

Karon Beach 26

Poo Island

4028

Chalong 30

Chalong Bay

Nga Cape

Kata Beach 27

Kata Noi Beach

Wiset Rd.

Makham Bay

TO PHI PHI ISLANDS AND KRABI

Nai Harn 28

Man Island

Ka Point

Rawai Beach ■

Ko Lone

Dok Mai Island

Phromthep Cape ■

Mai Thon Island

Andaman Sea

29 **Ko Hae**

0   4 miles

0   6 km

A pleasant picnic spot, **Nam Tok Ton Sai Waterfall** is a few minutes off the main road. It's a popular spot all year, but the falls are most impressive during the rainy season.

Nakha Noi

26 km (16 mi) northeast of Phuket Town.

By taking the road east at the crossroads you'll arrive at Ban Po Bay, where you can take a 20-minute boat ride to Nakha Noi, quiet island with fine sandy beaches. After you tour the island you can take in a show at a pearl farm that reveals how the tiny orbs are extracted from oysters. The show begins at 11 AM.

Mai Khao Beach

20 *37 km (23 mi) northwest of Phuket Town.*

North of Nai Yang Beach you'll find Mai Khao Beach. This is Phuket's northernmost beach, once a haven for giant sea turtles who laid their eggs here between November and February. Now the turtles have been displaced by the tourists staying in the resorts.

Lodging

$$$$ ⊡ **J. W. Marriott Resort & Spa.** The Marriott claims to have the island's longest stretch of shoreline, so if water sports are your passion you'll feel right at home here. The resort has all the amenities you'd expect from the well-regarded chain, including rooms of great comfort but little individuality. Nevertheless, if attentive service, a full range of activities, and a fine beach are what you want, then you really can't go wrong. ⊠ *Moo 3, 83110,* ☎ *076/338000,* WEB *www.phuket. com/marriott. 265 rooms. 2 restaurants, café, room service, minibars, cable TV, in-room VCRs, 4 tennis courts, pool, gym, health club, hair salon, sauna, spa, beach, windsurfing, boating, 2 bars, lobby lounge, shop, baby-sitting, laundry service, business services, airport shuttle, car rental, travel services. AE, MC, V.*

Nai Yang Beach

21 *34 km (20 mi) northwest of Phuket Town.*

Nai Yang Beach is really a continuation south of Mai Khao—making a 10-km (6-mi) stretch of sand. Casuarina trees line the gently curving shore. There's a few resorts, but little else to disturb the peace—apart, perhaps, from aircraft diverted from their normal flight path to the nearby airport.

Lodging

$$$$ ⊡ **Pearl Village Resort.** Set on 35 acres of landscaped gardens between a national park and a broad sandy beach, Pearl Village Resort is a relaxing retreat. As you stroll around the grounds you'll encounter streams, ponds, and a vast swimming pool. Rooms are large and airy, furnished with light woods and bamboo. All have views of the gardens or the beach. ⊠ *Nai Yang Beach, 83140,* ☎ *076/327006,* FAX *076/327338. 226 rooms. 2 restaurants, room service, minibars, cable TV, driving range, 4 tennis courts, pool, gym, health club, hair salon, massage, sauna, beach, windsurfing, boating, bicycles, horseback riding, 2 bars, shop, baby-sitting, laundry service, Internet, business services, convention center, airport shuttle, car rental, travel services. AE, MC, V.*

$$ ⊡ **Crown Nai Yang Suite Hotel.** This all-suites hotel is not directly on the beach, but the sands of Nai Yang are a short walk away. What the modern hotel lacks in beach frontage it makes up for with its lovely setting in a verdant forest. Rooms are decorated in light woods and pastel colors. A full range of sports facilities is at your doorstep. ✉ *117/ Moo 1, National Park Rd., 83140,* ☎ *076/327420,* FAX *076/ 327322. 96 rooms. 2 restaurants, coffee shop, minibars, cable TV, 2 tennis courts, pool, gym, sauna, dive shop, billiards, bar, baby-sitting, laundry service, airport shuttle, car rental, travel services. AE, MC, V.*

Bang Thao Beach

㉒ *22 km (14 mi) northwest of Phuket Town.*

Once the site of a tin mine, Bang Thao Beach now glistens with the more precious metals worn by its affluent visitors. The once quiet bay is now one of the island's major destinations. A free shuttle service brings visitors between the five resorts that line the shore.

Dining and Lodging

$$$$ ✕⛩ **Banyan Tree Phuket.** Of the quintet of resorts on Laguna Beach, this is the most exclusive—and expensive. Your secluded villa has a bathroom that is as big as the bedroom. An outdoor shower for rinsing off after a swim is a nice addition. Teak floors and locally woven fabrics remind you that you are in Thailand. The king-size bed is on a raised platform so that you can gaze out onto your garden. The most expensive villas also have their own private pools. Rejuvenating treatments in the spa include herbal massages. If you prefer, have a masseuse rub you down in your private gazebo. ✉ *33 Moo 4 Srisoonthorn Rd., Cherngtalay, Thalang, 83110,* ☎ *076/324374,* FAX *076/324356,* WEB *www. banyantree.com. 104 villas. 2 restaurants, café, minibars, cable TV, in-room VCRs, 18-hole golf course, 5 tennis courts, pro shop, aerobics, gym, hair salon, massage, beach, windsurfing, boating, bicycles, billiards, squash, 2 bars, shops, baby-sitting, dry cleaning, laundry service, business center, airport shuttle, car rental, travel services. AE, DC, MC, V.*

$$$$ ✕⛩ **Dusit Laguna.** Flanked by two lagoons, this luxury hotel has an unbeatable location. It's popular with those who like the fact that while the resort itself is restful, lively nightlife is nearby. The nicely decorated rooms have huge windows opening onto private balconies. The baths are spacious enough for two. On the terrace the evening begins with a beachfront barbecue, then moves on to dancing to the latest beats. European fare is served at the Junkceylon; Thai cuisine, accompanied by traditional music, is served in the Ruen Thai restaurant. ✉ *390 Srisoonthorn Rd., Cherngtalay, Thalang, Phuket 83110,* ☎ *076/324320; 02/ 236–0450 in Bangkok;* FAX *076/324174,* WEB *www.dusitgroup.com. 233 rooms, 7 suites. 4 restaurants, minibars, cable TV, putting green, 2 tennis courts, pool, gym, hair salon, beach, windsurfing, boating, laundry service, meeting rooms, airport shuttle, travel services. AE, DC, MC, V.*

$$$ ✕⛩ **Sheraton Grande Laguna.** Everything about this resort is grand— even the free-form swimming pool, which meanders through the grounds before opening up into two immense basins. The resort is an island within an island, surrounded by a lovely lagoon. The large, airy rooms, furnished in cane and other light woods, let you escape from the crowds on the long beach. Even more private are the one- or two-bedroom villas that overlook tropical gardens. The trio of restaurants cater to all tastes; Thai dishes are served in the Chao Lay restaurant, built on stilts over the lagoon. ✉ *Bang Thao Bay, 10 Moo 4 Srisoonthorn Rd., Cherngtalay, Thalang, Phuket 83110,* ☎ *076/324101,* FAX *076/324108,* WEB *www.sheraton.phuket.com. 258 rooms, 85 suites. 3 restaurants, 2 cafés, room service, minibars, cable TV, 18-hole golf course, 4 tennis courts, pro shop, 2 pools, gym, health club, massage, beach, windsurfing, boating, 2 bars, nightclub, shop, playground, dry cleaning, laundry service, Internet, airport shuttle, car rental, travel services. AE, DC, MC, V.*

Pansea Beach

★ ㉓   *21 km (12 mi) northwest of Phuket Town.*

South of Bang Thao you'll find this long stretch of shore in a protected bay. Separated from the rest of the coast, Pansea Beach has the feeling of a private enclave. Hidden among the palm trees you'll find two of the most luxurious lodgings on the island.

Even more secluded is **Surin Beach,** just south of Pansea Beach. It has a long stretch of golden sand, but the strong currents mean it isn't the best for swimming. On the headland south of Surin you'll find several romantic coves. You climb down the rocks to find tiny beaches surrounded by palms. If you're lucky, you'll have it all to yourself. One particularly peaceful cove is called Laem Sing.

Dining and Lodging

$$$$ ✕⊞ **Amanpuri Resort.** You'd be hard-pressed to find a more elegant hotel in Thailand—nor one quite as expensive (the nightly rate for the largest of the villas is nearly $7,000). The reception area, with beautifully polished teak floors, is completely open so that you can enjoy the breezes off the ocean. Here you'll find two palm-shaded restaurants overlooking the black-tiled swimming pool. Choose between rooms in secluded hillside pavilions or immense villas with broad eaves and swooping roofs. Each suite has a private sundeck with a gazebo. From the split-level bar you have stunning sunset views. ⊠ *Phuket 83110,* ☎ *076/324333; 02/287–0226 in Bangkok; 800/447–7462 in U.S;* ⃞ᴬ⃞ˣ *076/324100,* ⃝ᵂᴱᴮ *www.amanpuri.com. 40 pavilions, 30 villas. 2 restaurants, minibars, cable TV, in-room VCRs, 2 tennis courts, pool, gym, hair salon, massage, spa, beach, windsurfing, boating, marina, 2 bars, shops, baby-sitting, dry cleaning, laundry service, airport shuttle, car rental, travel services. AE, MC, V.*

$$$$ ⊞ **Chedi.** Almost completely hidden by a grove of coconut palms, this
★   resort has more than 100 thatch-roof cottages overlooking a quiet beach. You know this place is special when you walk into the lobby, which has a sweeping view of the Andaman Sea. A hexagonal pool is set amid the tropical flora. Should you long for a bit more privacy, each of the cottages has its own sundeck. The interiors, with shining wood floors and woven palm walls, are pleasantly uncluttered. ⊠ *118 Moo 3, Cherngtalay, Phuket 83110,* ☎ *076/324017,* ⃞ᶠᴬˣ *076/324252,* ⃝ᵂᴱᴮ *www.phuket.com/chedi. 110 chalets. Restaurant, café, minibars, cable TV, 2 tennis courts, pool, windsurfing, boating, shop, baby-sitting, dry cleaning, laundry service, Internet, business services, meeting rooms, airport shuttle, car rental, travel services. AE, DC, MC, V.*

Kamala Beach

㉔   *18 km (11 mi) west of Phuket Town.*

South of Bang Thao you reach Kamala Beach, a curving strip of coral sand backed by coconut palms. Unlike the more upscale enclaves to the north, Kamala Beach has some reasonably priced accommodations. A crumbling dirt road leads over a rugged cliff to Patong—it's passable, but a much easier route is the better maintained road that sweeps down the west coast.

☾   The island has its own theme park, **Phuket Fantasea,** where the kids can ride the elephants while you poke among the shops. In the evening there's a Las Vegas–type extravaganza with dozens of dancers performing modern and classical routines, 30 elephants going through their paces, magicians doing tricks, acrobats spinning above the crowd—well, you get the picture. The night ends with a fireworks display. The park's Golden Kinaree restaurant boasts the island's biggest buffet. ✉ *99 Moo 3,* ☎ *078/271222.* ⚏ *Admission.* ⊙ *Wed.–Sun. 5:30 PM–11:30 PM.*

Dining and Lodging

¢ ✕ **White Orchid.** Beyond the Kamala Hotel, where the road peters out
★ to a rutted track, is this little restaurant. There are only six or seven tables under a thatched roof and two more under palm trees at the water's edge. The menu is limited to what the owner, named Eed, buys that day in the market. Whatever is on the menu, make sure to start with the spring rolls. If she has tiger prawns, that's your best bet for an entrée. Although most of what she and her sister cook is Thai, she whips up a couple of Western dishes as well. ✉ *Kamala Bay,* ☎ *01/892–9757. MC, V.*

$ ⌸ **Kamala Dreams.** For reasonably priced accommodation on Kamala Beach, this attractive two-story house is one of the best options. The eight studio apartments, simply but comfortably furnished, have huge picture windows with views of the nearby mountains or the sea. A footbridge gives direct access from the gardens to the beach. ✉ *74/ 1 Moo 3, 83121,* ☎ *01/891–4293. 8 apartments. Restaurant, kitchenettes, microwaves, refrigerators, cable TV. AE, MC, V.*

Patong

㉕ *13 km (8 mi) west of Phuket Town.*

You'd hardly believe it today, but Patong was once the island's most remote beach, completely cut off by the surrounding mountains. A boat was the only way to reach Phuket Town. In 1959 a highway was completed that linked the two towns, and the tranquil beachfront was bought up by developers who knew the beautiful beach wouldn't stay a secret for long. Today Patong is virtually indistinguishable from Pattaya and other tourist destinations.

When it comes to Patong, you either love it or hate it. There is a cluster of luxury hotels, upscale restaurants, and even some smart nightspots, but Patong is mostly a crowded, noisy destination for those on package holidays. There's little local culture here. If you want nothing more than American burgers, English fish-and-chips, or German beers, then this is your scene.

Families find much to do in Patong, from waterskiing during the day to exploring the overpriced night market in the evening. But Patong is also known for its raunchy revelry. There are more than 150 bars and clubs in a half-mile radius of Patong's notorious Soi Bangla. Some first-time visitors are shocked by the decadent displays, not only in the dark corners of the windowless bars but in the open-air nightspots that jam the sois. Tour buses from the resorts let you sample it all from a safe distance.

Like Pattaya, Patong also has a a vibrant gay scene. There are also drag shows—lavish productions that put to shame many in Las Vegas—that attract everyone.

Dining and Lodging

$$ ✕ **Baan Rim Pa.** If you suffer from vertigo, take a pass on this restaurant. You dine on a terrace that clings to a cliff at the north end of Patong Beach. There are tables set back from the edge, but you'll then miss the gorgeous ocean views. The food is among the best Phuket has to offer—no wonder, as the head chef launched the Thai Cooking School. Here he has constructed set menus to make ordering simpler for those

unfamiliar with Thai food. They've turned down the heat on many favorites, so you may be disappointed if you like spicier fare. ⊠ *100/7 Kalim Beach Rd.,* ☎ *076/340789. AE, MC, V.*

$–$$ ✕ **Chao Lay.** Perched on a bluff overlooking the Andaman Sea, this open-front restaurant is an ideal spot to enjoy fantastic views. The Thai cooking also happens to be outstanding. Dishes include excellent *tom kha gai* (spicy chicken soup), delicate *mee krob* (thin noodles), and great grilled seafood. The restaurant is part of the Coral Beach Hotel. ⊠ *104 Moo 4,* ☎ *076/321106. Reservations essential. AE, DC, MC, V.*

$–$$ ✕ **Mallee's Seafood Village.** In the center of Patong, this restaurant serves up a wide range of seafood, from charcoal-grilled fish in banana leaves to steamed fish in tamarind sauce. If you have a hankering for Chinese food, try the shark steak in a green-pepper sauce. On the other hand, you may simply want to sit at one of the sidewalk tables and indulge in pancakes with honey. ⊠ *94/4 Taweewong Rd.,* ☎ *076/ 321205. AE, DC, MC, V.*

¢–$ ✕ **Suang Sawan.** Since they cater mostly to foreigners, Phuket's Thai restaurants are usually not as good (or as cheap) as in other parts of Thailand. More often than not, what distinguishes the eateries here is location. This is the case with Suang Sawan. Sitting high above the sea, the seafood restaurant's panoramic view of the coastline makes this a splendid place to dine. Try the *pla gaprong nam manao* (sea bass steamed in a spicy lime broth). ⊠ *255 Phrabarama Rd.,* ☎ *076/ 344175. AE, MC, V.*

$$$ ✕🏨 **Diamond Cliff Hotel.** Far from the madding crowds, this hotel in the northern section of Patong is one of the smartest places to stay. Mammoth rocks along the shore separate the beach into several private coves. The pool, built on a ledge above the main part of the hotel, provides an unobstructed view of the coast. Rooms are spacious and full of light, accentuating the hotel's open feel. Dining is taken seriously, with fresh seafood cooked in European or Thai style. ⊠ *61/9 Kalim Beach, Kathu District, Phuket 83121,* ☎ *076/340501; 02/246–4515 in Bangkok;* 𝗙𝗔𝗫 *076/340507,* 𝗪𝗘𝗕 *www.thailandhotels.net/diamondcliff. 140 rooms. Restaurant, room service, minibars, cable TV, pool, gym, massage, boating, bar, lobby lounge, laundry service, travel services. AE, MC, V.*

$$ 🏨 **Phuket Cabana.** This hotel's chief attraction is its unbeatable location, right in the middle of the city facing the beach. Modest rooms are in chalet-type bungalows furnished with rattan furniture. The Charthouse restaurant serves Western food and a smattering of Thai dishes. There's a good tour desk and a reputable dive shop to arrange outings. ⊠ *80 Taweewong Rd., Phuket 83121,* ☎ *076/340138,* 𝗙𝗔𝗫 *076/ 340178. 80 rooms. Restaurant, minibars, cable TV, pool, dive shop, airport shuttle, travel services. AE, MC, V.*

$ 🏨 **Palm View Lodge.** If you want to enjoy days at the beach and nights in the clubs without having to stay in the thick of things, then this might be the answer—an English-run hotel on a quiet residential street five minutes from the shore. Ground-floor rooms open out directly to the garden. There's no dining room, but a neighboring restaurant will deliver to your room or to a table beside the pool. The tiled rooms are simply but stylishly furnished with cane furniture. ⊠ *135/1 Namai Rd., 83150,* ☎ *076/344837,* 𝗙𝗔𝗫 *076/345088. 12 rooms. Refrigerators, cable TV, pool. MC, V.*

Nightlife

With the varied nightlife in Patong, it's no surprise to find a sensational drag show here. The famous **Simon Cabaret** (⊠ *8 Sirirach Rd.,* ☎ *076/ 342011*) treats you to a beautifully costumed and choreographed show. It's stylish, sophisticated, and hugely entertaining—well worth crossing the island to see. There are two shows daily, at 7:30 and 9:30.

Karon Beach

26 *20 km (12 mi) southwest of Phuket Town.*

Just south of Patong is beautiful Relax Bay, surrounded by verdant hills and virtually taken over by the huge Le Meridien. Cruise ships occasionally anchor offshore, doubling the number of vacationers. A little ways farther south is Karon Beach, divided into Karon Noi (Noi means small) and Karon Yai (Yai means large). Because of its good swimming and surfing, Karon Yai is becoming increasingly popular. Several hotels have sprung up here, making it virtually indistinguishable from the island's others beaches.

Dining and Lodging

$$ ✕ **On the Rock.** Built on the rocks overlooking Karon Beach, this three-level restaurant is one of the best of the island. Baby reef sharks glide lazily in an aquarium, glancing occasionally in your direction. Seafood is the specialty, so you won't go wrong ordering the *her thalee kanom khrok* (mackerel with fresh tomato and onion) and the *pla goh tod na phrik* (snapper in a pepper and chili sauce) with rice. Those not partial to Thai fare have a wide choice of Italian dishes. ⊠ *South end of Karon Beach,* ☎ *076/381625. AE, MC, V.*

$$$$ 🏨 **Le Meridien.** There are more bars, cafés, and restaurants in this hotel than in many small towns. Its range of outdoor diversions—everything from tennis to waterskiing—means you never have to leave the property. There are hundreds of guests at any given time, yet the resort never feels too crowded, thanks to its thoughtful design. Two huge wings are where you'll find the sumptuous rooms, which are furnished in teak and rattan. Most have sea views, others overlook the pair of pools. ⊠ *Box 277, Phuket 83000,* ☎ *076/340480,* ⦶ *076/340479. 470 rooms. 7 restaurants, room service, minibars, in-room data ports, cable TV, driving range, golf privileges, 4 tennis courts, 2 pools, gym, health club, massage, dive shop, boating, waterskiing, boccie, squash, volleyball, 3 bars, laundry service, meeting rooms, travel services. AE, DC, MC, V.*

$$$ 🏨 **Karon Beach Resort.** There's a homey feel to this beach resort, possibly because it is smaller than most on the island. The rooms are furnished with indigenous woods and with bright fabrics. All overlook the tropical gardens or the beach. Water-sports fans have a huge choice of distractions. Golfers have privileges at the nearby links. ⊠ *120/5 Moo 4, Patak Rd., 8300,* ☎ *076/330006,* ⦶ *076/330529. 80 rooms. Restaurant, room service, minibars, refrigerators, cable TV, golf privileges, pool, massage, beach, windsurfing, boating, parasailing, waterskiing, babysitting, laundry service, car rental, travel services. AE, MC, V.*

$$$ 🏨 **Marina Phuket.** These cozy bungalows, straddling the divide between
★ Karon Beach and Kata Beach, all have verandas with views from their private balconies of the palm-lined shore. Those closer to the beach are bit more spacious than those up the hill. All have traditional furnishings that include some interesting paintings by locals. The pool, nestled among rock outcroppings, is surrounded by tropical foliage. The main restaurant is among Phuket's finest, while a second serves very good Thai cuisine as musicians play classical music. ⊠ *47 Karon Rd., Phuket 83100,* ☎ *076/330493 or 076/330625,* ⦶ *076/330516 or 076/330999,* 🕸 *www.marinaphuket.com. 104 rooms. 2 restaurants, minibars, cable TV, pool, beach, dive shop, snorkeling. AE, MC, V.*

$$–$$$ 🏨 **Phuket Orchid Resort.** This resort is set slightly inland, but the beach is just a short walk away. The lack of a beachfront brings the rates down considerably. The lagoonlike pools and the adjoining open-air restaurant are the big attractions. The walled grounds give the resort seclusion from the hustle and bustle of the busy street outside. ⊠ *128/4 Moo 3, Patak Rd., 83100,* ☎ *076/396519,* ⦶ *076/396526. 411 rooms.*

Restaurant, cable TV, minibars, 2 pools, shops, baby-sitting, laundry service, meeting rooms, car rental, travel services. AE, MC, V.

$ 🏠 **Karon Beach Inn.** If you don't mind a 15-minute walk to the beach, you may feel right at home at this friendly guest house. The lack of an ocean view is compensated for by very reasonable rates. Rooms are modern, with extras you don't often find in this price range, such as cable TV. Baths have only showers, but are otherwise well equipped. ✉ *33/63 Moo 1, Patak Rd., 83100,* ☎ *076/398066,* FAX *076/398067,* WEB *www.karonbeachinn.com. 18 rooms. Minibars, refrigerators, cable TV. No credit cards.*

$ 🏠 **Ruan Thep Inn.** Just a stone's throw from the beach is a cluster of modest bungalows. A small restaurant more than satisfies your appetite, although there are plenty more eateries a short walk away. ✉ *120/4 Moo 4, Patak Rd., Phuket 83000,* ☎ *076/330281. 14 rooms. Restaurant. V.*

Kata Beach

🔵 *22 km (13 mi) southwest of Phuket Town.*

Protected by promontories at either end, Karon Beach has calm waters that make it a great spot for swimming. Sheltered by forest-clad hills, it's an incredibly peaceful place. It's still possible to find a deserted section of sand to watch the blazing sunsets. Things are changing, however. The success of Club Meditérranée has led to the building of other large hotels.

Lodging

$$$ 🏠 **Kata Beach Resort.** Personalized service is the secret of this big resort set along a broad section of Kata Beach. The staff works hard to make you feel at home. All rooms have balconies overlooking either the tropical gardens or the sandy beach, but if you want the best views reserve one of the expansive suites. The airy dining room serves a voluminous buffet, and for fine à la carte dining there's the stylish Nero Restaurant. ✉ *5/2 Moo 2, Patak Rd., Phuket 83100,* ☎ *076/330530,* FAX *076/330128,* WEB *www.katagroup.com. 267 rooms. 3 restaurants, cable TV, pool, health club, beach, boating, windsurfing, volleyball, conference center. AE, MC, V.*

$$$ 🏠 **Kata Thani.** Practically all of Kata Noi Beach has been engulfed by this mammoth resort. All the generously sized rooms have balconies facing the beach, but the hotel is so large that you might have to walk down some long corridors before you can really enjoy the view. Between the main building and the golden beach are expansive lawns and two large pools, one with a swim-up bar. There are restaurants nearby, as well as three hotel dining rooms. ✉ *3/24 Patak Rd., Kata Noi, Phuket 83100,* ☎ *076/330124,* FAX *076/330426,* WEB *www.phuket. com/katathani. 433 rooms. 3 restaurants, 4 tennis courts, 2 pools, health club, beach, windsurfing. AE, MC, V.*

$$$ ✕🏠 **Mom Tri's Boathouse & Restaurant.** With rooms that look onto
★ Kata Beach, this small hotel is a very comfortable retreat. Ask for a room garden estate, where six villas share a quiet spot atop a cliff. Meals served here are prepared to order by the eponymous owner's personal chef. The restaurants, with a reputation that extends far beyond Phuket, are said to share the region's largest wine cellar. For an after-dinner drink, try the relaxing bar right on the sand. ✉ *2/2 Patak Rd., Phuket 83100,* ☎ *076/330015; 02/253–8735 in Bangkok;* FAX *076/330561,* WEB *www.theboathousephuket.com. 33 rooms, 6 villas. 3 restaurants, minibars, cable TV, beach, bar, travel services. AE, DC, MC, V.*

$ ✕🏠 **Friendship Bungalows.** A short walk from the beach, these two rows of single-story buildings contain modestly furnished but spotlessly clean rooms. Those with air-conditioning cost a bit more, but the extra expense is worth it during the hot summer nights. The owners are extremely hospitable, making sure you feel right at home. The small restaurant on a terrace serves excellent local fare. ⊠ *6/5 Patak Rd., Phuket 83130,* ☎ *076/330499. 23 rooms. Restaurant. No credit cards.*

Nai Harn

★ ㉘ *18 km (11 mi) southwest of Phuket Town.*

South of Kata Beach the road cuts inland across the hills before it drops into yet another beautiful bay, Nai Harn. Protected by Man Island, this harbor is a popular anchorage for yachts. On the north side of the bay is the gleaming white Royal Meridien Phuket Yacht Club. The view from the terrace of the sun dropping into the Andaman Sea is superb. The public beach, with a few vendors selling snacks, is good for taking a dip.

From the top of the cliff at **Phromthep Cape,** the southernmost point on Ko Phuket, you are treated to a view of Nai Harn Bay and much of the coastline. At sunset, the view from here is superb. This evening pilgrimage has become so popular that a row of souvenir stands lines the parking lot. Once you get away from the congestion you can enjoy the colors of the setting sun in solitude.

Not far from Kata Beach is **Rawai Beach,** where you'll find a picturesque fishing village set in a coconut grove. At the southern end of Rawai Beach lies the village of **Chao Le,** whose inhabitants are sometimes called *chao nam,* or water people, by the rest of the island's inhabitants. The chao nam are believed to be descended from a band of pirates who attacked 17th-century trading ships entering these waters. Of the three chao nam villages on Phuket, the one near Rawai Beach is the easiest to visit.

Dining and Lodging

$$$$ ✕🖬 **Royal Meridien Phuket Yacht Club.** Rather than mimic the local style of architecture, this hotel has a sleek look that wouldn't be out of place in Bangkok. Beyond this modern exterior are the usual amenities, from a health club to a hair salon. The guest rooms are ample, with separate sitting areas and enormous terraces with sea views. Make a point of dining in the Chart Room, an open-air restaurant that overlooks the bay. Try the baked fish stuffed with prawns in a tasty mixture of Thai spices. ⊠ *Nai Harn Beach, Phuket 83130,* ☎ *076/ 381156; 02/251–4707 in Bangkok; 071/537–2988 in U.K.; 800/526– 6566 in U.S.;* 🅵🅰🆇 *076/381164,* 🆆🅴🅱 *www.lemeridien-yachtclub.com. 100 rooms, 8 suites. 2 restaurants, room service, minibars, cable TV, 2 tennis courts, pool, health club, hair salon, massage, spa, beach, snorkeling, windsurfing, boating, laundry service, business center, car rental, travel services. AE, DC, MC, V.*

Ko Hae

㉙ *8 km (5 mi) offshore from Chao Le.*

Cruise boats leave Rawai and Chalong, farther up the coast, for the popular island of Ko Hae (Coral Island). Just 30 minutes from the mainland, it has crystal-clear water for snorkeling and superb beaches for sunbathing.

North of Ko Hae is Ko Lone, another island reached by boat from Rawai or Chalong.

Lodging

$–$$ ⊡ **Coral Island Resort.** Make your friends back home jealous with a postcard from this island hideaway. The steep-eaved bungalows, built in the traditional manner, are set on a beach. The furnishings are comfortable without being flashy, as is the case in many Thai resorts. The water is almost always calm, so this is the place for water sports. The diving is sensational. ⊠ *50/4 Vises Rd., Moo 5, Rawai,* ☎ *076/ 281060,* FAX *076/381957. 64 rooms. Restaurant, café, pool, dive center, billiards. MC.*

Chalong

③⓪ *11 km (7 mi) south of Phuket Town.*

The waters in horseshoe-shape Chalong Bay are usually calm, as the entrance is guarded by Ko Lone and Ko Hae. That's why yachts making passage from Europe to Asia often head here. From the jetty you can catch a ferry to Ko Hae and Ko Lone. Boats also make the short run over to Ko Raya, a small, tranquil island not far from shore. The island has a couple of spotless beaches, Ao Tok (best for sunsets) and Ao Siam.

Not far from Chalong Bay you'll find **Wat Chalong,** the largest and most famous of Phuket's 20 Buddhist temples. It enshrines gilt statues of two revered monks who helped quell an 1876 rebellion. They are wrapped in brilliant saffron robes.

Dining

$–$$ ✕ **Jimmy's Lighthouse Bar & Grill.** This very popular restaurant is still a hangout for sailors, though many of the old salts now go next door to the marina. The remaining crowd is largely tourists. The place is good both for lunch and dinner. ⊠ *45/33 Chao Fa Rd.,* ☎ *076/381709. No credit cards.*

$ ✕ **Kan Eang.** There are now two branches of this restaurant in Chalong. Thais make a point of patronizing Kan Eang 1 (on Viset Road), ★ as the food is more authentic than at the neighboring Kan Eang 2. It's also closer to the bay. Grab a palm-shaded table next to the seawall and order some delicious grilled fish. Be sure that your waiter understands whether or not you want yours served *pet* (spicy hot). Succulent and sweet crabs should be a part of any meal here. ⊠ *44/1 Viset Rd.,* ☎ *076/381212;* ⊠ *9/3 Chaofa Rd.,* ☎ *076/381694. AE, MC, V.*

OFF THE   **THE SIMILAN ISLANDS –** Teeming with interesting marine life, these atoll-
BEATEN PATH like islands off the northwest coast of Phuket offer some of the world's
best snorkeling and diving, rivaling the Seychelles and the Maldives.
There is good visibility at depths of up to 120 ft. Tour operators in
Phuket offer cruises of two or three nights geared toward both divers
and sun-seekers. The islands are part of a national park, so there are no
hotels. On the mainland (a 70-minute ferry ride) more than two dozen
small lodgings dot the coast between the villages of Takua Pah and
Khao Lak. You can get there on a good 90-km (54-mi) coast road. For
20 km (12 mi) of the way the road skirts the coastal Tha Muang National Park, where—at Turtle Beach—giant leatherbacks come ashore to
lay their eggs from November to March.

PHUKET BAY

Ko Phuket's popularity endures, but more and more visitors are cutting their visits to the island short and moving to less packed places.

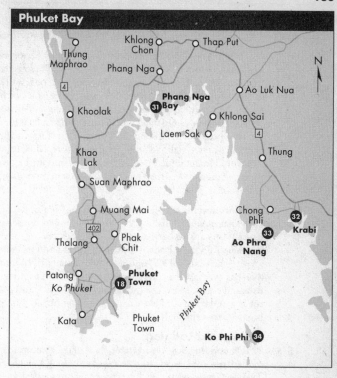

Phuke Bay

Phang Nga Bay, made famous by the James Bond movie *The Man with the Golden Gun,* lies at the northern tip of Phuket Bay. There are dozens of little islands to explore, as well as offshore caves and startling karst formations rising out of the sea. Take time to appreciate the sunsets, which are particularly beautiful on the island of Ko Mak.

The provincial capital of Krabi sits on the northeastern shore of Phuket Bay. Once a favorite harbor for smugglers bringing in alcohol and tobacco from Malaysia, the town has been transformed into a gateway to the nearby islands, particularly Ko Lanta and Ko Phi Phi, as well as beaches like Ao Phra Nang.

Just down the road from Krabi, Ao Phra Nang was first discovered by backpackers about a decade ago. Now it's being rediscovered by developers. Modern hotels have already replaced most of the thatched bungalows, and the rutted roads have now been paved. Further growth can be expected following the opening of the airport.

The islands of Ko Phi Phi were once idyllic retreats, with secret silver-sand coves, unspoiled stretches of shoreline, and limestone cliffs dropping precipitously into the sea. They were an insider's destination, known only to a few travelers who were in the know. But then the islands were portrayed in *The Beach* (2000). By the time the film had been released on DVD, Phi Phi was a hot property. Lovely beaches are still to be found, but most are now in the hands of developers. You can still stay in a moderate-price bungalow a few steps from the ocean, but not for much longer.

Numbers in the text correspond to numbers in the margin and on the Phuket Bay map.

Phang Nga Bay

★ ③① *100 km (62 mi) north of Phuket, 93 km (56 mi) northwest of Krabi.*

The best way—actually, the only way—to visit Phang Nga Bay is by boat. Talk with one of the travel agencies on Phuket that offers half-day tours of the area, or you can hire your own boat and spend as long as you want. There are two inlets, just before you reach the town of Phang Nga, where you can arrange for long-tail boats. Most tour buses go to the western inlet, where you can rent a boat for about B1,300 for two hours. The second inlet sees fewer foreign tourists, so the prices are better—about B800 for three hours. Most tourists don't arrive from Phuket until 11 AM, so if you get into the bay earlier you can explore it in solitude. To get an early start, you may want to stay overnight in the area.

There are several key sights around Phang Nga Bay. The island of **Ko Panyi** has a Muslim fishing village consisting of houses built on stilts. Restaurants are no bargain, tripling their prices for tourists. Beautiful **Ko Phing Kan,** now known locally as James Bond Island, is well worth a visit. The island of **Ko Tapu** resembles a nail driven into the sea. **Kao Kien** has overhanging cliffs covered with primitive paintings of elephants, fish, and crabs. Many are thought to be at least 3,500 years old. **Tham Lot** is a stalactite-studded cave that has an opening large enough for boats to pass through.

Dining and Lodging

$-$$ ✕⌂ **Phang Nga Bay Resort Hotel.** Each of the comfortable rooms at this modern resort have private terraces overlooking a jungle-ringed estuary. The four levels are set back to ensure picture-perfect view from everywhere. The nearest beaches are more than 1 km (½ mi) away, but the hotel operates a boat that brings you there. Rooms are conventionally but comfortably furnished, with all modern amenities. The restaurant, which has a terrace overlooking the water, serves Thai, Chinese, and Western dishes. ⊠ *20 Thaddan Panyee, 82000,* ☎ *076/411067 or 01/917–4147,* ₣ᴀ̅х *076/412057. 88 rooms. Restaurant, coffee shop, refrigerators, cable TV, 2 tennis courts, pool, billiards, dance club. AE, MC, V.*

Krabi

③② *867 km (538 mi) south of Bangkok, 180 km (117 mi) southeast of Phuket, 43 km (27 mi) by boat east of Ko Phi Phi.*

Krabi is a pleasant place to visit, but most pause just long enough to cash traveler's checks, arrange onward travel, and catch up on the news at one of the restaurants on Uttarakit Road. The locals are determined to keep Phuket-style development at bay, and so far—despite the opening of an airport 12 km (7 mi) from town—they are succeeding.

Between Krabi and Ao Nang Beach lies **Susan Hoi** (Fossil Beach), aptly named for the 75-million-year-old shells that have petrified into bizarrely shaped rock slabs.

Lodging

¢ ⌂ **Garden House.** A cluster of white-washed, red-roof cottages facing each other across a small lane, Garden House is a very pleasant overnight option. The management knows the area, so this is a good place to plan the next stage of a tour. Rent a bike if you'd like to explore the coast on two wheels. ⊠ *40 Hemthanon Rd., 81000,* ☎ *075/611265,* ₣ᴀ̅х *075/631250. 4 rooms. Bicycles, travel services. No credit cards.*

¢ ⌂ **Grand Tower Hotel.** It's hardly grand, but the accommodations at this five-story hotel are perfectly adequate for an overnight stay. Rooms are cooled by fans or air-conditioners, so make sure to state your preference. The café serves basic Western fare. Many of the long-distance private bus companies stop here. The employees at the tour desk are knowledgeable about the area and are happy to help you plan your visit. ⊠ 73/1 Uttarakit Rd., ☎ 075/611741, 𝐅𝐀𝐗 075/611741. 40 rooms. Restaurant, refrigerators, cable TV, travel services. MC, V.

¢ 🖬 **Thai Hotel.** Miss the boat to Phuket? If you need an inexpensive place to stay overnight, you might look at this hotel in Krabi. The location, just a block from the pier, couldn't be more convenient. Rooms are cozy and comfortable. ⊠ 7 Isara Rd., 81000, ☎ 075/612128, 𝐅𝐀𝐗 075/ 620564. 151 rooms. Restaurant. MC, V.

Ao Phra Nang

★ ㉝ 20 km (12 mi) from Krabi Town.

Even with the development, the beaches here are some of Thailand's most attractive. Especially fascinating are dozens of limestone karsts that rise like pillars out of the ocean. Days here are spent lounging on the beach. The snorkeling and scuba diving are good, particularly around Turtle Island and Chicken Island. Long-tail boats lining the beaches take you to other islands or to other beaches along the coast.

West of Ao Phra Nang Bay is **Haad Noppharat Thara,** a more secluded beach that's famous for its rows of casuarina trees. You can walk out to the little rocky island at low tide, but don't linger there too long. When the tide comes in, so does a current. For total seclusion, hire a long-tail boat to take you to the offshore islands.

Dining and Lodging

$$$$ ✕🖬 **Rayavadee Premier Resort.** Scattered across 26 landscaped acres, ★ this magnificent resort is set in coconut groves with white-sand beaches on three sides. The resort is on the mainland, but is accessible only by boat (20 minutes from Krabi or 10 minutes from Ao Phra Nang). Circular pavilions built in traditional Thai style have spacious living rooms with curving staircases that lead up to opulent bedrooms and sumptuous baths with huge, round tubs. Some of the best rooms have secluded gardens with private hot tubs. Two restaurants assure variety—the beachfront Krua Pranang, set in a breezy pavilion, serves outstanding Thai and Chinese food. ⊠ 67 Mu 5, Susan Hoy Rd., Tambol Sai Thai, Krabi 81000, ☎ 075/620740, 𝐅𝐀𝐗 075/620630, 𝐖𝐄𝐁 www.rayavadee.com. 100 pavilions. 2 restaurants, room service, in-room safes, minibars, cable TV, in-room VCRs, pool, massage, spa, beach, boating, laundry service. AE, DC, MC, V.

$–$$ ✕🖬 **Krabi Resort.** What was once a small collection of thatched cottages on Ao Phra Nang has mushroomed into a sprawling resort. Rows of attractive wood bungalows are staggered back from the beach. Furnishings are wood and wicker. A two-story building at the back of the property offers 40 standard rooms for the same price as the bungalows. A pool sits in the center of the tropical garden. The restaurant, popular with guests from other hotels, is alongside the beach. It specializes in local seafood. ⊠ 55–57 Pattana Rd., Amphoe Muang, Krabi 81000, ☎ 075/637030; 02/208–9165 in Bangkok; 𝐅𝐀𝐗 075/637051. 103 rooms. Restaurant, minibars, cable TV, pool, boating, nightclub. AE, DC, MC, V.

$ ✕🖬 **Emerald Bungalows.** On the quiet beach of Haad Noppharat Thara, just west of Ao Phra Nang, is this array of bungalows. Those facing the beach are the best (and most expensive). The seafood restaurant is the place for socializing. ⊠ Haad Noppharat Beach, Moo 4, (2/1 Kongca Rd., Krabi 81000), ☎ 01/956–2566. 36 rooms. Restaurant. No credit cards.

$$–$$$ 🏨 **Phra Nang Inn.** When selecting a room at this inn on the shore of Ao Phra Nang Beach, you can choose between the coconut wing and the betel-nut wing. The difference? Well, the rooms in the former are constructed from coconut palms, while those in the latter—well, you get the picture. The look of the rooms (jute and even seashells are incorporated into the design) is typical of the resort, which has a wonderfully kooky vibe (even the bar, called the 25 Million Year Pub, is a little odd). The rooms are vaguely Victorian looking (some even have four-poster beds), but they're actually quite comfy. ✉ *119 Moo 2, Krabi 91000,* ☎ *075/637130,* 🅵🅰🆇 *075/637134,* 🆆🅴🅱 *www.phranginn.com. 83 rooms. 2 restaurants, room service, minibars, cable TV, pool, hot tub, snorkeling, boating, laundry service, airport shuttle, travel services. AE, DC, MC, V.*

$$ 🏨 **Ao Nang Seafront Thai Resort.** A complete renovation in 2001 turned this into a very stylish ensemble of bungalows. The best of the bunch face the sea, and the rest overlook the pool and tropical gardens. The bungalows, cozier than the two-story villas, are decked out in dark tropical woods and richly colored fabrics. ✉ *273 Moo 2, Beach Rd., 81000,* ☎ *075/637591,* 🅵🅰🆇 *075/637359,* 🆆🅴🅱 *http:// aonang-thairesort.com. 36 rooms. Restaurant, refrigerators, bar. MC.*

$ 🏨 **Ao Nang Villa.** A modern three-story hotel has taken the place of the handful of the original bungalows that once stood on this spot. Right on the beach, the hotel is in a pleasant garden embracing a good-size pool. The restaurant, next door in a garden of its own, serves dinner both under its roof and under the stars. ✉ *113 Ao Phra Nang Beach, Krabi 81000,* ☎ *075/637270,* 🅵🅰🆇 *075/637274. 62 rooms. Restaurant, minibars, cable TV, tennis court, pool. MC, V.*

¢ 🏨 **Ban Ao Phra Nang Resort.** The best rooms at this palm-shaded hotel overlook the glittering pool. Those at the back have less to offer. The staff is friendly and helpful. The beach and the main street of Ao Phra Nang are nearby. Meals are served buffet-style. ✉ *31/3 Moo 2, Krabi 81000,* ☎ *075/637072,* 🅵🅰🆇 *075/637070. 108 rooms. Restaurant, refrigerators, cable TV, pool. MC, V.*

¢ 🏨 **Jinda Guest House.** Inexpensive lodgings are hard to find in Ao Phra Nang, but a short walk from the beach you'll find this collection of cottages. It's not luxurious, but manages to be quite cozy. The owner speaks a little English. ✉ *247/6 Moo 2, Krabi 81000,* ☎ *01/607–8556. 9 rooms with shared bath. No credit cards.*

Ko Phi Phi

㉞ *90 mins by boat southeast of Phuket Town, 2 hrs by boat southwest of Krabi.*

Of the two largest islands, only **Phi Phi Don** is inhabited. It's shaped like a butterfly, consisting of two hilly masses linked by a 2-km (1-mi) sandbar. Most hotels are found here, where boats dock at a village called Ton Sai. As no vehicles are allowed on the island, you'll probably disembark here. In the evening you can stroll along the sandbar, where small restaurants display the catch of the day on huge blocks of ice. Later in the evening, bars and discos cater to those in the mood to party.

The most popular way to explore the islands is by either a large cruise boat or a smaller long-tail boat. One of the most exciting trips is to the other large island, **Phi Phi Lae.** The first stop is Viking Cave, a vast cavern of limestone pillars covered with crude drawings thought to have been made at least 200 years ago by Portuguese, Dutch, or Scandinavian explorers. The boat continues on, gliding by cliffs rising vertically out of the sea, for an afternoon in Maya Bay. Here the calm waters, dotted with colorful coral, are ideal for swimming and snorkeling.

You can take a 45-minute trip by long-tail boat to circular **Bamboo Island,** with a superb beach around it. The underwater colors of the fish and the coral are brilliant. The island is uninhabited, but you can spend a night under the stars.

Dining and Lodging

Restaurants on Phi Phi consist of a row of closely packed cafés. The menus include mostly fish dishes—you choose your freshly caught fish, and the chef cooks it according to your instructions. Prices are below B150 per person, including a couple of beers. The open-air restaurants to the left of the pier cost a bit more, but the food is essentially the same.

$$$–$$$$ ✕⊡ **Holiday Inn Resort.** The sumptuously furnished bungalows share 20 acres of tropical gardens along a nearly deserted beach. The terrace restaurant, serving Thai, Chinese and European cuisines, has splendid views of the sea. Fish is, of course, the specialty. ⊠ *Cape Laemthong, 81000,* ☎ *01/476–3787; 076/214654 in Phuket,* FAX *076/ 215090 in Phuket,* WEB *www.krabi-hotels.com/holidayinnpp. 77 rooms. Restaurant, room service, in-room safes, minibars, cable TV, 2 tennis courts, pool, hot tub, massage, sauna, beach, snorkeling, windsurfing, boating, 2 bars, shops, baby-sitting, laundry service, travel services. AE, MC, V.*

$$$ ⊡ **Pee Pee Island Village.** Coconut palms tower over this cluster of small thatched bungalows on the northern cape. You'll find the same amenities in other lodgings on the island, but the atmosphere here is more laid-back. On the other hand, the views are less impressive. Water sports are a big draw, especially the diving. ⊠ *Cape Laemthong, 81000,* ☎ *01/476–7517; 076/215014 in Phuket;* FAX *01/229–2250. 65 rooms. Restaurant, minibars, cable TV, snorkeling, boating, travel services. AE, V.*

$$–$$$ ⊡ **PP Princess.** Although it's only a short walk from Phi Phi Don's pier, this attractive cluster of stylish bungalows feels miles away. The quiet retreat sits in a coconut plantation overlooking Lohdalum Bay. The teak-floor suites, furnished with teak and rattan and covered in rich fabrics, are flooded with light from the picture windows. French doors lead out to your private balcony. The main building houses a very attractive restaurant, Mai Thai, which serves up delicious seafood. A second restaurant, the Princess, is right on the beach. A pair of bars specialize in tropical cocktails. ⊠ *Lohdalum Bay, 81000,* ☎ *075/ 622079,* FAX *075/612188,* WEB *www.ppprincess.com. 79 rooms. Restaurant, cable TV, minibars, refrigerators, dive shop, snorkeling, windsurfing, boating, fishing, 3 bars, laundry service, Internet, travel services. AE, DC, MC, V.*

$–$$ ⊡ **Cabana Hotel.** This rambling resort, clasped between two beaches in a sandy embrace, would have been a perfect setting for *The Beach.* Ocean breezes make air-conditioning superfluous except during the rare steamy nights. All the nicely furnished rooms have balconies or terraces looking out over the tropical gardens and palm-fringed pool. ⊠ *Ton Sai Beach, 81000,* ☎ *075/620634; 02/691–4137 in Bangkok;* FAX *075/612132,* WEB *www.phiphicabana-hotel.com. 80 rooms. Restaurant, pool, beach, windsurfing, bar. AE, DC, MC, V.*

$ ⊡ **Chao Koh Phi Phi Lodge.** One of the best budget options on the island, Chao Koh Phi Phi Lodge is a collection of basic but comfortable bungalows near Tonsai Bay. The deluxe rooms have extras like air-conditioning that make them worth the added expense. The beachfront restaurant is a big draw in the evenings, serving excellent seafood at moderate prices. The friendly team that runs the lodge also operates a boat service to Krabi. ⊠ *Tongsai Bay, 81000,* ☎ *075/501821,*

FAX *075/236616*, WEB *www.kohphi-phi.com. 47 rooms. Restaurant, minibars, cable TV, hair salon, massage, dive shop, boating, shops, Internet, travel services. MC, V.*

¢ 🏠 **Phi Phi Lanah Beach Club.** Those who insist there are no more budget accommodations on Phi Phi Don should take a look at this palm-shaded resort. The thatched bungalows are so isolated that you can only get to them by boat. If you're looking for the unspoiled part of Phi Phi, this is the place. There are few amenities, and baths are communal, however, rooms have fans and mosquito nets. The young and friendly team that runs the place includes two chefs who delight in teaching you to cook Thai favorites. Another member is a masseuse. ✉ *196/1-3 Phuket Rd., Phuket 83000,* ☎ *01/737–1501 or 01/737–5441,* FAX *01/891–8304,* WEB *www.phiphilanahbeachclub.com. 12 rooms. Restaurant, beach, billiards, Ping-Pong, volleyball. No credit cards.*

SOUTHERN BEACHES A TO Z

To research prices, get advice from other travelers, and book travel arrangements, visit www.fodors.com.

AIR TRAVEL

Thai Airways flies from Bangkok to Chumphon (four times a week), Ko Samui (17 flights a day), Krabi (two flights a day), Ko Phuket (16 flights a day), Ranong (one flight a day), Surat Thani (two flights a day) and Trang (one flight a day). Bangkok Airways also operates daily flights from Bangkok to Ko Samui. There are also direct flights from Chiang Mai to the most popular destination in the south. Thai Airways has one daily flight from Chiang Mai to Phuket, and Bangkok Airways has two flights daily from Chiang Mai to Ko Samui. Both Thai Airways and Bangkok Airways have daily flights between Phuket and Koh Samui.

Flights to Phuket and Ko Samui are expensive, with one-way tickets from Bangkok costing B3,000–B4,000. Phuket and Ko Samui are both busy international airports—Phuket has daily flights from Hong Kong, Perth, Singapore, Taipei, Tokyo, and some European gateways, while tiny Ko Samui has daily flights to Singapore and Phnom Penh. Reservations to Phuket and Ko Samui are essential during holiday season.

Bangkok Airways has a daily flight from Ko Samui, which lands at U-Tapao Airport, 50 km (30 mi) east of Pattaya.
➤ CARRIERS: **Bangkok Airways** (✉ Ko Samui, ☎ 077/425012; ✉ Phuket, ☎ 076/212311 or 076/212341). **Thai Airways** (✉ Ko Samui, ☎ 077/273355; ✉ Krabi, ☎ 076/620070; ✉ Phuket, ☎ 076/211195).

AIRPORTS AND TRANSFERS

While most travelers head to the international airports at Ko Samui and Phuket, there are also airports at Chumphon, Krabi, and Surat Thani. Flights to these smaller airports are often cheaper, so ask your travel agent before you book your ticket.

Koh Samui's airport is at the northern tip of the island. It's a 10-minute drive to the resorts of Bangkrak and Bophut. Taxis meet all arrivals. Trips to various parts of the island usually are a fixed rate of B200. Some hotels have airport transfers, but they are not always complimentary. Make sure to ask before you get in.

Phuket's airport is also at the northern end of the island. Most of the hotels are on the west coast—check whether yours offers a free shuttle. Taxis meet all incoming flights. Fares are higher than in Bangkok; expect to pay B700 to Patong, Kata or Karon, up to B400 to Phuket town. There is also frequent minibus service to Phuket town, Patong, Kata, and Karon that costs between B80 and B120.

The Hua Hin airport reopened in 2001 after extensive renovation. Only charter flights currently land here, however. There is also talk of re-opening Trat Airport, which would make trips to Ko Chang easier.

➤ AIRPORT INFORMATION: **Chumphon** (☎ 077/591263). **Hua Hin** (☎ 032/520343). **Ko Samui** (☎ 077/245601). **Krabi** (☎ 075/636541). **Phuket** ☎ 076/205397). **Surat Thani** (☎ 077/253500).

BOAT AND FERRY TRAVEL

A reasonably priced network of passenger boats shuttle between the mainland and the islands as well as between the different islands. The best and most reliable of them are run by Songserm Travel. From Surat Thani, express boats depart for Thong Sala on Ko Pha Ngan at 7 AM, 9 AM, and 2 PM, stopping en route at Na Thon on Ko Samui. From Chumphon, two ferries (one express taking 2 hours and one slower boat taking 6 hours) travel daily to Ko Tao and continue on to Ko Pha Ngan and Ko Samui. (These ferries are often cancelled during monsoon season, so call ahead.) From Na Thon on Ko Samui, an express boat leaves at 9 AM daily for the 2½-hour trip to Ko Pha Ngan and continues on to Ko Tao. A speedboat leaves Bophut on Ko Samui daily at 8:30 AM for the 2-hour trip to Ko Tao. Long-tail boats can also be hired at Na Thon and Bophut to reach any of the islands, but you'll have to bargain over the fare.

From Makham Bay on Phuket, boats depart twice a day (8:30 and 1:30) for the 2-hour journey to Ko Phi Phi. Two boats a day (10 and 2) make the 2-hour trip between Krabi and Phi Phi. One daily boat (8:30) runs from Ao Phra Nang to Ko Phi Phi.

➤ BOAT AND FERRY LINES: **Songserm Travel** (✉ 121/7 Soi Chapermla, Phyathai Rd., Bangkok 10400, ☎ 02/252–9654 or 02/251–8994; ✉ Ferry terminal, Thong Sala, Ko Pha Ngan, ☎ 077/281639; ✉ 64/1–2 Na Thon, Ko Samui, ☎ 077/421316; ✉ 51 Satoon Rd., Phuket Town, ☎ 076/222570, FAX 076/214391; ✉ Ferry terminal, Surat Thani, ☎ 077/272928).

BUS TRAVEL

The region is served by a network of buses departing from Bangkok. Those headed to Pattaya, Ban Phe (where you catch boats bound for Ko Samet), Chantaburi, and Trat (where ferries to Ko Chang depart) leave from the Eastern Bus Terminal. Buses to Hua Hin, Chumphon, Surat Thani (both departure points for Ko Samui and other islands), Krabi, and Phuket leave from the Southern Bus Terminal.

Buses also transport you between destinations in the south. A daily bus travels from Phuket to Surat Thani, arriving in time for the ferry to Ko Samui. There's also service between Phuket and Krabi, Trang, Hat Yai, and Satun.

The distances covered are great, so bus trips to the southern beaches take many hours. The trip from Bangkok to Krabi, for example, takes at least 12 hours. If you are pressed for time, flying is a much quicker option.

➤ BUS STATIONS: **Chantaburi** (✉ Saritidet Rd.). **Chumphon** (✉ Tha Tapao Rd.). **Hua Hin** (✉ Dechanuchit Rd.). **Krabi** (✉ Chao Fa Rd.). **Pattaya** (✉ Pattaya Clang Rd.). **Phuket** (✉ Ranong Rd.). **Surat Thani** (✉ Taladmai Rd.).

CAR RENTALS

Phuket is the only island where you might want a car to get around. On all the other islands, independent travelers are better off on a motorbike. All hotels can arrange for rentals, and many have booking offices on the premises. Look for Avis, Budget, and Hertz at the airports in Ko Samui and Phuket.

Two reputable local companies are SMC Car Rental, with an office in Phuket, and TA Car Rental, based in Ko Samui.
➤ AGENCIES: **Avis** (✉ Krabi Airport, Krabi, ☎ 075/691941; ✉ Phuket Airport, Phuket, ☎ 076/351244). **Budget** (✉ Ko Samui Airport, Ko Samui, ☎ 077/427188; ✉ Phuket Airport, Phuket,, ☎ 076/205396). **Hertz** (✉ Phuket Airport, Phuket, ☎ 076/205396). **SMC Car Rental** (✉ Phuket Airport, Phuket, ☎ 076/693038). **TA Car Rental** ✉ Choengmon Beach, Ko Samui, ☎ 077/245129).

CAR TRAVEL

It's a long drive south from Bangkok, but once you're out of the capital all you have to do is follow the compass due south. There's only one highway as far south as Chumphon, where it divides into one road following the Andaman Sea coast to Phuket and another snaking along the Gulf of Thailand to Surat Thani, where the ferries cross to Ko Samui. Phuket Town is 862 km (517 mi) from Bangkok, Surat Thani is 674 km (404 mi). Allow 13 hours for the drive to Phuket, 10 hours for the drive to Surat Thani.

The resorts along the Eastern Gulf are much closer, making a car trip here more reasonable. For example, the drive to Pattaya takes between two and three hours.

EMERGENCIES

If you are on the mainland, Surat Thani Hospital has a good reputation. On Phuket try Bangkok Phuket Hospital.
➤ EMERGENCY NUMBERS: **Tourist Police** (☎ 077/421281 in Ko Samui; 076/219878 in Phuket; 077/281300 in Surat Thani).
➤ HOSPITALS: **Bangkok Phuket Hospital** (✉ 2/1 Hongyok Rd., Phuket Town, ☎ 076/254425). **Samui International Hospital** (✉ Chaweng Beach, Ko Samui, ☎ 077/421230). **Surat Thani Hospital** (✉ Surat-Phun Phin Rd., Surat Thani, ☎ 077/272231).

HEALTH

Health authorities have done a great job controlling mosquitoes around the southern resorts, but you'll still need a good supply of repellent. All accommodations, from luxury resorts to humble bungalows, either have screens on all windows and doors or at least mosquito netting over the beds.

Be careful at the beach, as the sun can be stronger than you think. Wear a hat and bring along plenty of sunscreen. Protective clothing while diving or snorkeling is a good idea, as accidentally brushing against or stepping on coral can be painful. Keep an eye out for dangerous creatures, especially jellyfish and sea urchins. If you are stung, seek medical attention immediately.

MAIL AND SHIPPING

The reception desk at your hotel will post your cards and letters, a much easier option than hunting down the nearest post office.
➤ POST OFFICES: **Hua Hin** (✉ Phetkasem Rd.). **Krabi** (✉ Uttarakit Rd.). **Pattaya** (✉ Soi Post Office). **Phuket** (✉ Phang Nga Rd.). **Surat Thani** (✉ Taladmai Rd.).

MONEY MATTERS

Banks are easy to locate in all mainland towns and in major resorts such as Krabi, Phuket (Patong, Karon Beach, and Kata Beach) and Ko Samui (Chaweng, Lamai, and Maenam). All banks will exchange foreign currency and most have ATMs. Remember that hotel exchange rates differ significantly from those at banks or currency exchange houses. The more remote the hotel, the less you'll get for your dollar.

TAXIS

There are no fleets of taxis on Phuket and Ko Samui—what you'll find are one-man operations which you must book by telephone. Taxis meet incoming flights at the airports in Phuket and Ko Samui. If you're likely to be needing a taxi during your stay, ask the driver for his card. The best and cheapest way of getting around on the islands, however, is by the ubiquitous songthaew.

TOUR OPERATORS

On Phuket a half-day sightseeing tour includes visits to Wat Chalong, Rawai Beach, Phromthep Cape, and Khao Rang. Other half-day tours take in the Thai Cultural Village and the cultured-pearl farms on Nakha Noi Island. Full-day boat tour travel is available to Phang Nga Bay and other islands. Make arrangements through your hotel.

One-day cruises to the Similan Islands are run by Songserm Travel. The trip takes about 10 hours from Phuket. Marina Divers runs trips for scuba enthusiasts to the Similan Islands. The Siam Cruise Co. operates two- and three-night cruises to the Similans on the *Andaman Princess.* The *Andaman Seafarer,* run by PIDC Divers, sets sail for four- and six-day trips.

Dive Deep runs trips from Ko Samui to Angthong National Marine Park and other destinations.
➤ TOUR OPERATORS: **Dive Deep** (✉ Chaweng Beach Resort, Ko Samui, ☎ 077/230155). **Marina Divers** (✉ Karon Villa Hotel, Karon Beach, Phuket, ☎ 076/381625). **PIDC Divers** (✉ 1/10 Viset Rd., Chalong Bay, Phuket, ☎ 076/381219). **Siam Cruise Co.** (✉ 33/10–11 Chaiyod Arcade, Sukhumvit Soi 11, Bangkok 10110, ☎ 02/255–8950). **Songserm Travel** (✉ 121/7 Soi Chapermla, Phyathai Rd., Bangkok 10400, ☎ 02/252–9654 or 02/251–8994; ✉ Ferry terminal, Thong Sala, Ko Pha Ngan, ☎ 077/281639; ✉ 64/1–2 Na Thon, Ko Samui, ☎ 077/421316; ✉ 51 Satoon Rd., Phuket Town, ☎ 076/222570, FAX 076/214391; ✉ Ferry terminal, Surat Thani, ☎ 077/272928).

TRAIN TRAVEL

A train from Bangkok's Hualamphong Station takes four long hours to reach Hua Hin. Trains leave Bangkok at 12:45 PM and 2:45 PM and depart Hua Hin for the return trip at 2:20 PM and 4 PM. Trains take four hours—it seems much longer—to reach Pattaya. The one daily train leaves Bangkok at 6:55 AM and arrives at 10:30 AM. It departs Pattaya for the return trip at 2:50 PM. If you're a train buff it's worth the trip. If not there are easier and quicker ways to travel. However, at B31 for the train there is nothing less expensive.

Many express trains from Bangkok's Hualamphong railway station stop at Surat Thani on their way south. The journey takes just under 12 hours, and the best trains are the overnighters that leave Bangkok at 6:30 PM and 7:20 PM, arriving in Surat Thani soon after 6 AM. First-class sleeping cabins are available only on the 7:20 train. Two express trains make the daily run up from Trang and Hat Yai in southern Thailand.

Surat Thani is the closest train station to Phuket. A bus service links the two cities. The State Railway of Thailand, in conjunction with Songserm Travel, issues a combined train and bus ticket to Phuket for B670. There's a similar deal for passengers headed to Ko Samui.

VISITOR INFORMATION

The Tourism Authority of Thailand has offices in several resorts in southern Thailand. You can drop by for maps and brochures, as well as information about local excursions.

➤ TOURIST INFORMATION: **Ko Samui** (✉ Na Thon, ☎ 077/421281). **Krabi** (✉ Uttarakit Rd., ☎ 075/612740). **Phuket** (✉ 73–75 Phuket Rd., Phuket Town, ☎ 076/212213). **Surat Thani** (✉ 5 Talat Mai Rd., ☎ 077/281828).

7 SIDE TRIP TO LAOS

Laos sways to a slow rhythm of life—
Vientiane is decidedly laid-back for a
capital city, Luang Prabang has enchanting
palaces and temples, and southern Laos
offers fascinating river journeys to thundering
waterfalls and small villages settled along
the banks of the Mekong Delta.

Updated by
David
Dudenhoefer
and
Robert Tilley

ALTHOUGH LAOS HAS OPENED ITSELF UP to international trade and tourism, it's still a secondary destination on most itineraries, and locals—not yet inured to countless visiting foreigners—volunteer assistance and a friendly welcome. Tourism professionals in Thailand and Laos have been energetically pushing a joint cooperation program, making it considerably easier for visitors to Thailand to plan a side trip to Laos. Much of the Thai part of this program is based in Chiang Mai, from where Luang Prabang and Vientiane are easily reached by air in 60–90 minutes. Most travel agents in Chiang Mai can set you up with a tour to Laos for as little as $250 (including airfare). You can also fly to Vientiane and Luang Prabang from Bangkok, or cross the Mekong at the Friendship Bridge in Nong Khai.

Despite a limited infrastructure, Laos is a wonderful country to visit. The Laotians are some of the friendliest, most gentle people in Southeast Asia—devoutly Buddhist, and traditional in many ways. And since their landlocked nation is so sparsely populated—less than six million people in area larger than Great Britain —its countryside is dominated by forested mountains. Laos has a rich culture and history, and though it's been a battleground many times in the past, is a peaceful, stable country today.

During the Vietnam War, the U.S. Air Force, in a vain attempt to disrupt the Ho Chi Minh Trail, dropped more tons of bombs on Laos than were dropped on Germany during World War II. Since the end of the Vietnam War, the People's Democratic Party has ruled the country, first on Marxist-Leninist lines and now on the basis of limited pro-market reforms. Overtures are being made to the outside, particularly to Thailand and China, to assist in developing the country—not an easy task.

Some changes are taking place. Vientiane has a new airport; visitors from most countries can now get a visa upon arriving; and the road from Vientiane to Luang Prabang, Laos's ancient capital, has been paved—though it still takes eight hours to make that serpentine, 150-mile journey. New hotels are opening, and the Friendship Bridge over the Mekong from Thailand's northern town of Nong Khai has made Vientiane, the capital, more accessible to trade from the south. Other border crossings have also opened up. The average annual per-capita income of $170 and a rugged landscape that makes transportation and communications extremely difficult have long made the countryside of Laos a sleepy backwater; but Luang Prabang has already become a busy tourist hub, and infrastructure is improving in other areas.

Pleasures and Pastimes

Architecture

Laotians are a very religious people, and the country's abundant Buddhist temples, are one of its main attractions. Those sacred sites are often works of art—collections of statues and structures that celebrate the human desire for perfection. They range from Luang Prabang's venerable Wat Xieng Thong, which dates from the 16th century, to relatively new, freshly painted wats in Vientiane. As interesting as their architecture and statuary may be, wats here are still principally centers of worship and study, which means the sound of chanting and the smell of incense may accompany you as you explore them. You'll also share them with devotees, or monks and novices in saffron robes, some of whom might be eager to practice their English with you.

Dining

It may not be as famous as Thai food, but Lao cuisine is often just as good. It is similar, though usually not as spicy. Since so much of the country is wilderness, there is usually game on the menu, such as venison or wild boar. Fresh river prawns and fish, such as the massive Mekong catfish (the world's largest fresh-water fish), are also standard fare. Though chilies are often used as a condiment, Lao cuisine also makes good use of ginger, lemon grass, coconut, tamarind, crushed peanuts, and fish paste. And if you tire of Lao food, both Vientiane and Luang Prabang have good French, Vietnamese, Chinese, Thai, and Indian restaurants, as well as bakeries that serve sandwiches made with fresh baguettes.

CATEGORY	COST*
$$$$	over $12
$$$	$9–$12
$$	$6–$9
$	$3–$6
¢	under $3

*per person, for a main course at dinner

Lodging

On the whole, hotels in Laos are a good deal. Though there's nothing in the country that approaches the resorts of Thailand and Malaysia, there are several charming lodges in historic buildings, and an abundance of guest houses that offer real bargains. Because the kip suffers from chronic devaluation, all hotel rates are in US dollars, as are the menus in their restaurants and bars. Some hotels even have higher rates for guests who pay their bills in kips.

CATEGORY	COST*
$$$$	over $150
$$$	$100–$150
$$	$50–$100
$	$25–$50
¢	under $25

*All prices are for a standard double room, excluding tax.

Exploring Laos

Laos has a small area of lowlands in the south; the rest of the country consists of central and northern mountain ranges and high plateaus. Much of the mountain terrain is impenetrable jungle, cut by rivers and ravines, and the only practical way of touring the country in anything less than a week is by plane. Fortunately, the national airline, Lao Aviation, runs frequent (and cheap) flights between the capital Vientiane and provincial cities such as Luang Prabang, Savannakhet, and Pakse.

There is no railroad and car rental services are nonexistent, so buses (or, for shorter journeys, taxis, chauffeur-driven cars or songthaews) are the only sensible means of land transport (motorcycles are *not* recommended). Bus services on the main routes are frequent and fares are very cheap, but it's a slow and uncomfortable way of getting around.

Since all the main cities and virtually all tourist sights lie on the Mekong River, boats offer an exotic and practical alternative—in fact, this legendary waterway is the busiest Laotian travel route. "Express" boats with noisy outboard motors and more leisurely "slow" boats ply sections of the river. The most popular tourist route is between Huay Xai on the northern Thai border and Luang Prabang, although it's possible to travel on cargo boats and barges as far south as Savannakhet, on the crossroads between Thailand and Vietnam, and Pakse, the southernmost city of Laos and gateway to Cambodia. Few tourists venture this far south in Laos, preferring the more mountainous north, but the region is rich in Khmer ruins.

Great Itinerary

If you limit your visit to the sights of Vientiane and Luang Prabang, a minimum of three days is required. Spend your first day exploring Vientiane, stay overnight and then head out the next morning for Luang Prabang. Two days here will give you a good introduction, but you should consider spending three or four days to take advantage of the growing number of day trip options.

When To Go

Most people visit Laos during the dry season, which runs from November through May, but the rainy season is warmer, greener, less expensive, and less crowded. Nights are chilly—sometimes down to 42°F—from November to February, so you'll want to bring some warm clothes if you visit then. It can get quite hot during the wet season, when it is often cloudy, though days can pass without a downpour. The rainiest months are July and August.

Vientiane

Vientiane is the quietest Southeast Asian capital, with a pace as slow as the Mekong River, which flows along the edge of town. It doesn't have the kind of imposing sights you find in Bangkok, but neither does it have the air pollution and traffic jams. In fact, there are many more bicycles and scooters than cars on the streets of Vientiane, and more trees than buildings lining them. The town's abundance of cement block buildings in need of paint give it the appearance of undevelopment, but scattered between those eyesores are remnants of elegant colonial French architecture and dozens of wats, where colorful Buddhist temples stand amidst coconut palms and flowering trees.

The **Sisaket Museum** is in an ancient, crumbling temple across the street from Wat Phra Keo. Built in 1818, the temple underwent some restoration in 1938, but is in need of more work. The paintings that once covered its interior walls have largely been destroyed by the ravages of time, but the intricately carved wooden ceiling and doors are still intact. Between the temple and the building that surrounds it, is a collection of no less than 10,136 Buddhas. ⊠ *Setthathirath Rd. at Mahosot St.,* ☎ *no phone.* ▣ *2,000 kip.* ۞ *Daily 8–12 and 1–4.*

To immerse yourself in Vientiane, visit the **Talat Sao,** or Morning Market, a vast indoor bazaar that is actually open all day. The bright, orderly emporium offers everything from hand-woven fabrics and wooden Buddha figures to electric rice cookers and tennis shoes. Though most of the shops cater to locals, there is also plenty to interest travelers, such as intricate gold and silver work, tee shirts, and antiques. ⊠ *Lane Xang Ave. at Khoun Boulom St.,* ☎ *no phone.* ۞ *7 AM–6 PM.*

That Luang, the city's most sacred monument, stands on the outskirts of town. A massive golden stupa that towers 147 feet high, it was built by King Setthathirath in 1566. The stupa is surrounded by a portico that holds various Buddha statues, and is flanked by two ancient wats; the survivors of the four wats that originally surrounded the stupa. That Luang is the site of a major festival held during November's full moon. ⊠ *North end of That Luang Rd.,* ☎ *no phone.* ▣ *2,000 kip.* ۞ *Tue.– Sun., 8–12 and 1–4.*

One of the city's oldest, and most impressive temples is **Wat Phra Keo,** and it has good reason for having a name so similar to the wat in Bangkok's Royal Palace. The original Wat Phra Keo here was built in

1565 to house the Emerald Buddha, which had been taken from the Thais by the Lao. The Buddha was recaptured by the Thai army in 1778, and taken to Bangkok. The present temple dates from 1936, and has become a national museum. On display are an array of Buddhas of different styles, some wonderful images of Khmer deities, and a 16th-century door carved with Hindu images. ⊠ *Setthathirath Rd. at Mahosot St.,* ☎ *no phone.* ⊡ *2,000 kip.* ☉ *Daily 8–12 and 1–4.*

Dining and Lodging

$ ✕ **Le Provençal.** This little bistro on Namphu (Fountain) Square belongs to a local family that lived in France for many years. Seating is available either in the air-conditioned interior, or on a patio overlooking the square. The menu is ample and almost exclusively French, with the exception of about a dozen pizzas. Try the *terrine du maison* to start, then sink your teeth into *poulet niçoise,* or a filet of fish *à la provençale.* Save room for dessert, such as crème caramel, or chocolate mousse. Note that lunch is served but the hours for it are short: 11:30 AM–2 PM. ⊠ *Nam Phu Square,* ☎ *021/219685. MC, V. Closed 2 PM–5:30 PM, and Sunday lunch.*

¢–$ ✕ **Kualao.** In a mansion one block east of Namphu Square, this is Vientiane's best Lao restaurant, despite its rather tacky decor. The food is quite good, and the vast menu ranges from *mokpa fork* (steamed fish with eggs, onions, and coconut milk wrapped in a banana leaf) to *gaeng panag* (a thick red curry with either chicken, pork, or beef). Photos and English descriptions facilitate ordering. Servings are small, so most people order various entrees, or set menus with seven to nine dishes, plus dessert and coffee. Lao folk dancing is performed nightly from 7 to 9. ⊠ *111 Samsenthai Rd.,* ☎ *021/215777. MC, V. Closed 2 PM–5 PM.*

$$$ ☷ **Settha Palace.** Built by the French in the 1930s, this was the country's premier hotel until it was expropriated in the 1970s. It was returned
★ to its original owners in the 1990s, when it underwent extensive renovation. Though the marble floors and fixtures are new, the owners respected the original design. Rooms have high ceilings, hardwood floors, oriental rugs, and are furnished with period pieces. Their tall windows open onto lush gardens that surround a large pool. The lobby, decorated with fine weaving and antiques, is adjacent to a small bar and elegant restaurant that specialized in Lao cuisine. ⊠ *6 Pang Kham St.,* ☎ *021/217581,* ℻ *021/217583,* 🕸 *www.setthapalace.com. 29 rooms. Restaurant, mini-bars, cable TV, pool, bar, laundry service, concierge, business services, meeting rooms, non-smoking rooms. BP. AE, MC, V.*

$$ ☷ **Tai-Pan.** With a convenient location in the heart of town near the Mekong River, and comfort at competitive rates, this hotel is popular with businessmen. Rooms are spacious and have dark parquet floors. The ground floor holds the reception, restaurant, and lounge, which are separated by potted plants and wooden dividers. Behind the building is a narrow garden and a small pool. ⊠ *2-12 Francois Ngin Rd.,* ☎ *21/216907,* ℻ *21/216223,* 🕸 *www.travelao.com. 44 rooms. Cable TV, pool, exercise equipment, laundry service, business services, meeting rooms, non-smoking floor. AE, MC, V.*

$ ☷ **Lane-Xang.** The hotel promotes itself as a five-star hotel at the cost of a three-star, but even those three aren't shining very brightly these days. The furnishings are worn, the ceilings need paint, and the bathrooms show the wear and tear of decades, but they're relatively large and clean. The staff is attentive and friendly, and if you don't mind the dog-eared appearance, it is a good deal, especially when you add in the complimentary breakfast, airport transfers, and nightly folk dancing show. The best rooms overlook the Mekong, though those all have two single beds. ⊠ *Fangum Rd.,* ☎ *021/214102,* ℻ *021/214108. 109* *rooms. Restaurant, cable TV, tennis court, pool, bar, laundry service, travel services. MC, V. BP.*

¢ ⊞ **Orchid Guesthouse.** Vientiane has an abundance of guest houses, but this is the only one that faces the river. The simple but spacious rooms have shiny tile floors and small desks. The bathrooms are cramped, but have hot water showers. Front rooms and a rooftop deck afford views of the Mekong. ⊠ *33 Fangum Rd.,* ☎ *021/252825,* ℻ *021/216588. 21 rooms. Fans, cable TV, breakfast room, laundry service; no air-conditioning in some rooms. No credit cards. CP.*

Luang Prabang

230 km (144 mi) north of Vientiane.

Most visitors to Laos don't go to see Vientiane, the present-day capital, but to visit its ancient capital of Luang Prabang, a sleepy town of about 68,000 inhabitants that sits high on the banks of a peninsula where the Nam Khan River flows into the Mekong. It is still Laos's religious and artistic capital and its combination of impressive natural surroundings, historic architecture, and friendly inhabitants make it one of the region's most pleasant towns. The city's abundance of ancient temples led UNESCO to declare it a world heritage site. Some 30 wats are scattered around town, making it a pleasant place to explore on a rented bicycle or on foot. But Luang Prabang's charm is not exclusively architectural—just as pleasant are its people, who seem to spend as much time on the streets as they do in their homes. Children play on the sidewalks while matrons gossip in the shade, young women in traditional dress zip past on motor scooters, and Buddhist monks in saffron robes stroll by with black umbrellas, to protect their shaven heads from the tropical sun.

Laotians aren't the only people you'll see on the streets of Luang Prabang, however. With each passing year, the increase in visitors seems to overwhelm the town during the November to April high season. Despite hundreds of guest houses, finding accommodation can be a challenge in peak season, and when you visit the main attractions, be prepared to be cheek to jowl with other tourists.

Though forested **Phousi Hill** has several shrines and temples on it, the main reason for ascending its 300 steps is to enjoy the view from the summit—a panorama of Luang Prabang, the Nam Khan and Mekong Rivers, and the surrounding mountains. It's a popular spot for watching the sunset— you'll want to bring insect repellent—but the view from atop old Phousi is splendid at any hour. ⊠ *Sisavangvong Rd.,* ☎ *no phone.* ▣ *5,000 kips.* ☉ *Daily dawn to dusk.*

The **Royal Palace,** in a walled compound across from Phousi Hill, is the former home of the Savang family, (King Savang Vattana and his children were exiled following the communist takeover in 1975). Its throne room has gilded furniture, walls covered with colorful mosaics, and various display cases filled with rare Buddhas and other artifacts. The walls of the king's reception room are decorated with scenes of traditional Laos life painted in 1930 by the French artist Alex de Fautereau. The Queen's reception room contains an eclectic assortment of items, including teacups presented by Mao Tse Tung, and medals from Lyndon Johnson. Also on display are excellent friezes removed from local temples, Khmer bong drums, and elephant tusks with carved images of the Buddha.

The museum's most prized exhibit is the Pha Bang, a gold Buddha just inches under 3 ft tall and weighing more than 100 pounds. Its history goes back to the first century, when it was cast in Sri Lanka; it was brought to Luang Prabang in 1353 as a gift to King Fa Bang. This event is celebrated as the introduction of Buddhism to Laos, and Pha Bang is venerated as the protector of the faith. At press time, an ornate temple called Ho Pha Bang was nearing completion by the entrance to the compound, and the venerated idol will be housed within it once it is ready. ⊠ *Sisavangvong Rd. across from Phousi Hill,* ☎ *071/212470.* ⊡ *10,000 kips.* ⊙ *Wed.–Mon., 8–11 and 1–4.*

The small but lovely **Wat Mai**, next to the Royal Palace compound, dates from 1797. It's four-tier roof is characteristic of Luang Prabang architecture, but more impressive is the gilded relief work covering the front of the building. Those intricate panels represent the life of the Buddha, but also include depictions of various Asian animals. ⊠ *Sisavangvong Rd.,* ☎ *no phone.* ⊡ *Free.* ⊙ *6 AM–7 PM.*

Luang Prabang's most important and impressive temple complex is **Wat Xieng Thong,** a collection of ancient buildings near the tip of the peninsula. Constructed in 1559, the main temple is one of the few structures to have survived centuries of marauding Chinese and Thais. Low, sweeping roofs overlap to make complex patterns and create a feeling of harmony and peace. The interior has decorated wooden columns and a ceiling covered with wheels of *dhamma*, representing the Buddha's teaching, but the exterior is just as impressive thanks to mosaics of colored glass that were added at the beginning of 20th century. Several small **chapels** at the sides of the main hall are also covered with mosaics and contain various images of the Buddha. The bronze 16th-century reclining Buddha was displayed in the 1931 Paris Exhibition. The mosaic on the back wall of that chapel commemorates the 2,500th anniversary of the Buddha's birth with a depiction of Lao village life. The chapel near the compound's east gate, with a gilded facade, contains the royal family's funeral statuary, including a 40-ft wooden boat used as a hearse. ⊠ *Souvannakhampoung Rd. at Sisaleumsak,* ☎ *no phone,* ⊡ *7,000 kips.* ⊙ *Daily 8–6.*

Dining and Lodging

The main road is lined with restaurants, but the side streets are well worth exploring. In addition to the hotels listed below, Luang Prabang has dozens of inexpensive, family-run guest houses of similar quality.

$–$$$ ✕ **L'Elephant.** When you can't face another serving of rice or spicy sauces, it's time to walk down the hill from the Villa Santi to this pleasant corner restaurant. The menu is traditional French, with a bit of Laotian influence, especially when it comes to the ingredients. Consider, for example, the *chevreuil au poivre vert* (local venison in a pepper sauce). There is always a three-course set meal, and several daily specials, which usually include fish fresh from the Mekong. Seating is available in the bright, airy dining room or on the sidewalk, behind a barrier of plants. Though primarily a dinner spot, the restaurant does serve lunch on weekends. ⊠ *Ban Vat Nong,* ☎ *071/252482. MC, V.*

$$$ ✕▣ **Villa Santi.** This 19th-century royal residence in the heart of town ★ was converted to a boutique hotel by the princess's son-in-law, who also built an identical annex around the corner and a resort outside of town. Guest rooms have hardwood furniture, and are decorated with handicrafts and fine weaving. The lovely garden courtyard doubles as a bar, and the second-floor restaurant, which has live folk music at dinner, serves Laotian and western cuisine. The resort, 3½ mi from town, recreates the traditional ambiance, but has larger rooms with balconies overlooking lily pools, lush gardens, rice paddies, and forested hills. ⊠ *Sakkarine Rd.,* ☎ *071/252157,* ℻ *071/252158,* ⓦⓔⓑ *www.villasantihotel.com. 64 rooms. Restaurant, in-room safes, minibars, no room phones, no room TVs, pool, bar, laundry service, concierge, airport shuttle, travel services, no-smoking rooms. BP. AE, MC, V.*

$ ✕🍽 **Tum Tum Cheng.** Though accommodations here don't rank among
★ this town's best, the restaurant definitely does. The intimate spot serves
an inventive menu of Laotian food, with such treats as Mekong catfish in a sweet ginger sauce and venison with mushrooms. Seating is
available inside on cushions or on the garden terrace, but is limited,
so making reservations is essential in the high season. Rooms are simple but sufficient—they're decorated with local handicrafts, but are short
on amenities, and have rather basic bathrooms. The location, a stone's
throw from Vat Xieng Thong, is perfect, and the owners, a Lao/Hun-
garian couple, are charming. ⊠ *Baan Xieng Thong,* ☎ FAX *071/253224.
10 rooms. Restaurant, no room phones, no room TVs, bicycles, laundry service. No credit cards.*

$$$ 🏨 **Grand Luang Prabang.** This Thai-owned hotel occupies the former
residence of Prince Petsarath, whose house stands amidst the hotel's new,
but traditionally designed buildings. It has an unmatched location on a
bend of the Mekong River, and though guest rooms are set back a bit,
most have river views. Rooms are spacious and have hardwood floors,
white marble baths, and sliding glass doors that open onto large balconies.
It's 2½ mi from Luang Prabang, just before the village of Xiengkeo; a
shuttle provides regular transportation to town. ⊠ *Ban Xiengkeo,* ☎
071/253852, FAX *071/253028,* WEB *www.grandluangprabang.com. 78
rooms. Restaurant, minibars, cable TV, pool, bicycles, bar, laundry ser-
vice, concierge, meeting rooms, airport shuttle, no-smoking rooms. AE,
MC, V. BP.*

$$ 🏨 **Le Calao Inn.** This small hotel, just down the street from Wat Xieng
Thong, was resurrected from a ruined mansion, originally built by a
Portuguese merchant in 1906. Four guest rooms upstairs open onto a
colonnaded veranda to views of the Mekong and the hills beyond. The
two rooms on the lower floor are larger—with three beds each—and
have private terraces, but are a bit dark. The ground floor and terrace
hold a restaurant that serves a combination of French and Asian fare.
⊠ *Mekong Rd.,* ☎ *071/212100,* FAX *071/212085. 6 rooms. Restaurant,
no room phones, no room TVs, laundry service. MC, V. BP.*

$$ 🏨 **L'hôtel Souvannaphoum.** Located on a busy street just outside the
historic peninsular area, this government-owned hotel is a bit dog-eared,
but a good value. The reception, an open-air restaurant, and a small
bar are in the ground floor of an old mansion; guest rooms are in a
newer building nearby. Rooms are big and fairly bright, with white wicker
furniture and doors that open onto small balconies overlooking trop-
ical greenery. Ask for a room at the back for more peace and quiet. ⊠
Photisarath Rd., ☎ *071/212200,* FAX *071/212577. 25 rooms. Restau-
rant, refrigerators, bar, laundry service, travel services. MC, V. BP.*

Pak Ou Caves

25 km (15 mi) up the Mekong from Luang Prabang.

Set in high limestone cliffs above the Mekong River are two sacred caves
filled with Buddha statues. The lower cave, **Tham Thing,** is accessible
from the river by a stairway and has enough daylight to allow you to
find your way around. The stairway continues to the upper cave,
Tham Phum, for which you will need a flashlight. The moderate ad-
mission charge includes a flashlight and a guide.

Slow boats make the three-hour journey to the caves from Luang Pra-
bang, many of them stopping at waterside villages for a perusal of the
rich variety of local handicrafts, a nip of *lao lao* (home-brewed rice
whiskey), and perhaps a bowl of noodles. Those in a hurry can catch
a speedboat from Luang Prabang to the caves—a noisy one-hour trip.
An alternative route is by bus or taxi to the town of Pak Ou, where

boats ferry visitors across the river to the caves. Pak Ou has several passable restaurants.

Kuang Si Waterfall

29 km (17 mi) south of Luang Prabang.

A series of cascades surrounded by lush foliage, Kuang Si is a popular spot with Lao and foreigners alike. Many visitors merely view the falls from the lower pool, where picnic tables and food vendors invite one to linger, but a steep path through the forest leads to pools above the falls that are the perfect spot for a swim, so bring your bathing suit. Tour operators and taxi drivers in Luang Prabang offer day trips that combine Kuang Si with the Pak Ou Caves. The drive there, past rice farms and small villages, is half the adventure.

Plain of Jars

96 km (60 mi) southeast of Luang Prabang.

The Plain of Jars is one of the world's most tantalizing mysteries and should rank among its major wonders. The broad, mountain-ringed plain northeast of Vientiane, is scattered with hundreds of ancient stone and clay jars, some estimated to weigh five or six tons. The jars are estimated to be at least 2,000 years old but to this day nobody knows who made them or why. They survived heavy bombing during the Vietnam War, and their sheer size has kept them out of the hands of antiquities-hunters. The vast plain is also difficult to reach, a hard day's drive along Highway 7 from either Vientiane or Luang Prabang. Travel operators in both cities (Diethelm Travel is the best) offer tours of this ilk, but the most comfortable route is by air to the tiny airfield of Phonesavanh, where a couple of hotels have basic but adequate accommodations, and a taxi can be hired for around $25 for the 30 km (19 mi) journey to the edge of the plain. Lao Aviation flies twice weekly from Vientiane or Luang Prabang to Phonesavanh.

Ban Huay Xai

297 km (185 mi) up the Mekong from Luang Prabang.

Growing in popularity is the Mekong River trip between Luang Prabang and Ban Huay Xai, across the river from Chiang Khong in Thailand. The scenery is splendid: high hills clad in foliage and rocky islands in mid-river are a continual feast for the eyes. Only a few villages line the river; these isolated pockets of habitation are havens of wonder. Only one village has established itself as a stopover for foreigners: Pakbeng, halfway between Luang Prabang and Ban Huay Xai. Once you arrive in Ban Huay Xai, a worthwhile side trip—and a good way to return to Thailand—is to cross the river to Chiang Khong and then take a bus to Chiang Rai, 60 km (37 mi) inland.

There are two ways to make the journey: either by regular boat, which holds about 50 passengers, or by speedboat, which seats about four. The regular boat takes 12 hours over two days. The night is spent at Pakbeng in very basic lodgings—guest houses with only cold water and limited electricity. The speedboats make the journey between Luang Prabang and Ban Huay Xai in six hours. Speedboats, while thrilling for the first hour, become extremely uncomfortable after the novelty wears off. Passengers must sit uncomfortably on hard seats; the engine noise is deafening (ear plugs are advised); and the wind and spray can be chilling. Take a warm, waterproof windbreaker, and get a life jacket and crash helmet with a visor from the boat driver. Another option is to journey to Pakbeng by speedboat, overnight at the village, and continue the following day by either speedboat or regular boat. For the regular boat, the fare is about $15; the speedboat is $35 per person. Only three slow boats make the trip per week.

For those not eager to repeat the long journey back to Luang Prabang, there is also a twice-weekly flight to the city from Ban Huay Xai.

Laos A to Z

To research prices, get advice from other travelers, and book travel arrangements, visit www.fodors.com.

AIR TRAVEL
You can fly from Bangkok to Vientiane on Thai Airways International, or directly to Luang Prabang on Bangkok Airways. The national airline, Lao Aviation, has daily flights between Vientiane and Bangkok as well as twice weekly flights to Chiang Mai. The departure tax is US$10.
➤ CARRIERS: **Bangkok Airways** (☎ 071/253253 in Luang Prabang; 02/229–3434 in Bangkok, WEB www.bangkokair.com). **Lao Aviation** (☎ 021/212057 in Vientiane; 02/236–9821 in Bangkok, WEB www.lao-aviation.com). **Thai Airways International** (☎ 021/225271 in Vientiane; 02/280–0060 in Bangkok, WEB www.thaiair.com).

AIRPORTS
Vientiane's Wattay Airport is about 4 km (2½ mi) from the city center. Luang Prabang's airport is 4 km (2½ mi) northeast of the city. Ban Huay Xai's airport is 9 km (5½ mi) south of town.
➤ AIRPORTS: **Luang Prabang airport** (☎ 071/212173). **Wattay Airport** (☎ 021/512028).

AIRPORT TRANSFERS
Tuk tuk rides will cost you 2,000–4,000 kips. Vientiane and Luang Prabang also have metered taxis.

BUS AND CAR TRAVEL
You can enter Laos from Northern Thailand by crossing the Friendship Bridge at Nong Khai. Buses and taxis wait on the Laotian side to make the run into Vientiane, 19 km (12 mi) away—about 350 baht by taxi.

BUSINESS HOURS
Business hours are 7–11:30 and 2–5:30 weekdays, and post offices keep the same schedule.

CUSTOMS AND DUTIES
Tourists are allowed to bring into Laos 200 cigarettes, 50 cigars, or ½ lb of tobacco, and one quart of spirits. Bringing in or taking out local currency is prohibited, as is the export of antiques and religious artifacts without a permit.

ELECTRICITY
The electrical current is 220 volts AC, 50Hz. Outside of Vientiane and Luang Prabang, electricity is uncertain, and even in Luang Prabang there are frequent late-afternoon outages in hot weather.

EMBASSIES AND CONSULATES
British, Canadian, and New Zealand residents should contact the respective embassies in Bangkok for assistance in Laos.
➤ UNITED STATES: **Embassy** (✉ BP 114, rue Bartholomé, Vientiane, ☎ 021/212 581).

➤ Australia: **Embassy** (✉ Nehru Rd., Ban Phonxy, Vientiane, ☎ 021/413600).

EMERGENCIES

For medical and police emergencies, use the services of your hotel. In serious medical emergencies, get to Thailand as quickly as possible. The best clinic in the country is Mahosot Hospital International Clinic in Vientiane, though you should go here only if you are unable to obtain assistance through your hotel. In the case of a lost passport, immediately notify your embassy.

➤ Hospital: **Mahosot Hospital International Clinic** (✉ Fa Ngoum Quay, ☎ 021/214022).

ETIQUETTE AND BEHAVIOR

Dress respectfully, and remove your shoes before entering a temple. Take your lead from these gentle, hospitable people and avoid displays of anger or confrontational behavior. Everyone should also avoid public displays of affection, which are considered offensive.

HOLIDAYS

New Year's Day (Jan. 1); Army Day (Jan. 24); Lao New Year (Water Festival, Apr. 13–15); Labor Day (May 1); National Day (Dec. 2).

LANGUAGE

In tourist hotels, the staff speak some English. You will also find a smattering of English speakers in the shops and restaurants. A few old-timers know some French. The national language, Lao, is tonal; although a few words are similar to Thai, most are not, and the alphabet differs.

MONEY MATTERS

COSTS

Anticipate spending $20–$150 for a double room with private bath, according to your tastes. Dinner in a Western restaurant should cost $8–$15; in a local restaurant, a meal may cost as little as $4–$6. A local beer runs $1–$2, according to the establishment. The average taxi trip costs a few dollars.

CURRENCY

The local currency is the kip, which continually drops against the dollar. Hence, dollars are preferred and are always used to pay hotel and airline bills. The Thai baht is accepted in Vientiane, Luang Prabang, and border towns. Kip cannot be changed back into a hard currency. At press time the official exchange rate was 240 kip to the Thai baht, and 9,800 kip for one US dollar. Credit cards are accepted at only the more expensive establishments.

CURRENCY EXCHANGE AND ATMS

Banks give better exchange rates than money changers. At press time there was one ATM in the country, at Vientiane's Banque Pour le Commerce Exterieur Lao (BPCE), one block south of Fountain Square on Pangkham Rd.

PASSPORTS AND VISAS

All visitors to Laos need a passport and visa. Some travelers still obtain their visas at the embassy in Bangkok, but if you fly into Vientiane, or Luang Prabang, you can get a visa at the airport. Visas cost $30, and you'll need to have a passport photo with you. You can also get a visa at the Friendship Bridge in Nong Khai, in Chiang Khong (near Chiang Rai), and in Khon Kaen in northeastern Thailand, though it can take a few hours to a day. The process takes one to two days in Bangkok, where you can pay a travel agency to do the foot work. Tourist visas ($10) are good for 30 days and can be extended for another 15. Sometimes the immigration officials want to see evidence of sufficient funds and an air ticket out of the country. Because the rules could change at a moment's notice, you might want to contact an Embassy of the Lao People's Democratic Republic beforehand.

➤ LAOTIAN EMBASSIES: **Australia** (⊠ 1 Dalman Crescent, O'Malley, ACT 2606, ☎ 026/286–4595). **Thailand** (⊠ 1-3 Soi Ramkhamhaeng 39, Bangkok, ☎ 02/539–6668). **United States** (⊠ Consular Section, 2222 S. St. NW, Washington, DC 20008, ☎ 202/667–0076).

SAFETY

As in all of Southeast Asia, it's advisable to drink bottled water (stay away from ice also) and keep away from uncooked foods. Laos is fairly free of crime in the tourist areas, though traveling by road puts you at risk of highway thieves. Trekking is increasingly popular in Laos, but beware: there are still unexploded bombs left over from the Vietnam War in southern Laos. Don't wander off of well-traveled trails. Don't photograph anything that may have military significance.

TELEPHONES

To call Laos from overseas, dial the country code, 856, and then the area code, omitting the first 0. The outgoing international code is 00, but IDD phones are rare. If you have to make an international call from Laos, use your hotel's switchboard. This is a good idea even for local calls, since there are few pay phones.

TIPPING

Give bellboys 5,000 kips. Guides expect a few (U.S.) dollars after a day of sightseeing. At tourist hotels, gratuities are included in the cost of meals and accommodation, but considering that most staff earn about $1 per day, it's nice to give them something extra.

TOURS AND PACKAGES

You can make tour arrangements (round-trip flight from Bangkok or Chiang Mai to Vientiane and Luang Prabang, hotels, guides, and visas) through travel agencies in Bangkok and Chiang Mai. Recommended tour companies with offices in Bangkok are Abercrombie & Kent, Diethelm Travel, and Journeys International. In Chiang Mai, Nam Khon Travel is the leading specialist in package tours to Laos.

➤ TOUR COMPANIES: **Abercrombie & Kent** (⊠ 1520 Kensington Rd., Suite 212, Oak Brook, IL 60521, ☎ 630/954–2944 or 800/323–7308, FAX 630/954–3324, WEB www.aandktours.com). **Diethelm Travel** (⊠ Kian Gwan II Bldg., 140/1 Wireless Rd., Bangkok, ☎ 02/255–9150, WEB www. diethelm-travel.com). **Journeys International** (⊠ 107 April Dr., Ann Arbor, MI 48103, ☎ 734/665–4407 or 800/255–8735, WEB www. journeys-intl.com). **Nam Khon Travel** (6 Chaiyaphoom Rd., Chiang Mai, ☎ 053/874321).

TRANSPORTATION AROUND LAOS

Though you can go by road from Vientiane to Luang Prabang, it takes seven to eight hours to make the 242-km (150-mi) trip along the meandering, but paved, road up into the mountains. Missing out on some great scenery, many people prefer to fly on Lao Aviation, which has two daily flights out of Vientiane for approximately $60 each way. Irregularly, river ferries also ply the waters between Vientiane and Luang Prabang; it takes three nights upstream and two nights coming down the Mekong. You can also charter a speedboat, but the discomfort keeps most from choosing this option.

You can cover Luang Prabang and even Vientiane on foot, but taxis and tuk-tuks are also available for about 1,000 kips for short trips.

Although there is a city bus service in Vientiane, schedules and routes are confusing for first-time visitors, so stick to taxis, tuk-tuks, and song-thaews (pickup trucks with benches in the back).

VISITOR INFORMATION

Diethelm Travel, which has offices in Vientiane and Luang Prabang, is your best source of information in Laos. The National Tourism Authority of the Lao People's Democratic Republic has offices in Vientiane and Luang Prabang, where they provide some printed materials, but little else. There is also a private website, (www.laos-hotels.com), with information about the big hotels.

➤ CONTACTS: **Diethelm Travel** (✉ Setthathirath Rd. at Namphu Square., Vientiane, ☎ 021/213833, WEB www.diethelm-travel.com; Sisavanguong Rd., Luang Prabang, ☎ 071/212277). **Luang Prabang Tourism Office** (✉ 72 Sisavangvong Rd., ☎ 071/212198). **National Tourism Authority of the Lao People's Democratic Republic** (✉ BP 3556, Avenue Lang Xang, Vientiane, ☎ 021/212248, WEB www.mekongcenter. com).

INDEX

Icons and Symbols

★ Our special recommendations
✕ Restaurant
🏨 Lodging establishment
✕🏨 Lodging establishment whose restaurant warrants a special trip
🐤 Good for kids (rubber duck)
☞ Sends you to another section of the guide for more information
⊠ Address
☎ Telephone number
🕘 Opening and closing times
💲 Admission prices

Numbers in white and black circles ③ ❸ that appear on the maps, in the margins, and within the tours correspond to one another.

NOTES

NOTES

NOTES

Fodor's Key to the Guides

America's guidebook leader publishes guides for every kind of traveler.
Check out our many series and find your perfect match.

Fodor's Gold Guides
America's favorite travel-guide series
offers the most detailed insider reviews
of hotels, restaurants, and attractions
in all price ranges, plus great background information, smart tips, and
useful maps.

Fodor's Road Guide USA
Big guides for a big country—the
most comprehensive guides to
America's roads, packed with places
to stay, eat, and play across the
U.S.A. Just right for road warriors,
family vacationers, and cross-country
trekkers.

COMPASS AMERICAN GUIDES
Stunning guides from top local writers
and photographers, with gorgeous
photos, literary excerpts, and colorful
anecdotes. A must-have for culture
mavens, history buffs, and new residents.

Fodor's CITYPACKS
Concise city coverage with a foldout
map. The right choice for urban travelers
who want everything under one cover.

Fodor's EXPLORING GUIDES
Hundreds of color photos bring your
destination to life. Lively stories lend
insight into the culture, history, and
people.

Fodor's POCKET GUIDES
For travelers who need only the essen-
tials. The best of Fodor's in pocket-size
packages for just $9.95.

Fodor's To Go
Credit-card–size, magnetized color
microguides that fit in the palm
of your hand—perfect for "stealth"
travelers or as gifts.

Fodor's FLASHMAPS
Every resident's map guide. 60 easy-
to-follow maps of public transit, parks,
museums, zip codes, and more.

Fodor's CITYGUIDES
Sourcebooks for living in the city:
Thousands of in-the-know listings for
restaurants, shops, sports, nightlife,
and other city resources.

**Fodor's AROUND THE CITY
WITH KIDS**
68 great ideas for family days,
recommended by resident parents.
Perfect for exploring in your own
backyard or on the road.

Fodor's ESCAPES
Fill your trip with once-in-a-lifetime
experiences, from ballooning in
Chianti to overnighting in the
Moroccan desert. These full-color
dream books point the way.

Fodor's FYI
Get tips from the pros on planning
the perfect trip. Learn how to pack,
fly hassle-free, plan a honeymoon
or cruise, stay healthy on the road,
and travel with your baby.

Fodor's Languages for Travelers
Practice the local language before
hitting the road. Available in phrase
books, cassette sets, and CD sets.

Karen Brown's Guides
Engaging guides to the most charming
inns and B&Bs in the U.S.A. and Europe,
with easy-to-follow inn-to-inn itineraries.

Baedeker's Guides
Comprehensive guides, trusted since
1829, packed with A–Z reviews and
star ratings.

At bookstores everywhere.   www.fodors.com/books